SURE... NO PROBLEM.
I'M ON MY WAY.
KCHAK
ZZCH
PFF

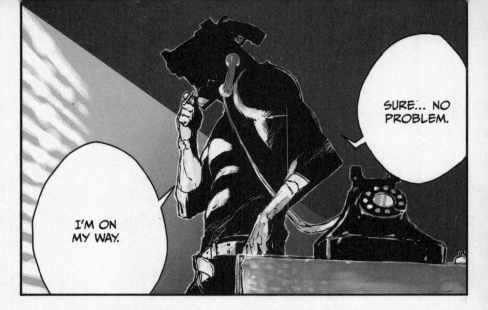

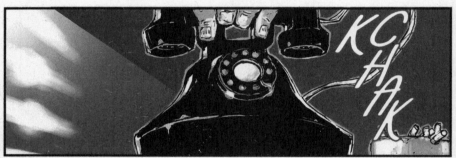

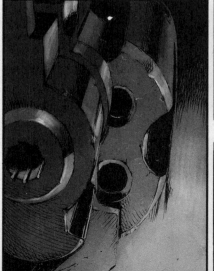

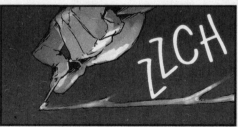

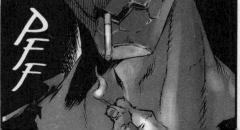

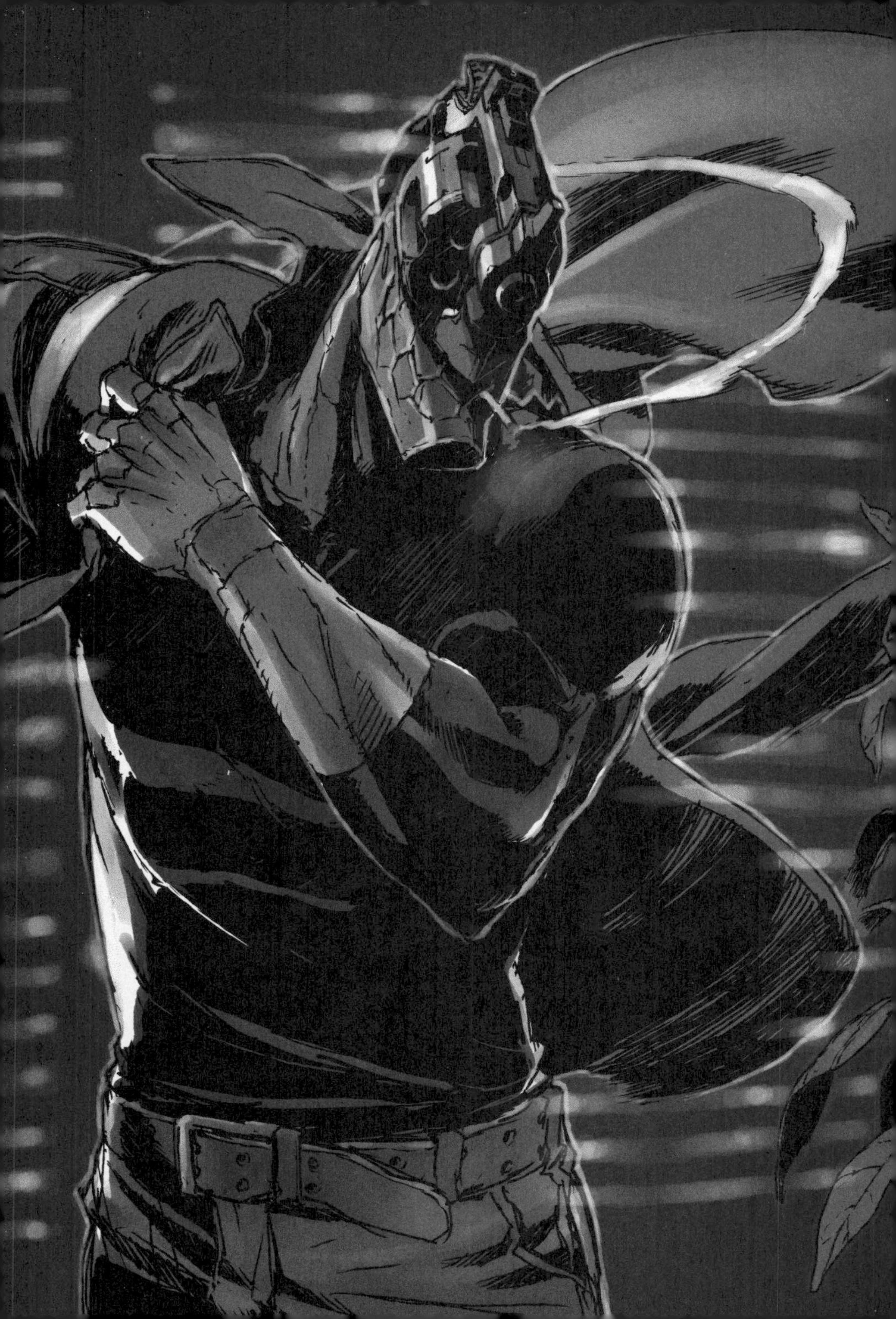

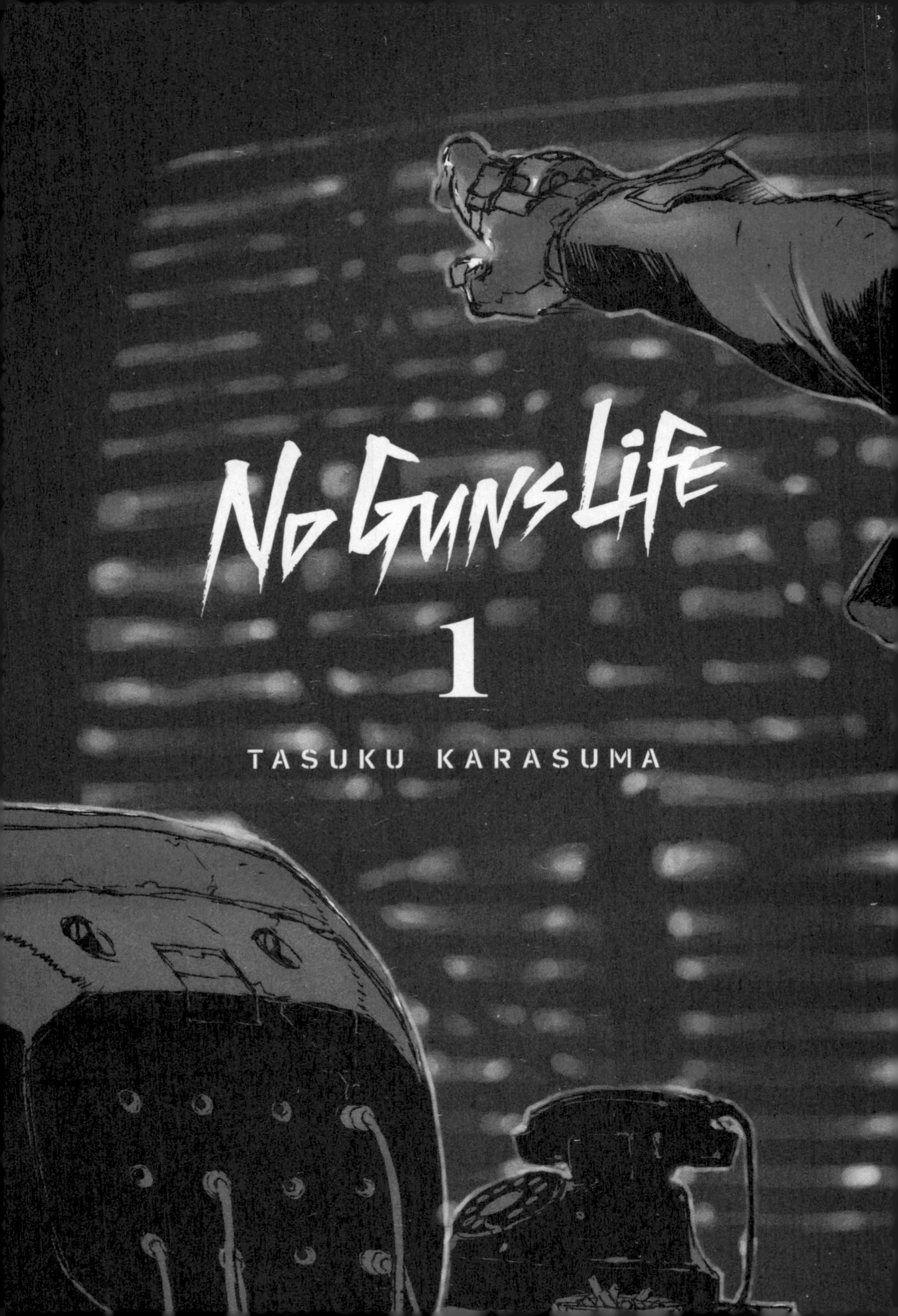
No Guns Life
1
TASUKU KARASUMA

CONTENTS

NO GUNS LIFE

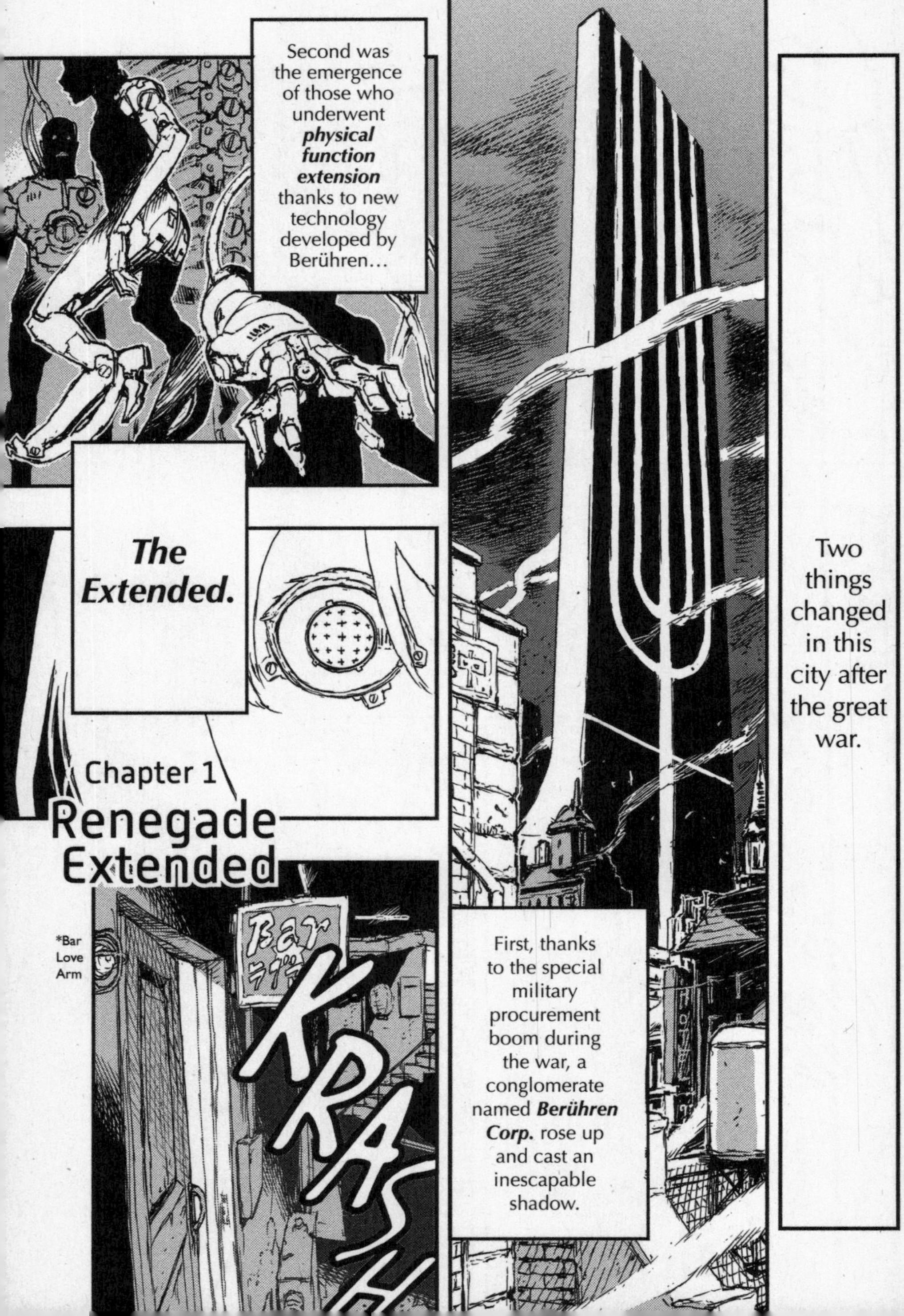
Two things changed in this city after the great war.
First, thanks to the special military procurement boom during the war, a conglomerate named **Berühren Corp.** rose up and cast an inescapable shadow.
Second was the emergence of those who underwent ***physical function extension*** thanks to new technology developed by Berühren…
The Extended.
Chapter 1
Renegade Extended
Bar
*Bar Love Arm
KRASH

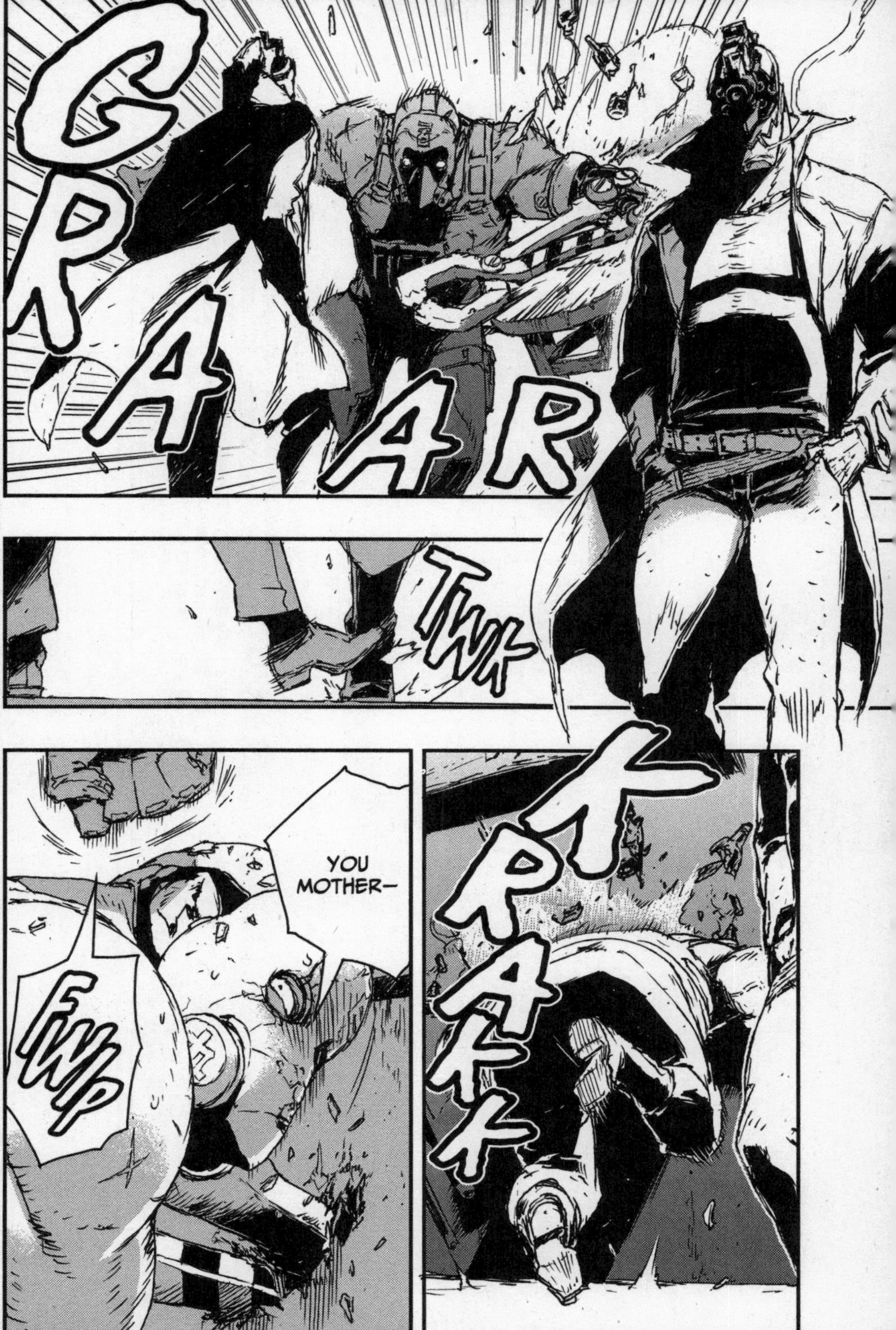
GRAAR
TWK
KRAKK
YOU MOTHER—
FWIP

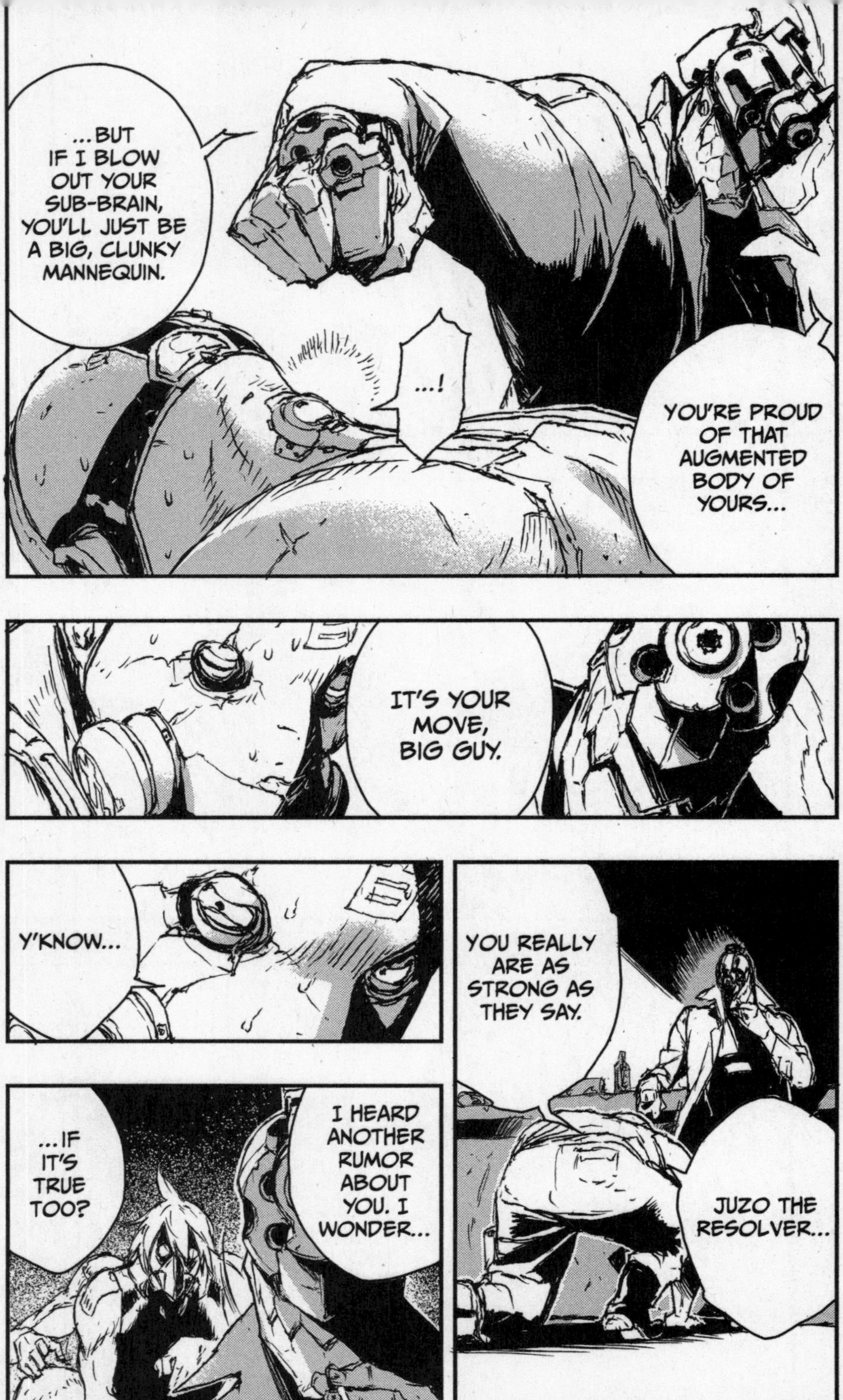
YOU'RE PROUD OF THAT AUGMENTED BODY OF YOURS...
...BUT IF I BLOW OUT YOUR SUB-BRAIN, YOU'LL JUST BE A BIG, CLUNKY MANNEQUIN.
...!
IT'S YOUR MOVE, BIG GUY.
YOU REALLY ARE AS STRONG AS THEY SAY.
JUZO THE RESOLVER...
Y'KNOW...
I HEARD ANOTHER RUMOR ABOUT YOU. I WONDER...
...IF IT'S TRUE TOO?

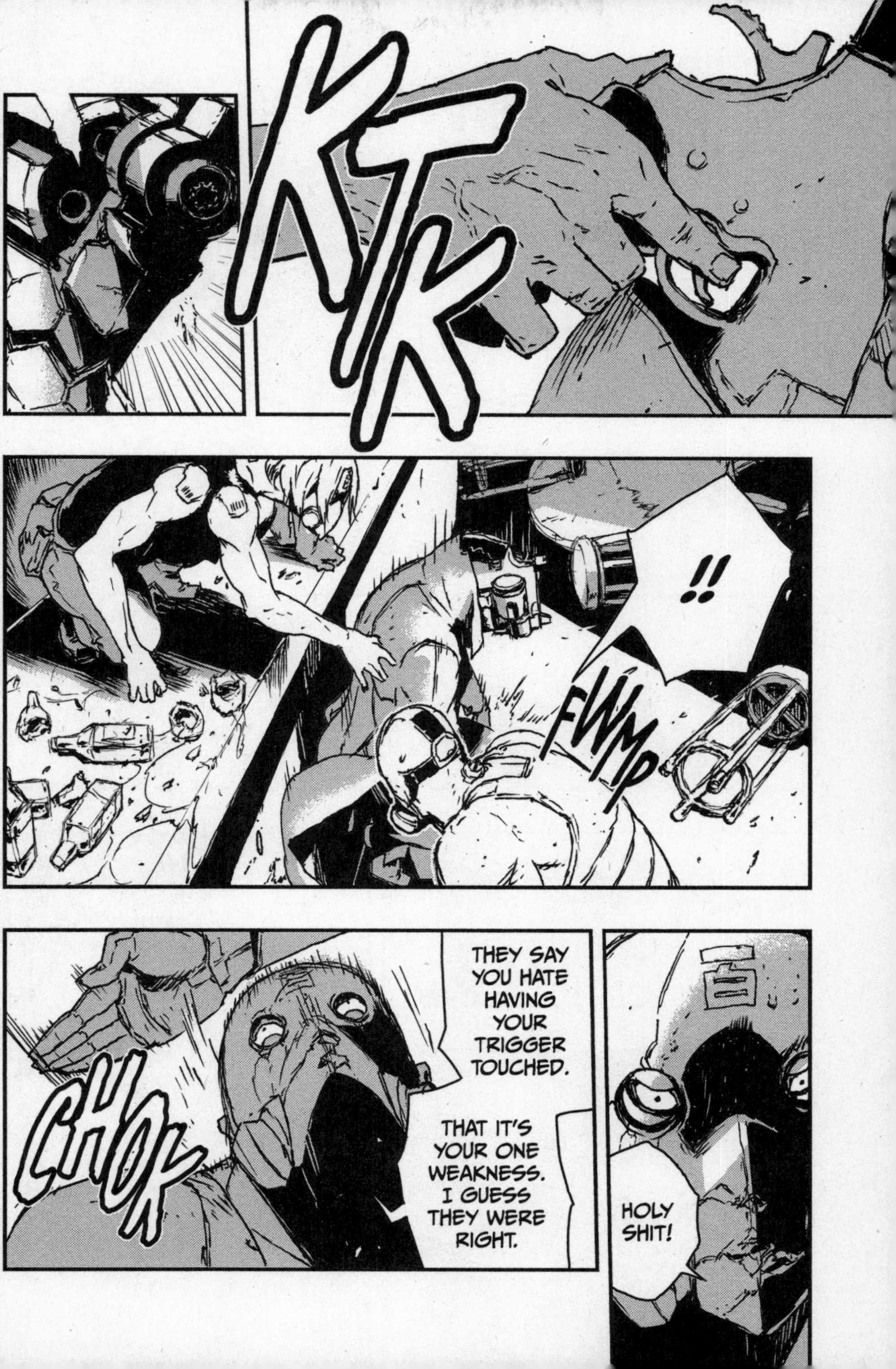
KTK
!!
FWMP
HOLY SHIT!
THEY SAY YOU HATE HAVING YOUR TRIGGER TOUCHED.
THAT IT'S YOUR ONE WEAKNESS. I GUESS THEY WERE RIGHT.
CHOK

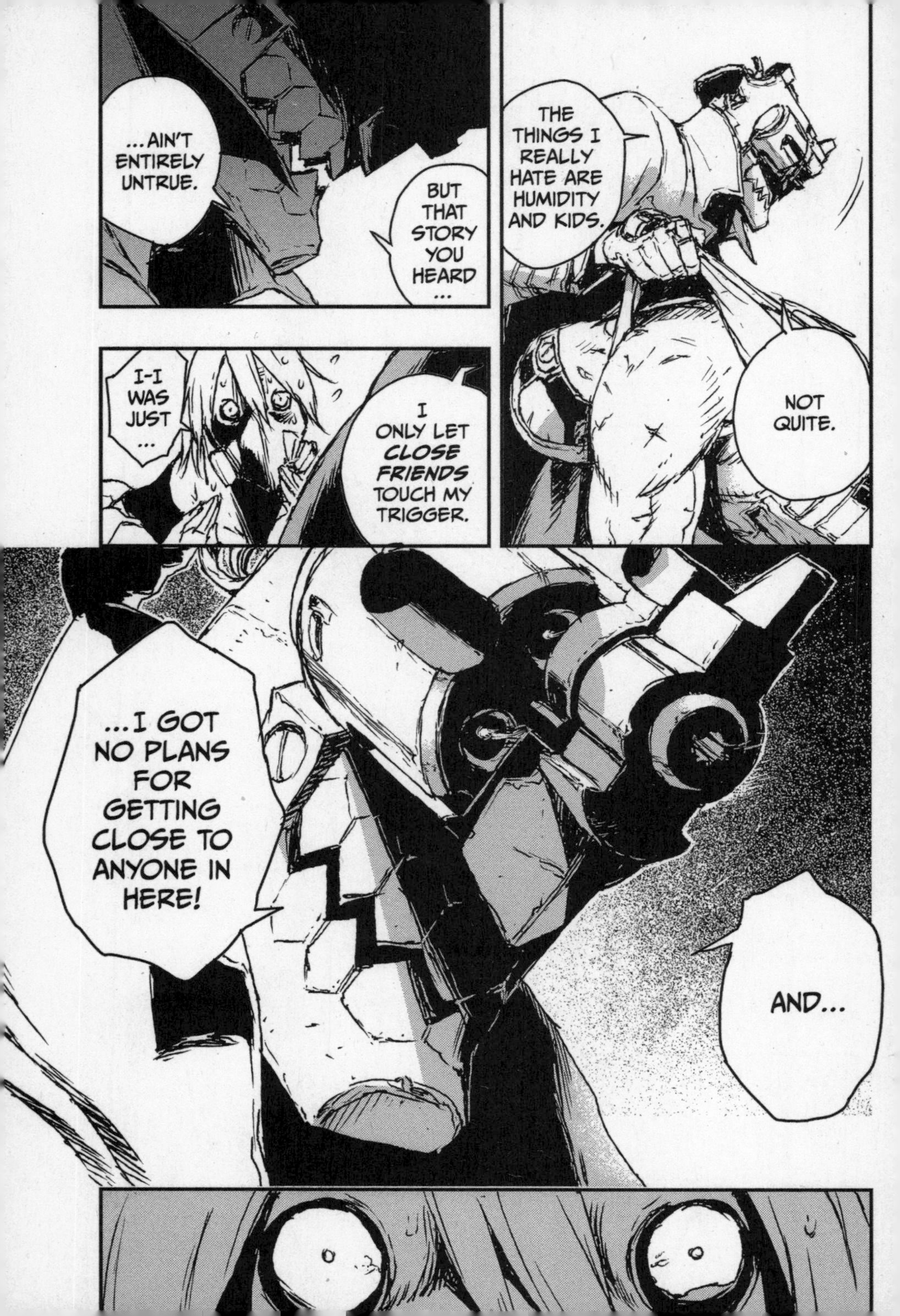
THE THINGS I REALLY HATE ARE HUMIDITY AND KIDS.
NOT QUITE.
BUT THAT STORY YOU HEARD ...
...AIN'T ENTIRELY UNTRUE.
I ONLY LET *CLOSE FRIENDS* TOUCH MY TRIGGER.
I-I WAS JUST ...
AND...
...I GOT NO PLANS FOR GETTING CLOSE TO ANYONE IN HERE!

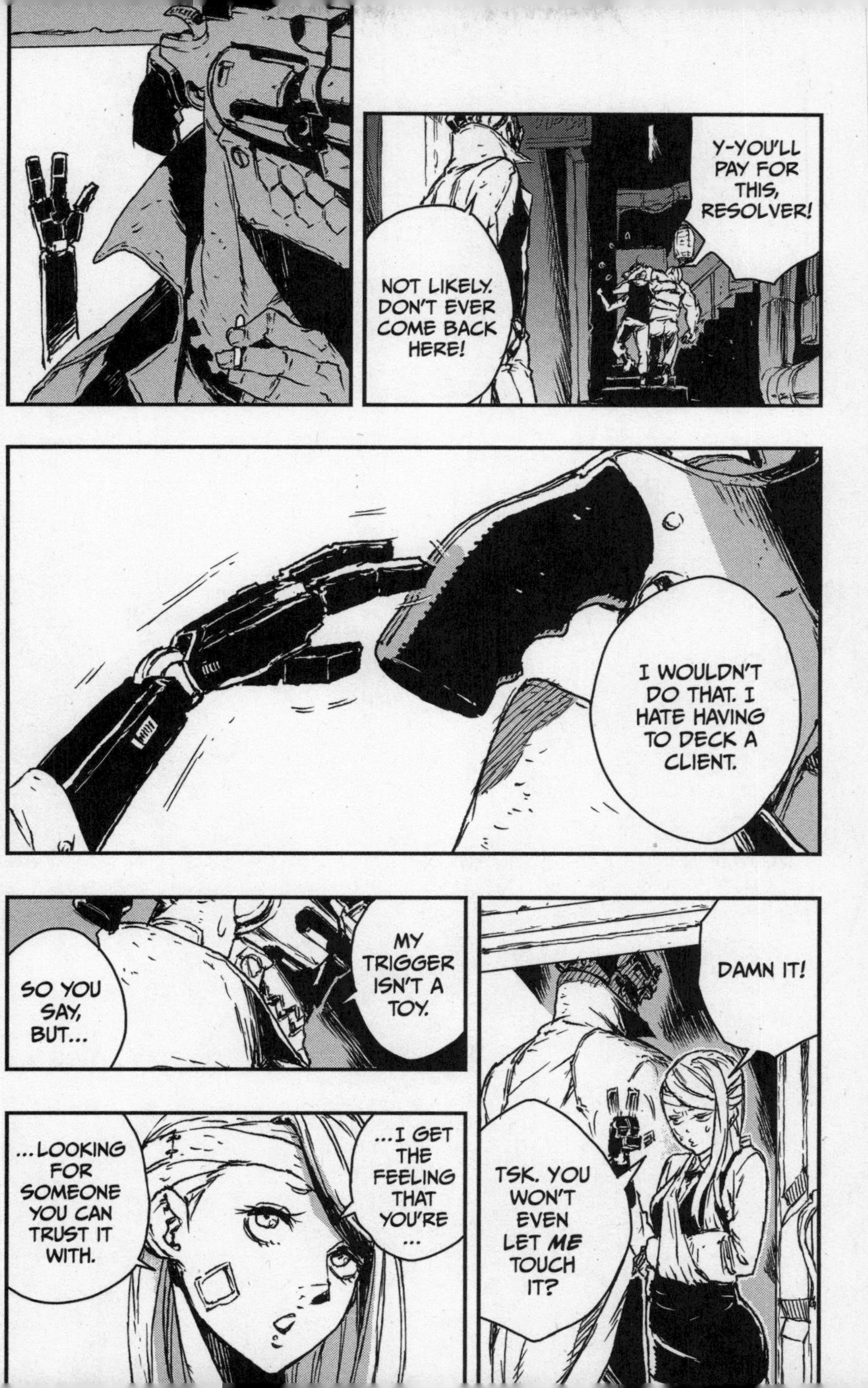
Y-YOU'LL PAY FOR THIS, RESOLVER!
NOT LIKELY. DON'T EVER COME BACK HERE!
I WOULDN'T DO THAT. I HATE HAVING TO DECK A CLIENT.
DAMN IT!
TSK. YOU WON'T EVEN LET *ME* TOUCH IT?
MY TRIGGER ISN'T A TOY.
SO YOU SAY, BUT...
...I GET THE FEELING THAT YOU'RE ...
...LOOKING FOR SOMEONE YOU CAN TRUST IT WITH.

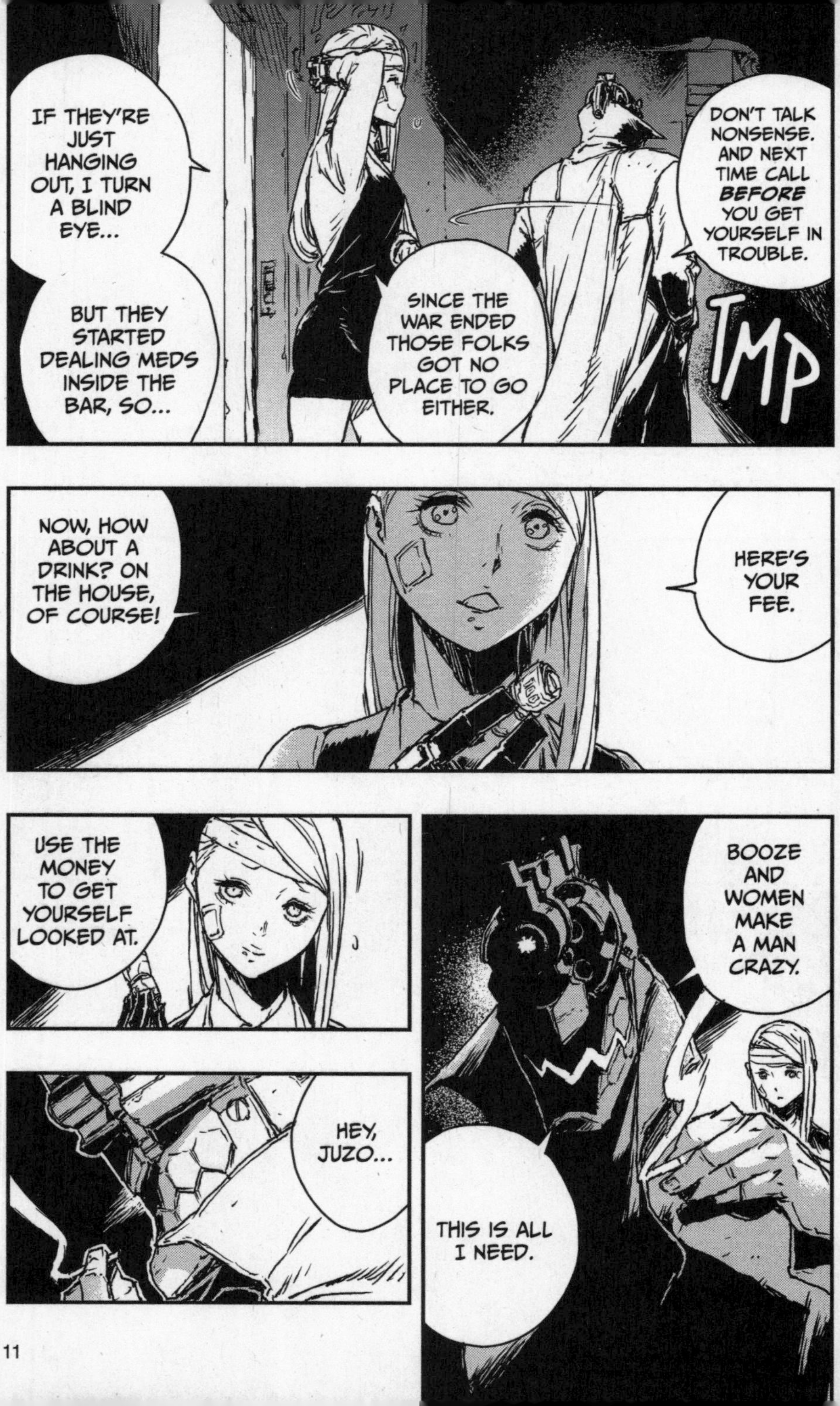
DON'T TALK NONSENSE. AND NEXT TIME CALL *BEFORE* YOU GET YOURSELF IN TROUBLE.
TMP
SINCE THE WAR ENDED THOSE FOLKS GOT NO PLACE TO GO EITHER.
IF THEY'RE JUST HANGING OUT, I TURN A BLIND EYE...
BUT THEY STARTED DEALING MEDS INSIDE THE BAR, SO...
HERE'S YOUR FEE.
NOW, HOW ABOUT A DRINK? ON THE HOUSE, OF COURSE!
BOOZE AND WOMEN MAKE A MAN CRAZY.
THIS IS ALL I NEED.
USE THE MONEY TO GET YOURSELF LOOKED AT.
HEY, JUZO...

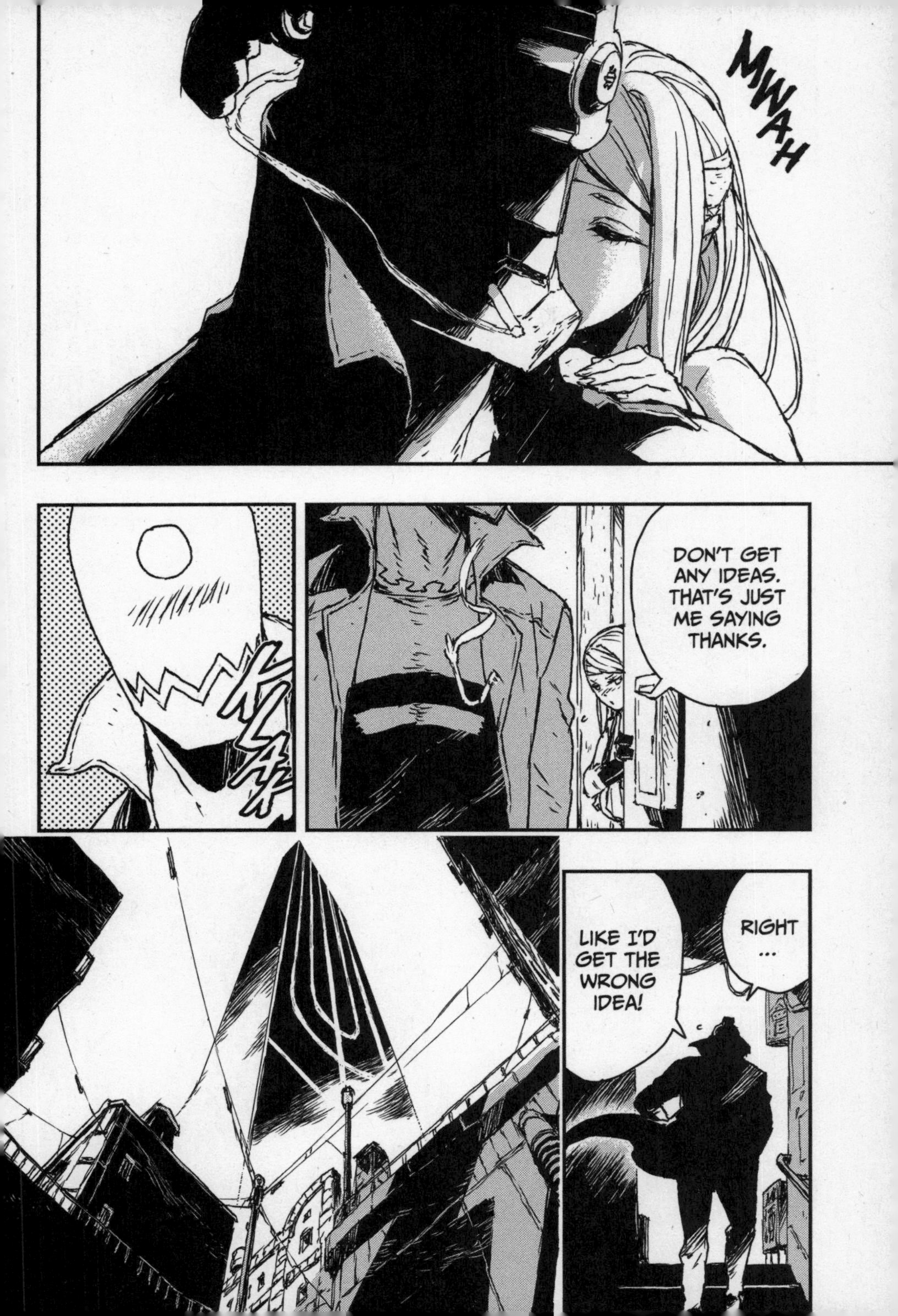
MWAH
DON'T GET ANY IDEAS. THAT'S JUST ME SAYING THANKS.
KLAK
RIGHT ...
LIKE I'D GET THE WRONG IDEA!

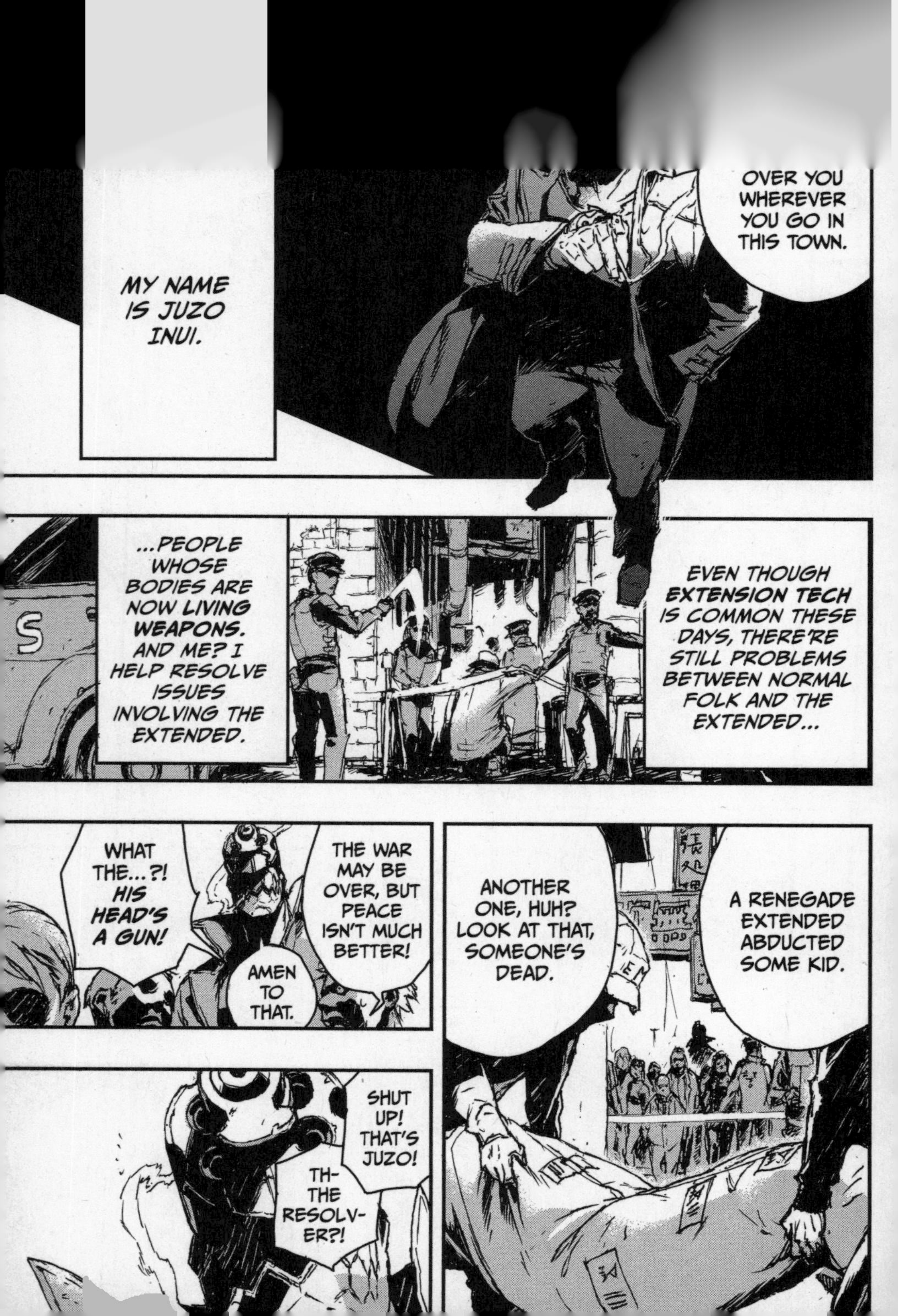
OVER YOU WHEREVER YOU GO IN THIS TOWN.
MY NAME IS JUZO INUI.
EVEN THOUGH EXTENSION TECH IS COMMON THESE DAYS, THERE'RE STILL PROBLEMS BETWEEN NORMAL FOLK AND THE EXTENDED...
...PEOPLE WHOSE BODIES ARE NOW LIVING WEAPONS. AND ME? I HELP RESOLVE ISSUES INVOLVING THE EXTENDED.
A RENEGADE EXTENDED ABDUCTED SOME KID.
ANOTHER ONE, HUH? LOOK AT THAT, SOMEONE'S DEAD.
THE WAR MAY BE OVER, BUT PEACE ISN'T MUCH BETTER!
WHAT THE...?! HIS HEAD'S A GUN!
AMEN TO THAT.
SHUT UP! THAT'S JUZO!
TH-THE RESOLVER?!

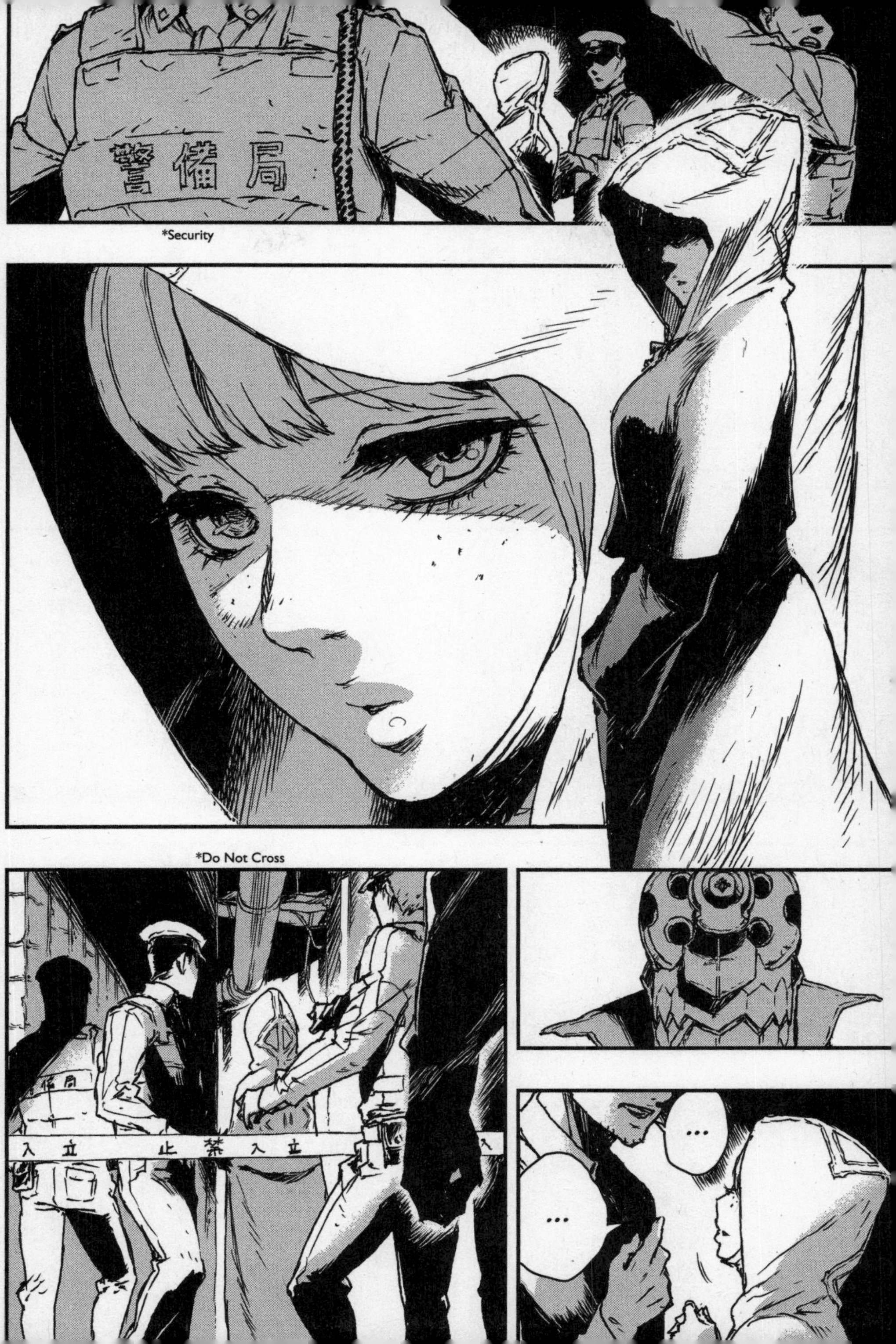
警備局
*Security
*Do Not Cross
...
...

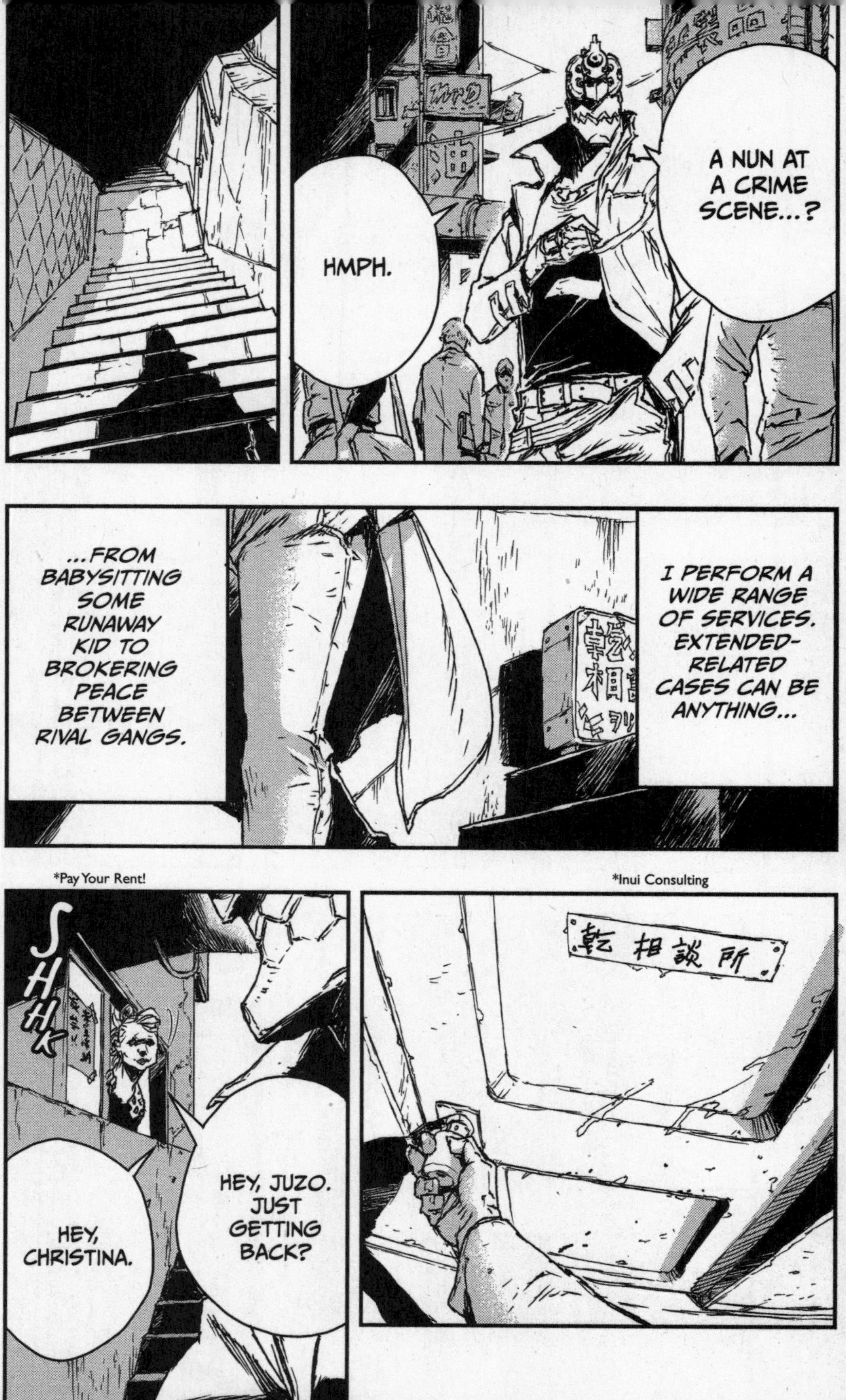
A NUN AT A CRIME SCENE...?
HMPH.
I PERFORM A WIDE RANGE OF SERVICES. EXTENDED-RELATED CASES CAN BE ANYTHING...
...FROM BABYSITTING SOME RUNAWAY KID TO BROKERING PEACE BETWEEN RIVAL GANGS.
*Inui Consulting
*Pay Your Rent!
SHHK
HEY, JUZO. JUST GETTING BACK?
HEY, CHRISTINA.

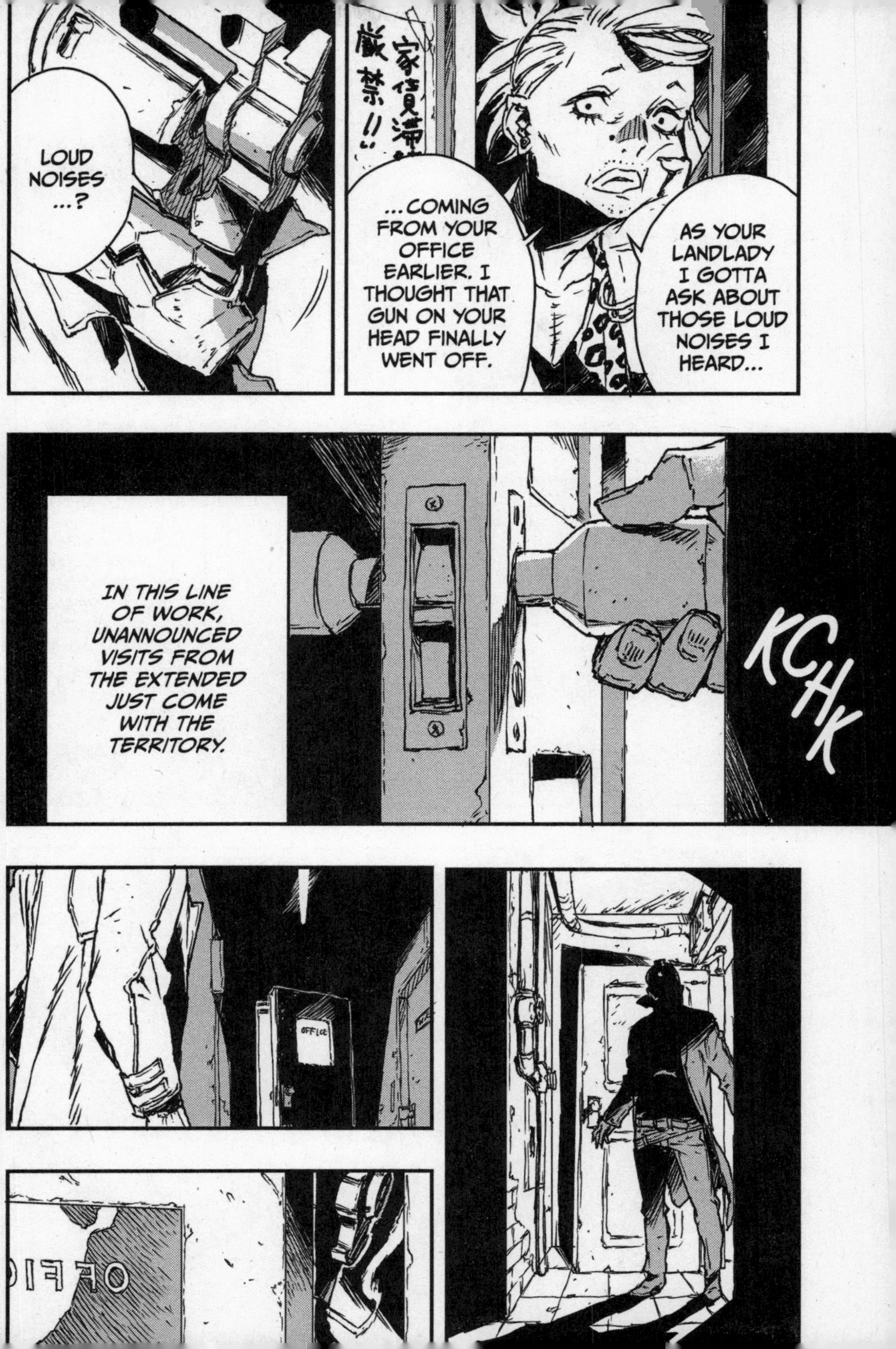
AS YOUR LANDLADY I GOTTA ASK ABOUT THOSE LOUD NOISES I HEARD...
...COMING FROM YOUR OFFICE EARLIER. I THOUGHT THAT GUN ON YOUR HEAD FINALLY WENT OFF.
家賃滞
厳禁!!
LOUD NOISES ...?
KCHK
IN THIS LINE OF WORK, UNANNOUNCED VISITS FROM THE EXTENDED JUST COME WITH THE TERRITORY.
OFFICE
OFFI

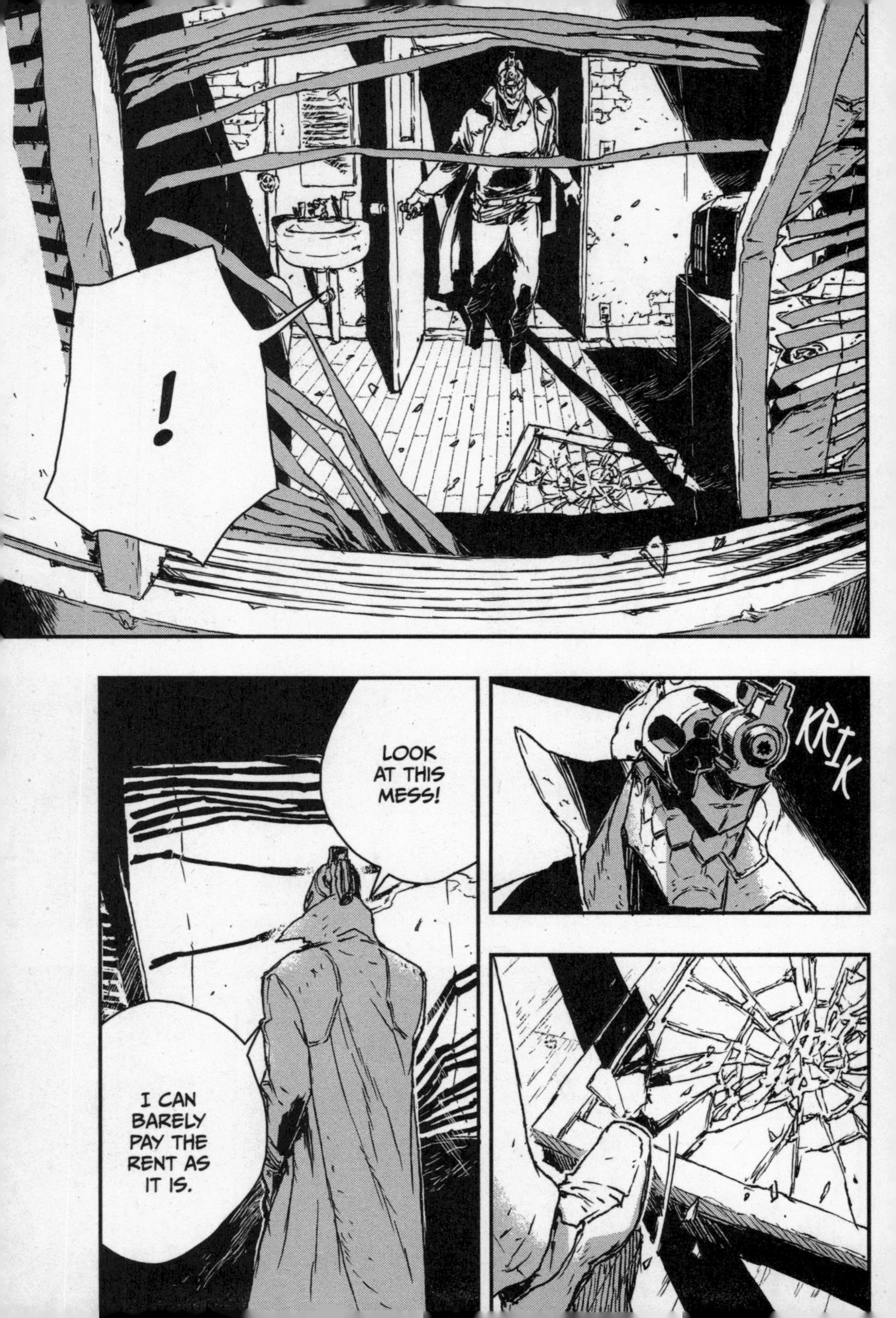
!
KRIK
LOOK AT THIS MESS!
I CAN BARELY PAY THE RENT AS IT IS.

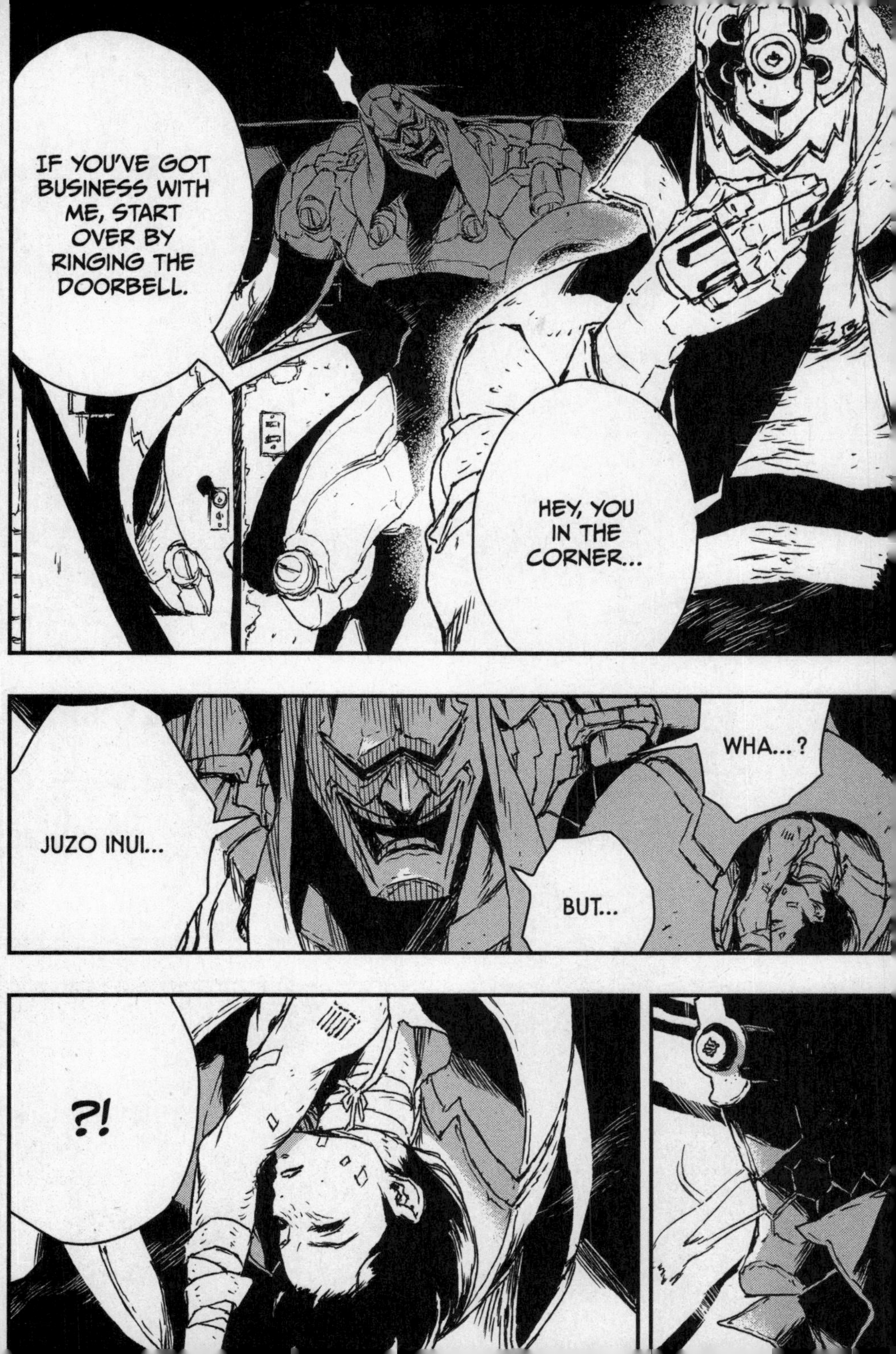
HEY, YOU IN THE CORNER...
IF YOU'VE GOT BUSINESS WITH ME, START OVER BY RINGING THE DOORBELL.
WHA...?
BUT...
JUZO INUI...
?!

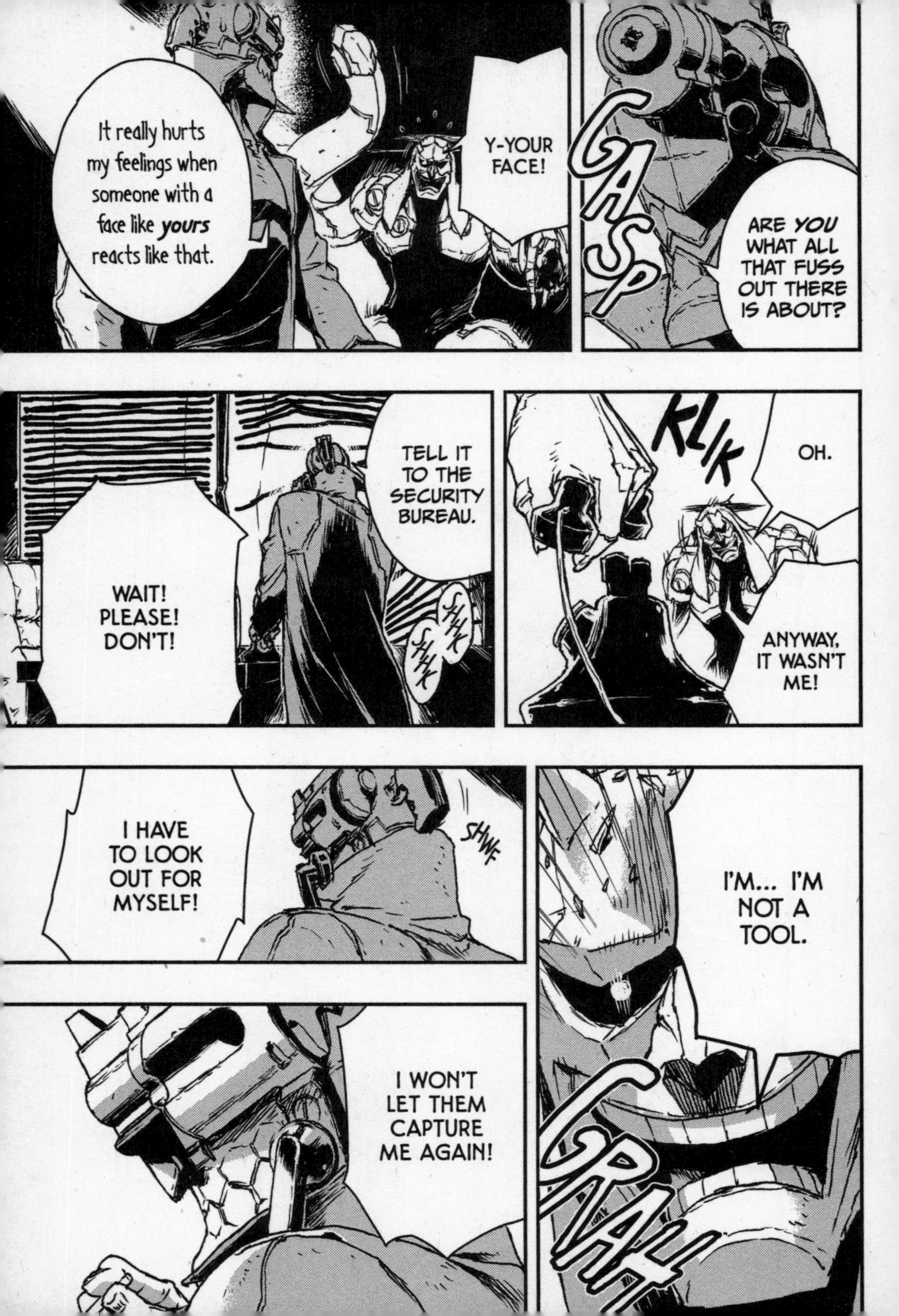
GASP
ARE *YOU* WHAT ALL THAT FUSS OUT THERE IS ABOUT?
Y-YOUR FACE!
It really hurts my feelings when someone with a face like ***yours*** reacts like that.
KLIK
OH.
ANYWAY, IT WASN'T ME!
TELL IT TO THE SECURITY BUREAU.
SHHK
SHHK
WAIT! PLEASE! DON'T!
I'M... I'M NOT A TOOL.
GRAH
SHWF
I HAVE TO LOOK OUT FOR MYSELF!
I WON'T LET THEM CAPTURE ME AGAIN!

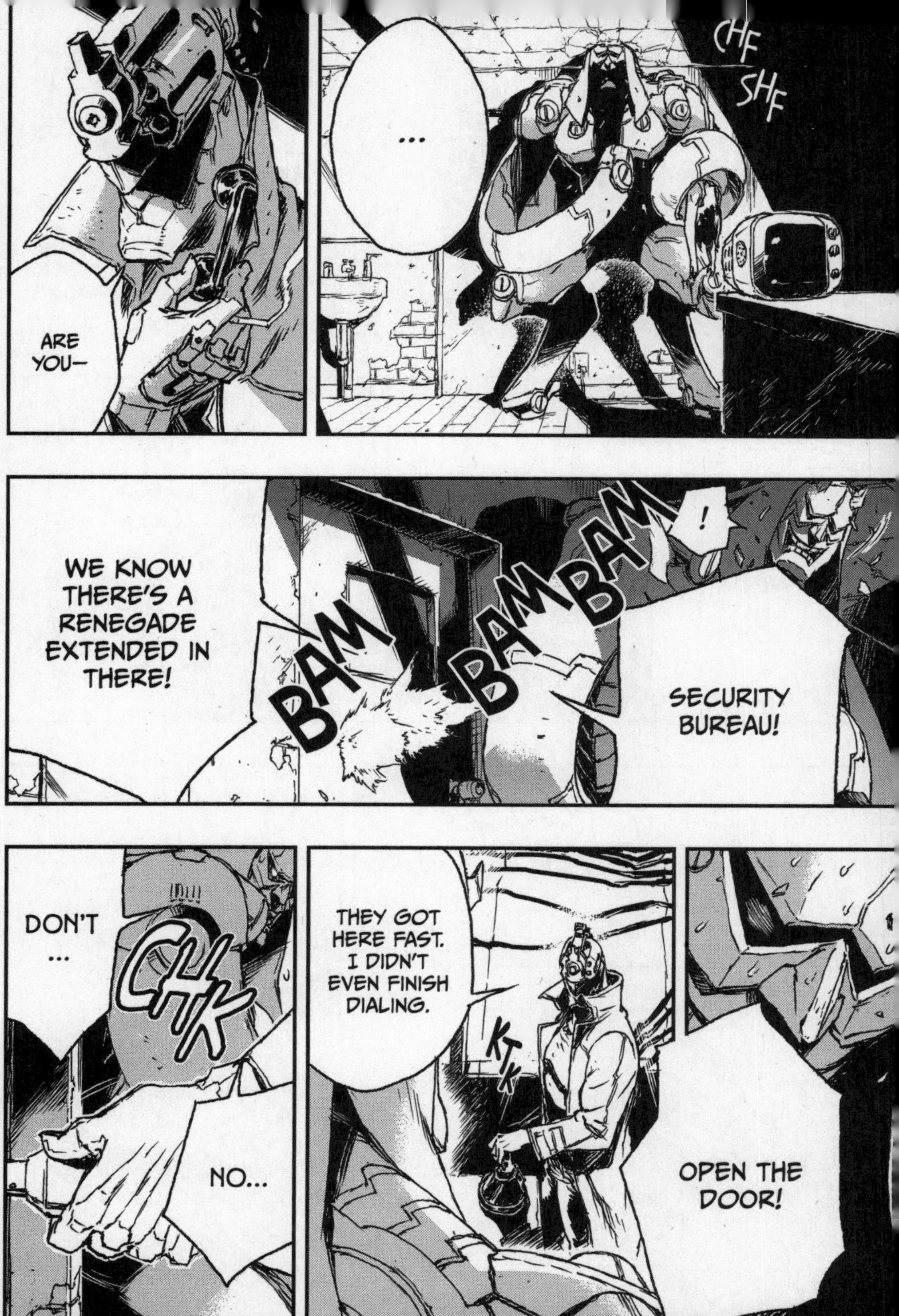
CHF SHF
...
ARE YOU—
!
SECURITY BUREAU!
BAM
BAM BAM
WE KNOW THERE'S A RENEGADE EXTENDED IN THERE!
OPEN THE DOOR!
THEY GOT HERE FAST. I DIDN'T EVEN FINISH DIALING.
KTK
DON'T ...
CHK
NO...

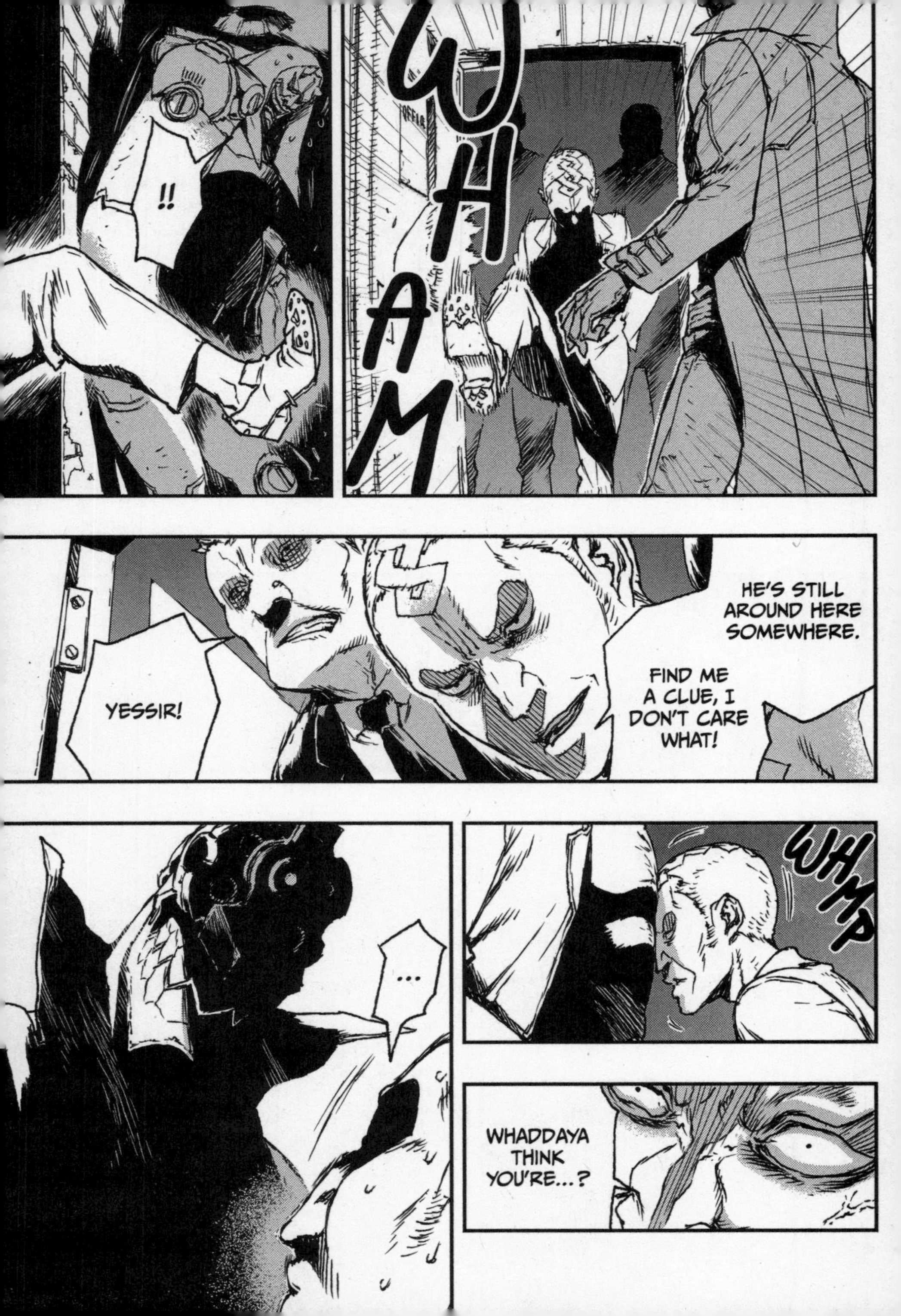
WHAM
!!
HE'S STILL AROUND HERE SOMEWHERE.
FIND ME A CLUE, I DON'T CARE WHAT!
YESSIR!
WHMP
WHADDAYA THINK YOU'RE...?
...

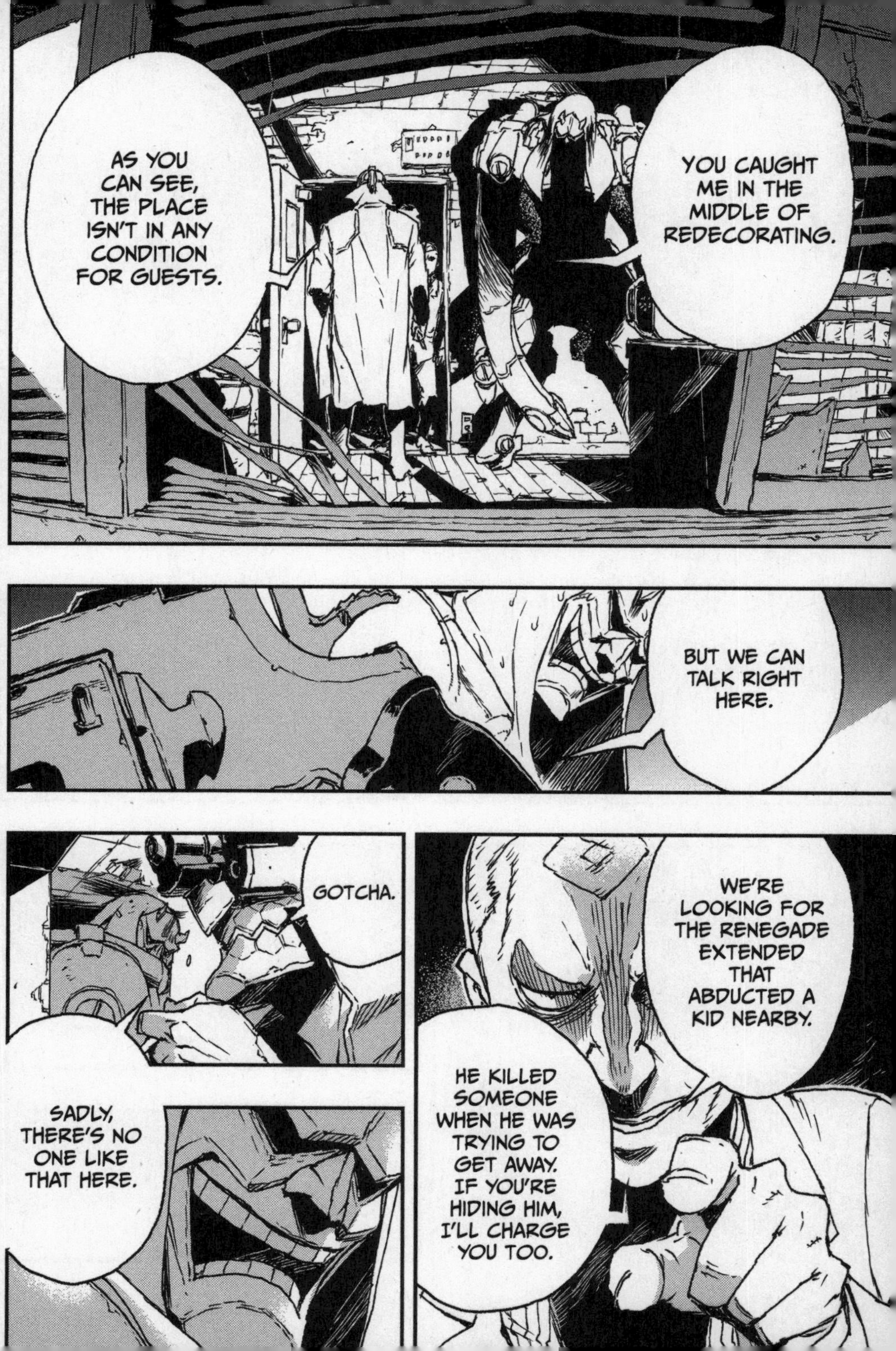
YOU CAUGHT ME IN THE MIDDLE OF REDECORATING.
AS YOU CAN SEE, THE PLACE ISN'T IN ANY CONDITION FOR GUESTS.
BUT WE CAN TALK RIGHT HERE.
WE'RE LOOKING FOR THE RENEGADE EXTENDED THAT ABDUCTED A KID NEARBY.
HE KILLED SOMEONE WHEN HE WAS TRYING TO GET AWAY. IF YOU'RE HIDING HIM, I'LL CHARGE YOU TOO.
GOTCHA.
SADLY, THERE'S NO ONE LIKE THAT HERE.

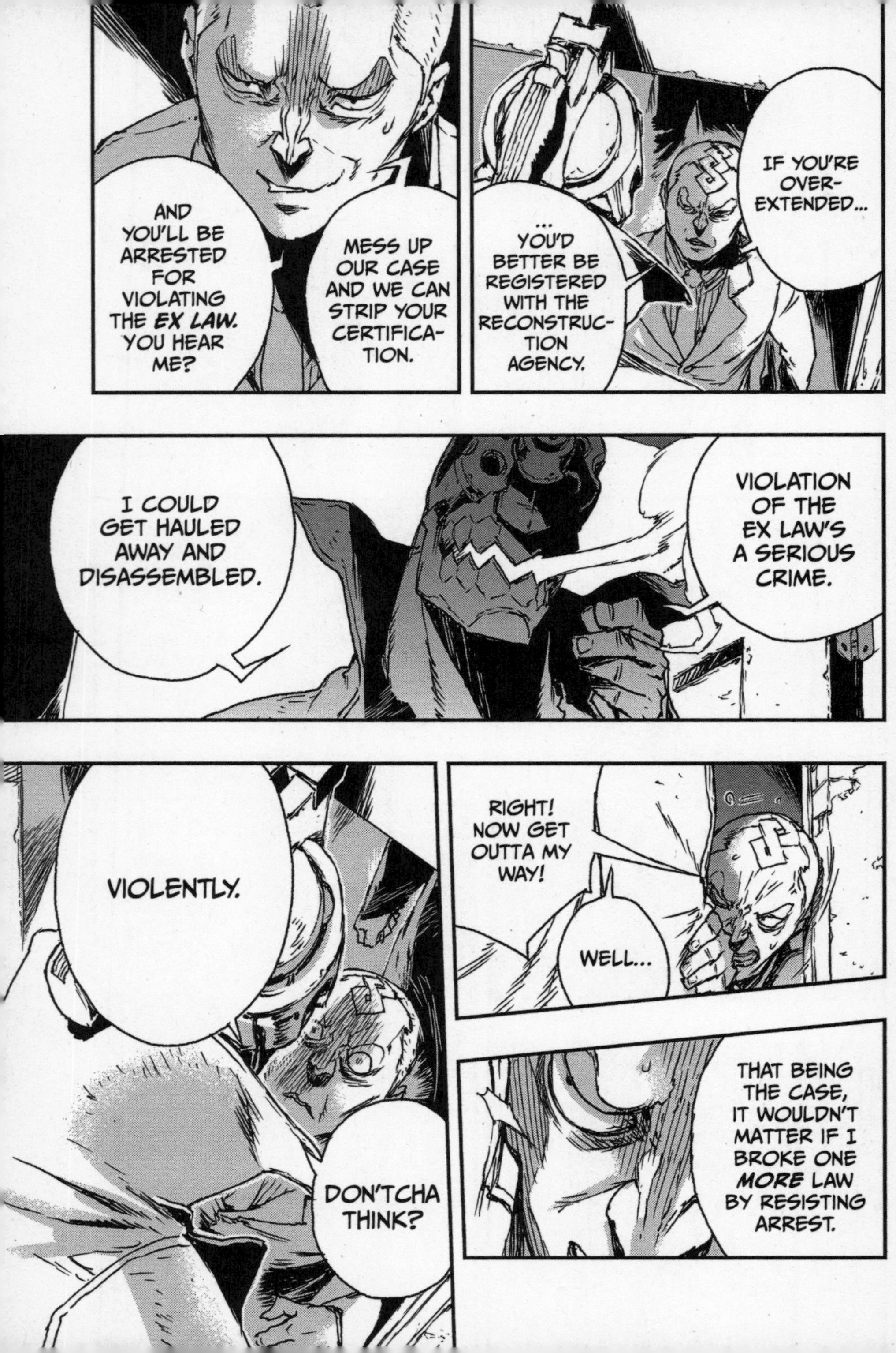
IF YOU'RE OVER-EXTENDED...
... YOU'D BETTER BE REGISTERED WITH THE RECONSTRUCTION AGENCY.
MESS UP OUR CASE AND WE CAN STRIP YOUR CERTIFICATION.
AND YOU'LL BE ARRESTED FOR VIOLATING THE *EX LAW.* YOU HEAR ME?
VIOLATION OF THE EX LAW'S A SERIOUS CRIME.
I COULD GET HAULED AWAY AND DISASSEMBLED.
RIGHT! NOW GET OUTTA MY WAY!
WELL...
THAT BEING THE CASE, IT WOULDN'T MATTER IF I BROKE ONE *MORE* LAW BY RESISTING ARREST.
VIOLENTLY.
DON'TCHA THINK?

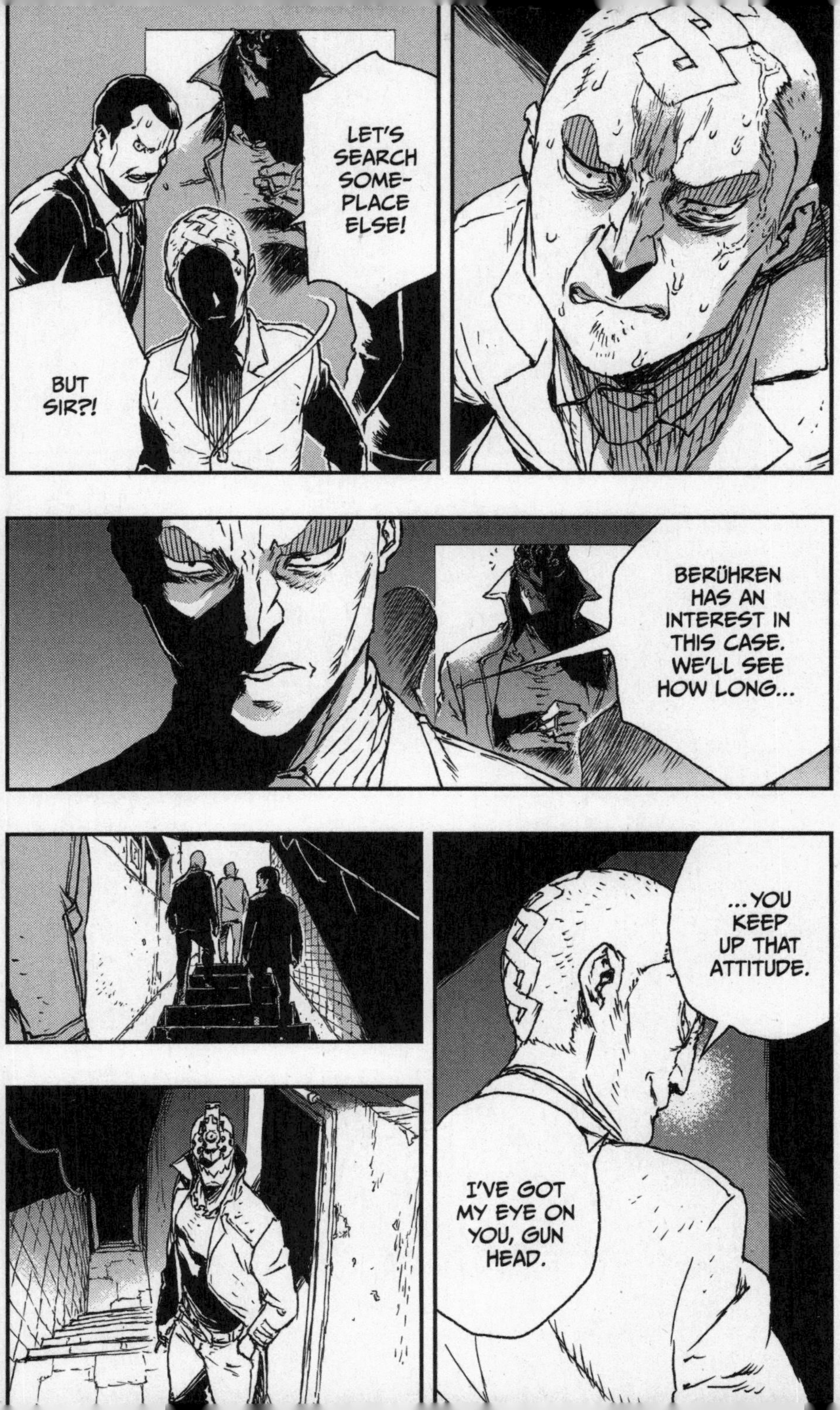
LET'S SEARCH SOME-PLACE ELSE!
BUT SIR?!
BERÜHREN HAS AN INTEREST IN THIS CASE. WE'LL SEE HOW LONG...
...YOU KEEP UP THAT ATTITUDE.
I'VE GOT MY EYE ON YOU, GUN HEAD.

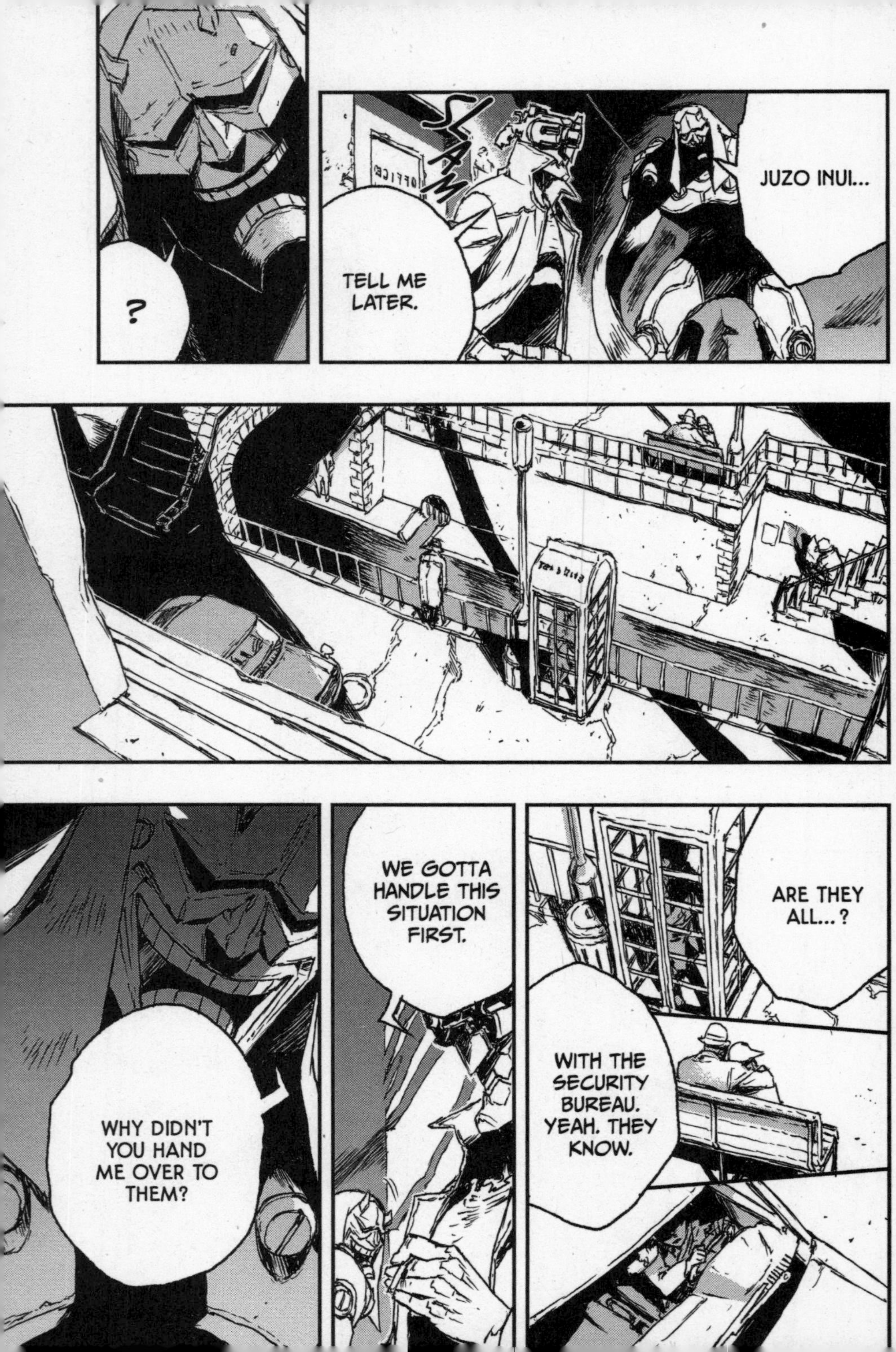
JUZO INUI...
SLAM
TELL ME LATER.
?
ARE THEY ALL...?
WITH THE SECURITY BUREAU. YEAH. THEY KNOW.
WE GOTTA HANDLE THIS SITUATION FIRST.
WHY DIDN'T YOU HAND ME OVER TO THEM?

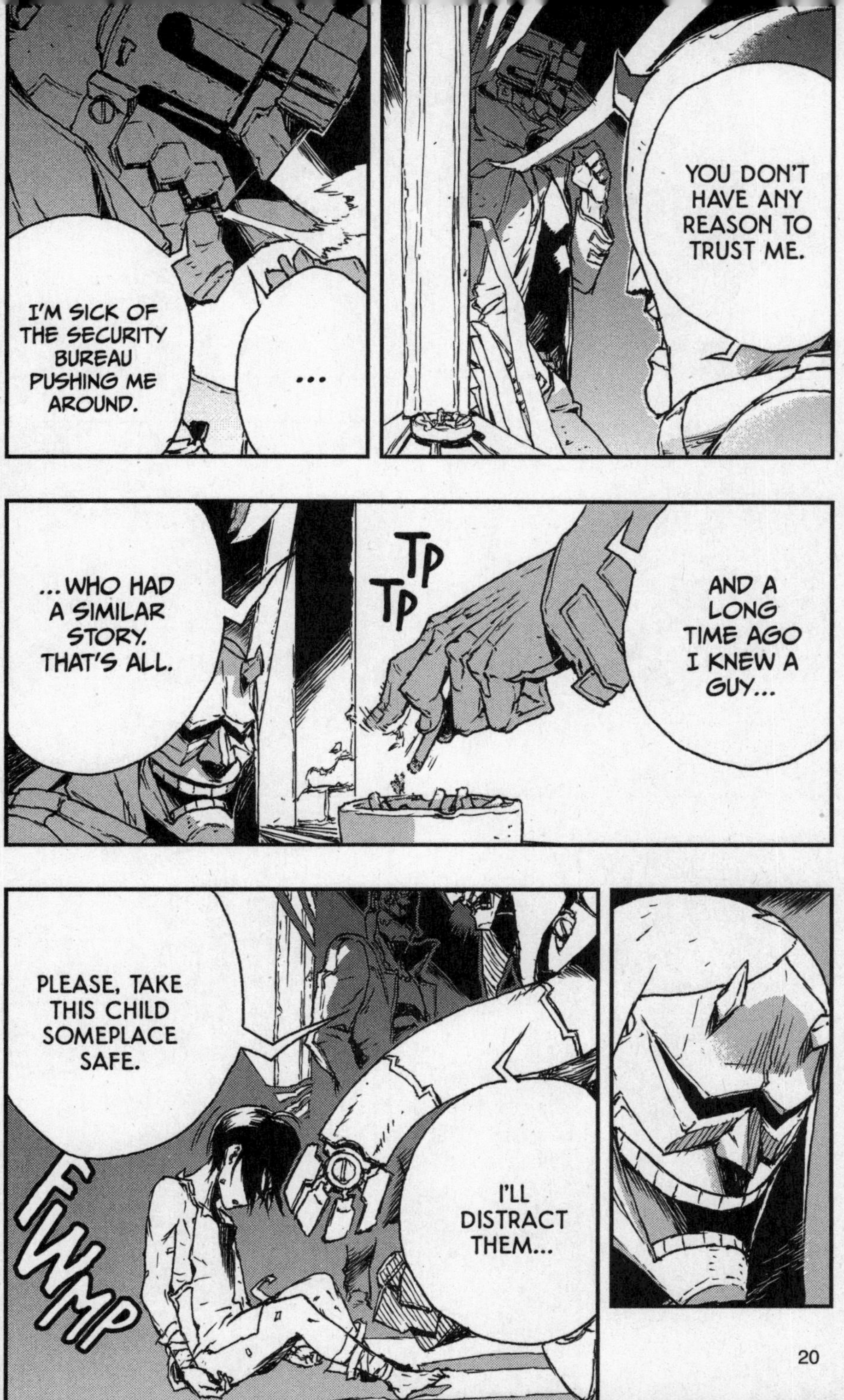
YOU DON'T HAVE ANY REASON TO TRUST ME.
...
I'M SICK OF THE SECURITY BUREAU PUSHING ME AROUND.
AND A LONG TIME AGO I KNEW A GUY...
TP TP
...WHO HAD A SIMILAR STORY. THAT'S ALL.
PLEASE, TAKE THIS CHILD SOMEPLACE SAFE.
I'LL DISTRACT THEM...
FWMP

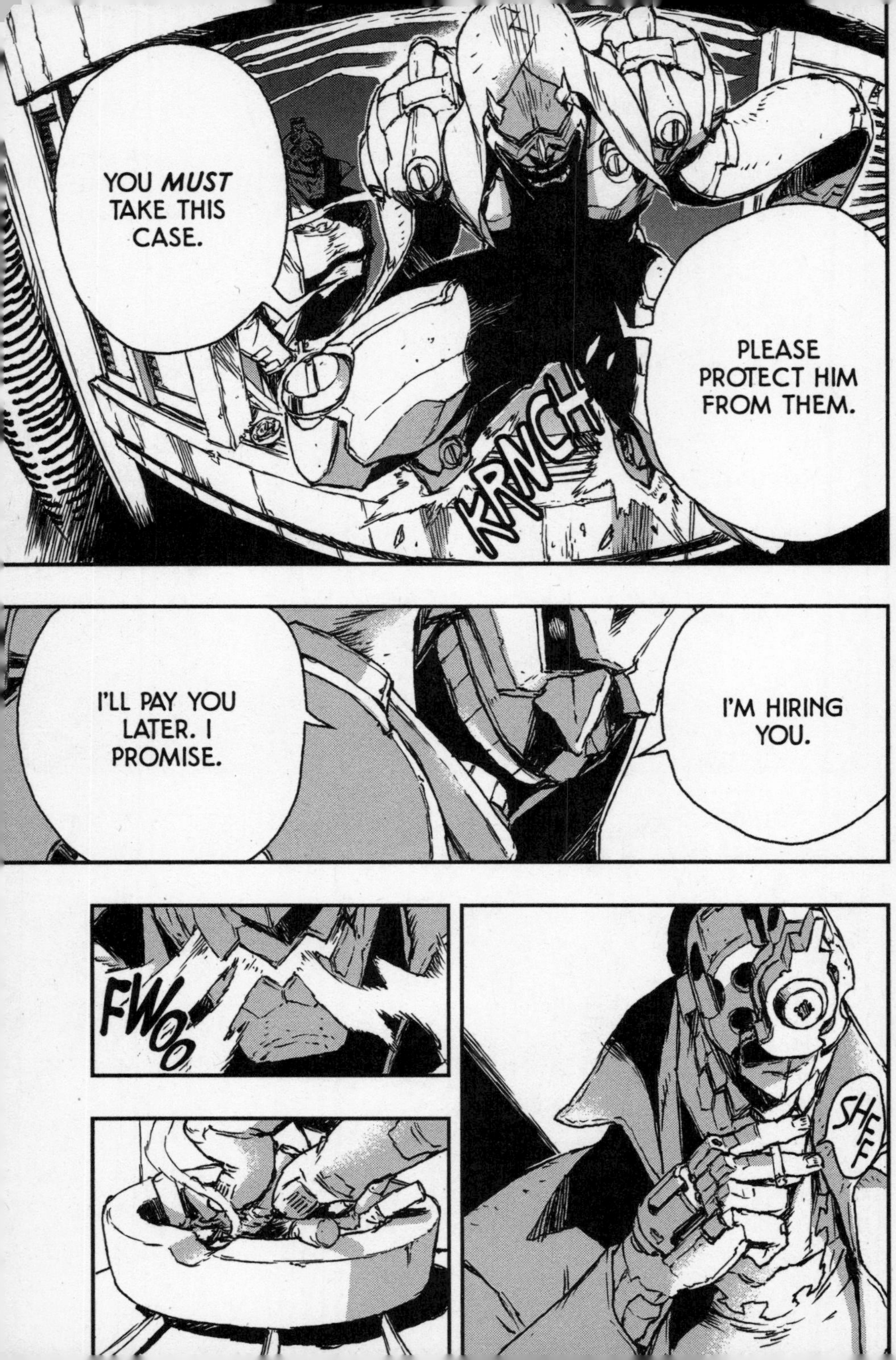
PLEASE PROTECT HIM FROM THEM.
YOU *MUST* TAKE THIS CASE.
KRNCH
I'M HIRING YOU.
I'LL PAY YOU LATER. I PROMISE.
SHEFF
FWOO

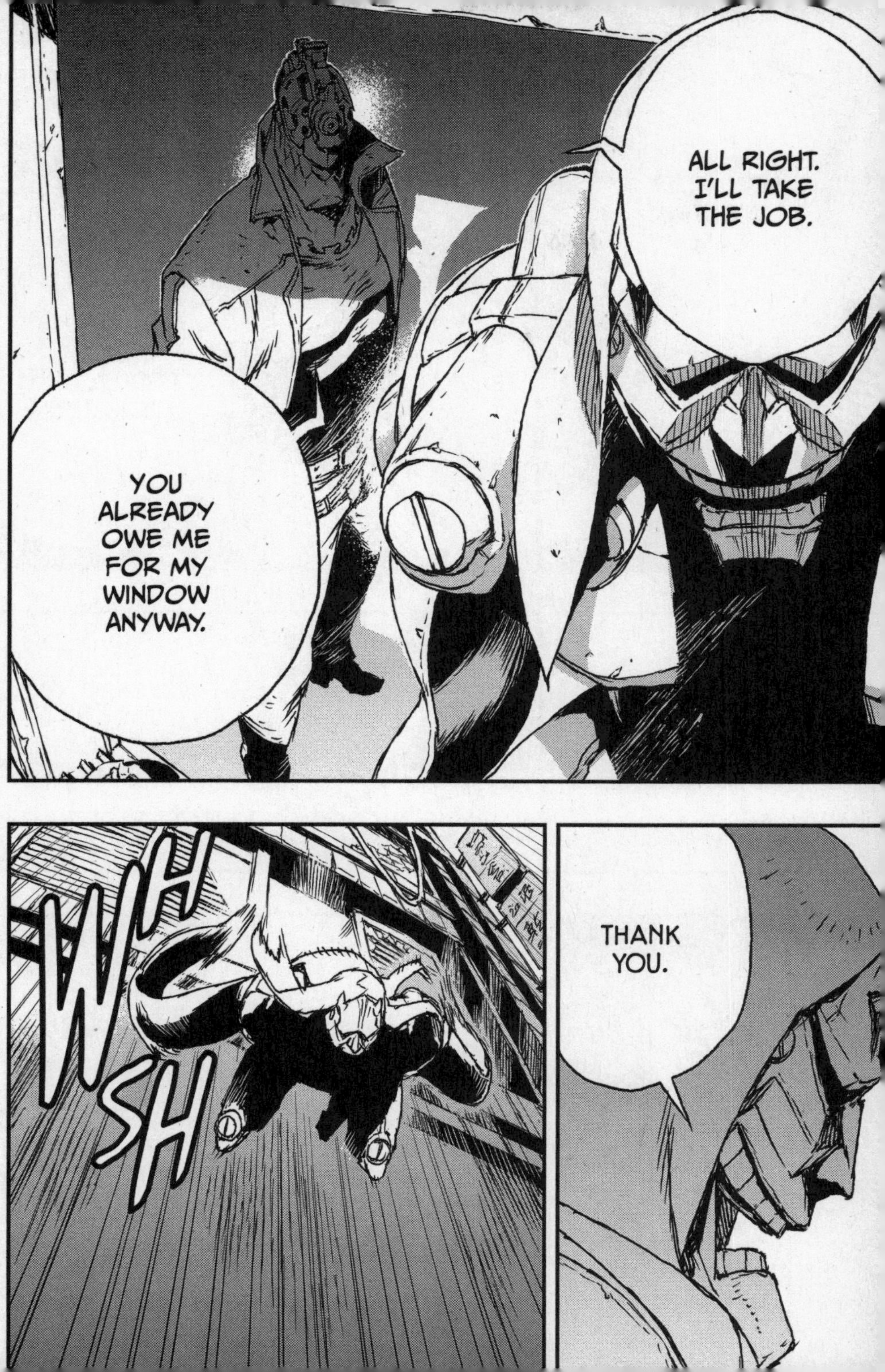
ALL RIGHT. I'LL TAKE THE JOB.
YOU ALREADY OWE ME FOR MY WINDOW ANYWAY.
THANK YOU.
WHSH

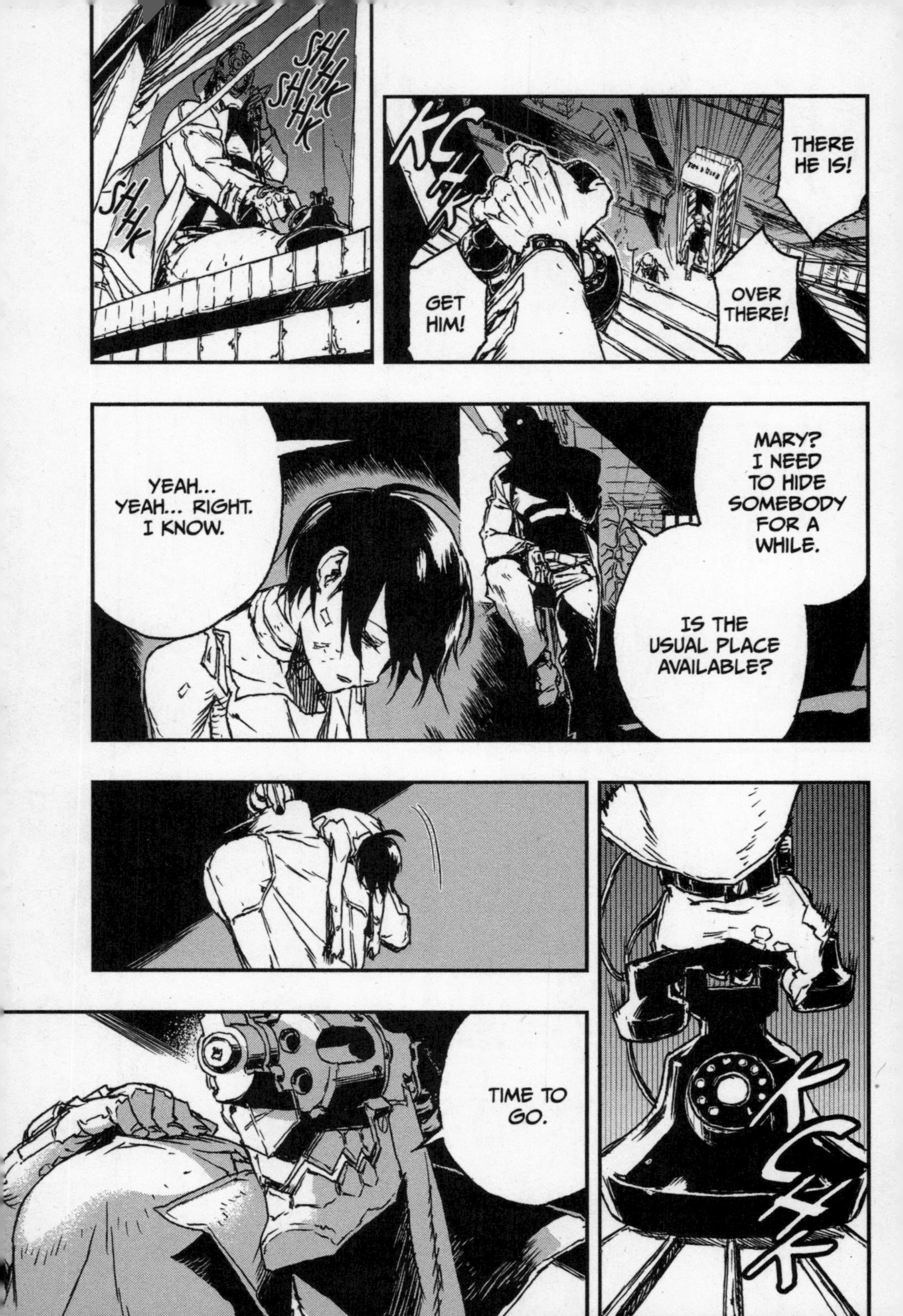
THERE HE IS!
KCHK
OVER THERE!
GET HIM!
SHHK SHHK
SHHK
MARY? I NEED TO HIDE SOMEBODY FOR A WHILE.
IS THE USUAL PLACE AVAILABLE?
YEAH... YEAH... RIGHT. I KNOW.
KCHK
TIME TO GO.

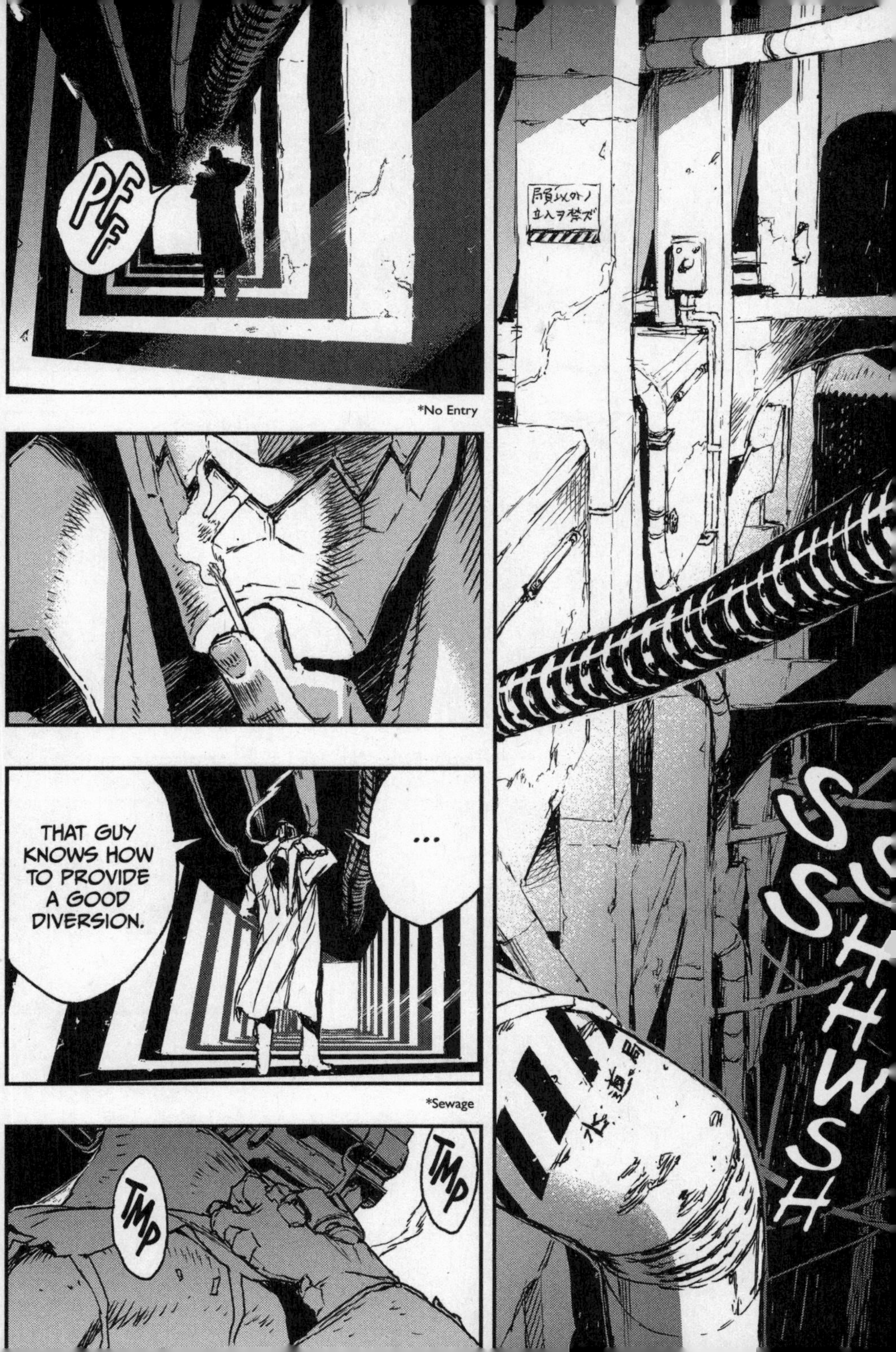
SHWSH
PFFF
*No Entry
THAT GUY KNOWS HOW TO PROVIDE A GOOD DIVERSION.
...
*Sewage
TMP
TMP

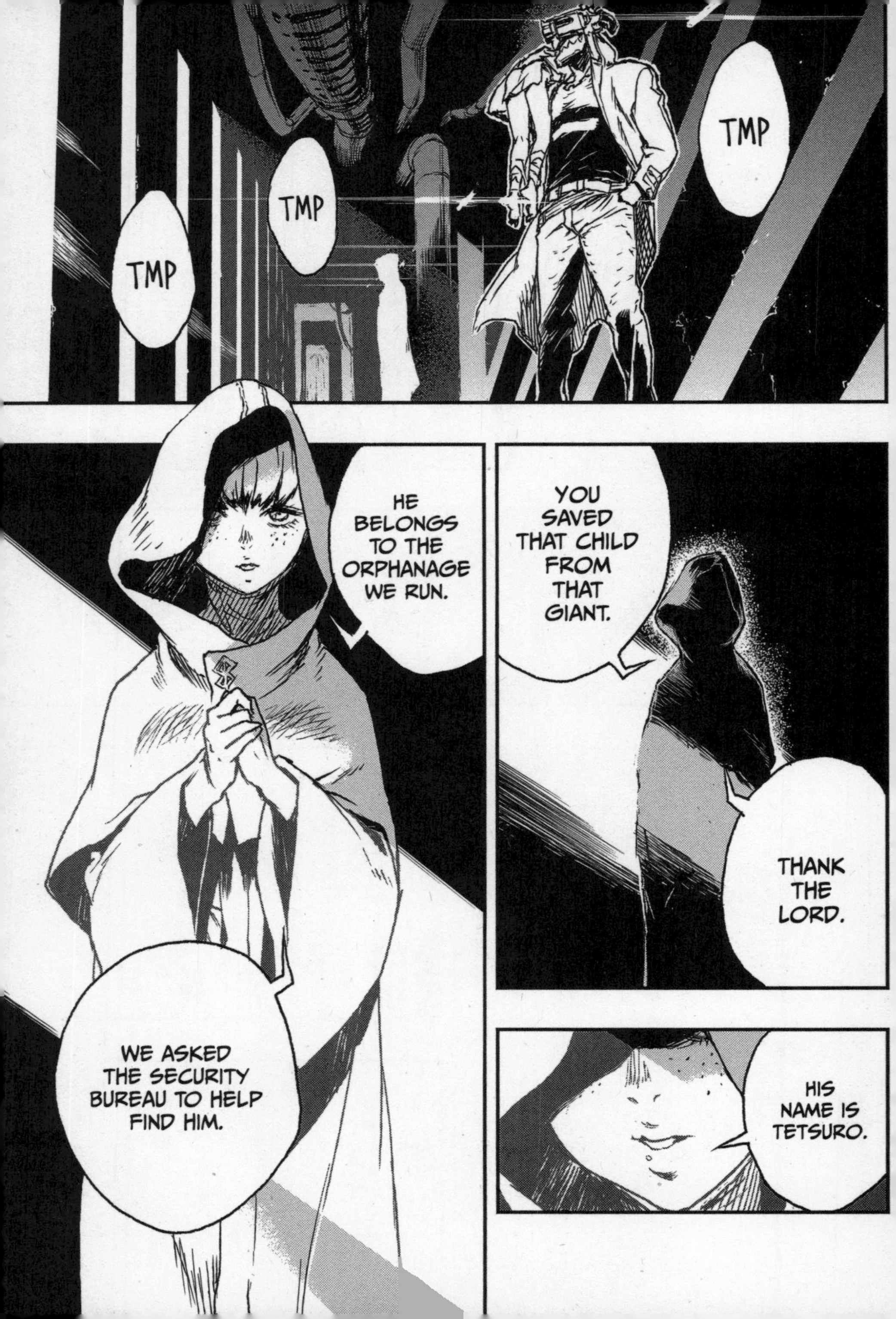
TMP
TMP
TMP
YOU SAVED THAT CHILD FROM THAT GIANT.
THANK THE LORD.
HIS NAME IS TETSURO.
HE BELONGS TO THE ORPHANAGE WE RUN.
WE ASKED THE SECURITY BUREAU TO HELP FIND HIM.

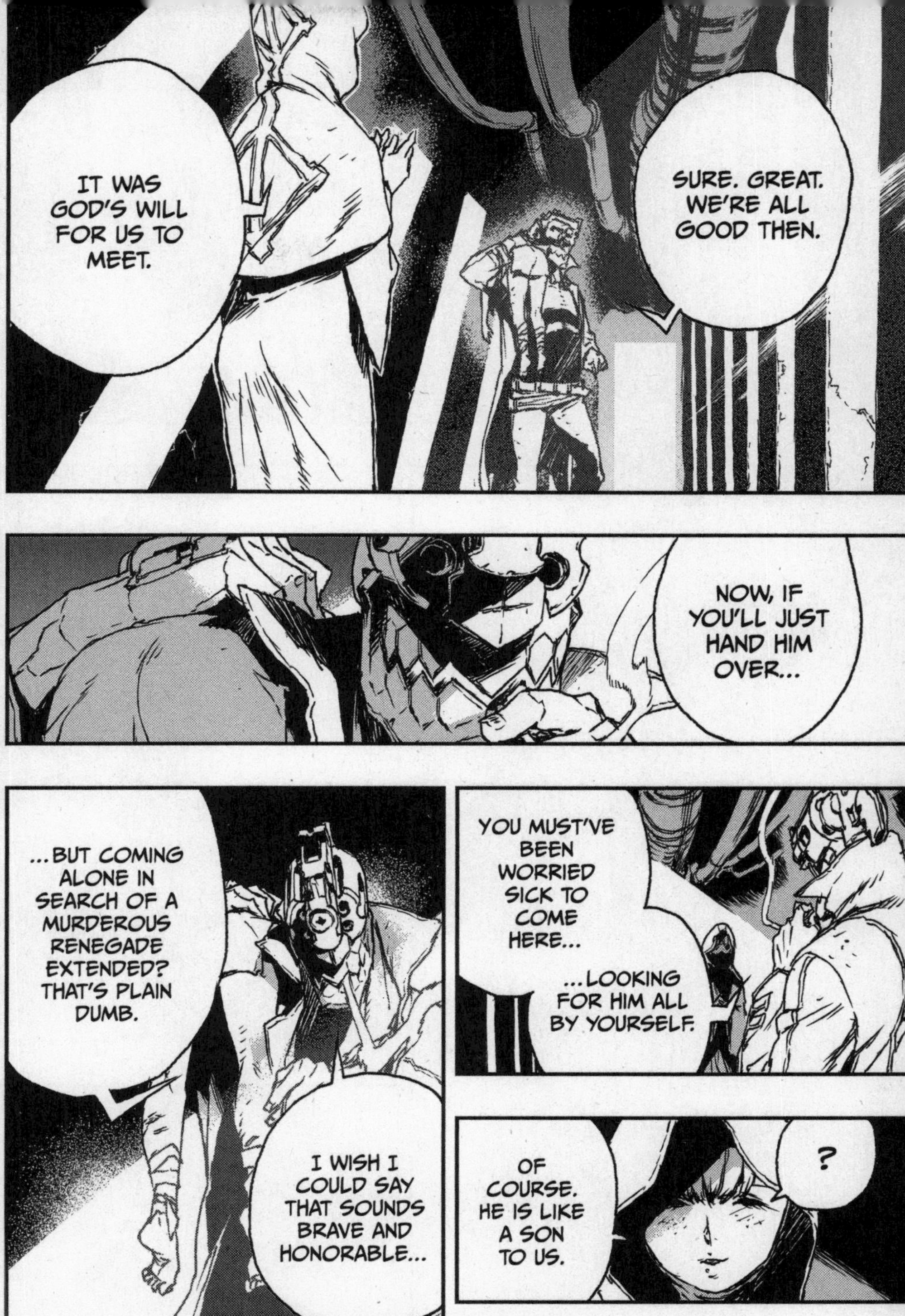
SURE. GREAT. WE'RE ALL GOOD THEN.
IT WAS GOD'S WILL FOR US TO MEET.
NOW, IF YOU'LL JUST HAND HIM OVER...
YOU MUST'VE BEEN WORRIED SICK TO COME HERE...
...LOOKING FOR HIM ALL BY YOURSELF.
?
OF COURSE. HE IS LIKE A SON TO US.
I WISH I COULD SAY THAT SOUNDS BRAVE AND HONORABLE...
...BUT COMING ALONE IN SEARCH OF A MURDEROUS RENEGADE EXTENDED? THAT'S PLAIN DUMB.

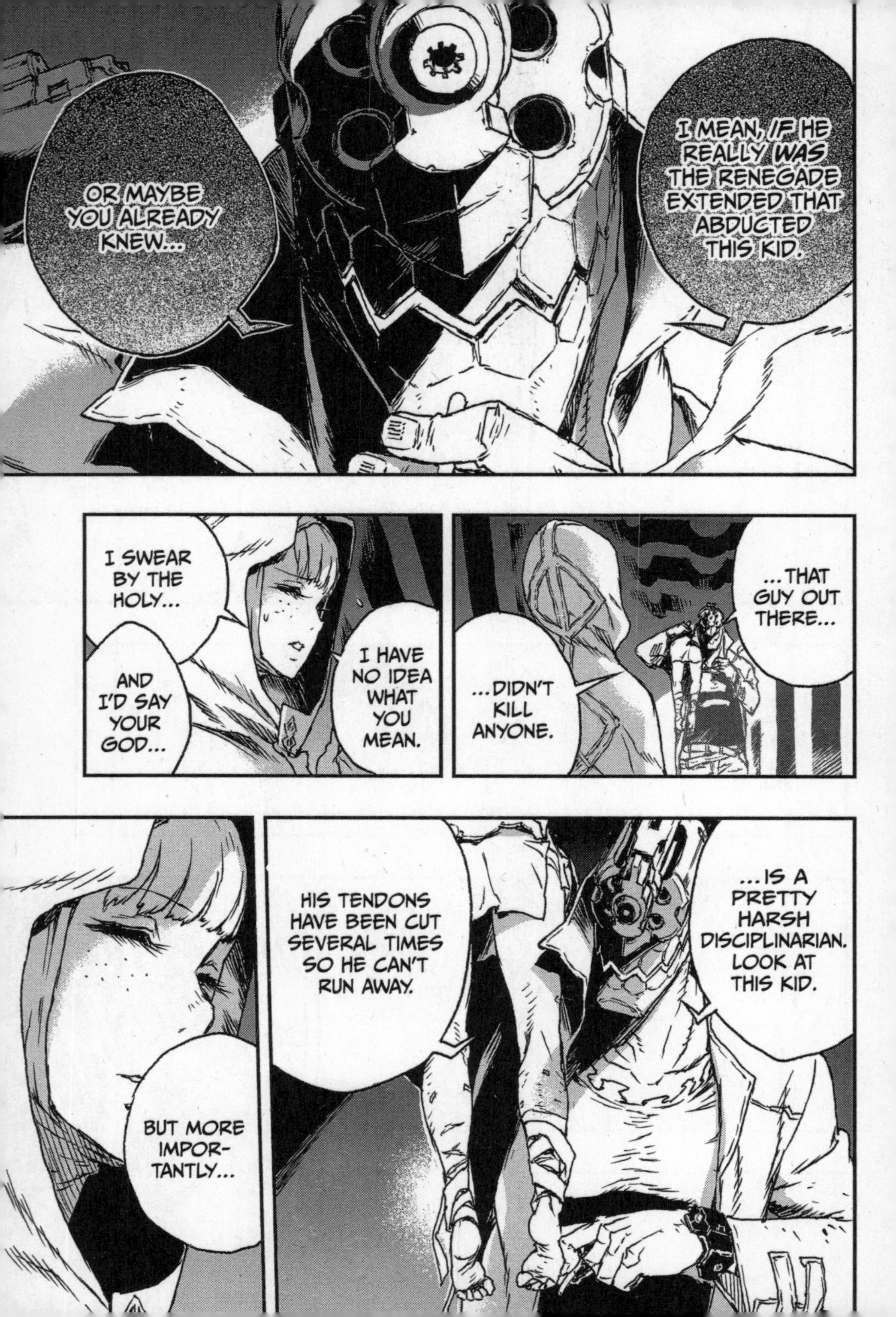
I MEAN, IF HE REALLY WAS THE RENEGADE EXTENDED THAT ABDUCTED THIS KID.
OR MAYBE YOU ALREADY KNEW...
...THAT GUY OUT THERE...
...DIDN'T KILL ANYONE.
I SWEAR BY THE HOLY...
I HAVE NO IDEA WHAT YOU MEAN.
AND I'D SAY YOUR GOD...
...IS A PRETTY HARSH DISCIPLINARIAN. LOOK AT THIS KID.
HIS TENDONS HAVE BEEN CUT SEVERAL TIMES SO HE CAN'T RUN AWAY.
BUT MORE IMPOR-TANTLY...

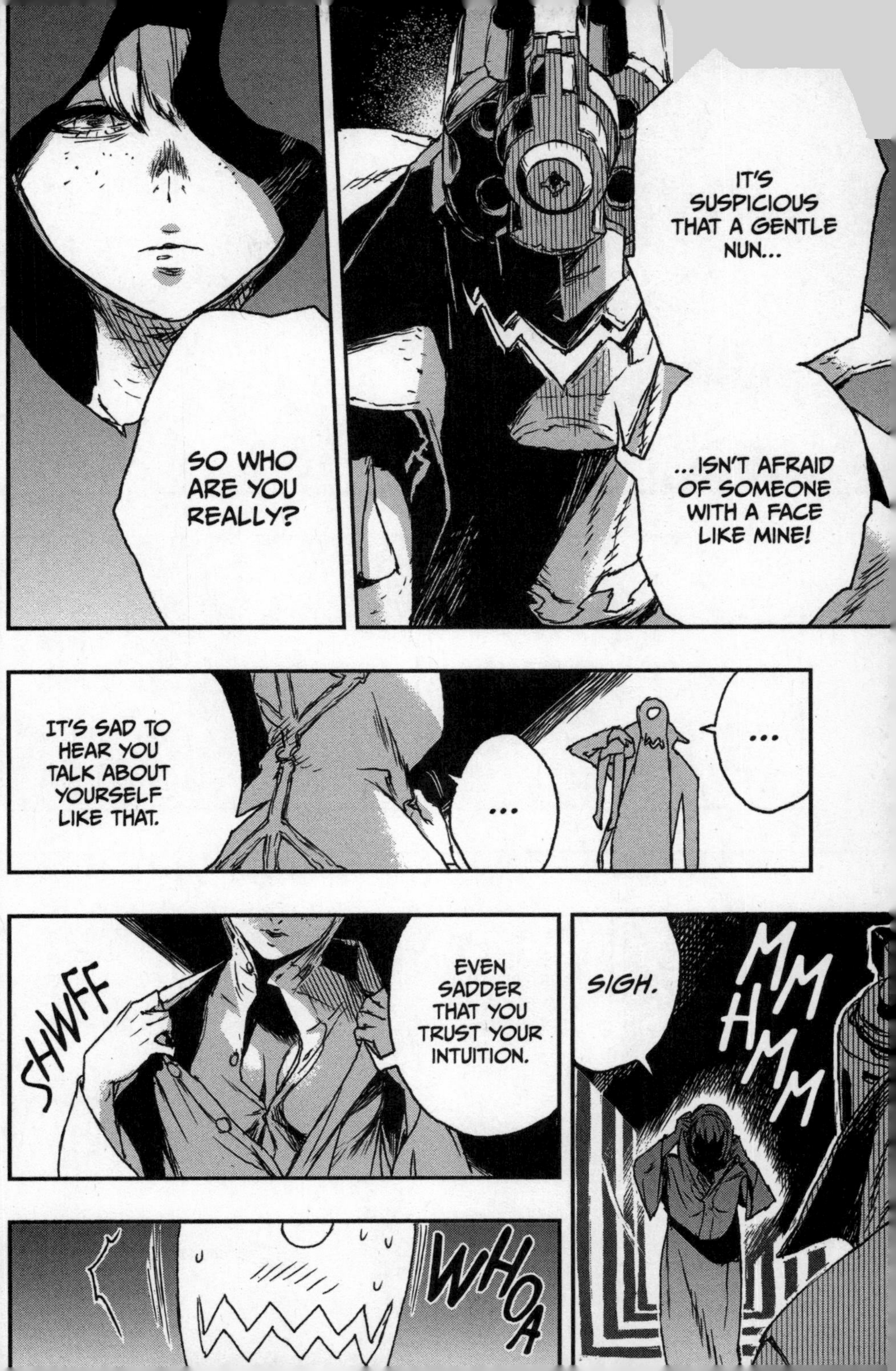
IT'S SUSPICIOUS THAT A GENTLE NUN...
...ISN'T AFRAID OF SOMEONE WITH A FACE LIKE MINE!
SO WHO ARE YOU REALLY?
...
...
IT'S SAD TO HEAR YOU TALK ABOUT YOURSELF LIKE THAT.
SIGH.
MMHMMM
EVEN SADDER THAT YOU TRUST YOUR INTUITION.
SHWFF
WHOA

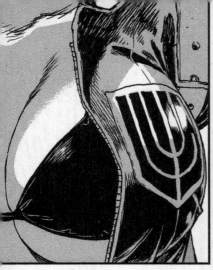

THAT
BADGE!

BECAUSE
IF YOU
DIDN'T...

...YOU'D HAVE
HANDED HIM
OVER TO ME...
AND I WOULDN'T
HAVE TO KILL
YOU NOW.

KCHK

YOU'RE WITH
BERÜHREN?!

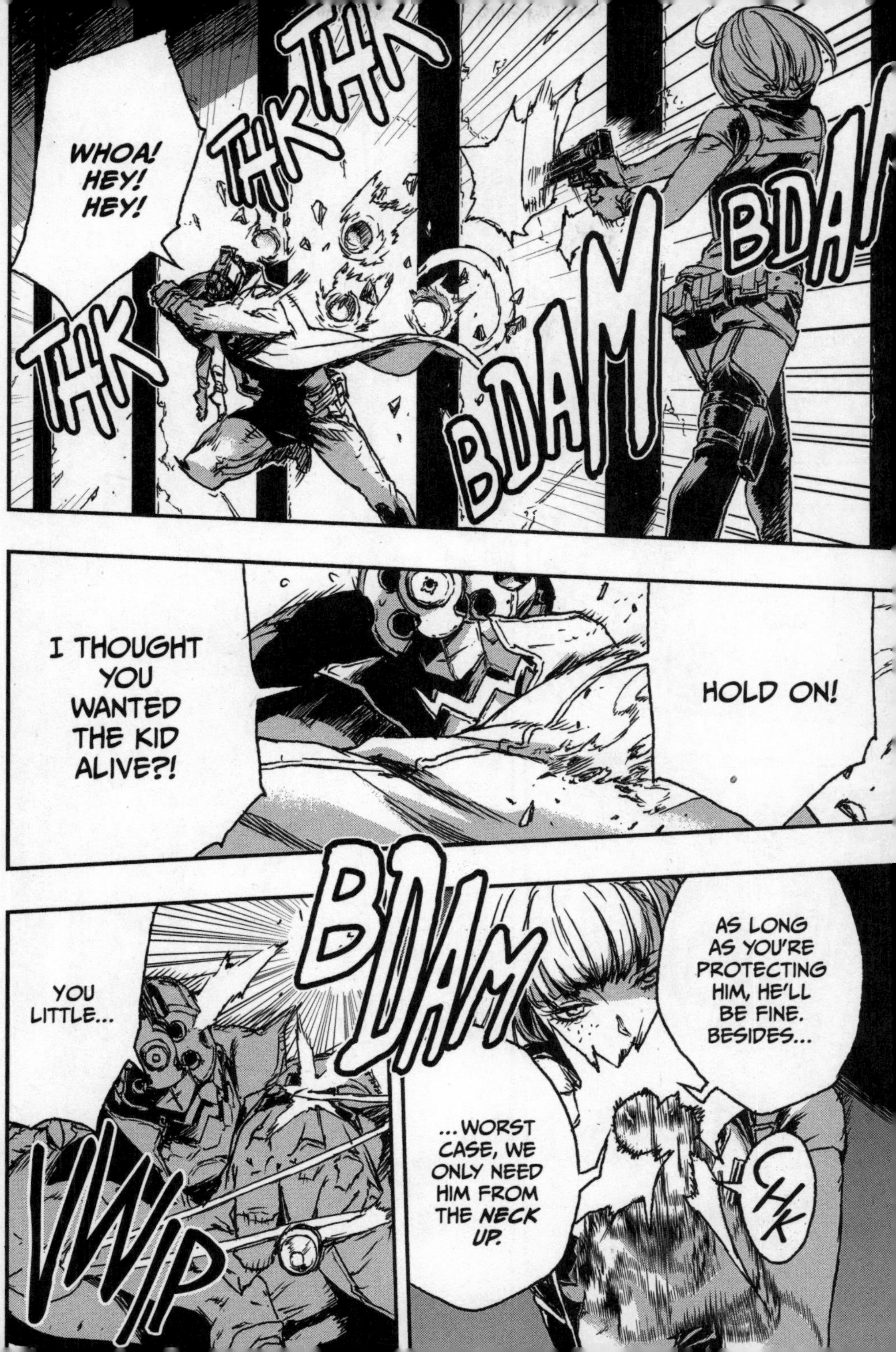
BDA
THK THK
BDAM
WHOA! HEY! HEY!
THK
HOLD ON!
I THOUGHT YOU WANTED THE KID ALIVE?!
AS LONG AS YOU'RE PROTECTING HIM, HE'LL BE FINE. BESIDES...
BDAM
YOU LITTLE...
CHK
...WORST CASE, WE ONLY NEED HIM FROM THE *NECK UP.*
VWIP

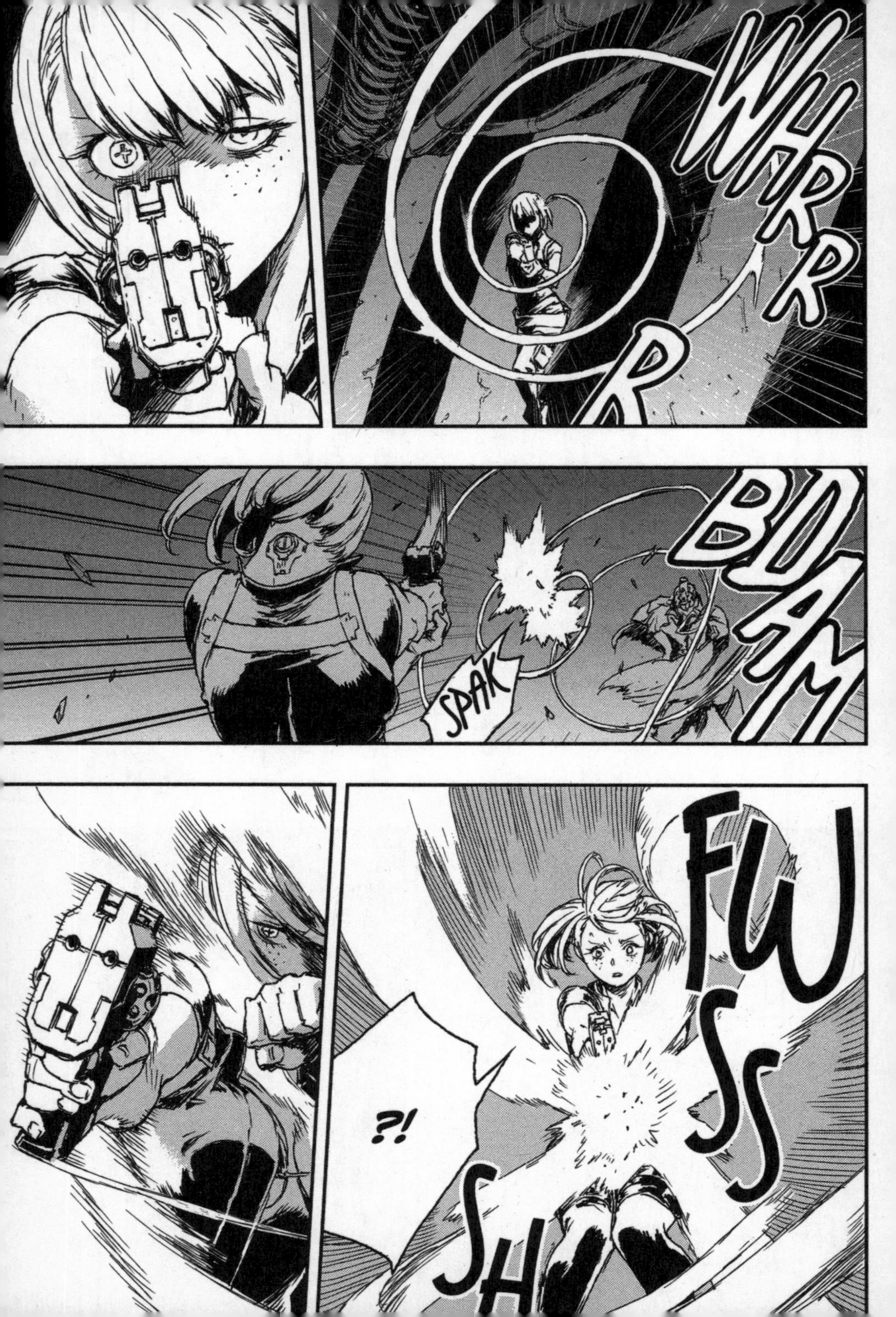
WHRRRR
BDAM
SPAK
FWSSSH
?!

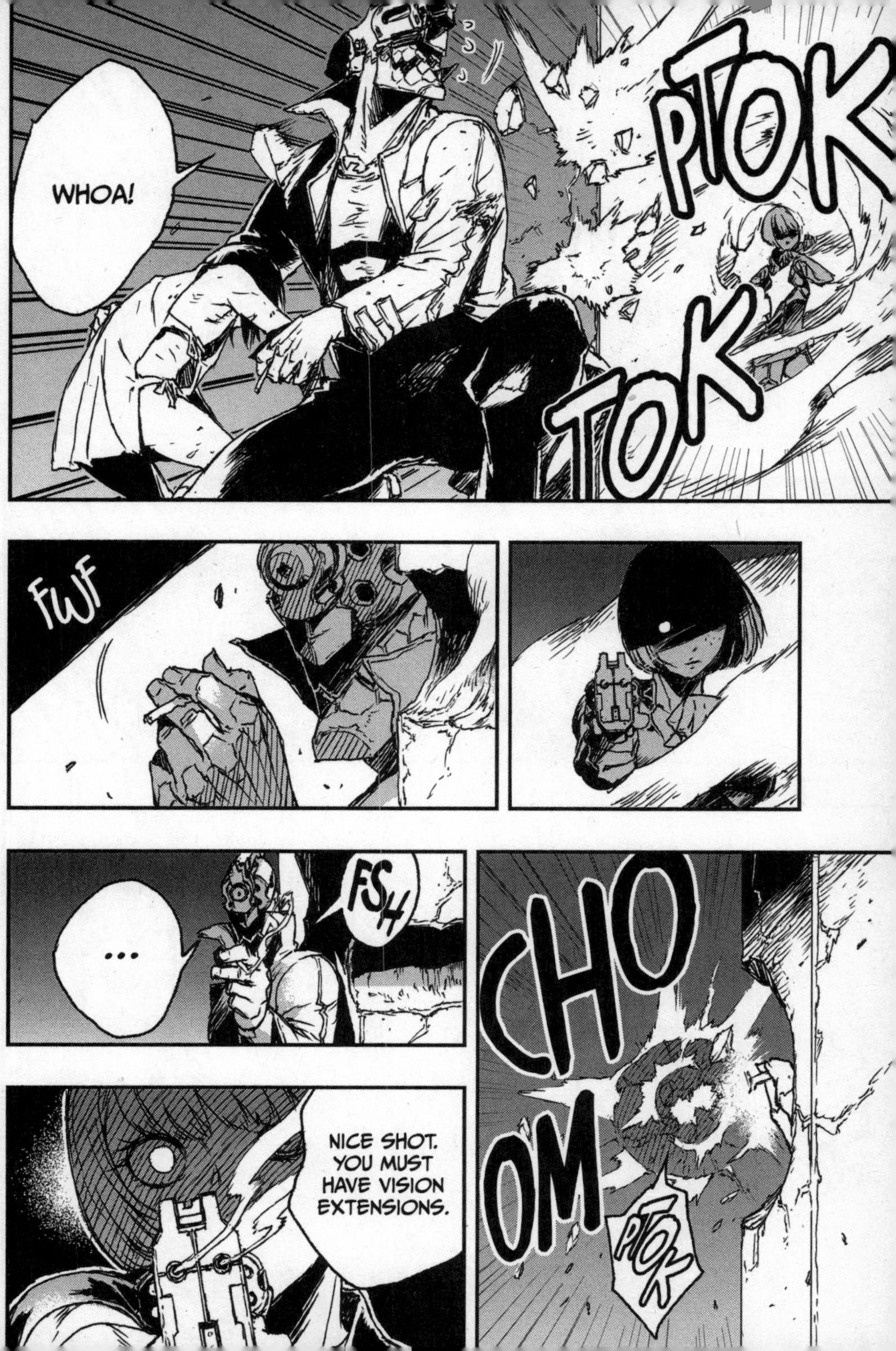
PTOK
TOK
WHOA!
FWF
CHOOM
PTOK
FSH
...
NICE SHOT. YOU MUST HAVE VISION EXTENSIONS.

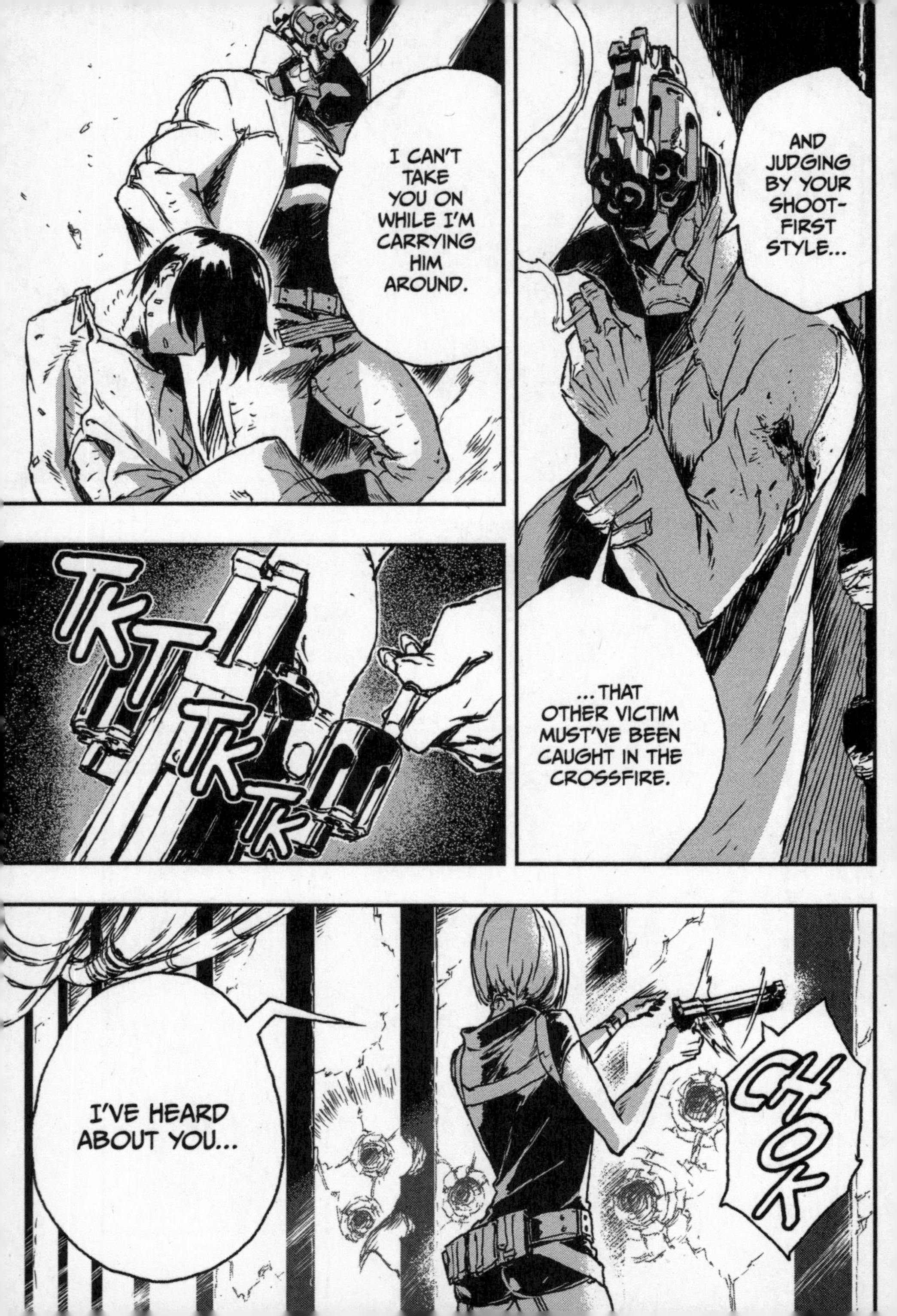
AND JUDGING BY YOUR SHOOT-FIRST STYLE...
...THAT OTHER VICTIM MUST'VE BEEN CAUGHT IN THE CROSSFIRE.
I CAN'T TAKE YOU ON WHILE I'M CARRYING HIM AROUND.
TKTKTK
CHOK
I'VE HEARD ABOUT YOU...

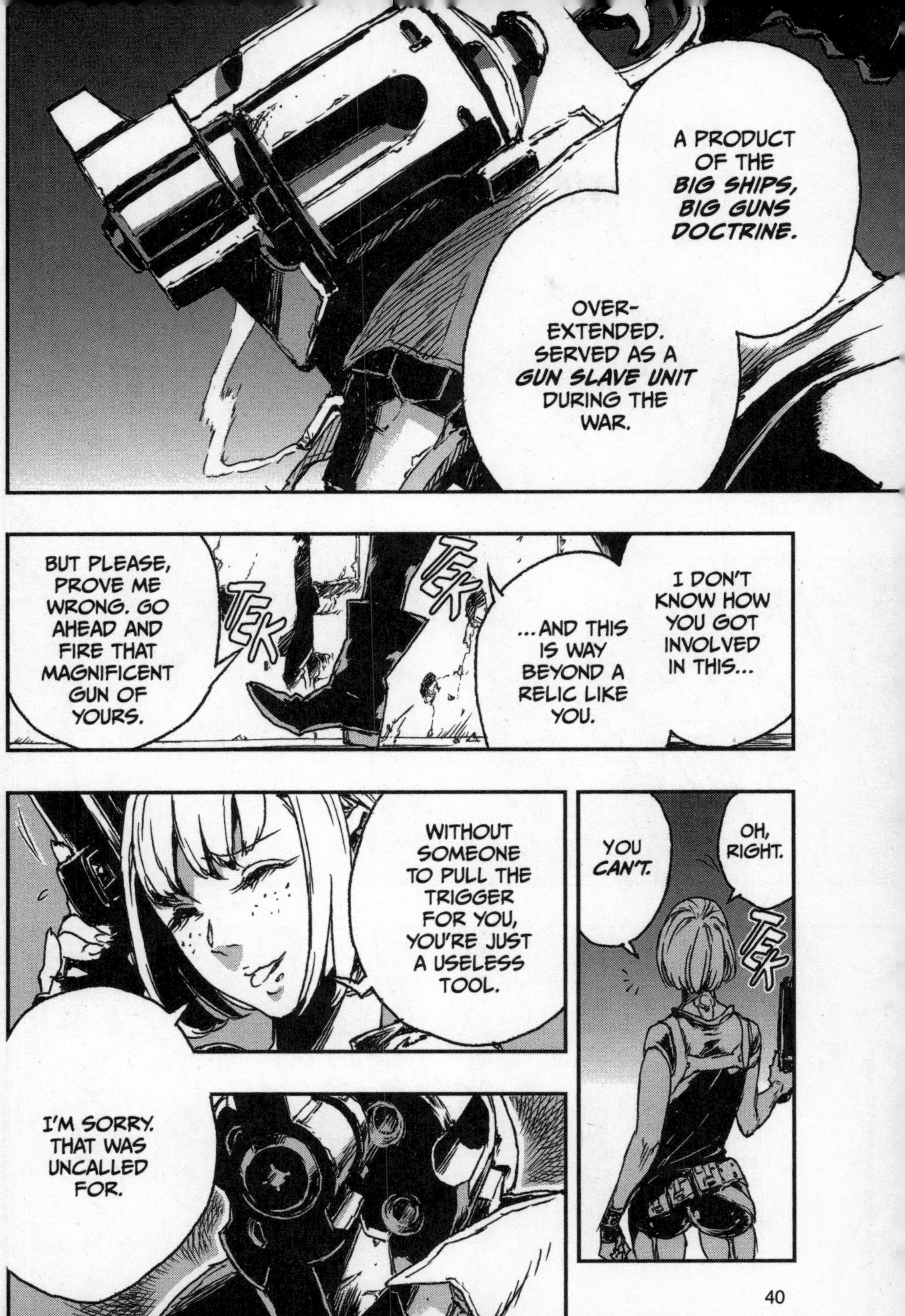
A PRODUCT OF THE *BIG SHIPS, BIG GUNS DOCTRINE.*
OVER-EXTENDED. SERVED AS A *GUN SLAVE UNIT* DURING THE WAR.
I DON'T KNOW HOW YOU GOT INVOLVED IN THIS...
...AND THIS IS WAY BEYOND A RELIC LIKE YOU.
TEK
TEK
BUT PLEASE, PROVE ME WRONG. GO AHEAD AND FIRE THAT MAGNIFICENT GUN OF YOURS.
OH, RIGHT.
YOU *CAN'T.*
TEK
WITHOUT SOMEONE TO PULL THE TRIGGER FOR YOU, YOU'RE JUST A USELESS TOOL.
I'M SORRY. THAT WAS UNCALLED FOR.

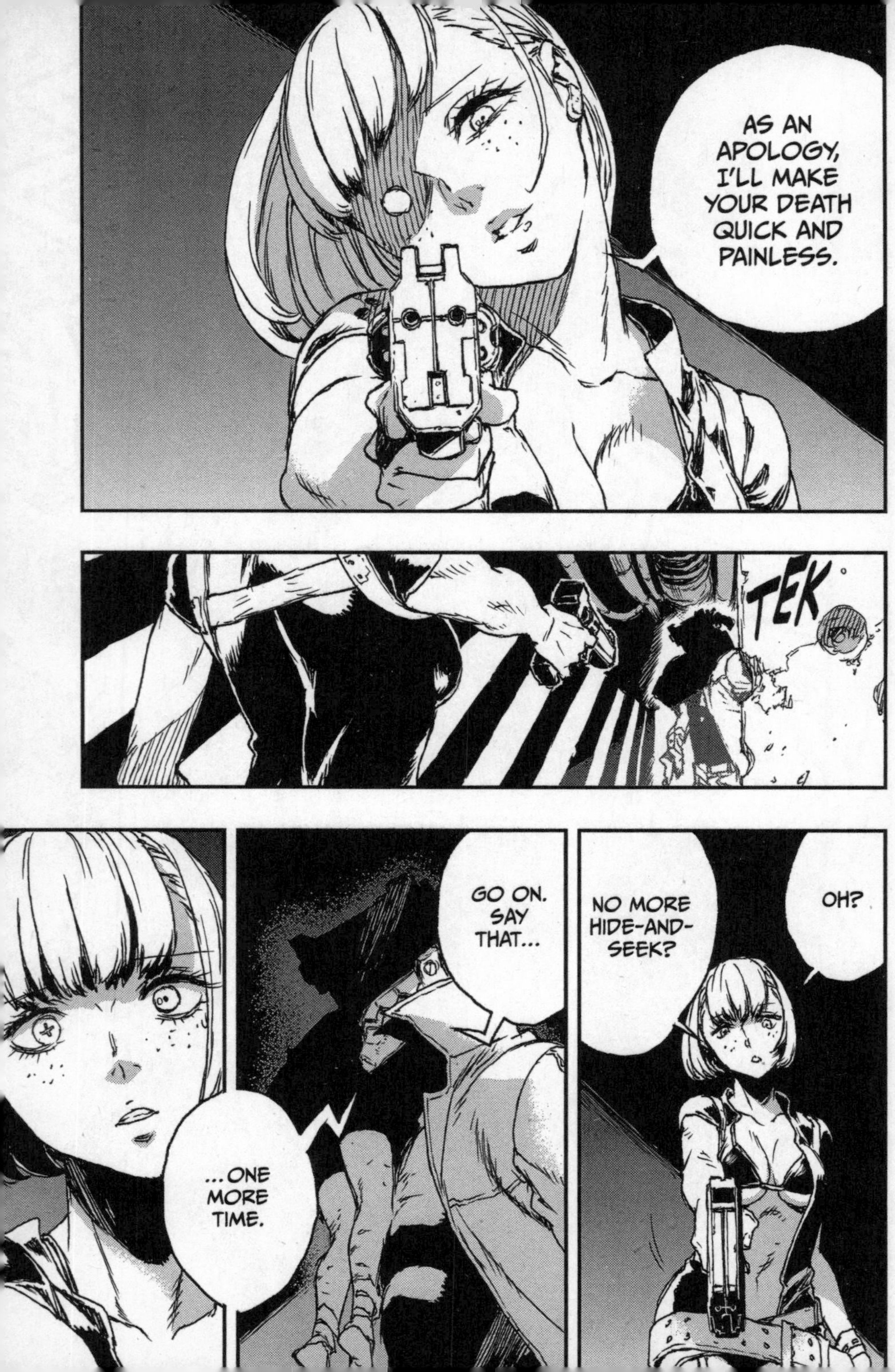
AS AN APOLOGY, I'LL MAKE YOUR DEATH QUICK AND PAINLESS.
TEK
OH?
NO MORE HIDE-AND-SEEK?
GO ON. SAY THAT...
...ONE MORE TIME.

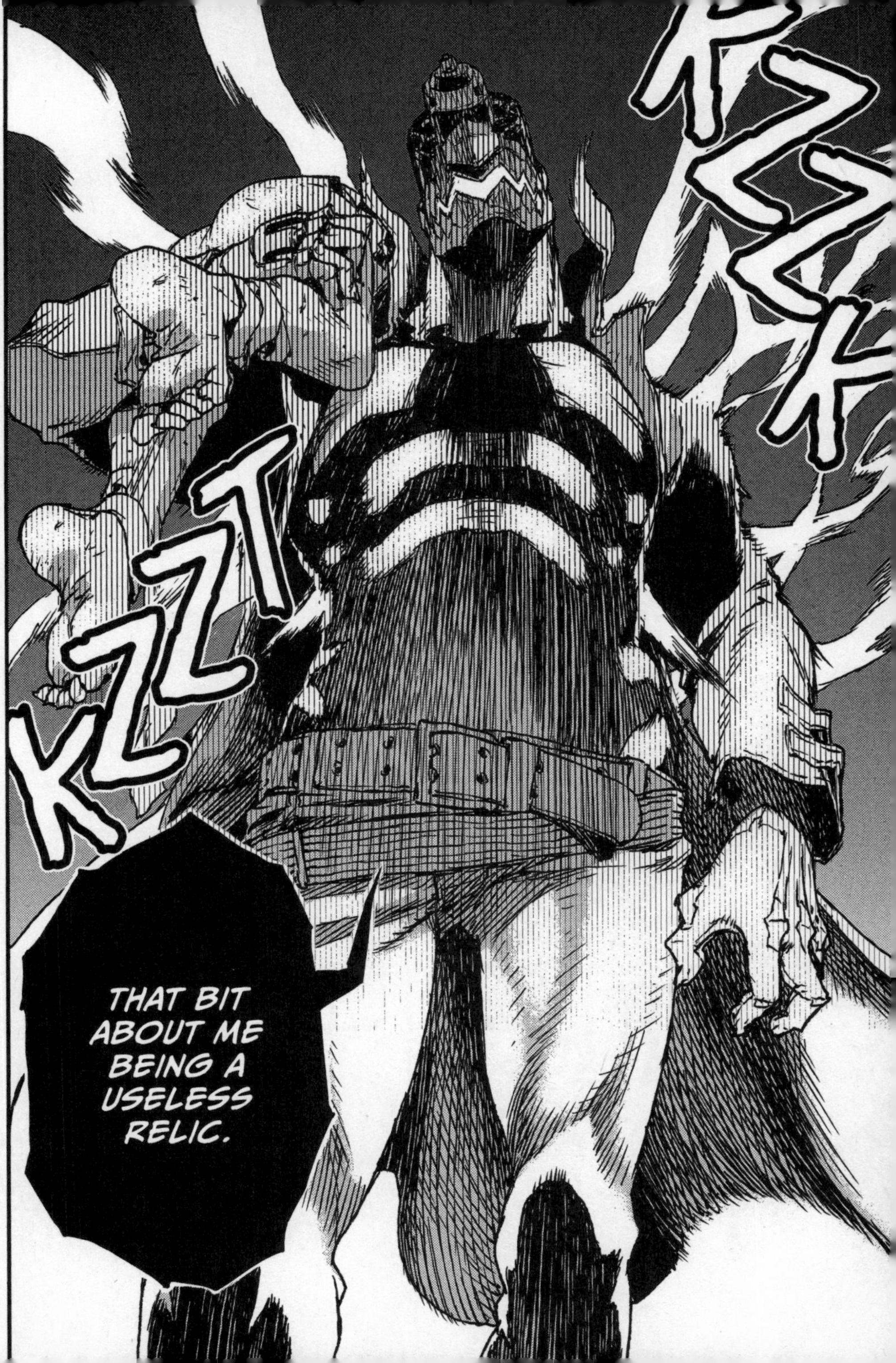
KZZT
THAT BIT ABOUT ME BEING A USELESS RELIC.

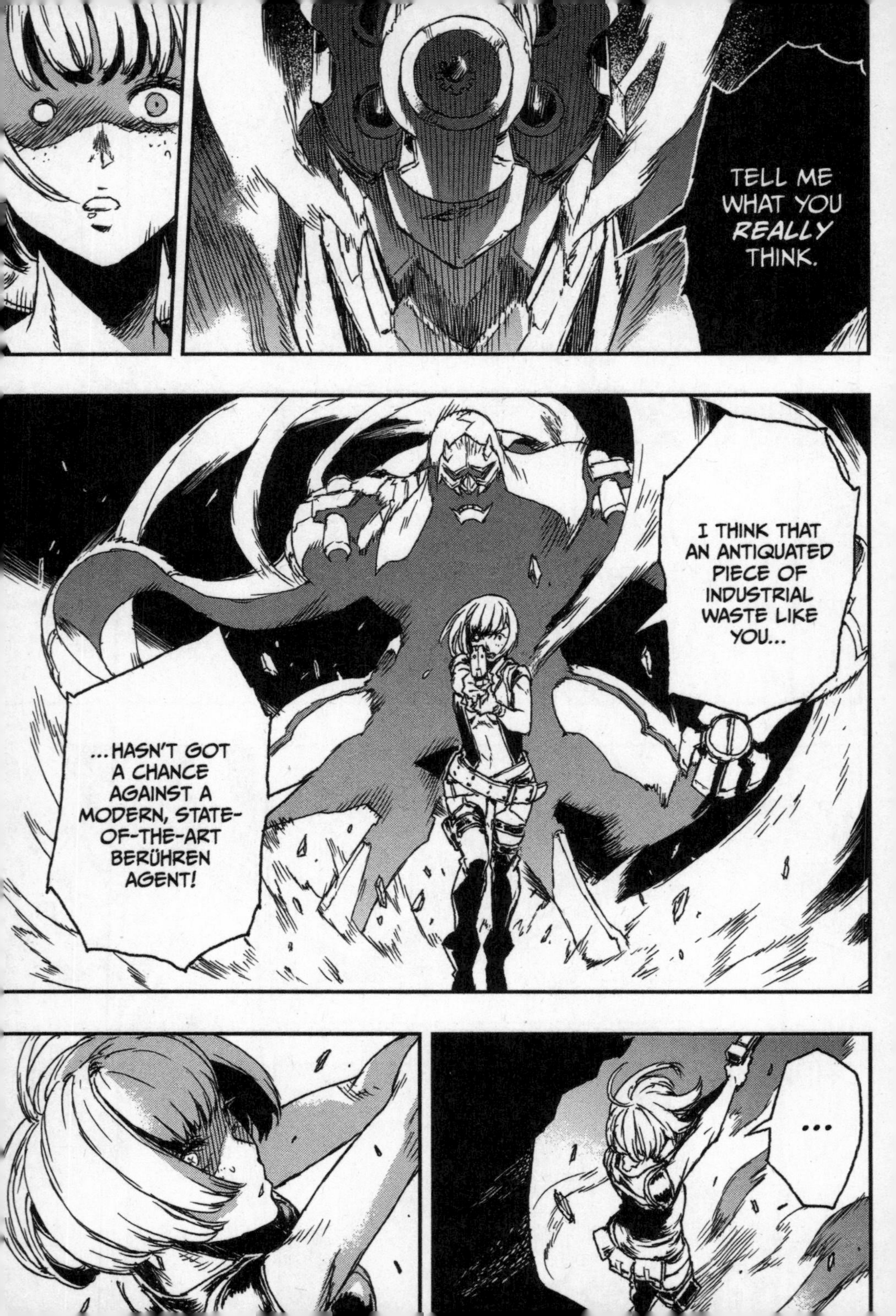
TELL ME WHAT YOU *REALLY* THINK.
I THINK THAT AN ANTIQUATED PIECE OF INDUSTRIAL WASTE LIKE YOU...
...HASN'T GOT A CHANCE AGAINST A MODERN, STATE-OF-THE-ART BERÜHREN AGENT!
...

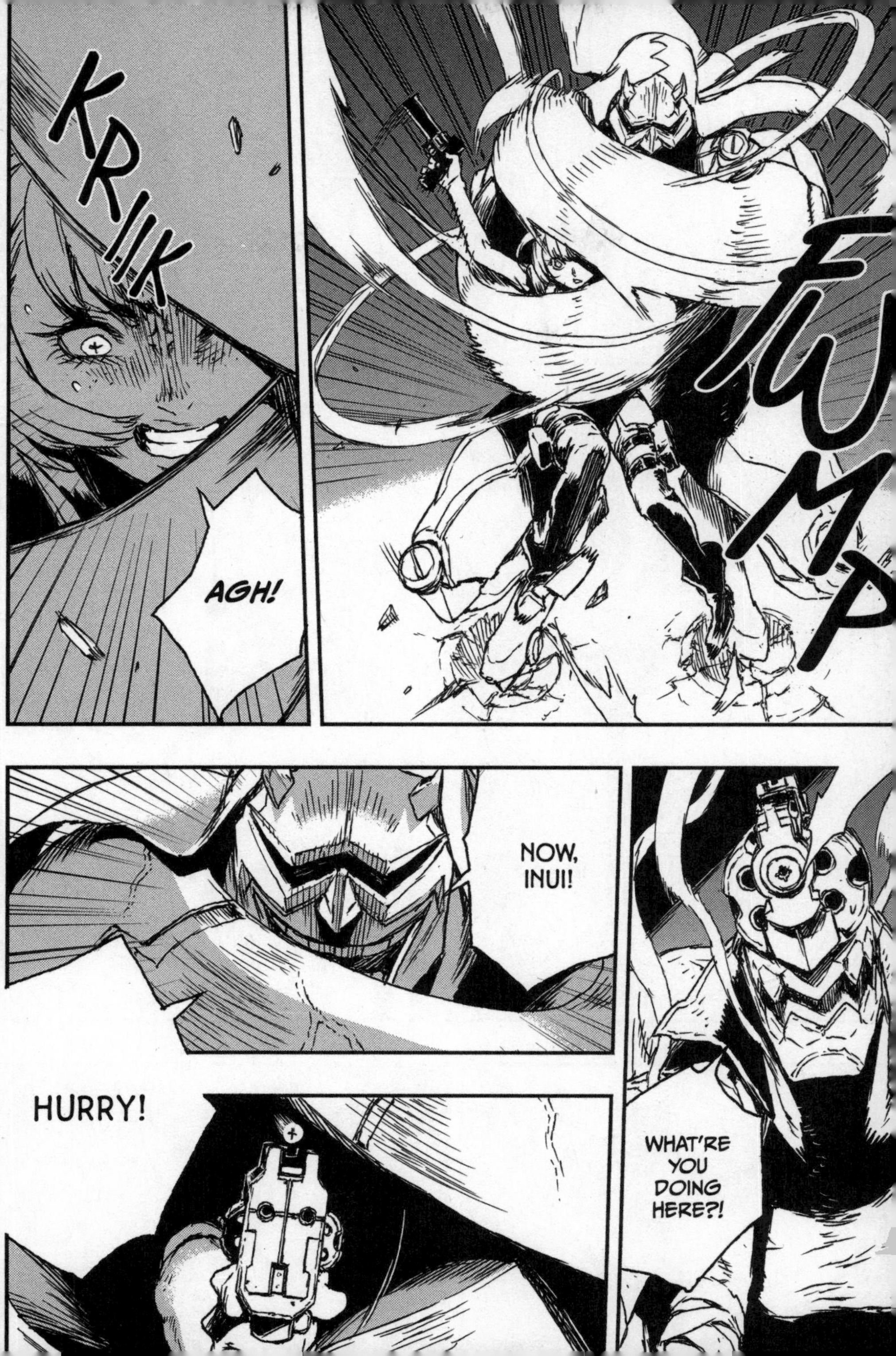
FWUMP
KRIIIK
AGH!
WHAT'RE YOU DOING HERE?!
NOW, INUI!
HURRY!

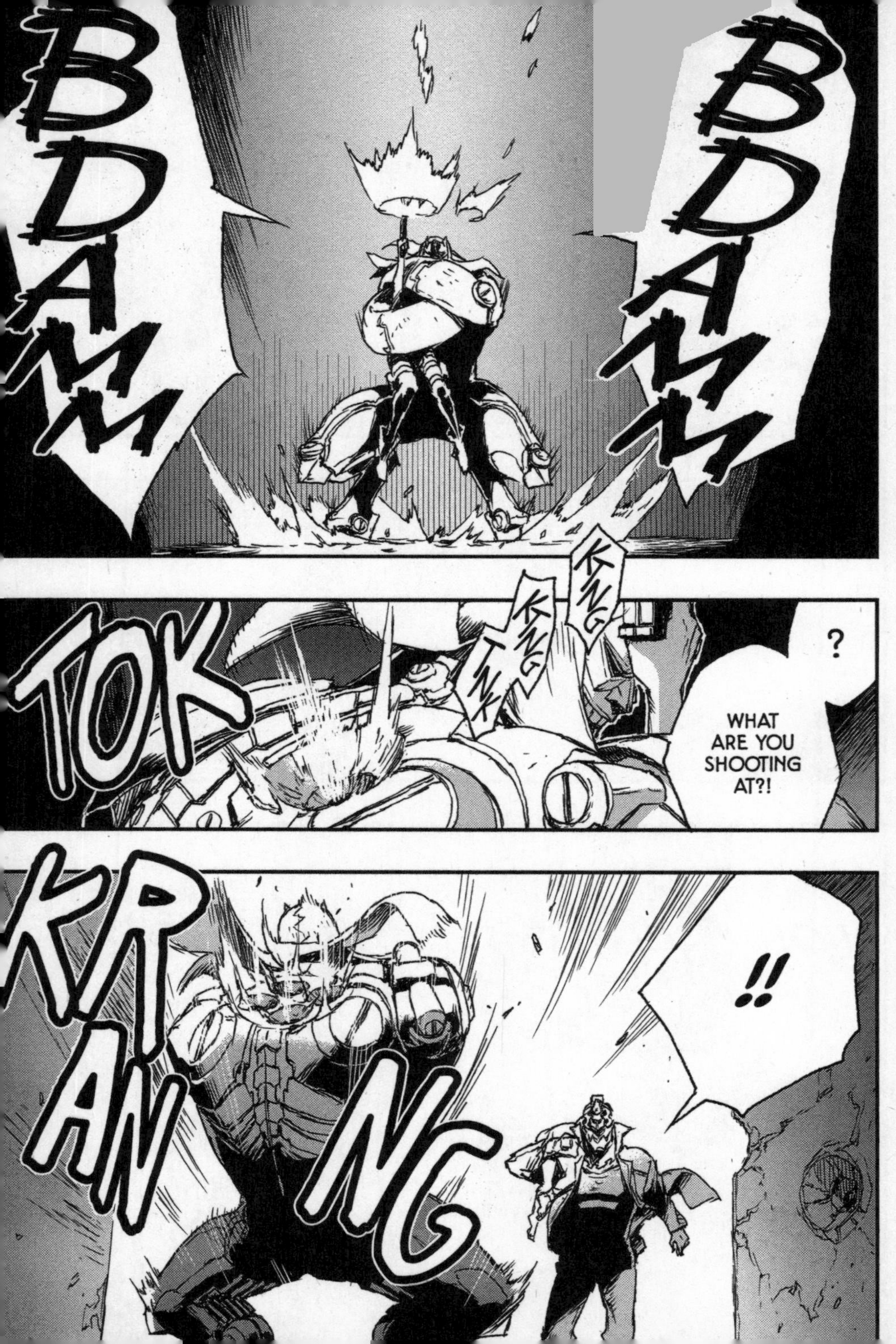
BDAMM
BDAMM
?
WHAT ARE YOU SHOOTING AT?!
KING
KING
TINK
TOK
!!
KRANANNG

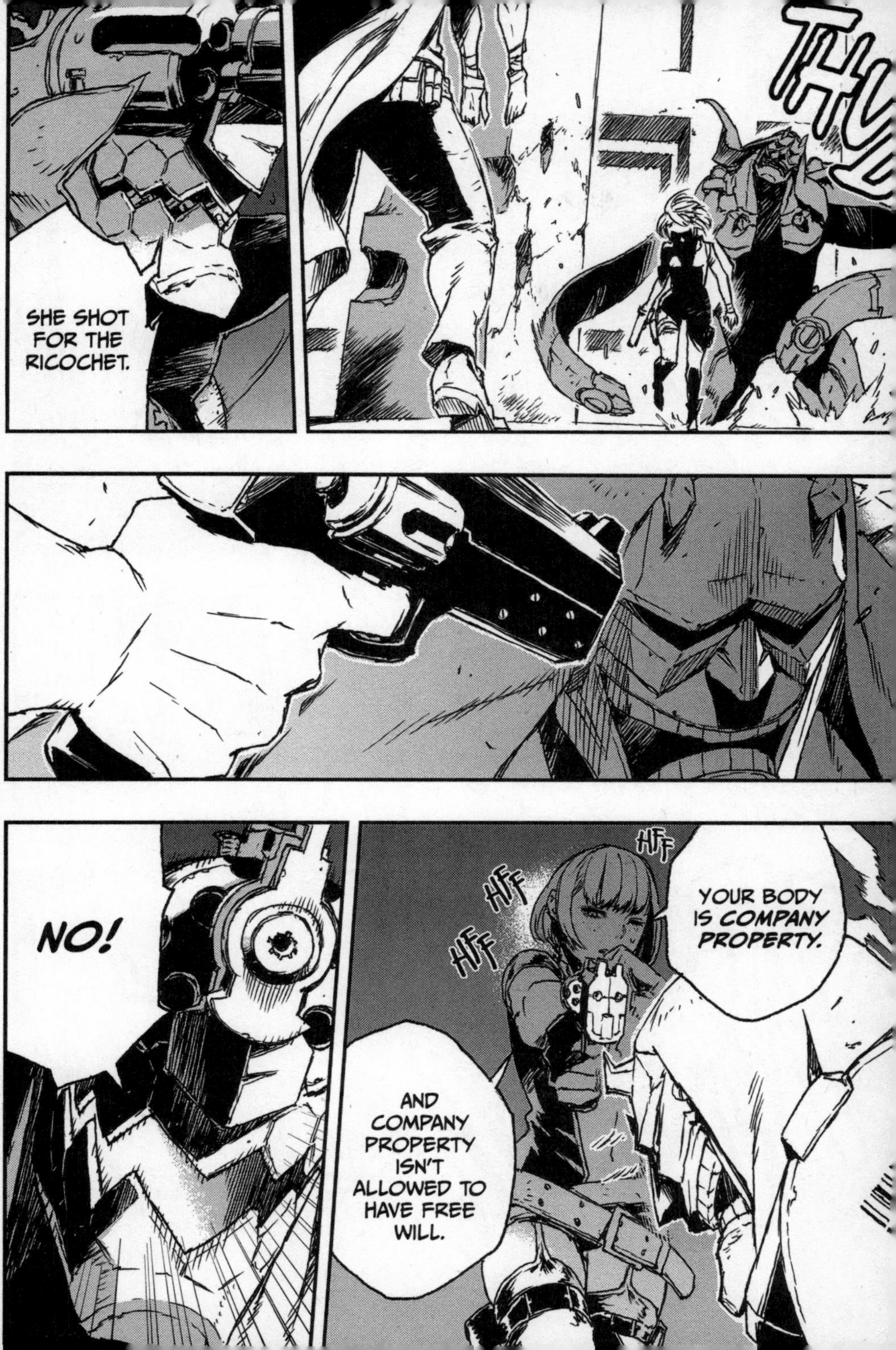
SHE SHOT FOR THE RICOCHET.
HFF
HFF
HFF
YOUR BODY IS COMPANY PROPERTY.
AND COMPANY PROPERTY ISN'T ALLOWED TO HAVE FREE WILL.
NO!

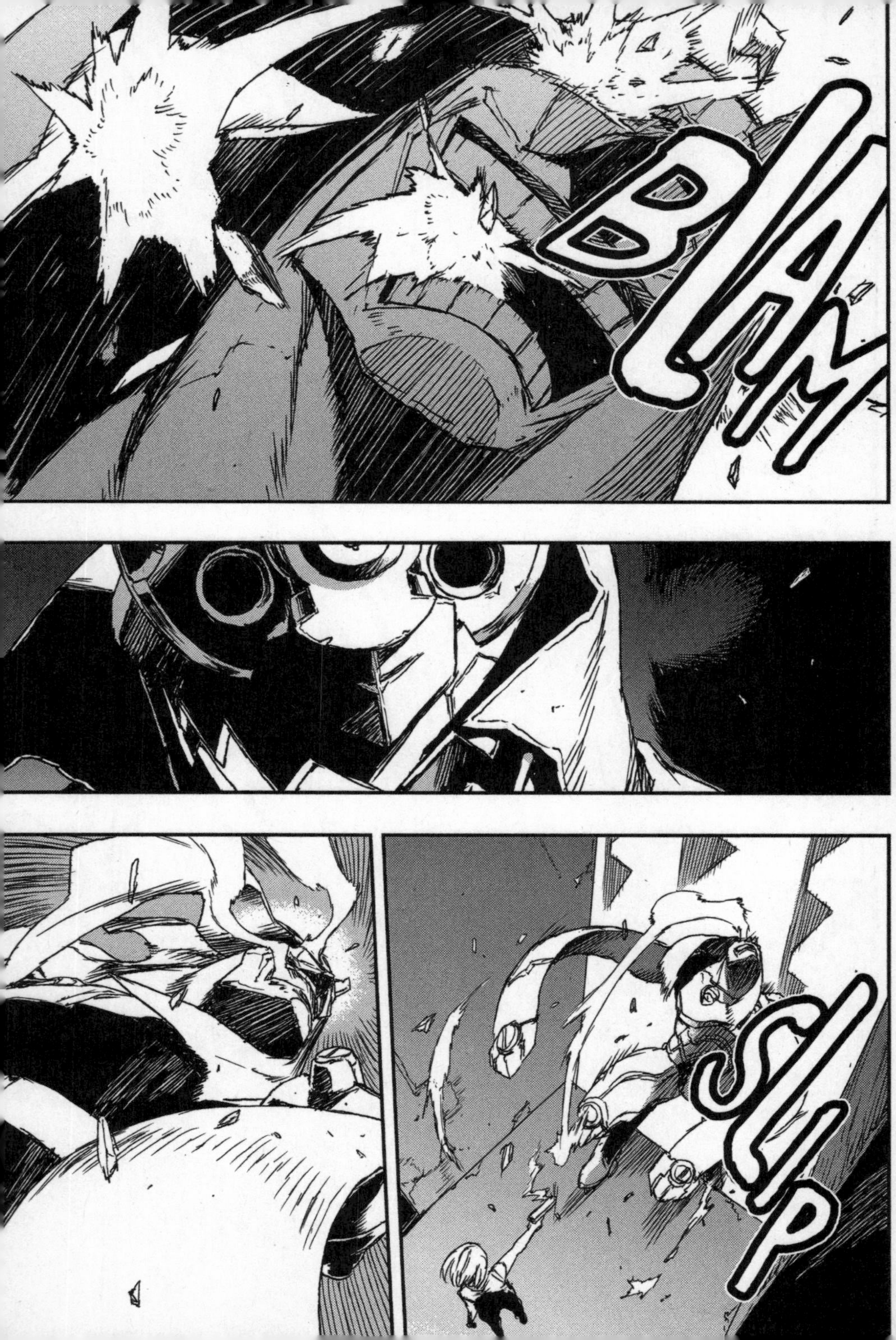
BLAM
SLIP

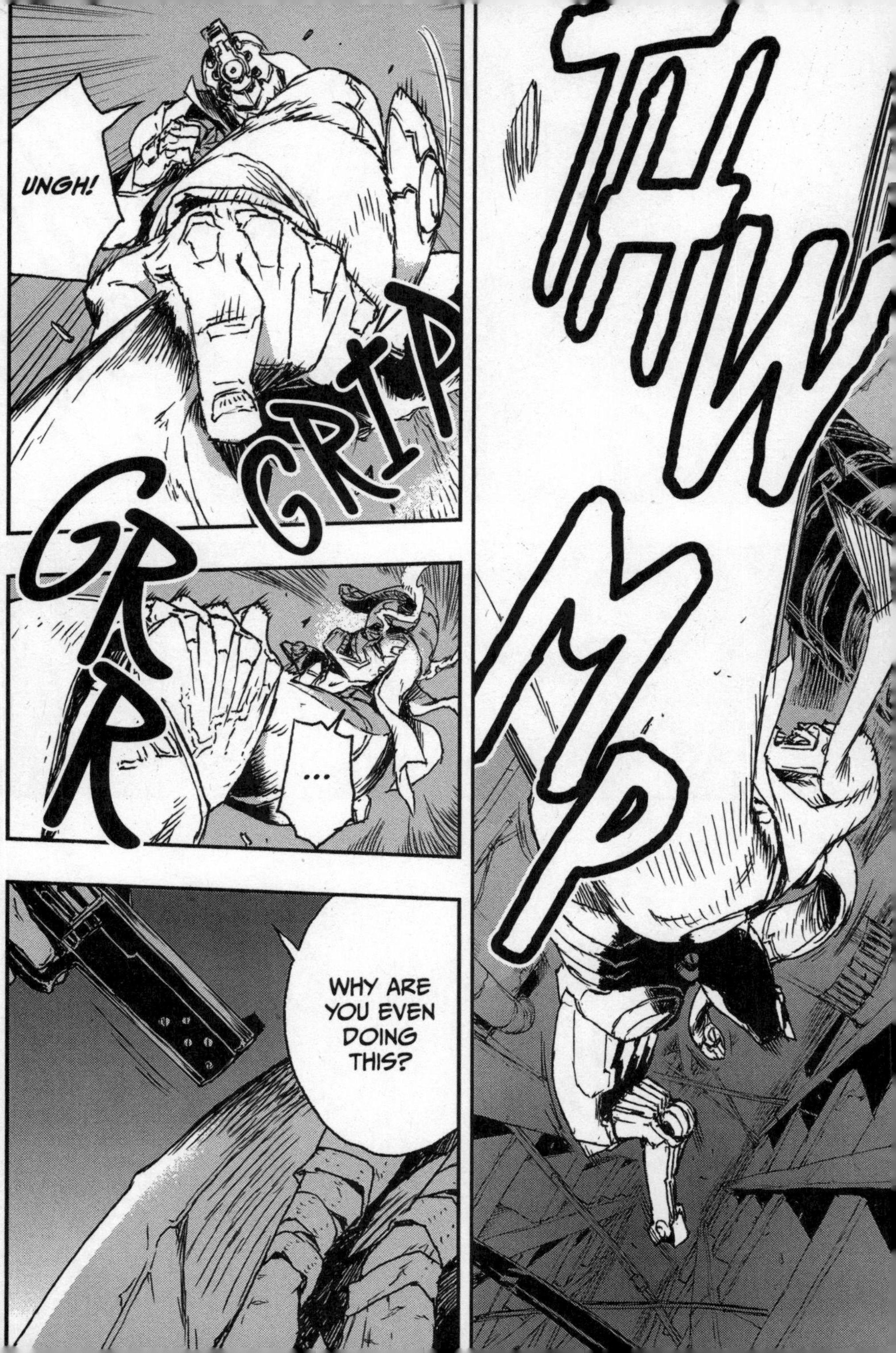
THWUMP
UNGH!
GRIP
GRR
...
WHY ARE YOU EVEN DOING THIS?

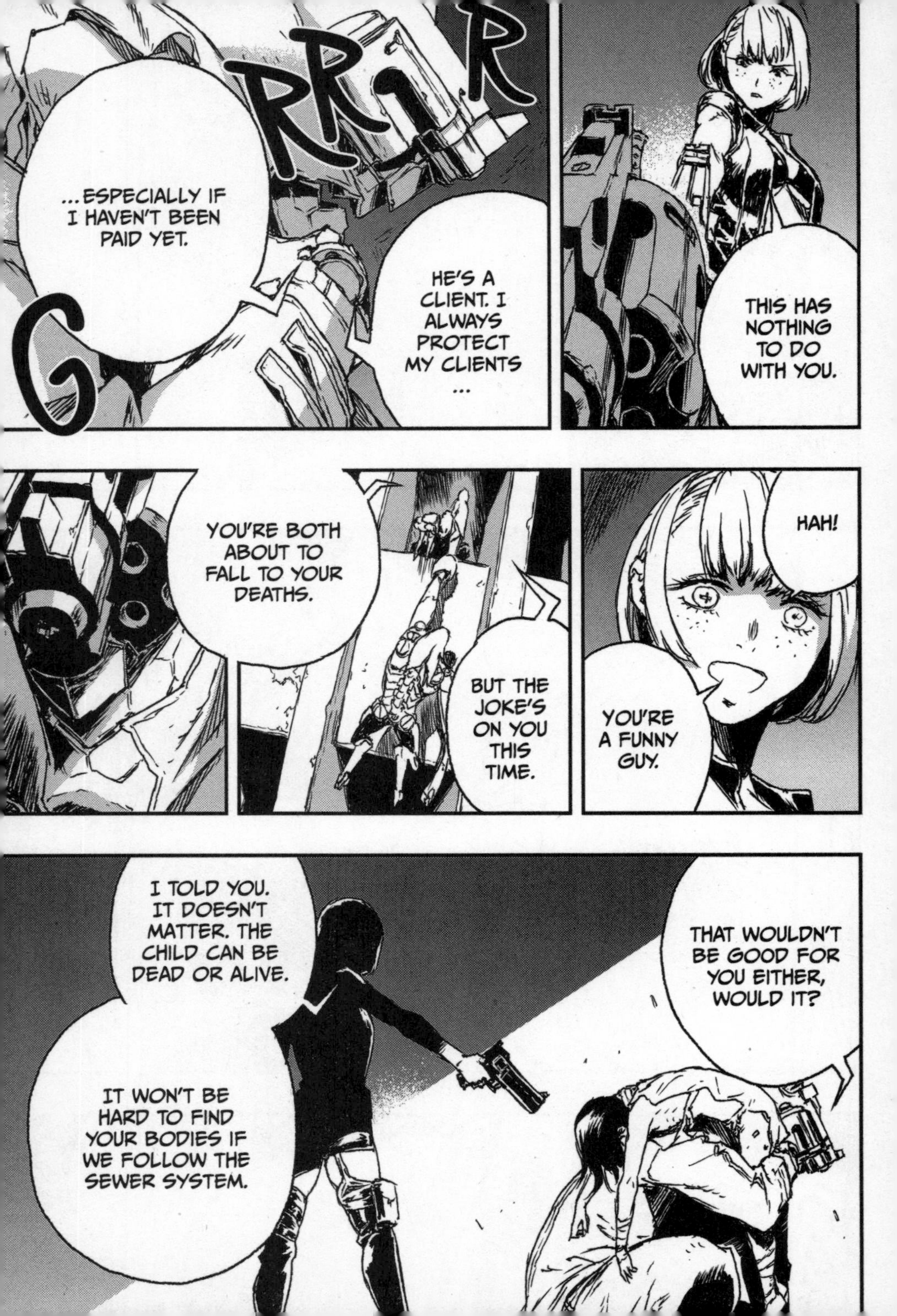
THIS HAS NOTHING TO DO WITH YOU.
HE'S A CLIENT. I ALWAYS PROTECT MY CLIENTS ...
...ESPECIALLY IF I HAVEN'T BEEN PAID YET.
GRRRR
HAH!
YOU'RE A FUNNY GUY.
BUT THE JOKE'S ON YOU THIS TIME.
YOU'RE BOTH ABOUT TO FALL TO YOUR DEATHS.
THAT WOULDN'T BE GOOD FOR YOU EITHER, WOULD IT?
I TOLD YOU. IT DOESN'T MATTER. THE CHILD CAN BE DEAD OR ALIVE.
IT WON'T BE HARD TO FIND YOUR BODIES IF WE FOLLOW THE SEWER SYSTEM.

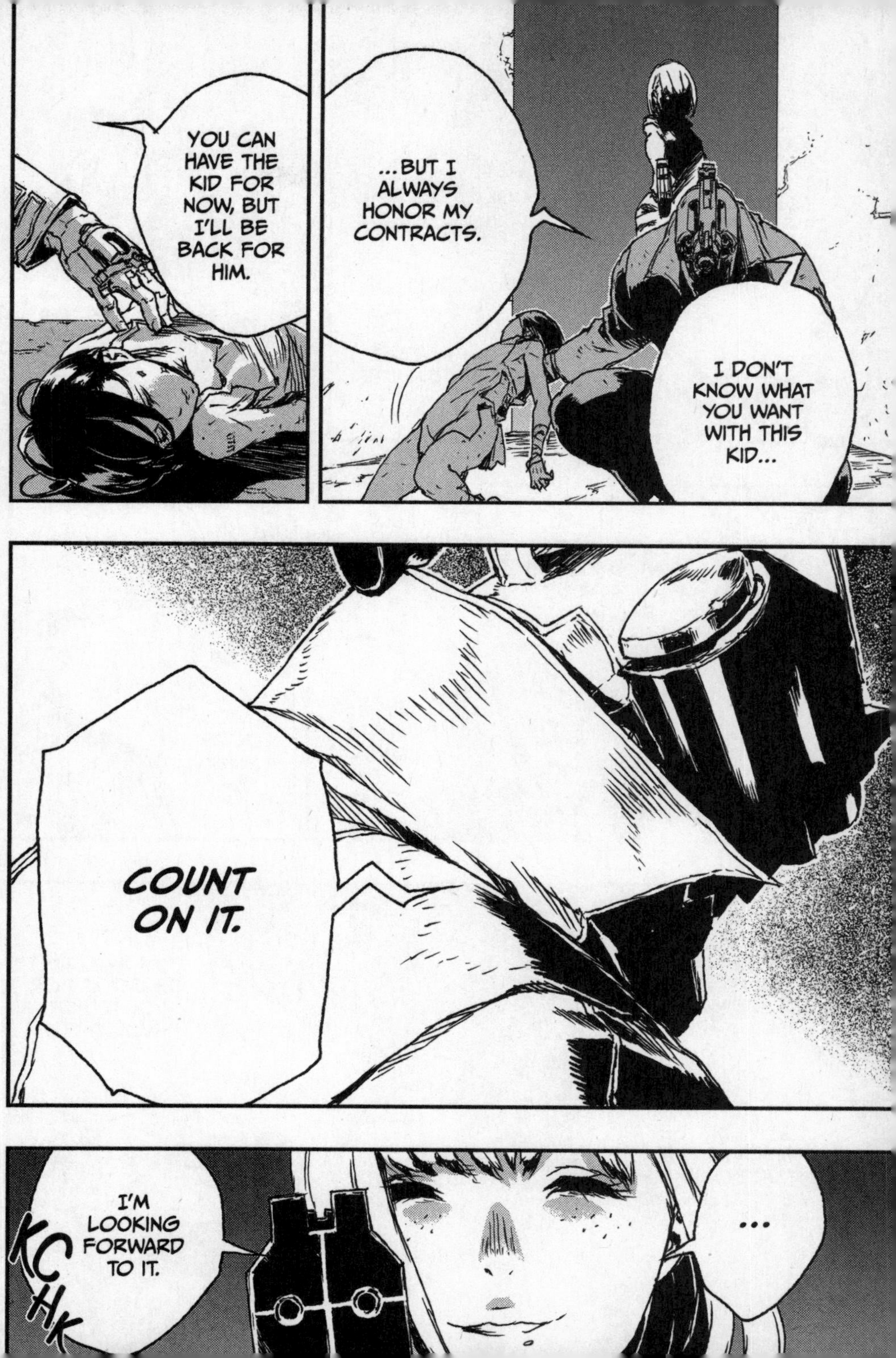
I DON'T KNOW WHAT YOU WANT WITH THIS KID...
...BUT I ALWAYS HONOR MY CONTRACTS.
YOU CAN HAVE THE KID FOR NOW, BUT I'LL BE BACK FOR HIM.
COUNT ON IT.
...
I'M LOOKING FORWARD TO IT.
KCHK

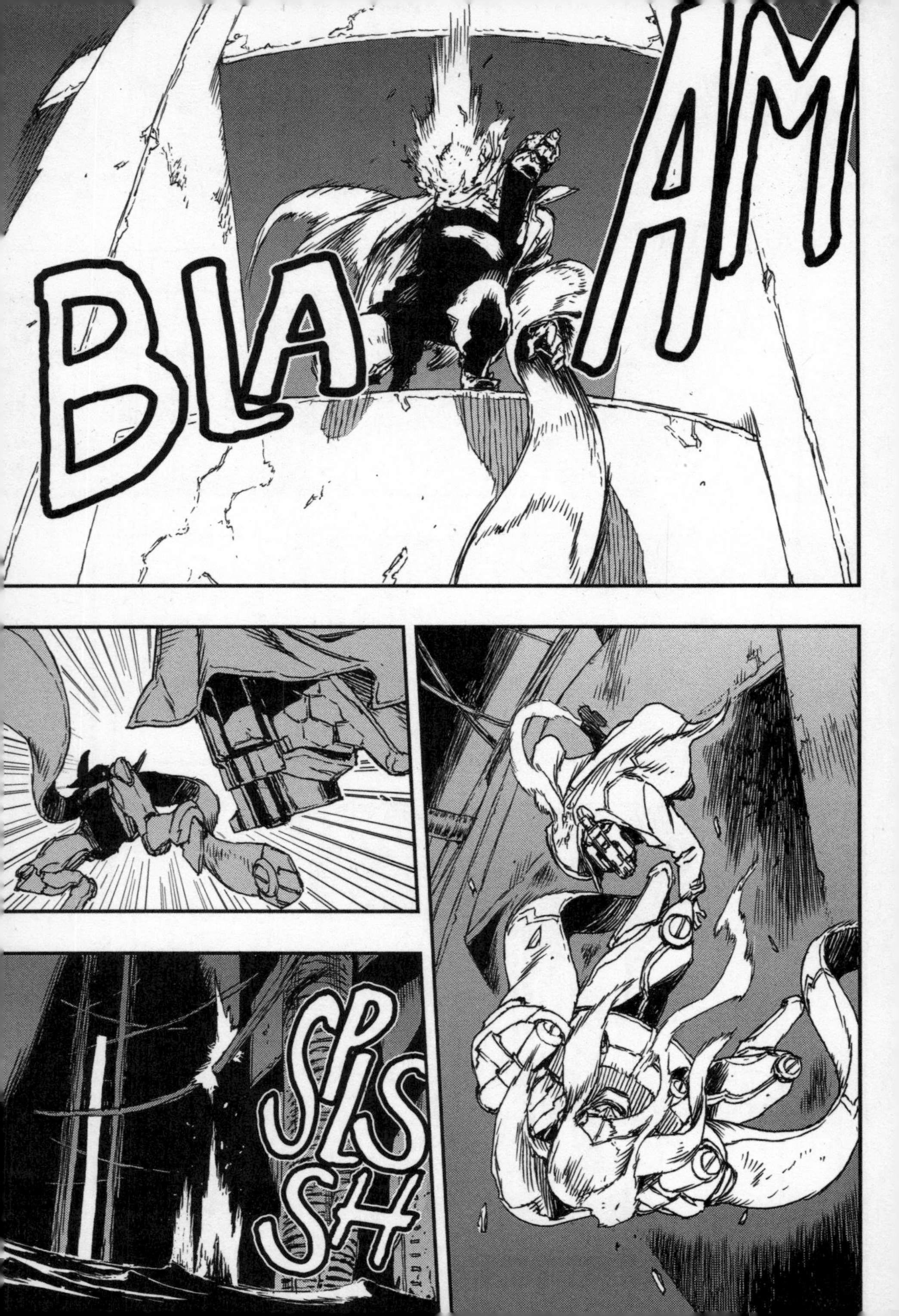
BLAAM
SPLSSH

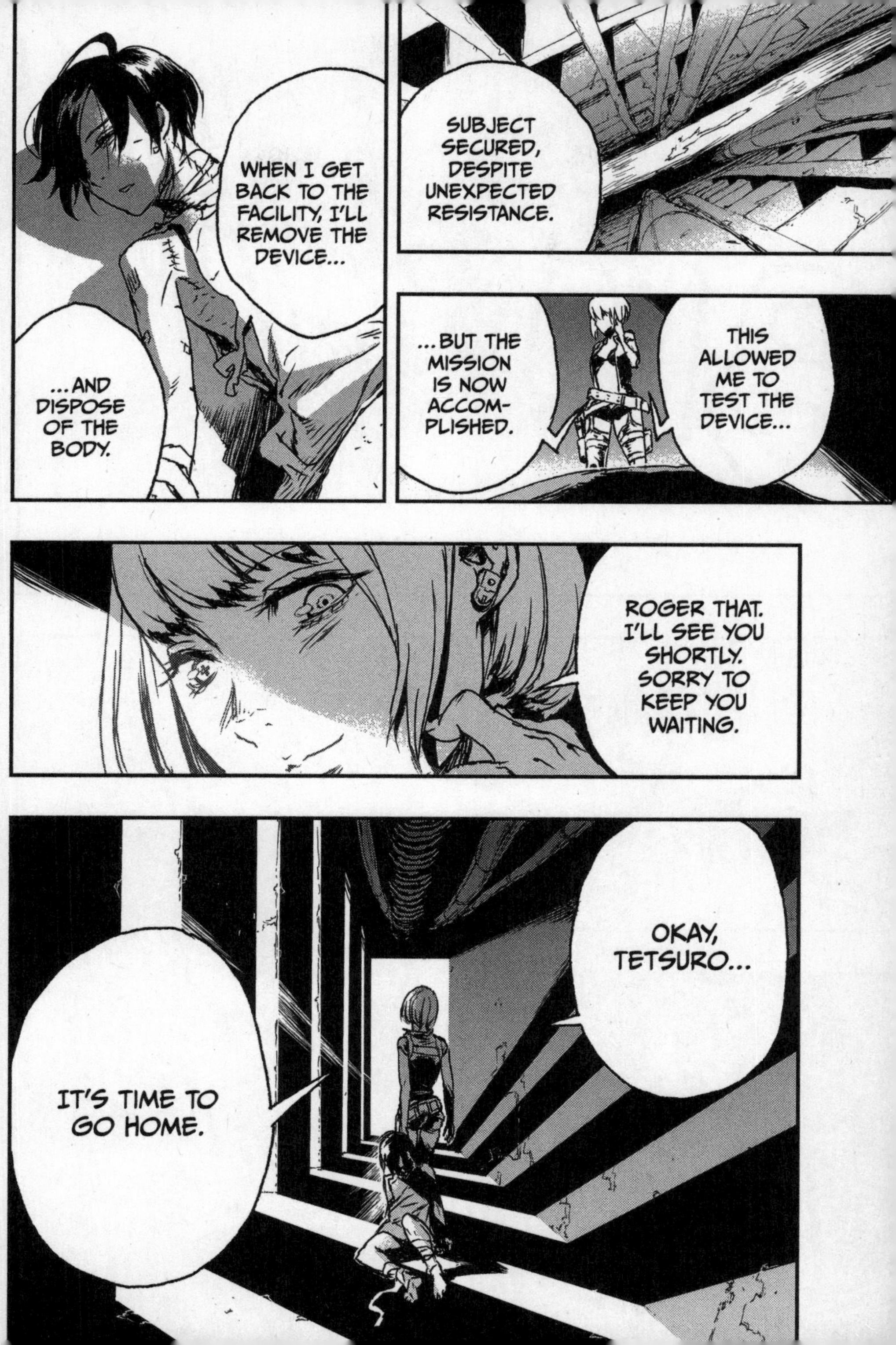
SUBJECT SECURED, DESPITE UNEXPECTED RESISTANCE.
THIS ALLOWED ME TO TEST THE DEVICE...
...BUT THE MISSION IS NOW ACCOMPLISHED.
WHEN I GET BACK TO THE FACILITY, I'LL REMOVE THE DEVICE...
...AND DISPOSE OF THE BODY.
ROGER THAT. I'LL SEE YOU SHORTLY. SORRY TO KEEP YOU WAITING.
OKAY, TETSURO...
IT'S TIME TO GO HOME.

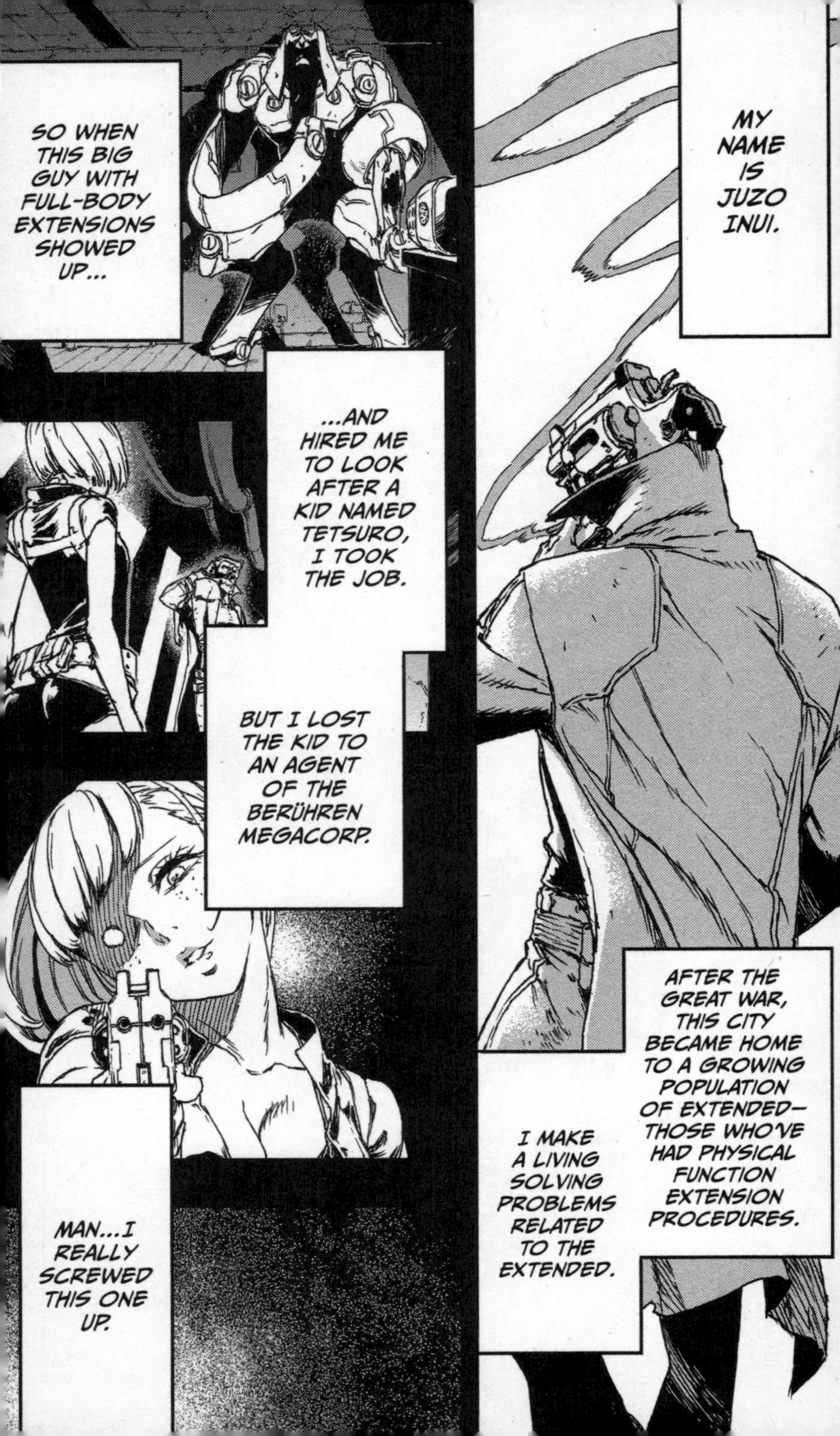
MY NAME IS JUZO INUI.
AFTER THE GREAT WAR, THIS CITY BECAME HOME TO A GROWING POPULATION OF EXTENDED—THOSE WHO'VE HAD PHYSICAL FUNCTION EXTENSION PROCEDURES.
I MAKE A LIVING SOLVING PROBLEMS RELATED TO THE EXTENDED.
SO WHEN THIS BIG GUY WITH FULL-BODY EXTENSIONS SHOWED UP...
...AND HIRED ME TO LOOK AFTER A KID NAMED TETSURO, I TOOK THE JOB.
BUT I LOST THE KID TO AN AGENT OF THE BERÜHREN MEGACORP.
MAN...I REALLY SCREWED THIS ONE UP.

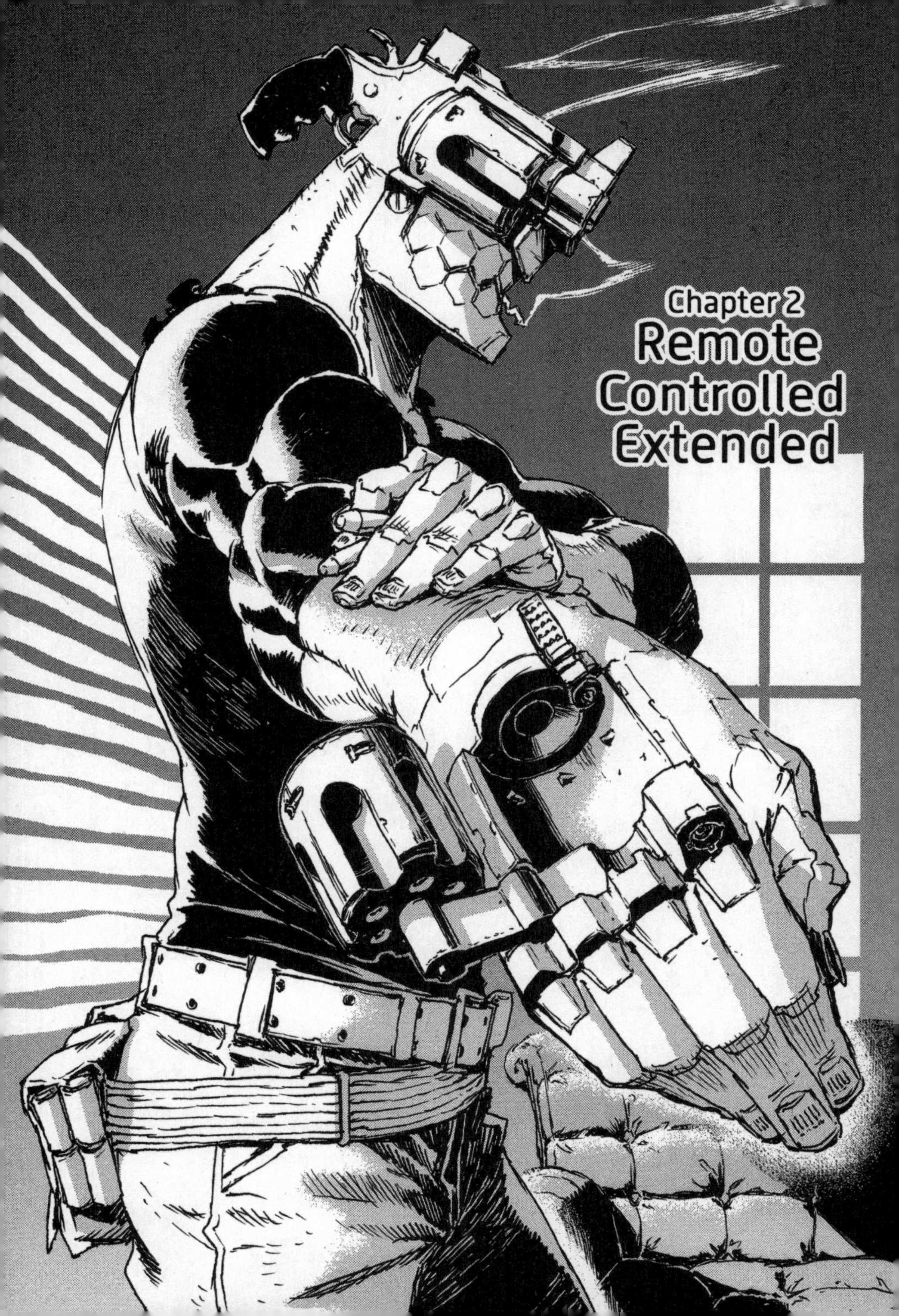
Chapter 2
Remote Controlled Extended

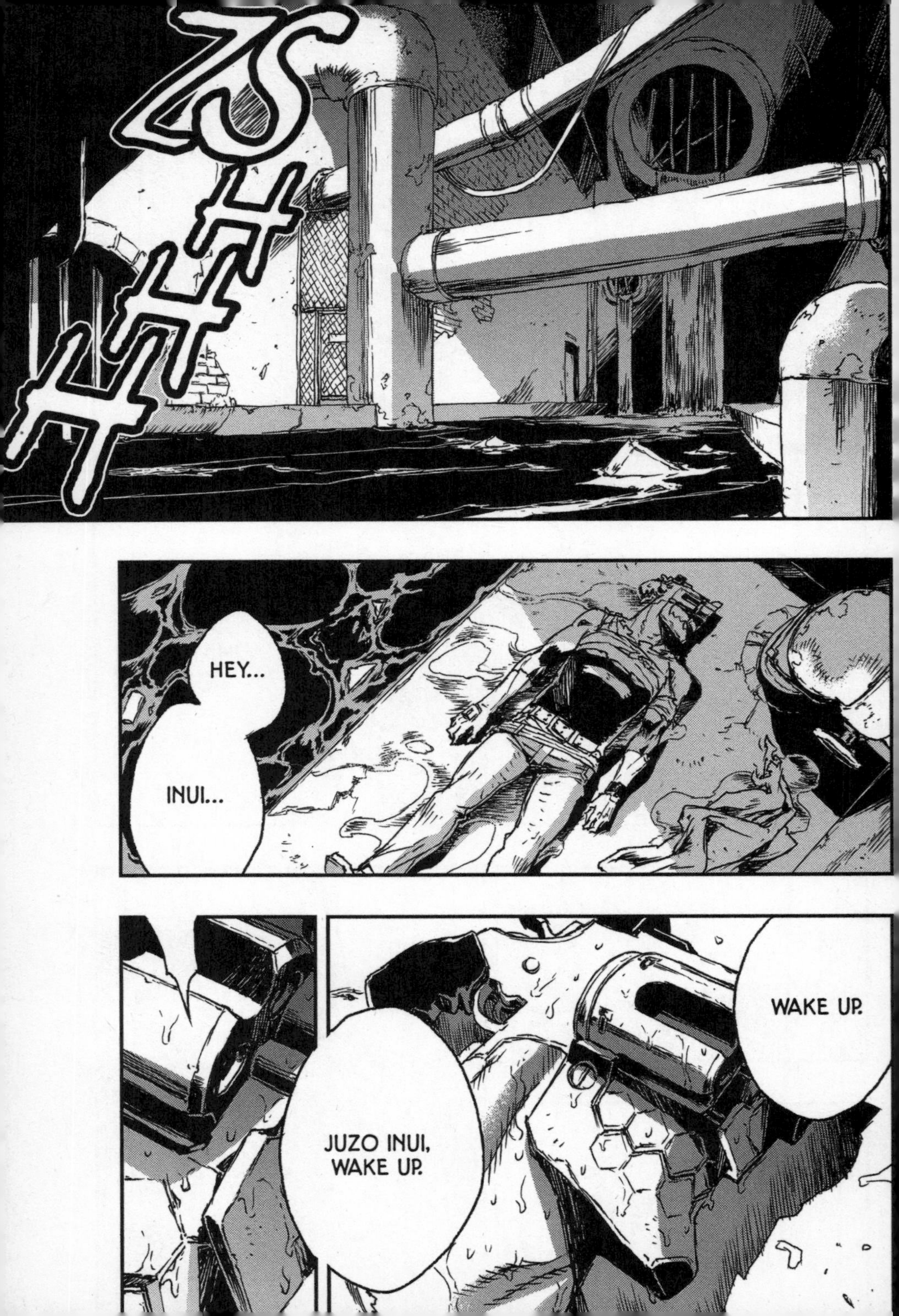
ZSHHHH
HEY...
INUI...
WAKE UP.
JUZO INUI, WAKE UP.

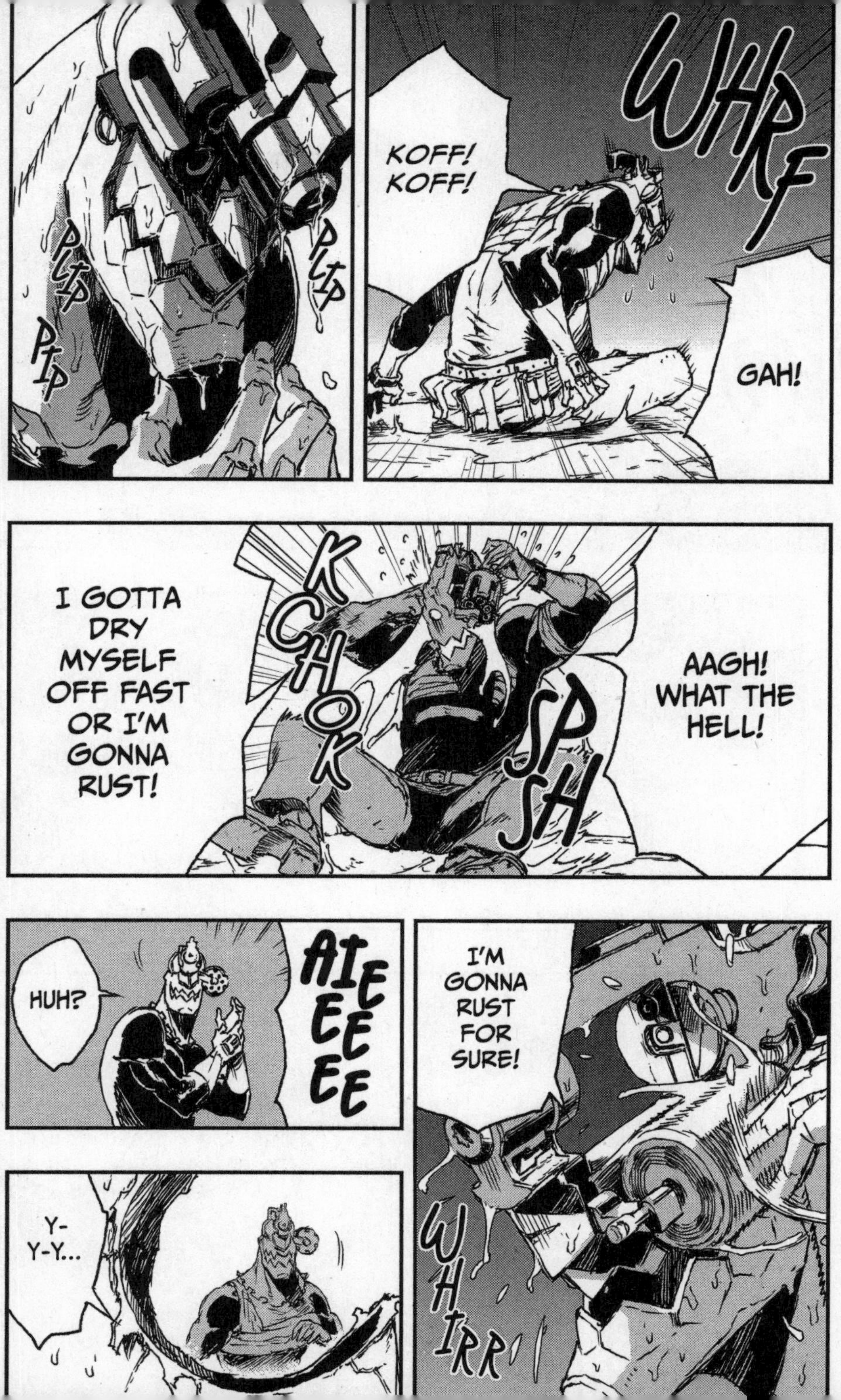
WHRF
KOFF! KOFF!
GAH!
PLIP
PLIP
PLIP
AAGH! WHAT THE HELL!
SPSH
KCHOK
I GOTTA DRY MYSELF OFF FAST OR I'M GONNA RUST!
I'M GONNA RUST FOR SURE!
WHIRR
AIEEEEE
HUH?
Y-
Y-Y...

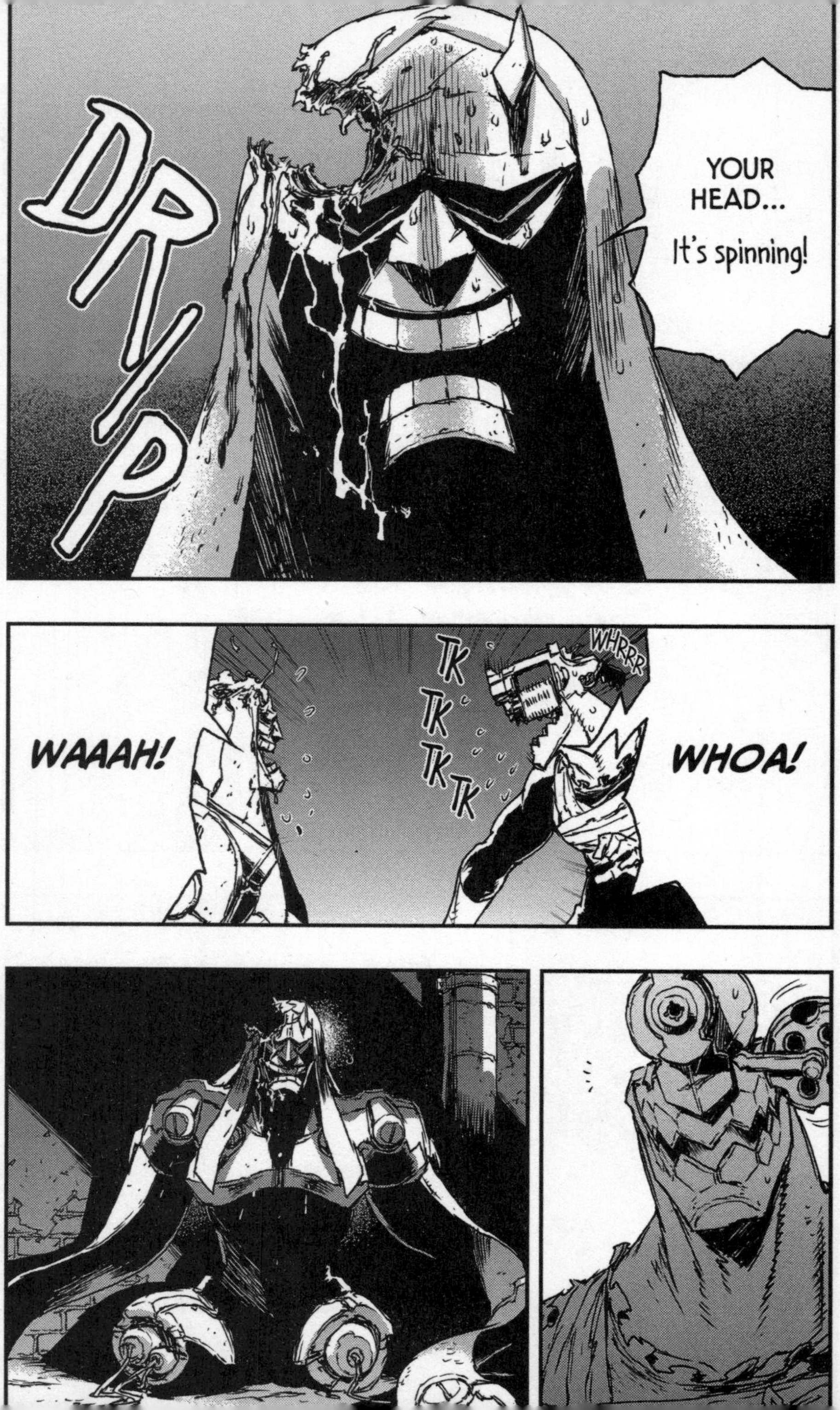
YOUR HEAD...
It's spinning!
DRIP
WHRRR
TK TK TK TK
WHOA!
WAAAH!

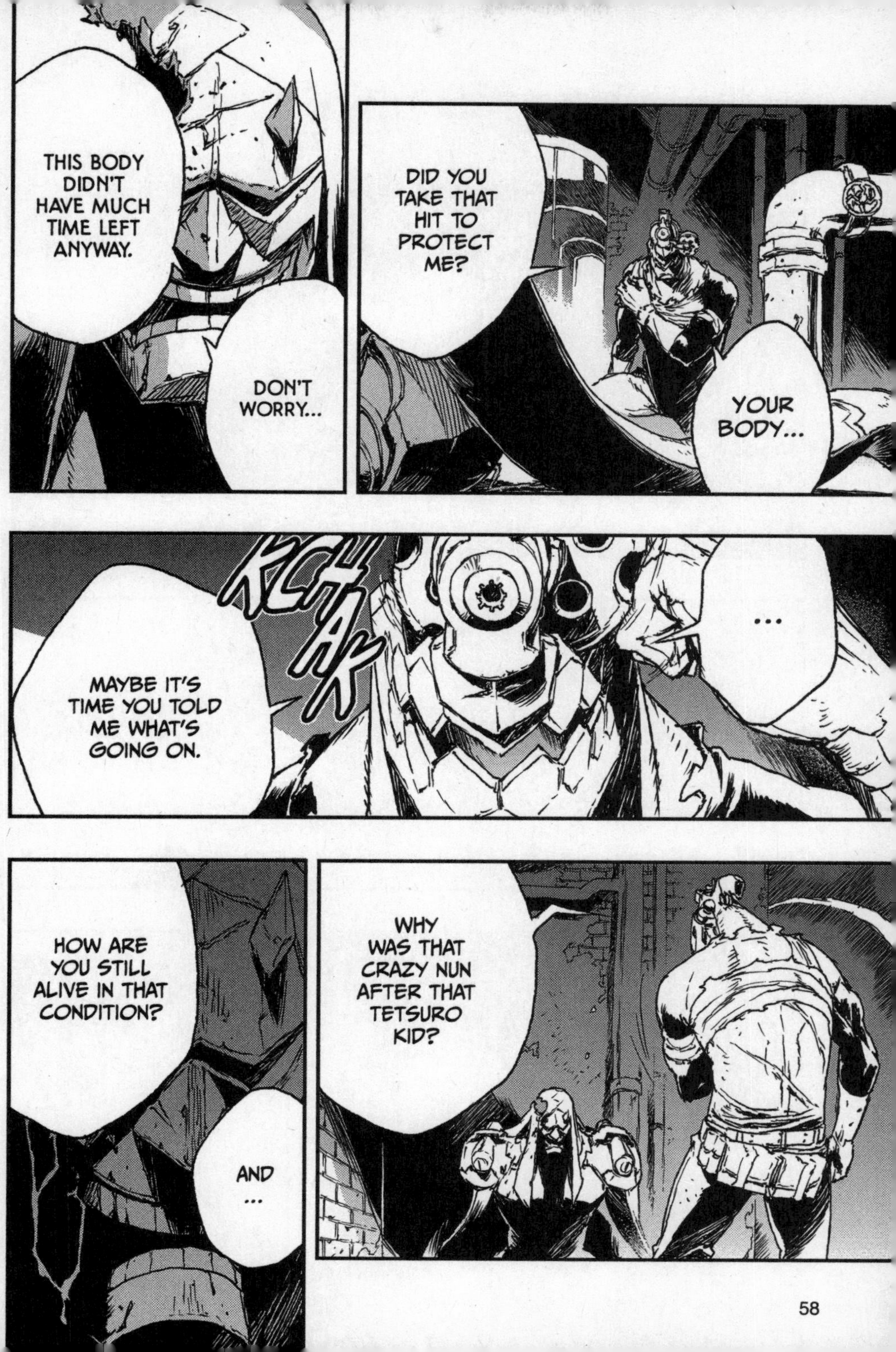
DID YOU TAKE THAT HIT TO PROTECT ME?
YOUR BODY...
THIS BODY DIDN'T HAVE MUCH TIME LEFT ANYWAY.
DON'T WORRY...
...
KCHAK
MAYBE IT'S TIME YOU TOLD ME WHAT'S GOING ON.
WHY WAS THAT CRAZY NUN AFTER THAT TETSURO KID?
HOW ARE YOU STILL ALIVE IN THAT CONDITION?
AND ...

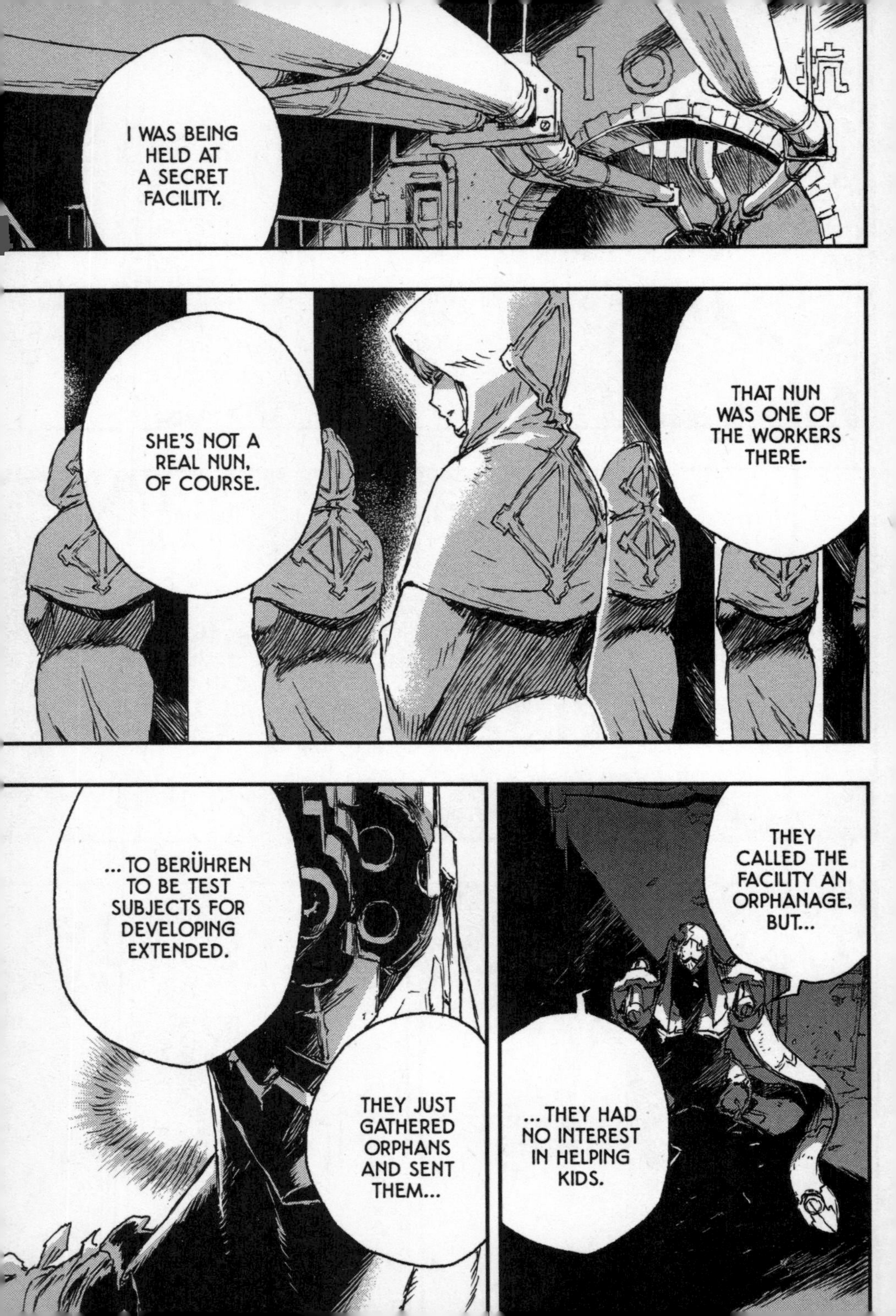

I WAS BEING HELD AT A SECRET FACILITY.
THAT NUN WAS ONE OF THE WORKERS THERE.
SHE'S NOT A REAL NUN, OF COURSE.
THEY CALLED THE FACILITY AN ORPHANAGE, BUT...
...THEY HAD NO INTEREST IN HELPING KIDS.
THEY JUST GATHERED ORPHANS AND SENT THEM...
...TO BERÜHREN TO BE TEST SUBJECTS FOR DEVELOPING EXTENDED.

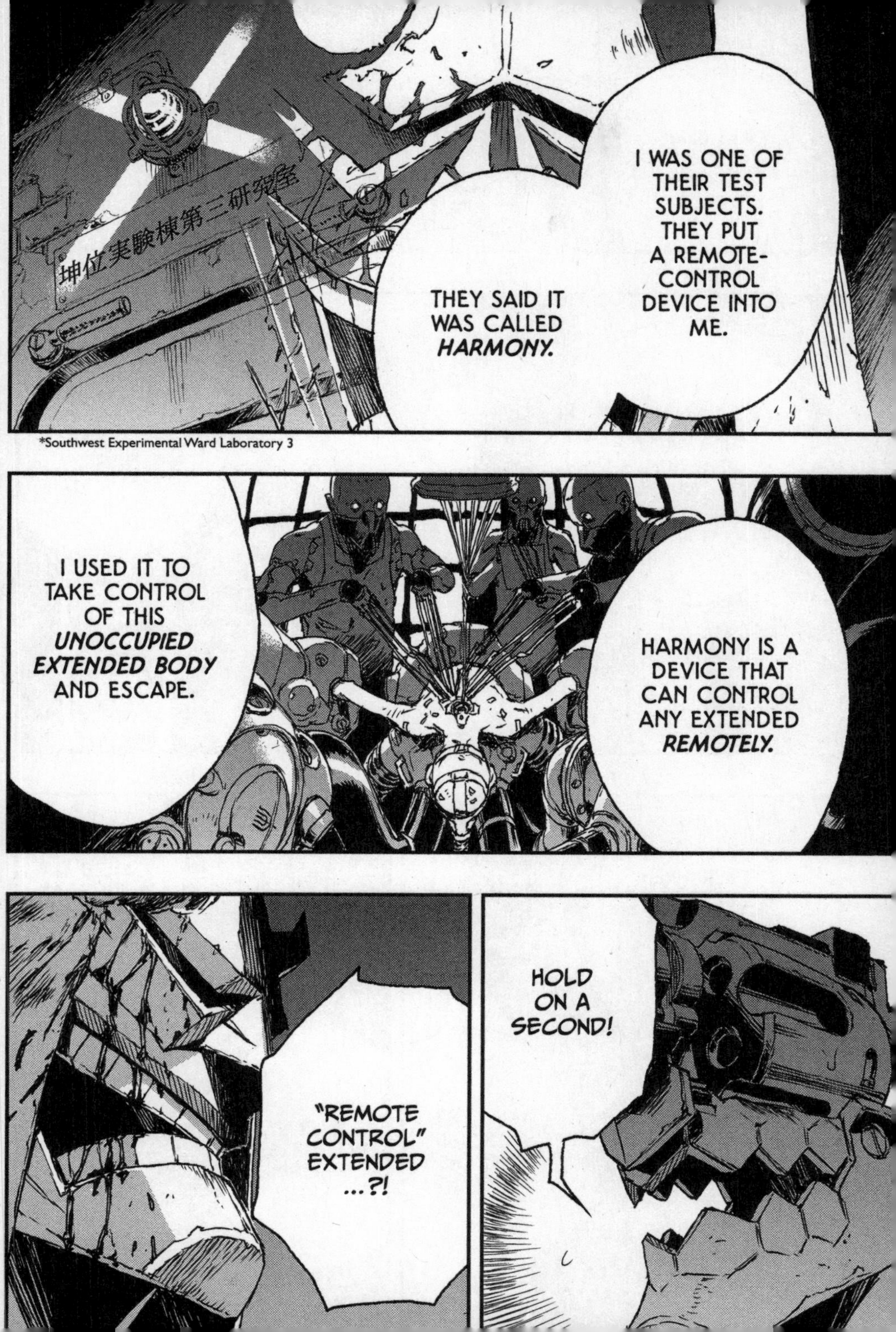
I WAS ONE OF THEIR TEST SUBJECTS. THEY PUT A REMOTE-CONTROL DEVICE INTO ME.
THEY SAID IT WAS CALLED *HARMONY.*
坤位実験棟第三研究室
HARMONY IS A DEVICE THAT CAN CONTROL ANY EXTENDED *REMOTELY.*
I USED IT TO TAKE CONTROL OF THIS *UNOCCUPIED EXTENDED BODY* AND ESCAPE.
HOLD ON A SECOND!
"REMOTE CONTROL" EXTENDED ...?!
*Southwest Experimental Ward Laboratory 3

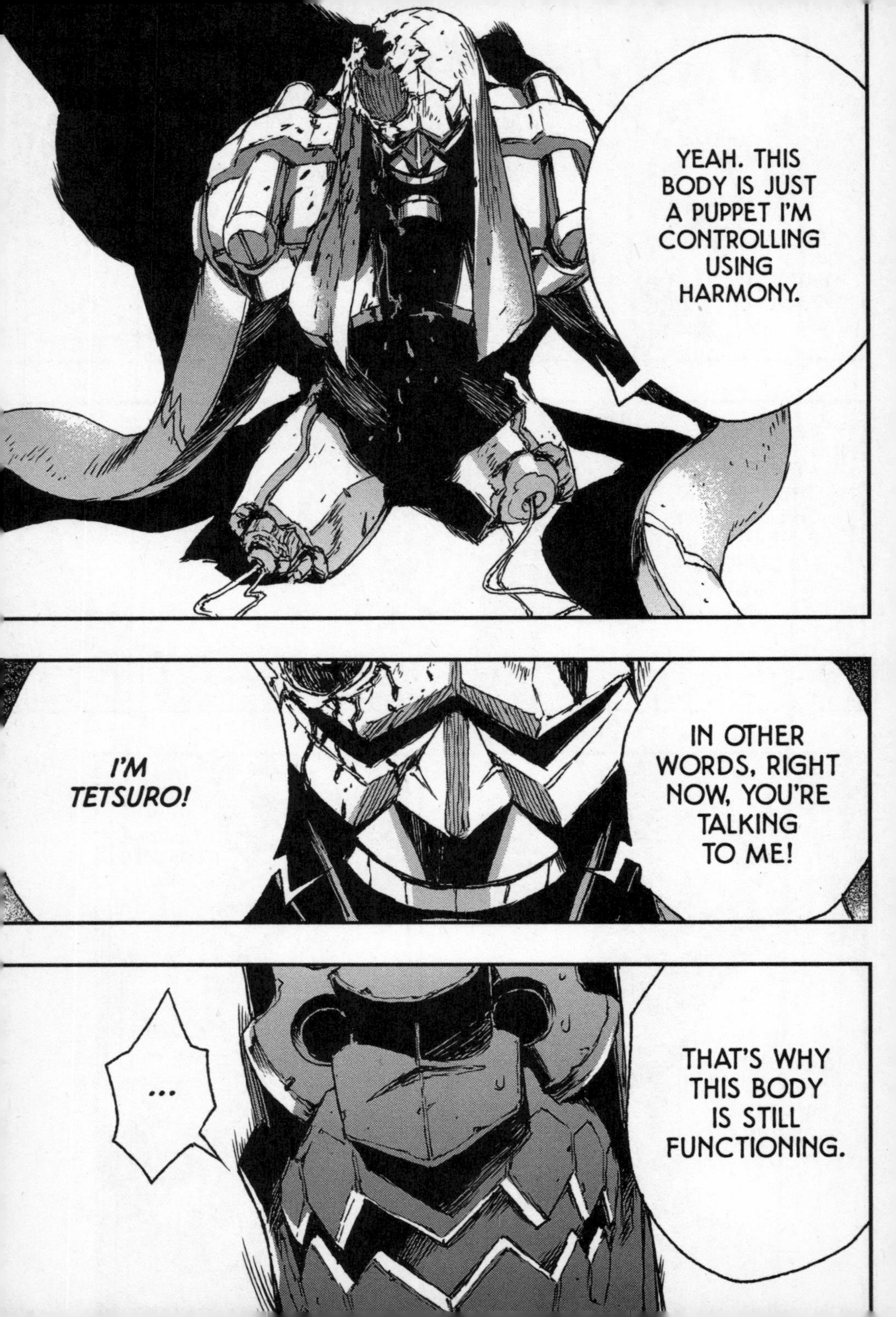
YEAH. THIS BODY IS JUST A PUPPET I'M CONTROLLING USING HARMONY.
IN OTHER WORDS, RIGHT NOW, YOU'RE TALKING TO ME!
I'M TETSURO!
THAT'S WHY THIS BODY IS STILL FUNCTIONING.
...

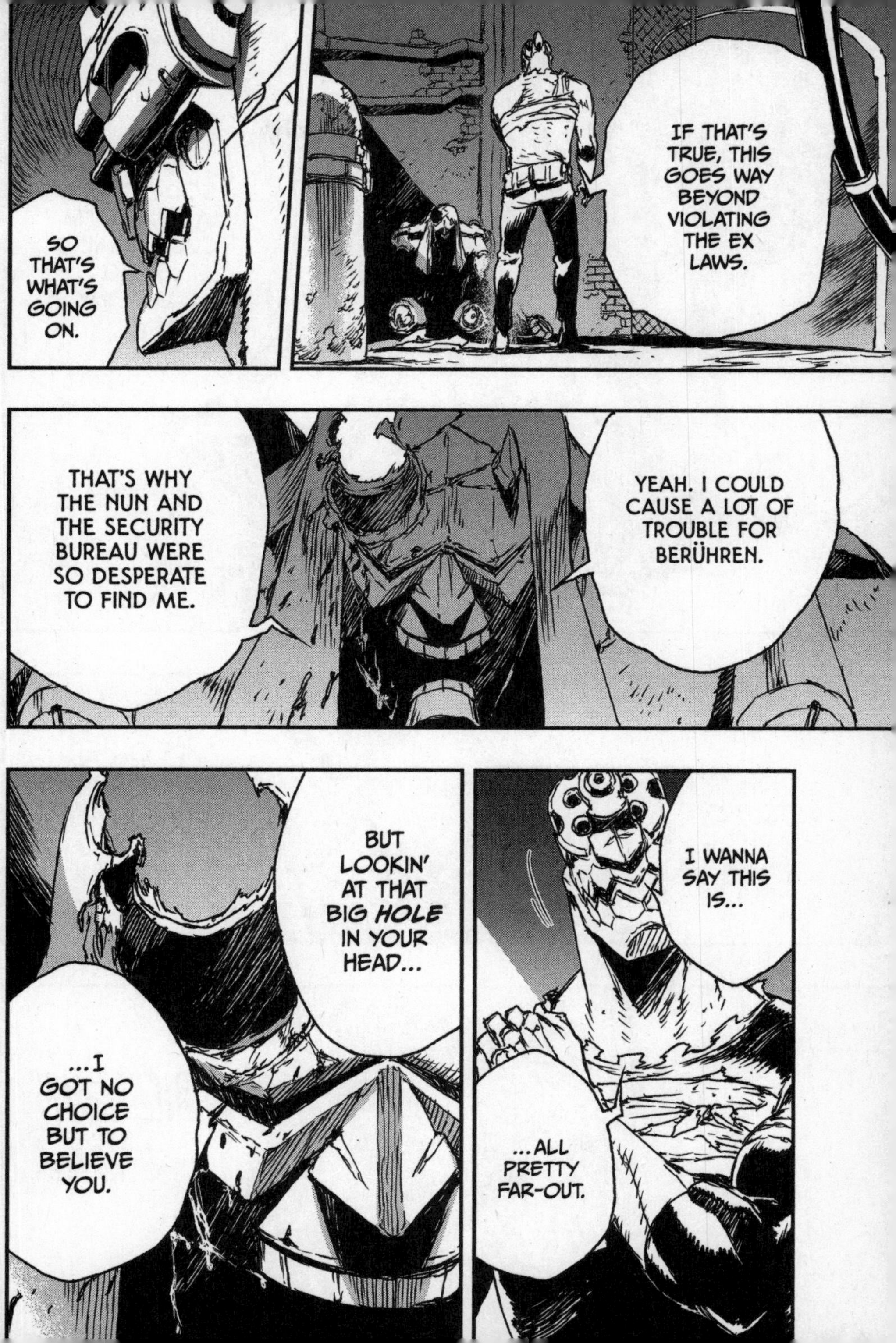
IF THAT'S TRUE, THIS GOES WAY BEYOND VIOLATING THE EX LAWS.
SO THAT'S WHAT'S GOING ON.
YEAH. I COULD CAUSE A LOT OF TROUBLE FOR BERÜHREN.
THAT'S WHY THE NUN AND THE SECURITY BUREAU WERE SO DESPERATE TO FIND ME.
I WANNA SAY THIS IS...
...ALL PRETTY FAR-OUT.
BUT LOOKIN' AT THAT BIG *HOLE* IN YOUR HEAD...
...I GOT NO CHOICE BUT TO BELIEVE YOU.

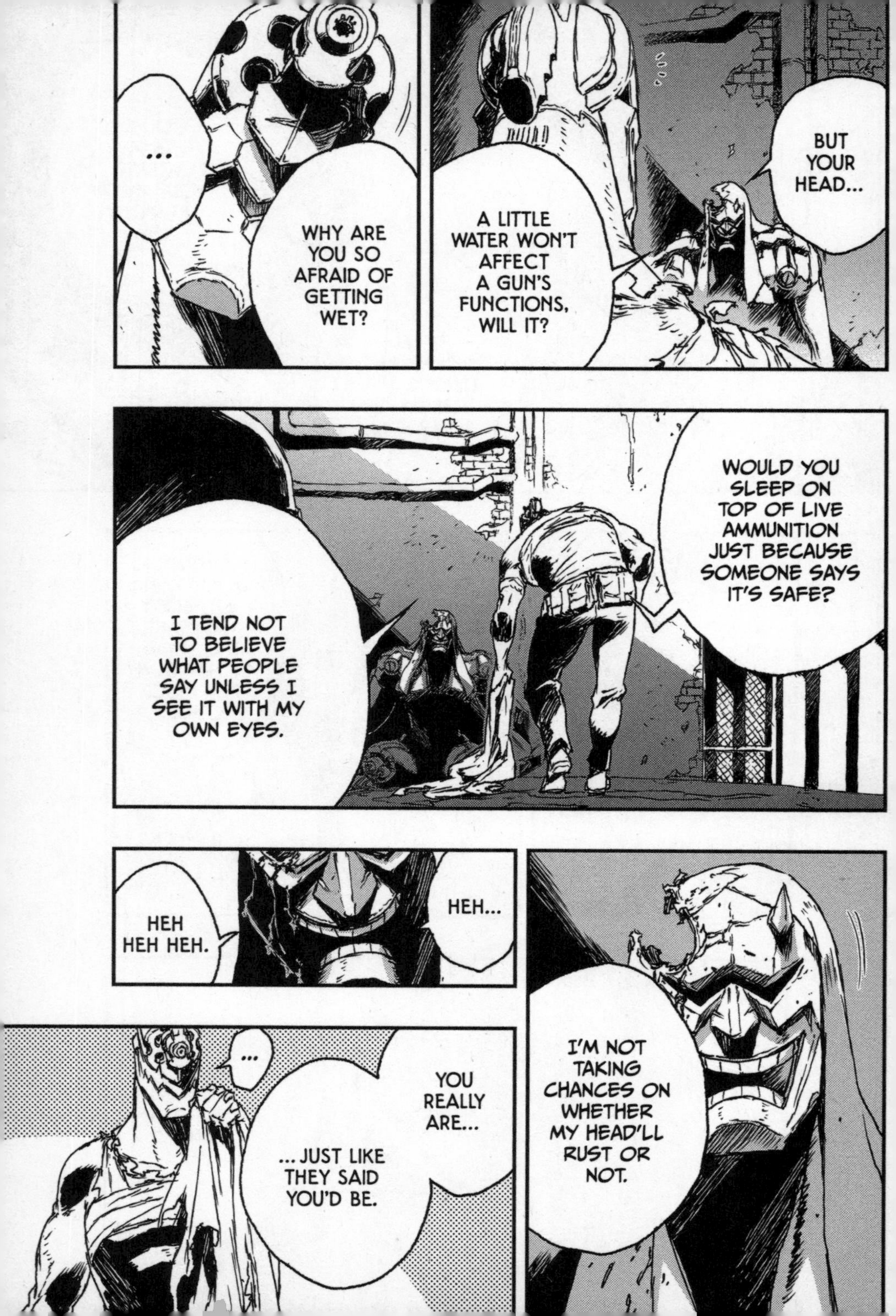
BUT YOUR HEAD...
A LITTLE WATER WON'T AFFECT A GUN'S FUNCTIONS, WILL IT?
...
WHY ARE YOU SO AFRAID OF GETTING WET?
WOULD YOU SLEEP ON TOP OF LIVE AMMUNITION JUST BECAUSE SOMEONE SAYS IT'S SAFE?
I TEND NOT TO BELIEVE WHAT PEOPLE SAY UNLESS I SEE IT WITH MY OWN EYES.
I'M NOT TAKING CHANCES ON WHETHER MY HEAD'LL RUST OR NOT.
HEH...
HEH HEH HEH.
YOU REALLY ARE...
...JUST LIKE THEY SAID YOU'D BE.
...

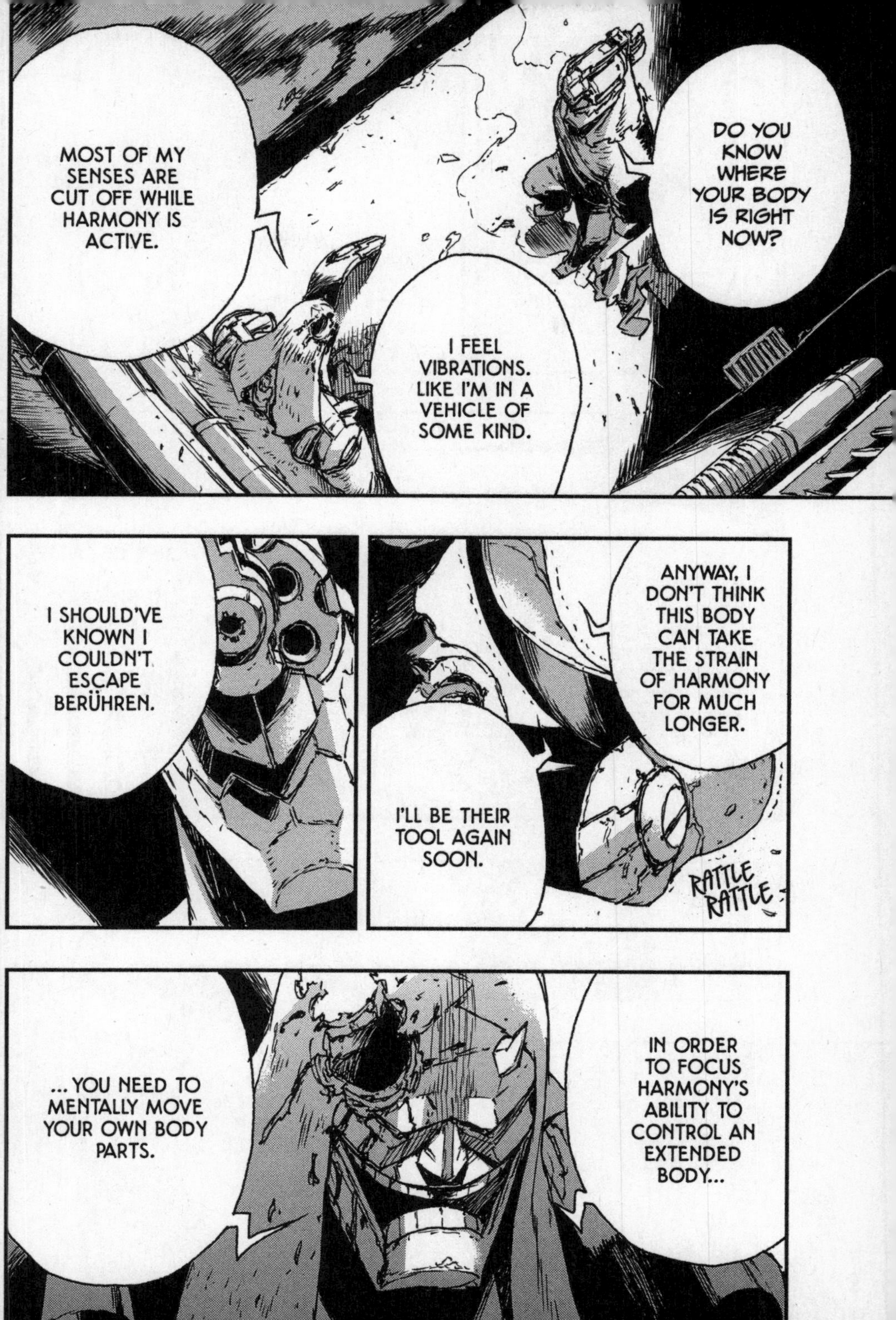
DO YOU KNOW WHERE YOUR BODY IS RIGHT NOW?
MOST OF MY SENSES ARE CUT OFF WHILE HARMONY IS ACTIVE.
I FEEL VIBRATIONS. LIKE I'M IN A VEHICLE OF SOME KIND.
ANYWAY, I DON'T THINK THIS BODY CAN TAKE THE STRAIN OF HARMONY FOR MUCH LONGER.
I'LL BE THEIR TOOL AGAIN SOON.
RATTLE RATTLE
I SHOULD'VE KNOWN I COULDN'T ESCAPE BERÜHREN.
IN ORDER TO FOCUS HARMONY'S ABILITY TO CONTROL AN EXTENDED BODY...
...YOU NEED TO MENTALLY MOVE YOUR OWN BODY PARTS.

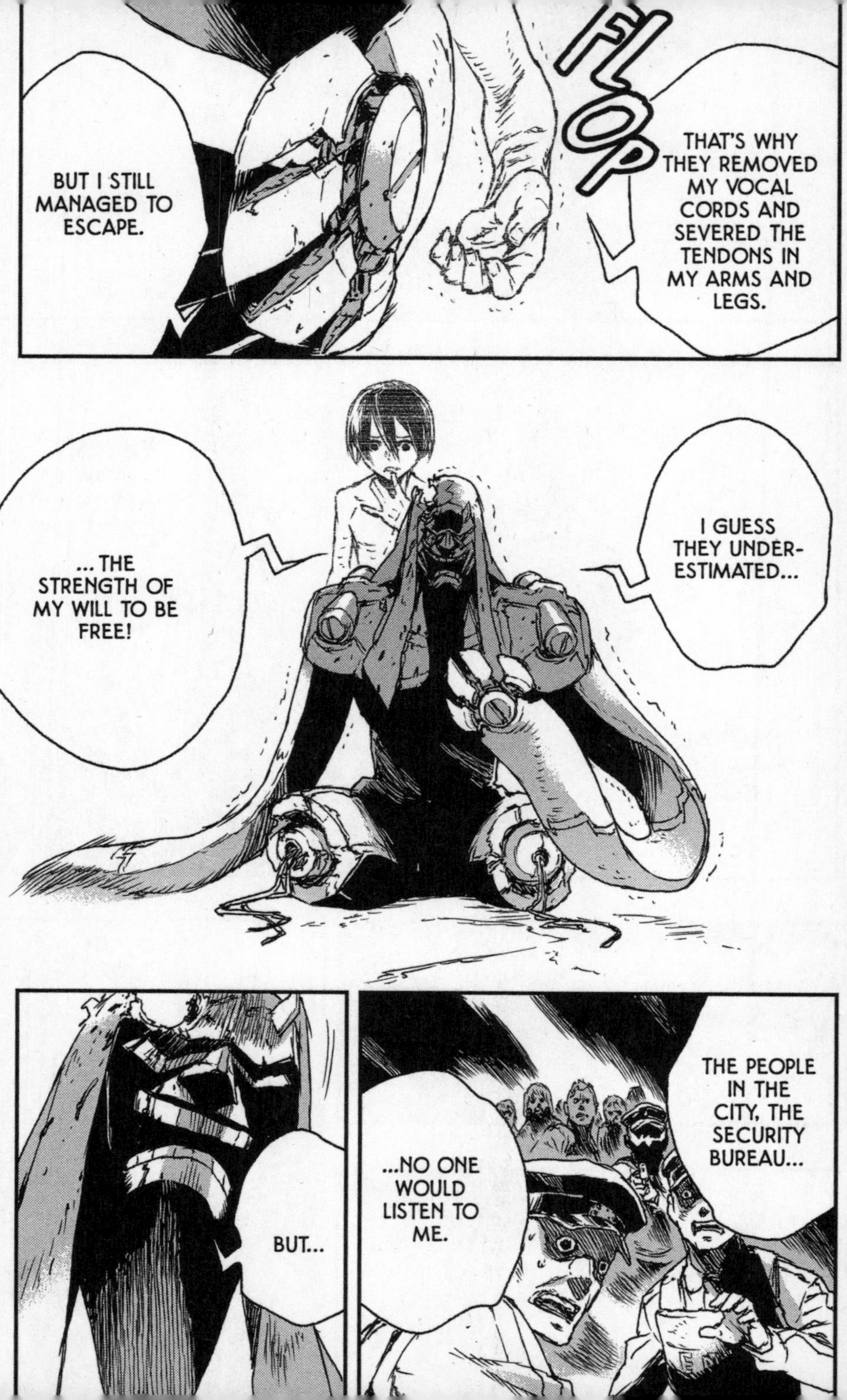
THAT'S WHY THEY REMOVED MY VOCAL CORDS AND SEVERED THE TENDONS IN MY ARMS AND LEGS.
FLOP
BUT I STILL MANAGED TO ESCAPE.
I GUESS THEY UNDER-ESTIMATED...
... THE STRENGTH OF MY WILL TO BE FREE!
THE PEOPLE IN THE CITY, THE SECURITY BUREAU...
...NO ONE WOULD LISTEN TO ME.
BUT...

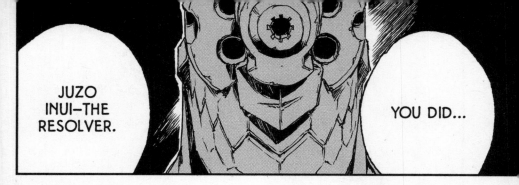

JUZO INUI—THE RESOLVER.

YOU DID...

THIS ISN'T HOW I THOUGHT IT WOULD END.

BUT I'M GLAD THAT I GOT...

... TO MEET YOU—

KLAK

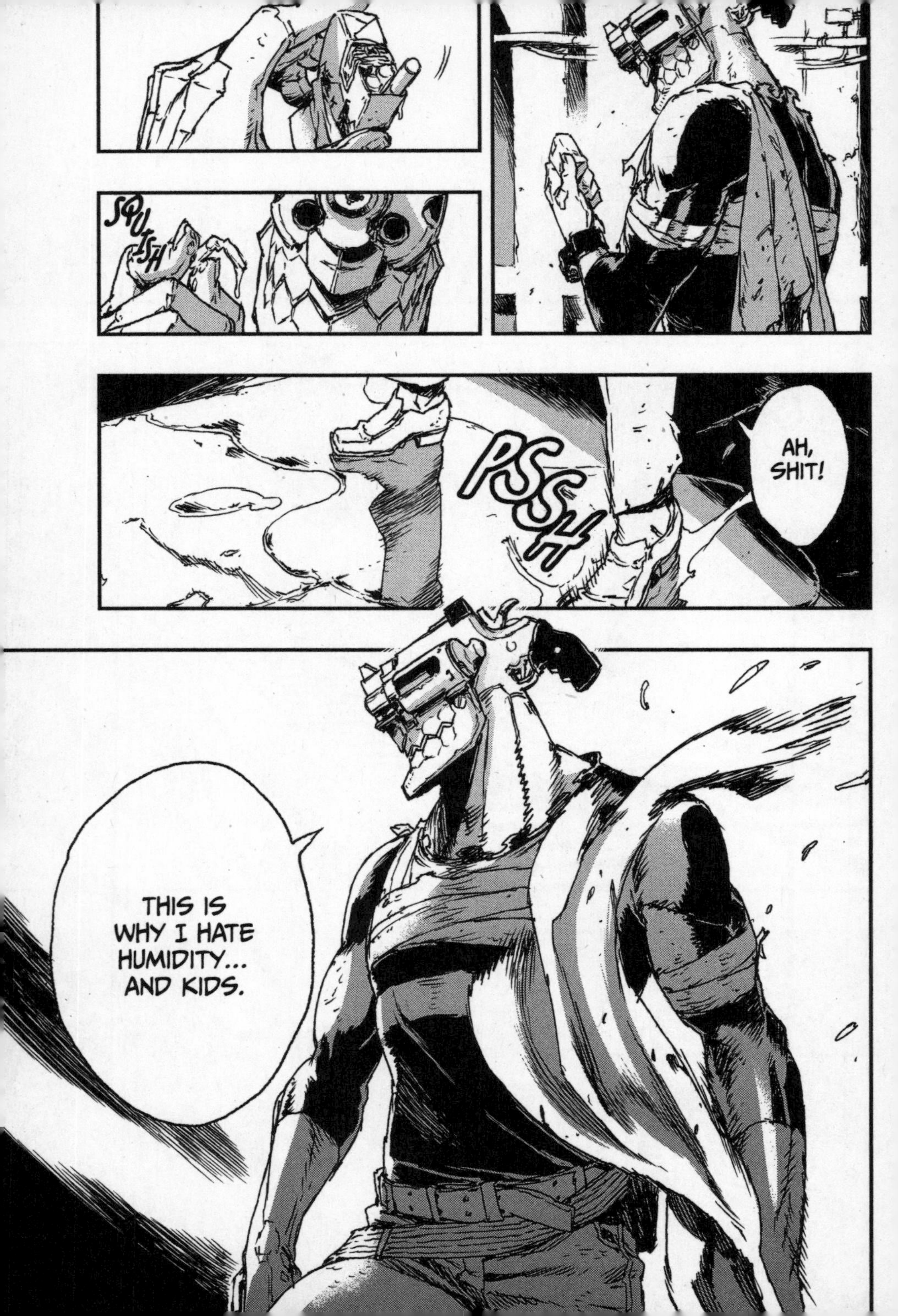
SQUISH
AH, SHIT!
PSSH
THIS IS WHY I HATE HUMIDITY... AND KIDS.

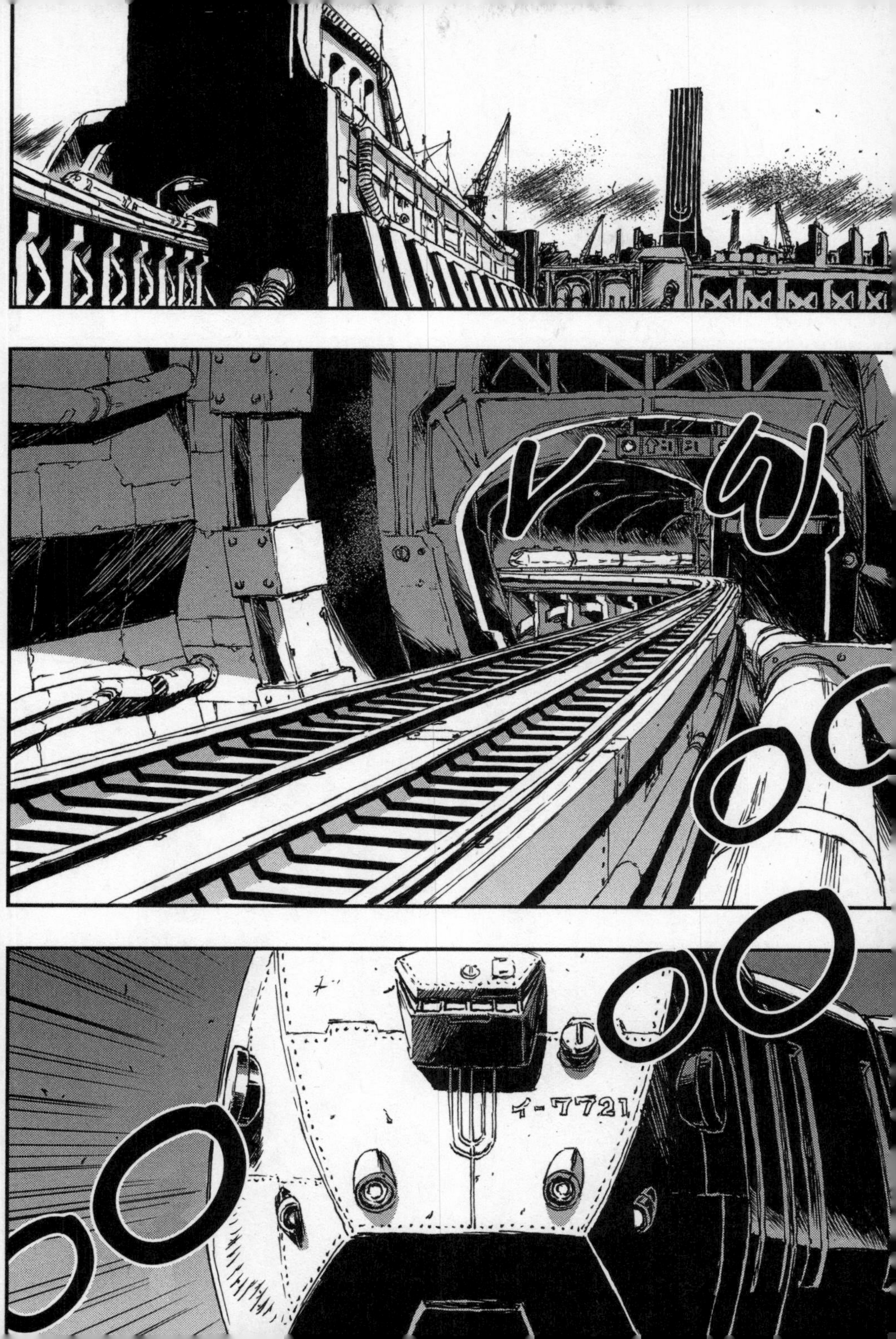
VWOOOOOO
イ-7721

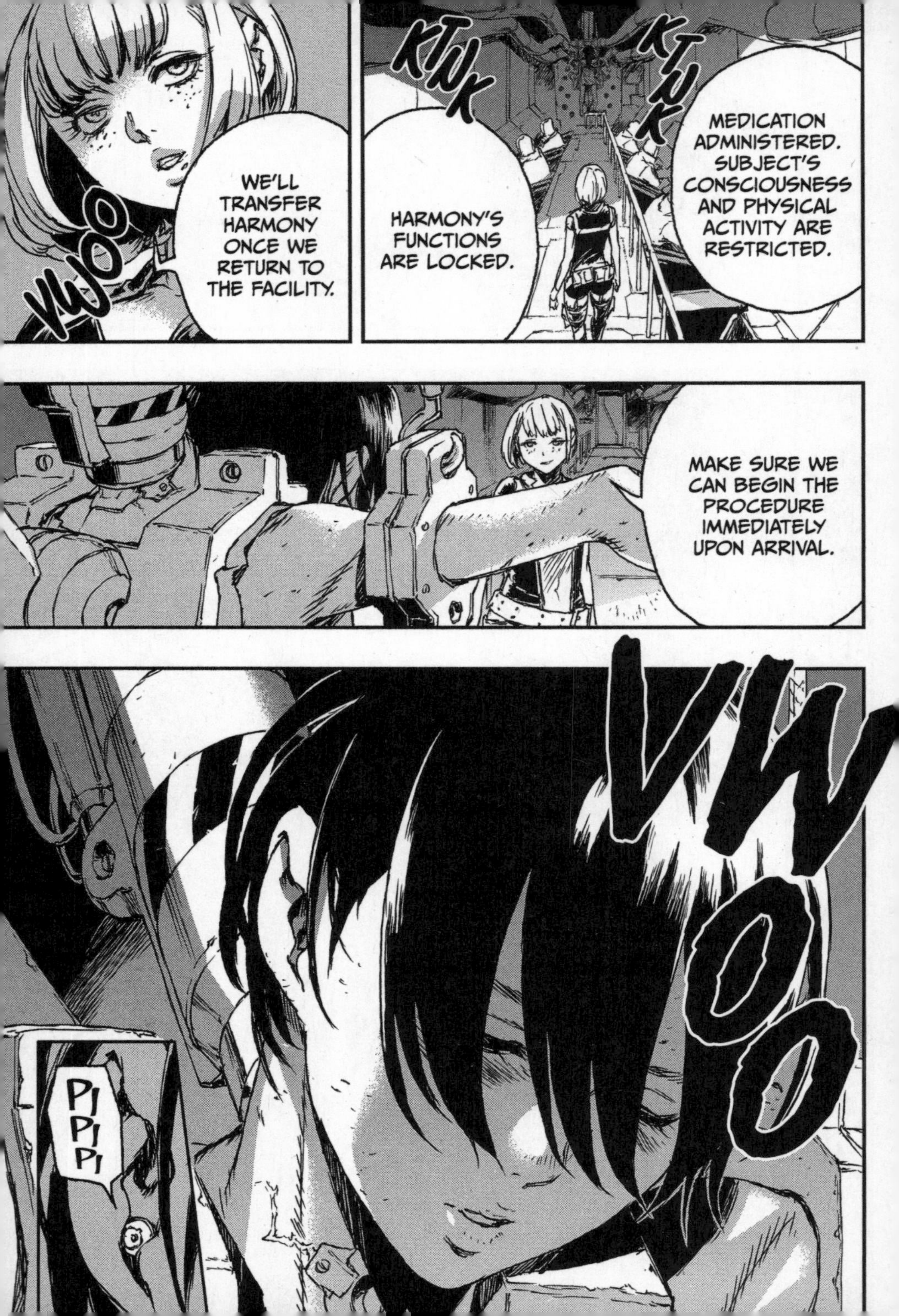
KTUNK
MEDICATION ADMINISTERED. SUBJECT'S CONSCIOUSNESS AND PHYSICAL ACTIVITY ARE RESTRICTED.
KTUNK
HARMONY'S FUNCTIONS ARE LOCKED.
WE'LL TRANSFER HARMONY ONCE WE RETURN TO THE FACILITY.
VWOO
MAKE SURE WE CAN BEGIN THE PROCEDURE IMMEDIATELY UPON ARRIVAL.
VWOOO
PIPIPI

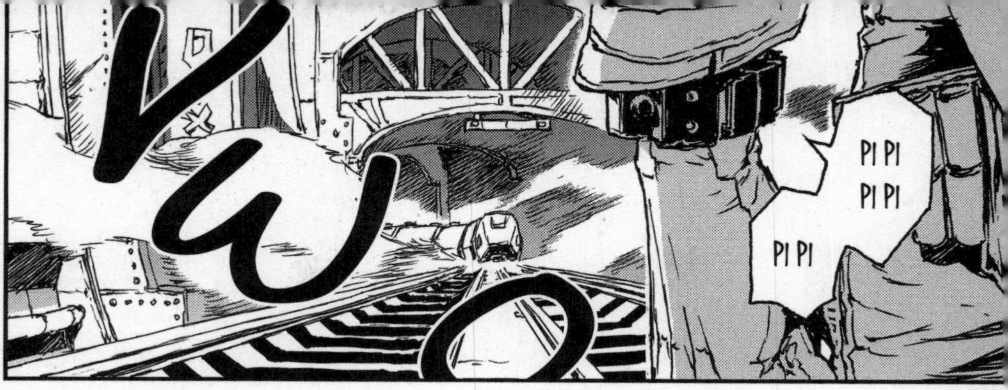
VWO
PI PI
PI PI
PI PI

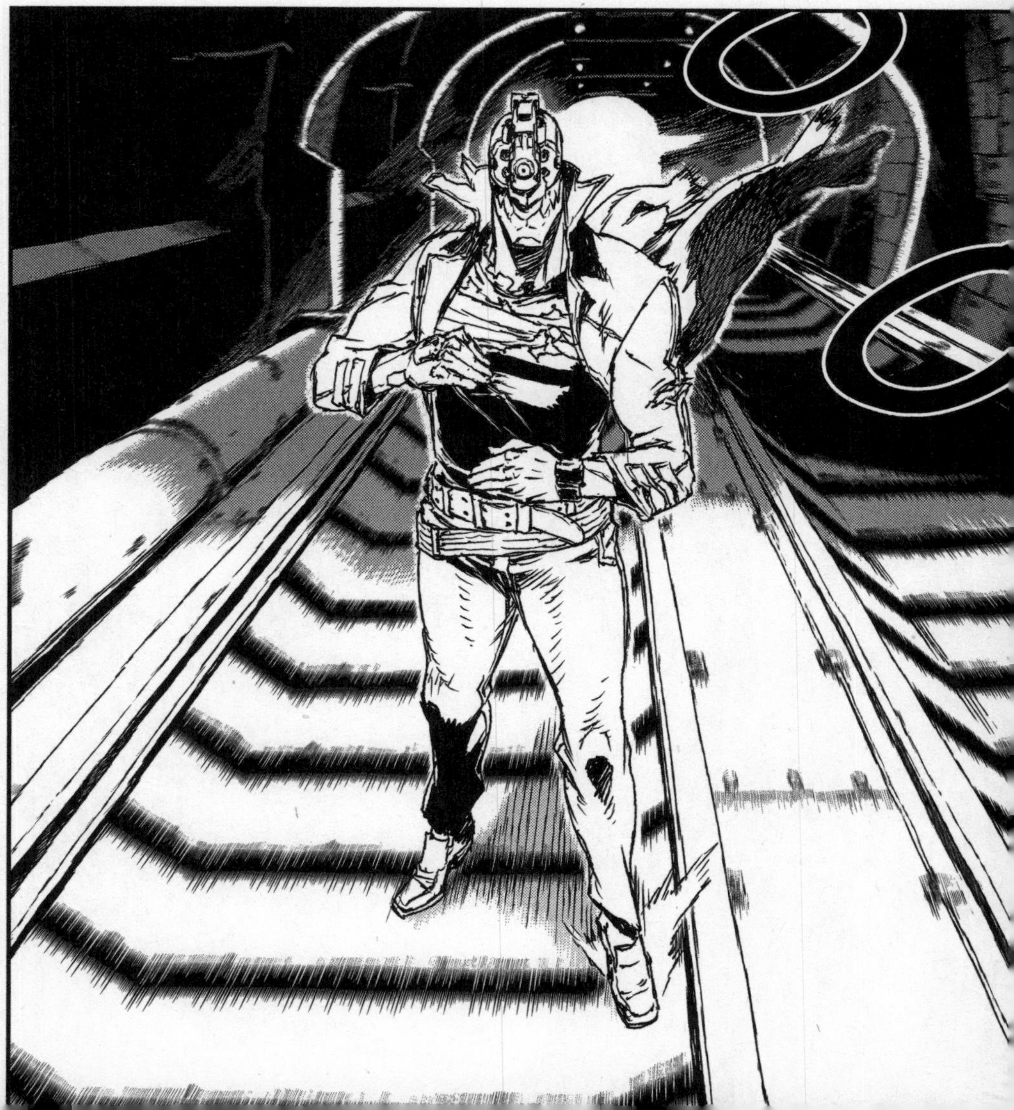
OO

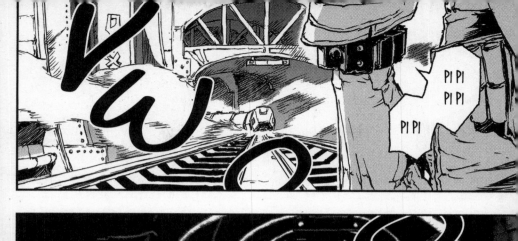

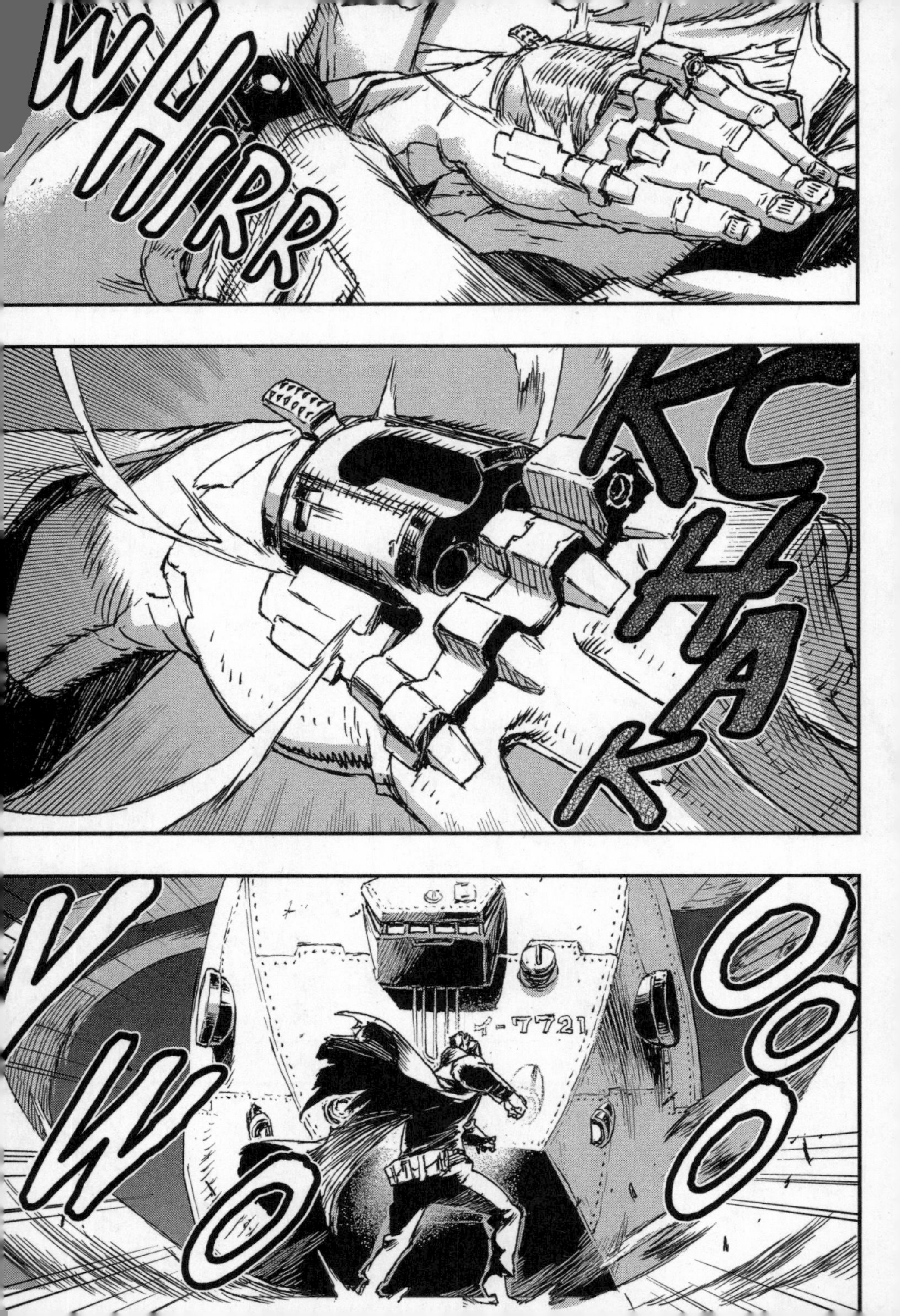
WHIRR
KCHAK
イ-7721
VWO
OOOO

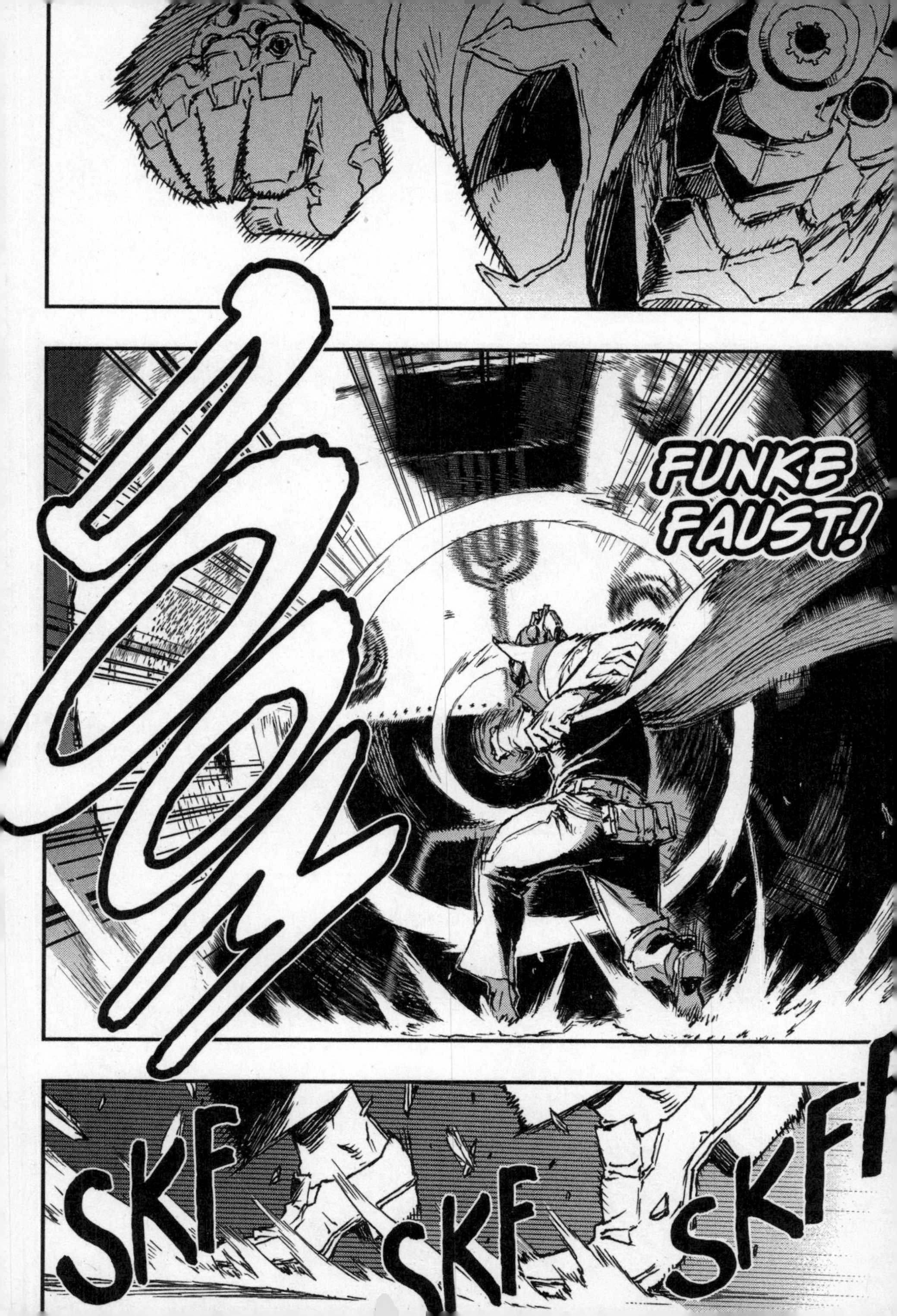
FUNKE
FAUST!
SKF
SKF
SKF

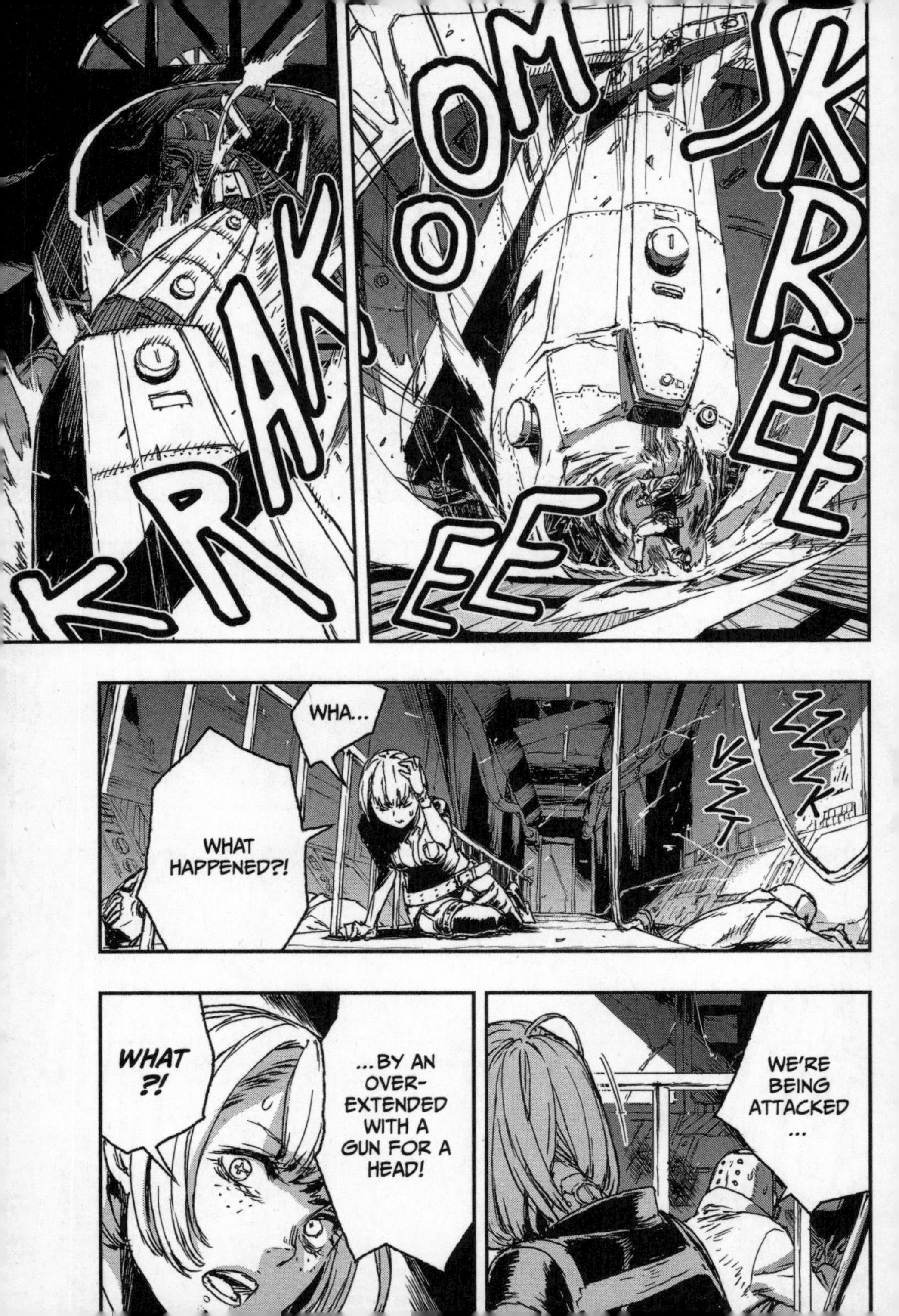
SKREEEEE
KRAKOOM
ZZZK
VZZT
WHA...
WHAT HAPPENED?!
WE'RE BEING ATTACKED ...
...BY AN OVER-EXTENDED WITH A GUN FOR A HEAD!
WHAT ?!

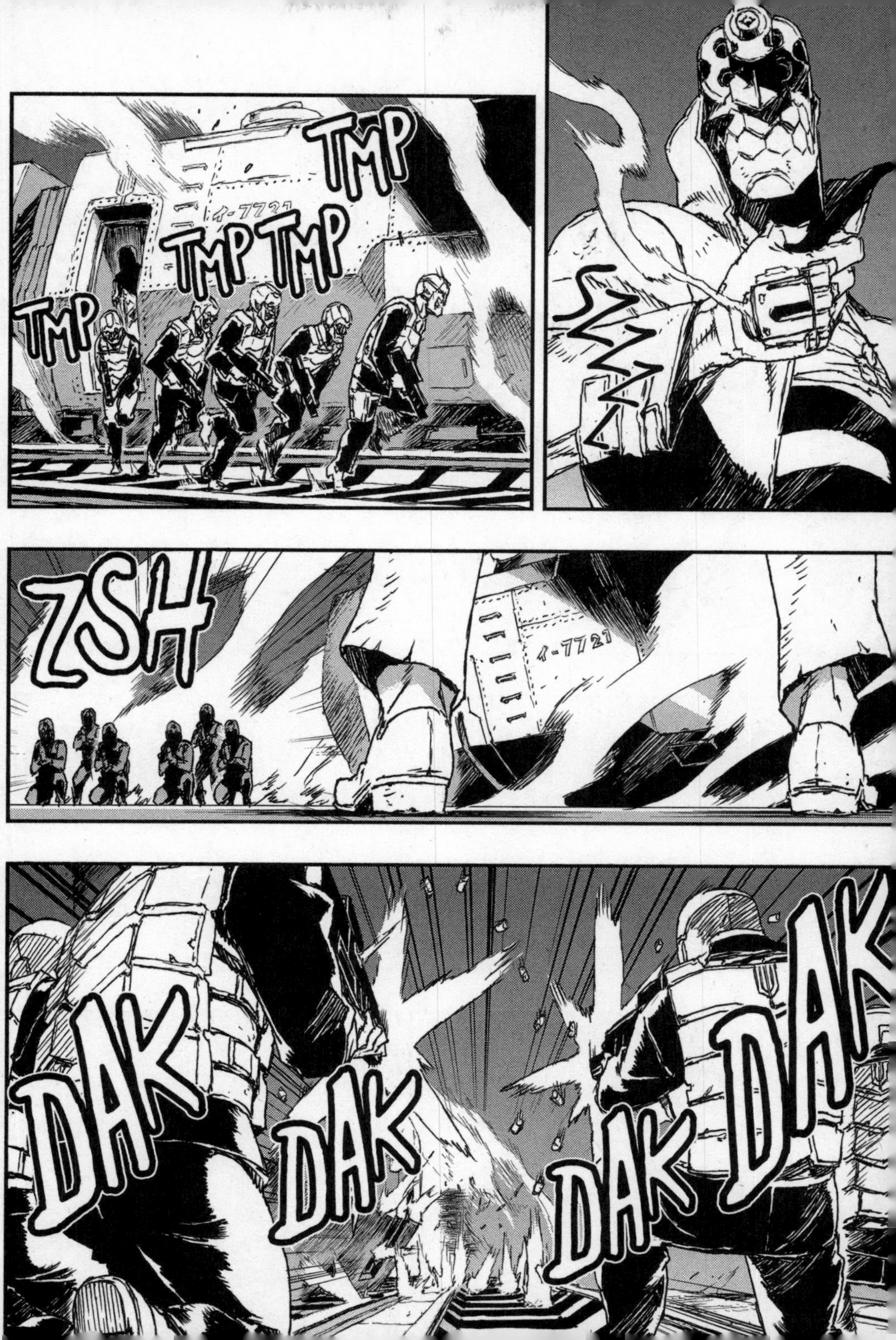
TMP
イ-7721
TMP TMP
TMP
ZSH
イ-7721
DAK
DAK
DAK
DAK

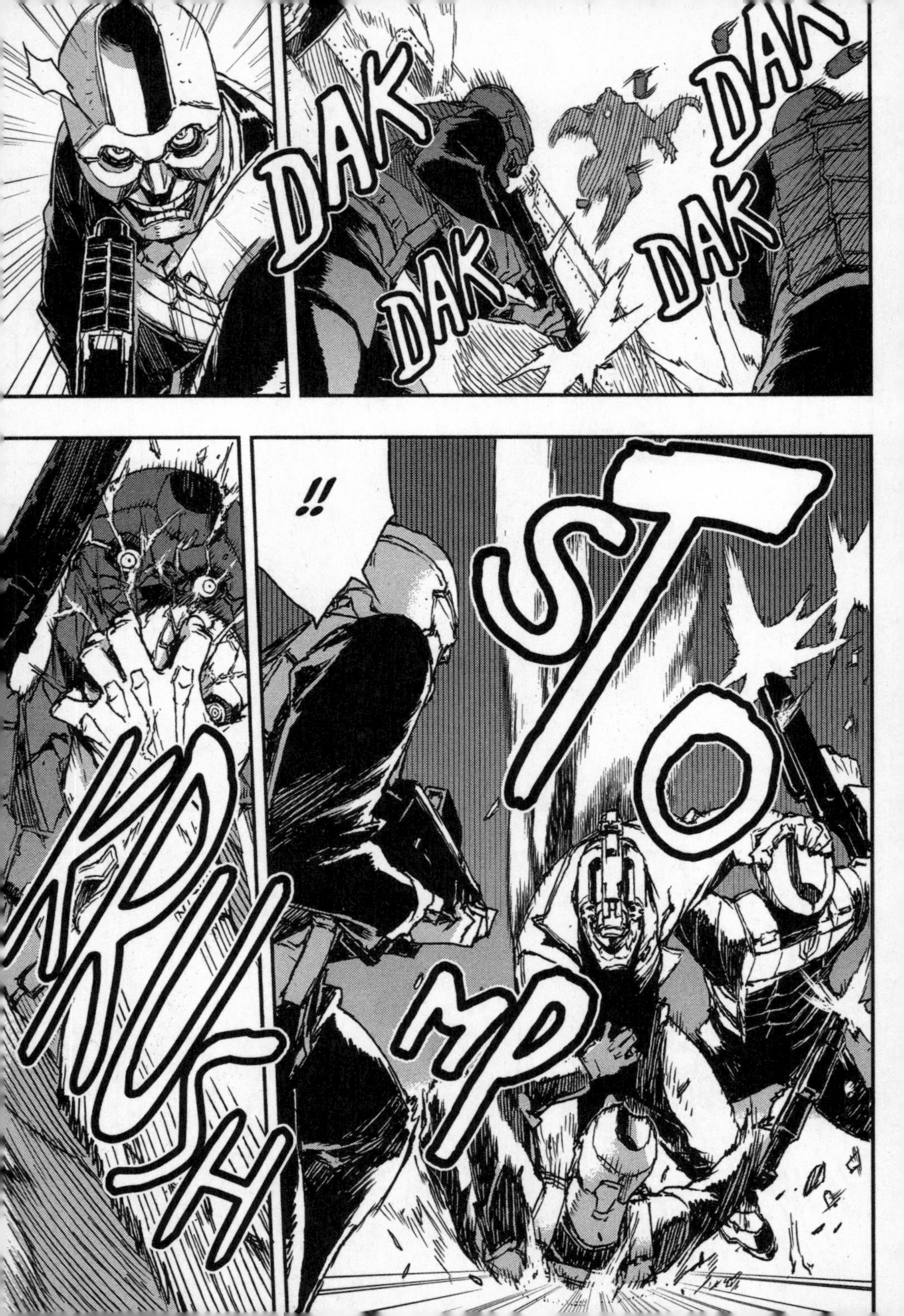
DAK
DAK
DAK
DAK
DAK
!!
STOMP
KRUSH

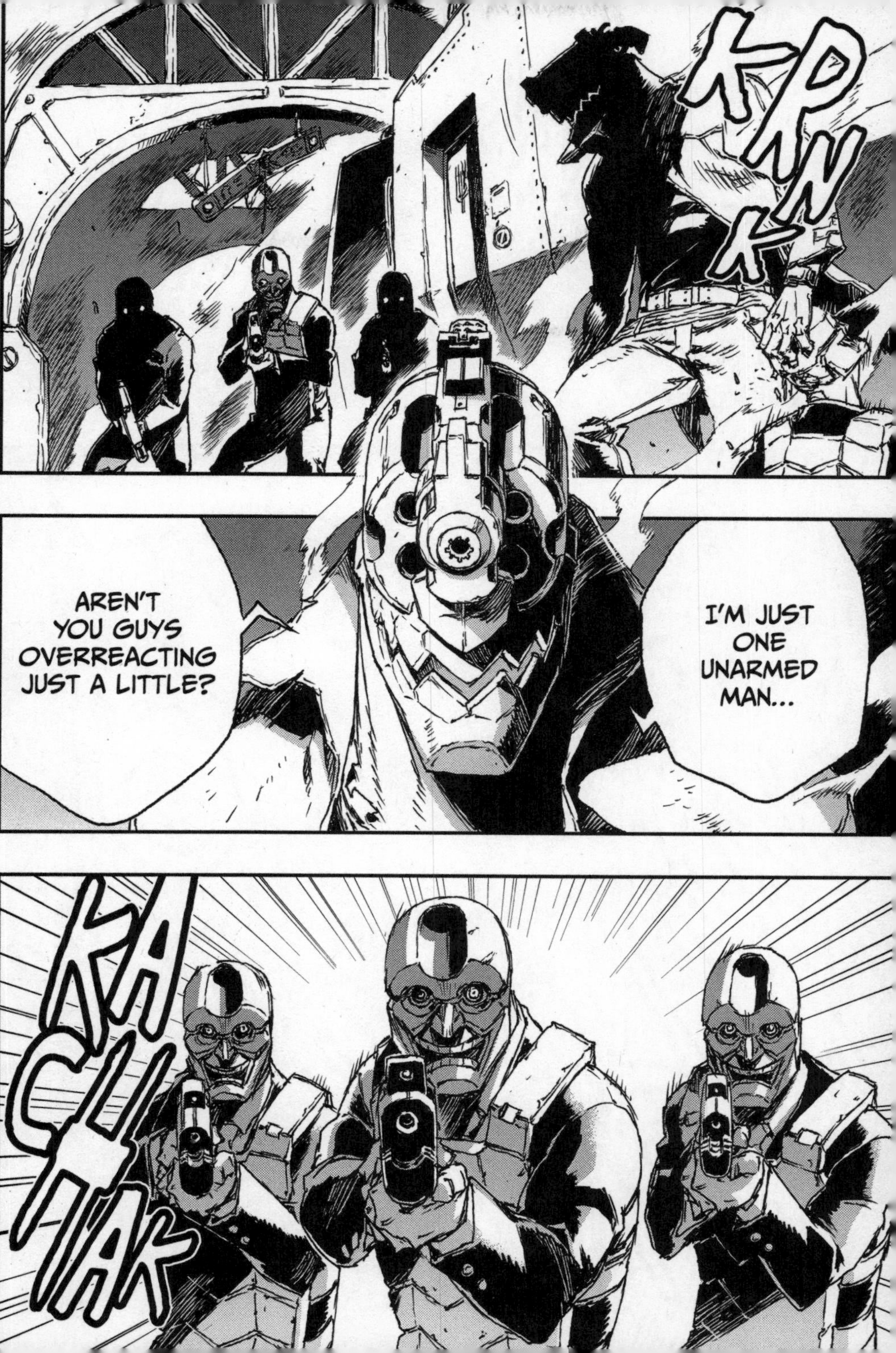
KPNK
I'M JUST ONE UNARMED MAN...
AREN'T YOU GUYS OVERREACTING JUST A LITTLE?
KACHAK

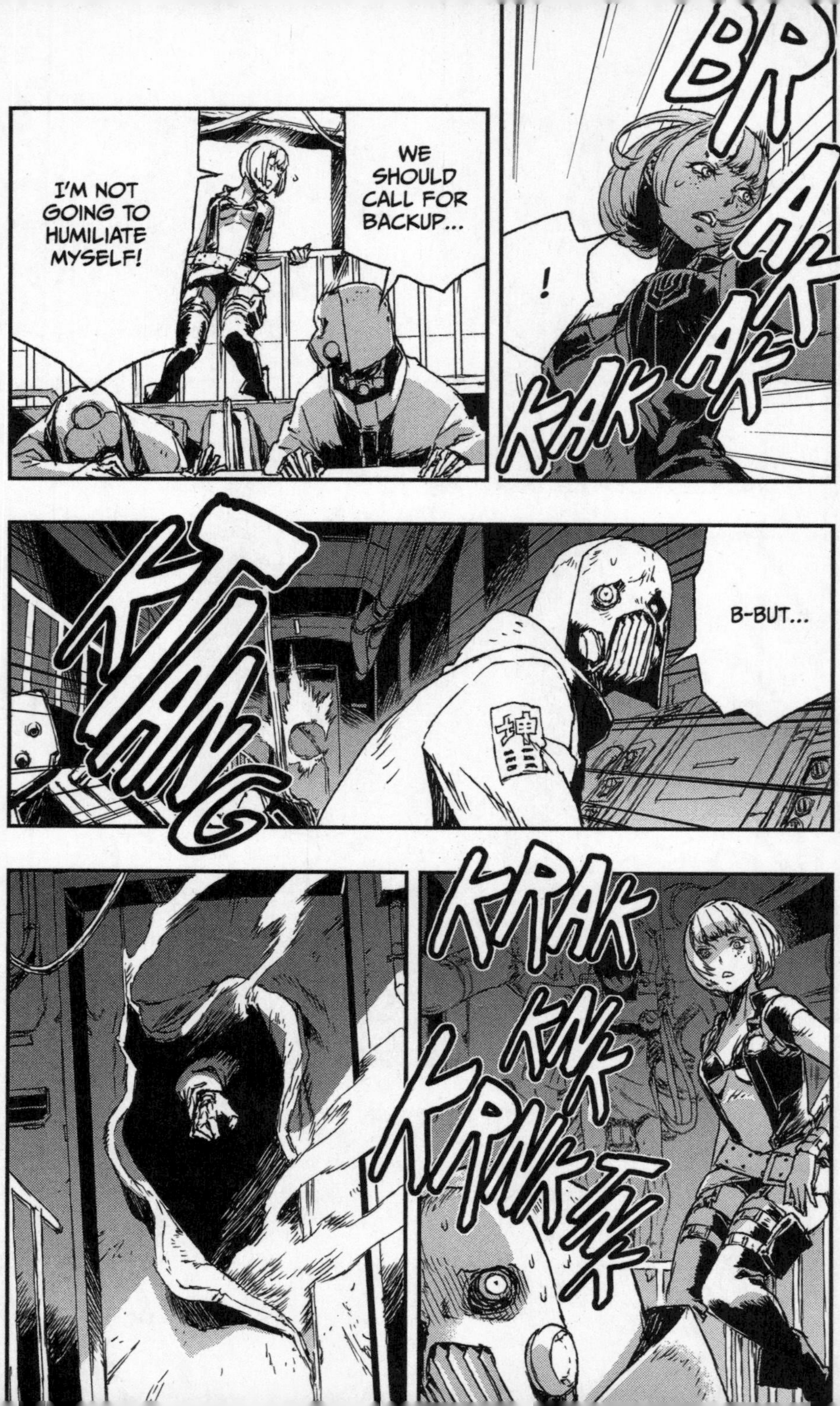
BRAKAKAK
KAK
!
WE SHOULD CALL FOR BACKUP...
I'M NOT GOING TO HUMILIATE MYSELF!
B-BUT...
KTANG
KRAK
KNK
KRNKTNK

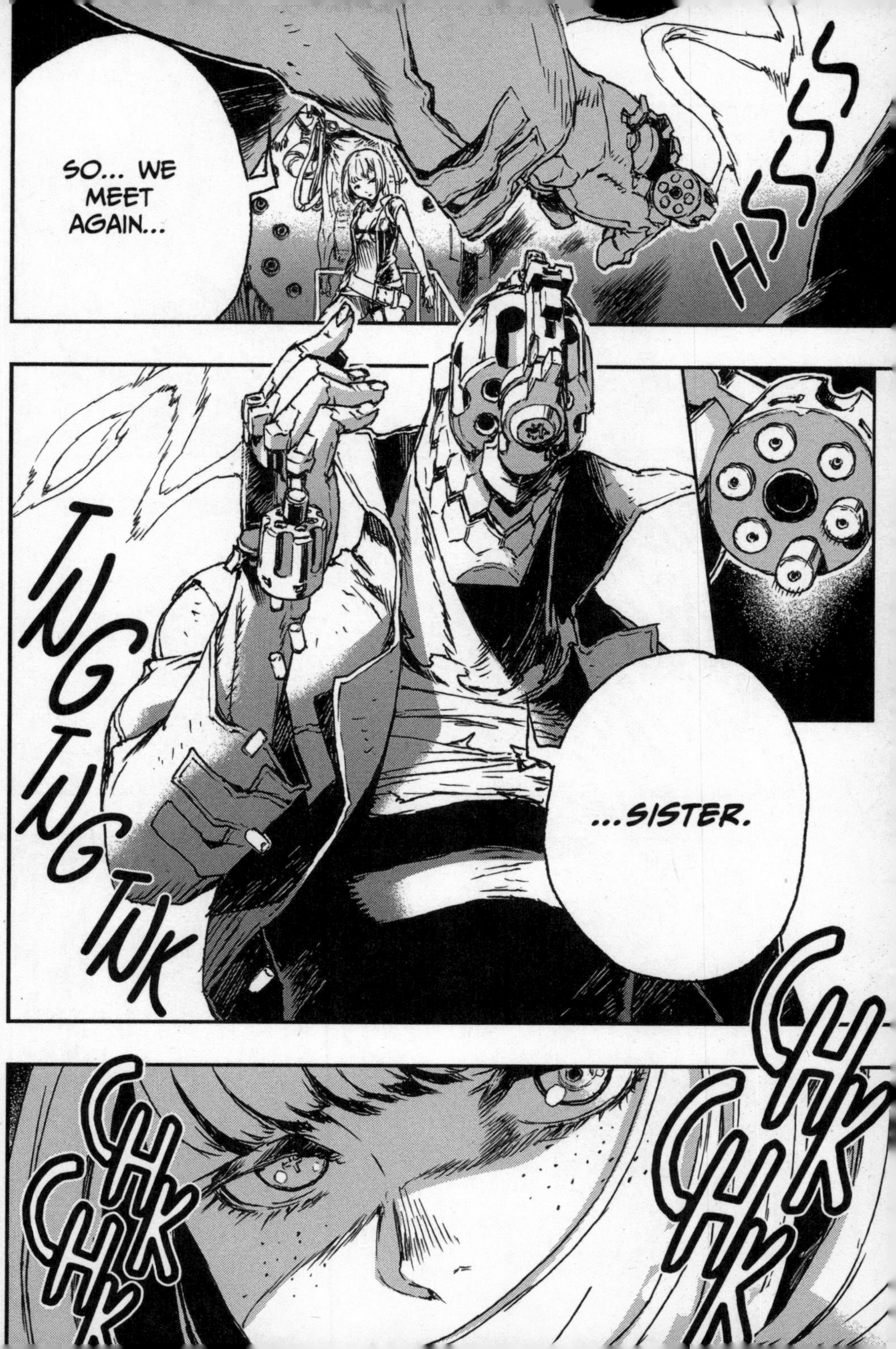
HSSS
SO... WE MEET AGAIN...
...SISTER.
TING TING TINK
CHK CHK
CHK CHK

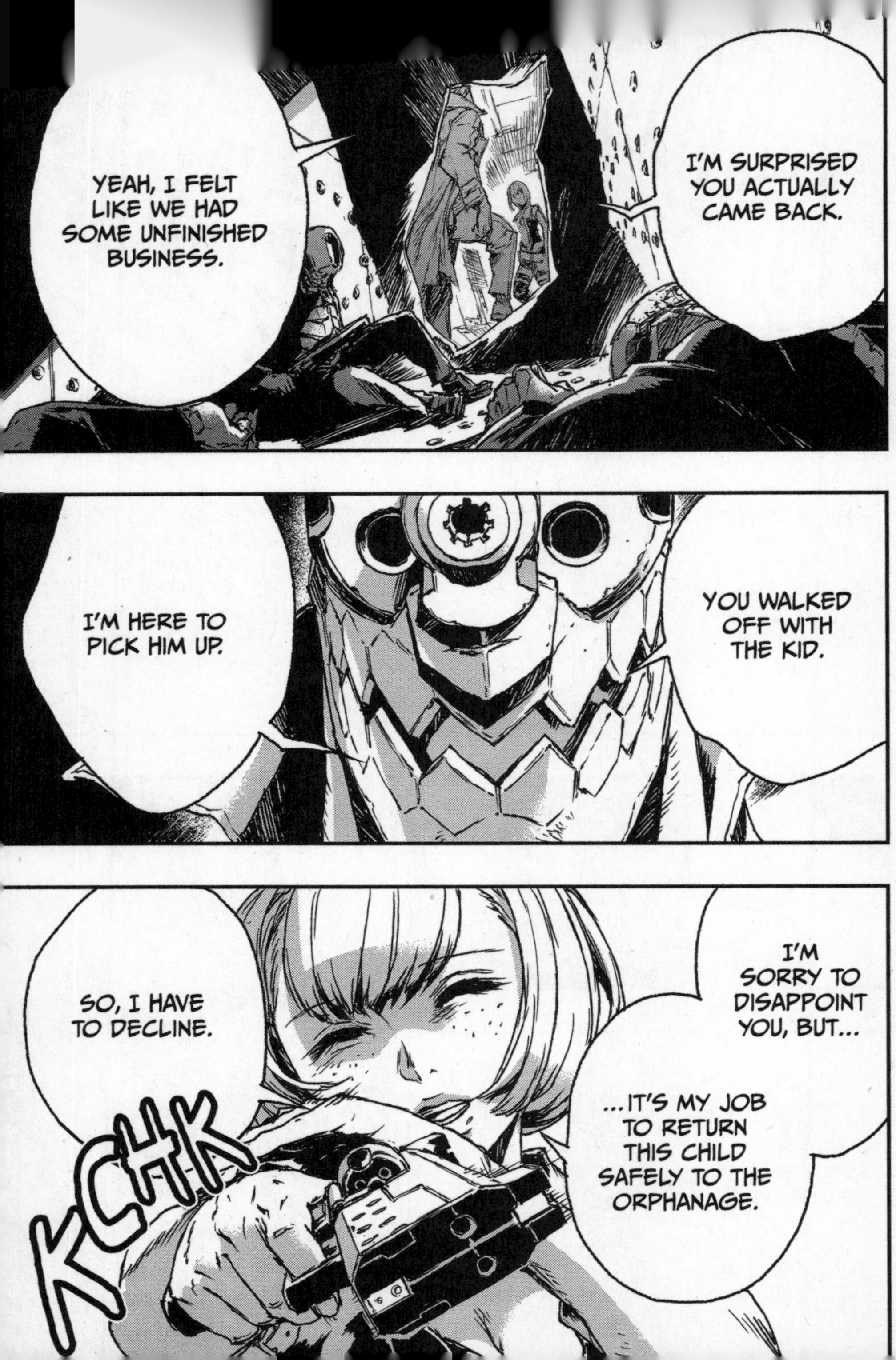
I'M SURPRISED YOU ACTUALLY CAME BACK.
YEAH, I FELT LIKE WE HAD SOME UNFINISHED BUSINESS.
YOU WALKED OFF WITH THE KID.
I'M HERE TO PICK HIM UP.
I'M SORRY TO DISAPPOINT YOU, BUT...
...IT'S MY JOB TO RETURN THIS CHILD SAFELY TO THE ORPHANAGE.
SO, I HAVE TO DECLINE.
KCHK

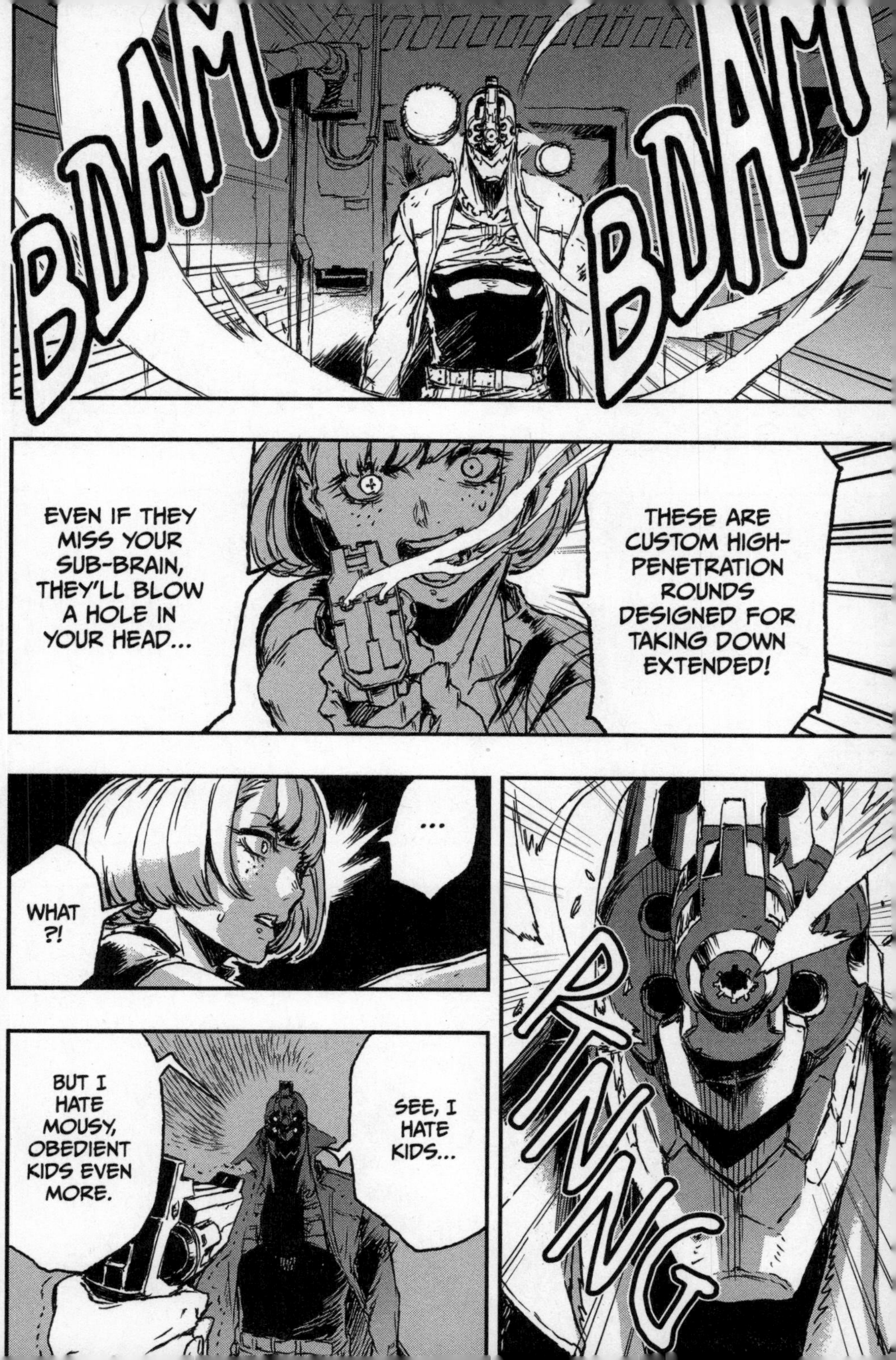
BDAM
BDAM
THESE ARE CUSTOM HIGH-PENETRATION ROUNDS DESIGNED FOR TAKING DOWN EXTENDED!
EVEN IF THEY MISS YOUR SUB-BRAIN, THEY'LL BLOW A HOLE IN YOUR HEAD...
PTNNG
...
WHAT?!
SEE, I HATE KIDS...
BUT I HATE MOUSY, OBEDIENT KIDS EVEN MORE.

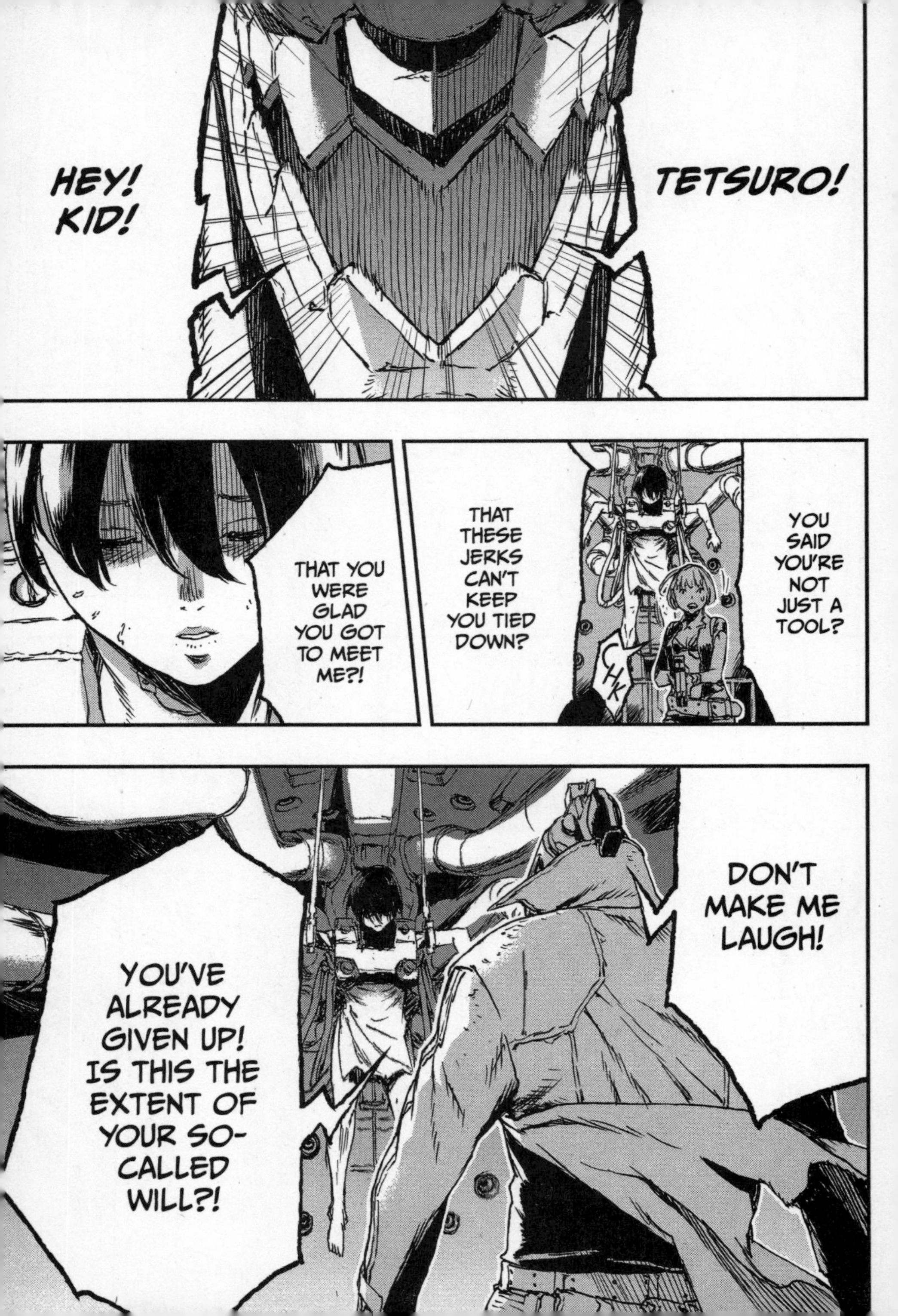
TETSURO!
HEY! KID!
YOU SAID YOU'RE NOT JUST A TOOL?
THAT THESE JERKS CAN'T KEEP YOU TIED DOWN?
CHK
THAT YOU WERE GLAD YOU GOT TO MEET ME?!
DON'T MAKE ME LAUGH!
YOU'VE ALREADY GIVEN UP! IS THIS THE EXTENT OF YOUR SO-CALLED WILL?!

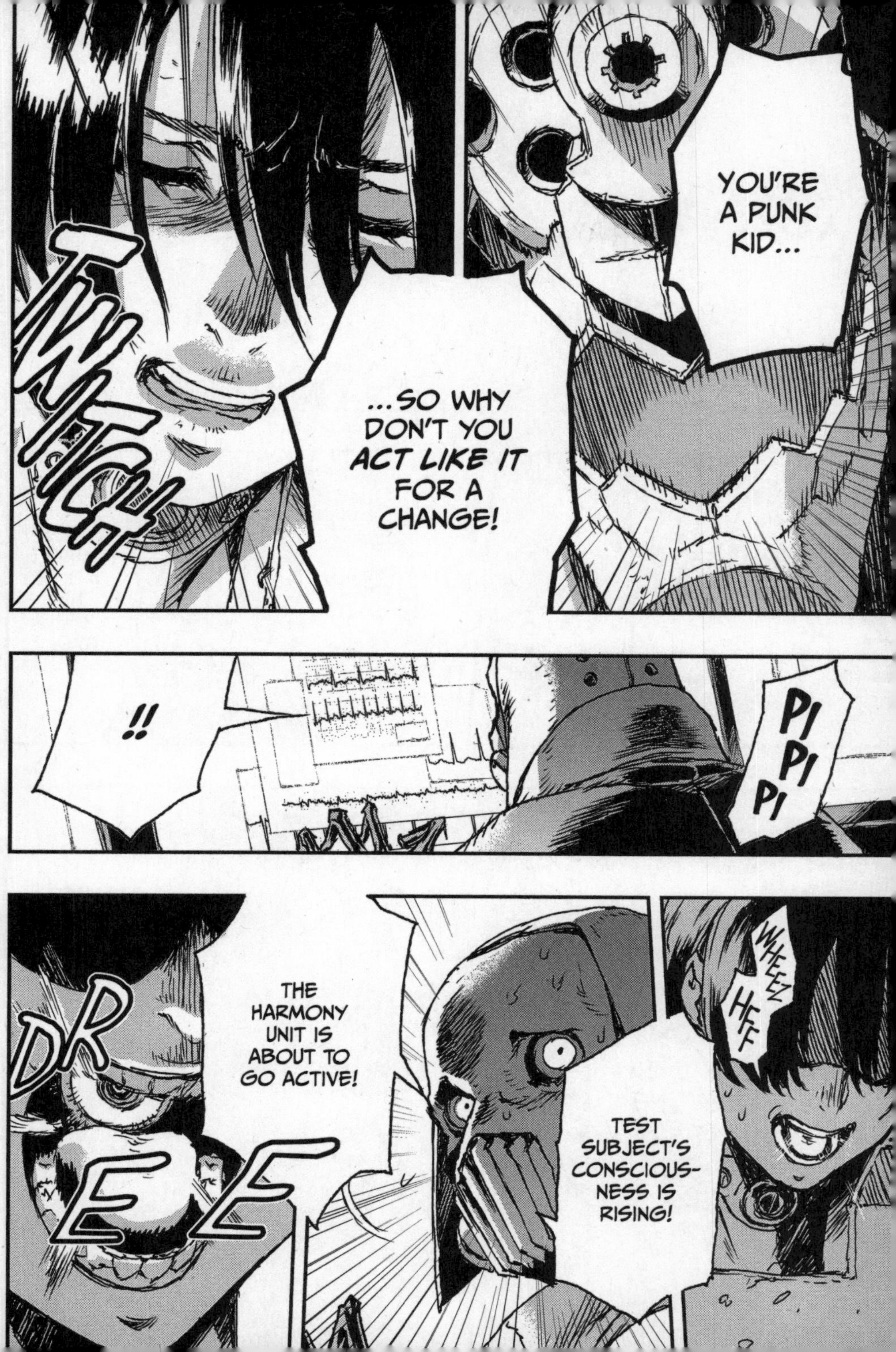
YOU'RE A PUNK KID...
...SO WHY DON'T YOU ACT LIKE IT FOR A CHANGE!
TWITCH
PI PI PI
!!
WHEEZ HEFF
TEST SUBJECT'S CONSCIOUS-NESS IS RISING!
THE HARMONY UNIT IS ABOUT TO GO ACTIVE!
DREE

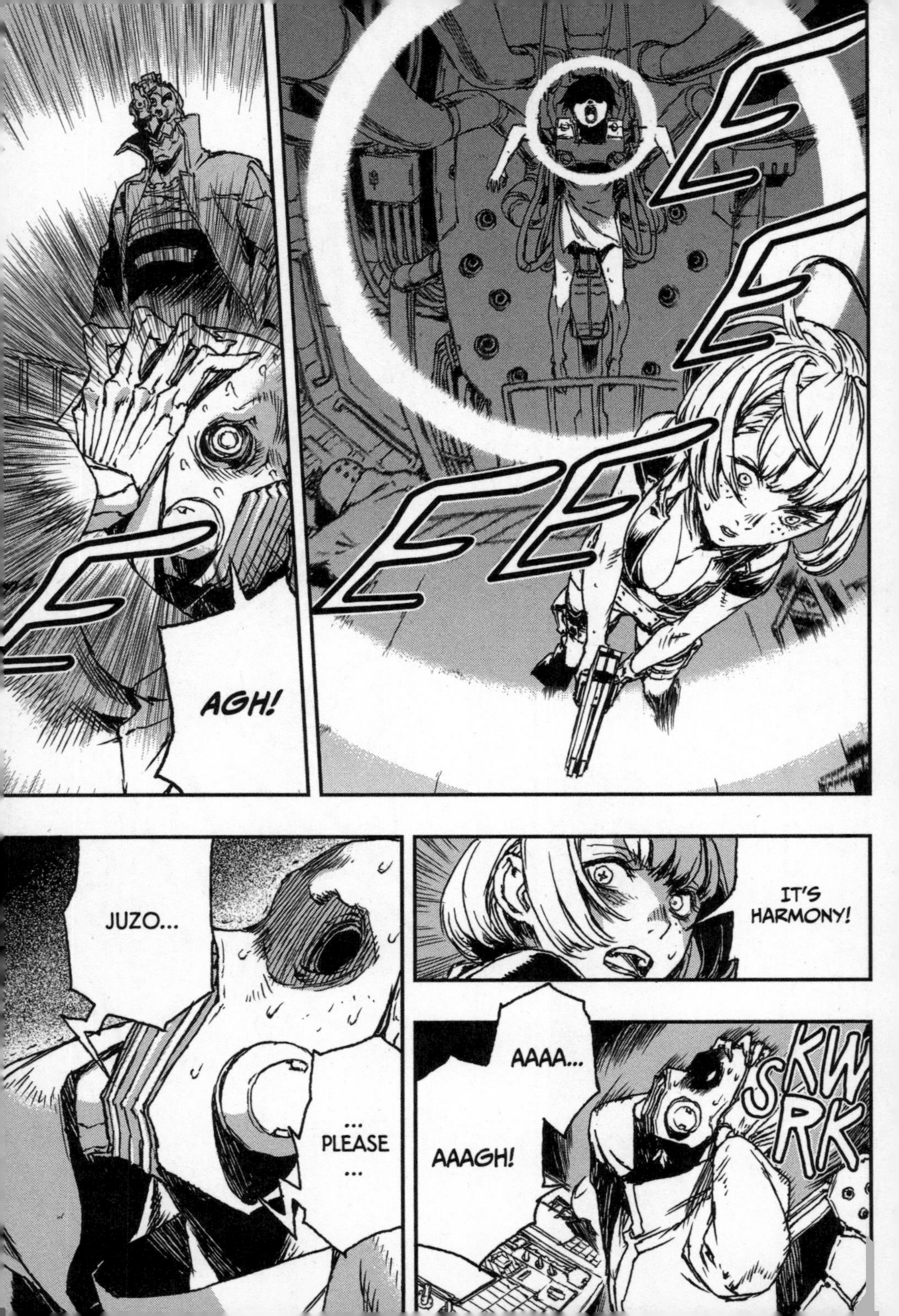
EEEEEEEE
AGH!
IT'S HARMONY!
AAAA...
AAAGH!
SKW SRK
JUZO...
... PLEASE ...

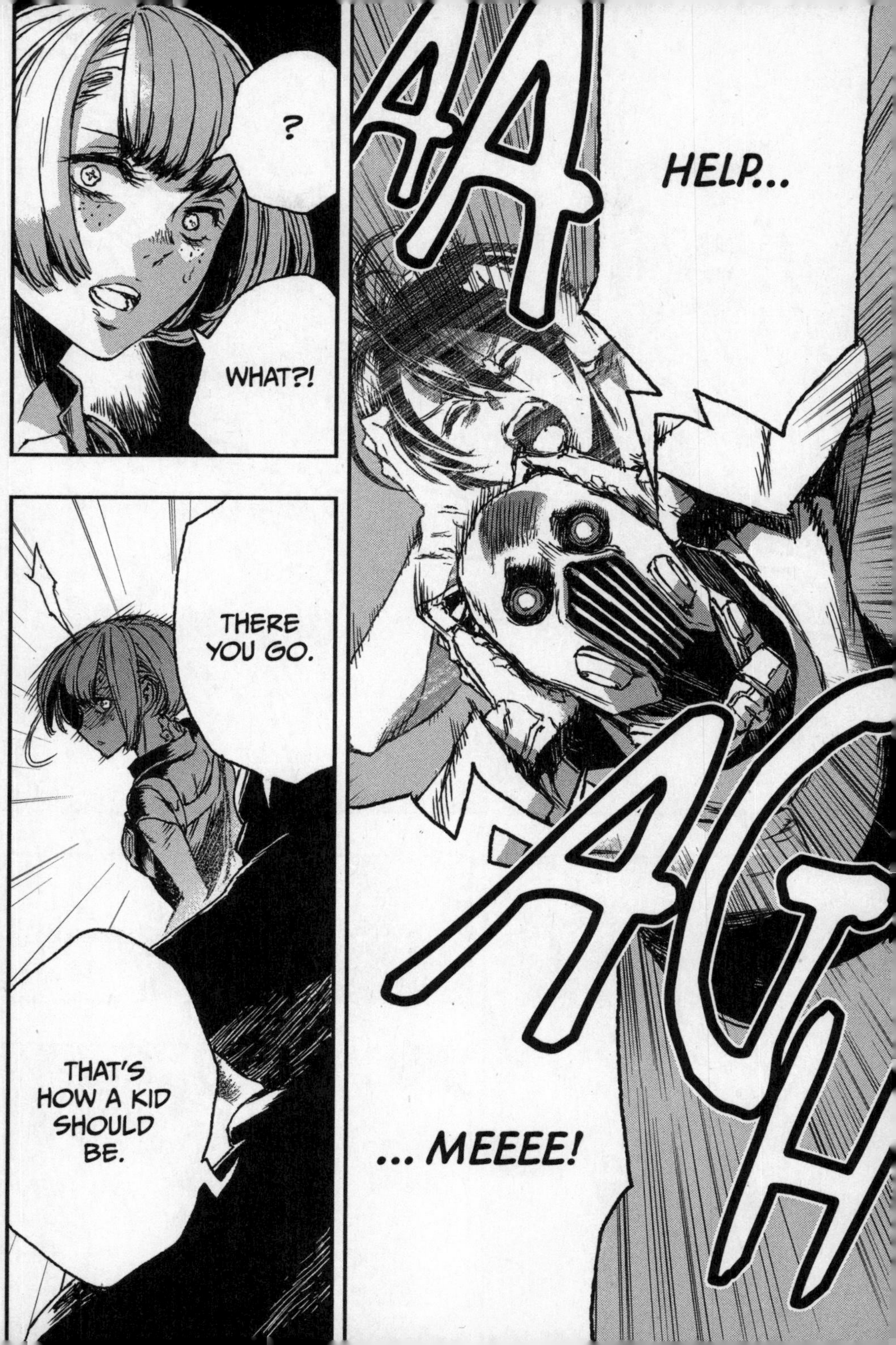
AA
HELP...
...MEEEE!
AAH
?
WHAT?!
THERE YOU GO.
THAT'S HOW A KID SHOULD BE.

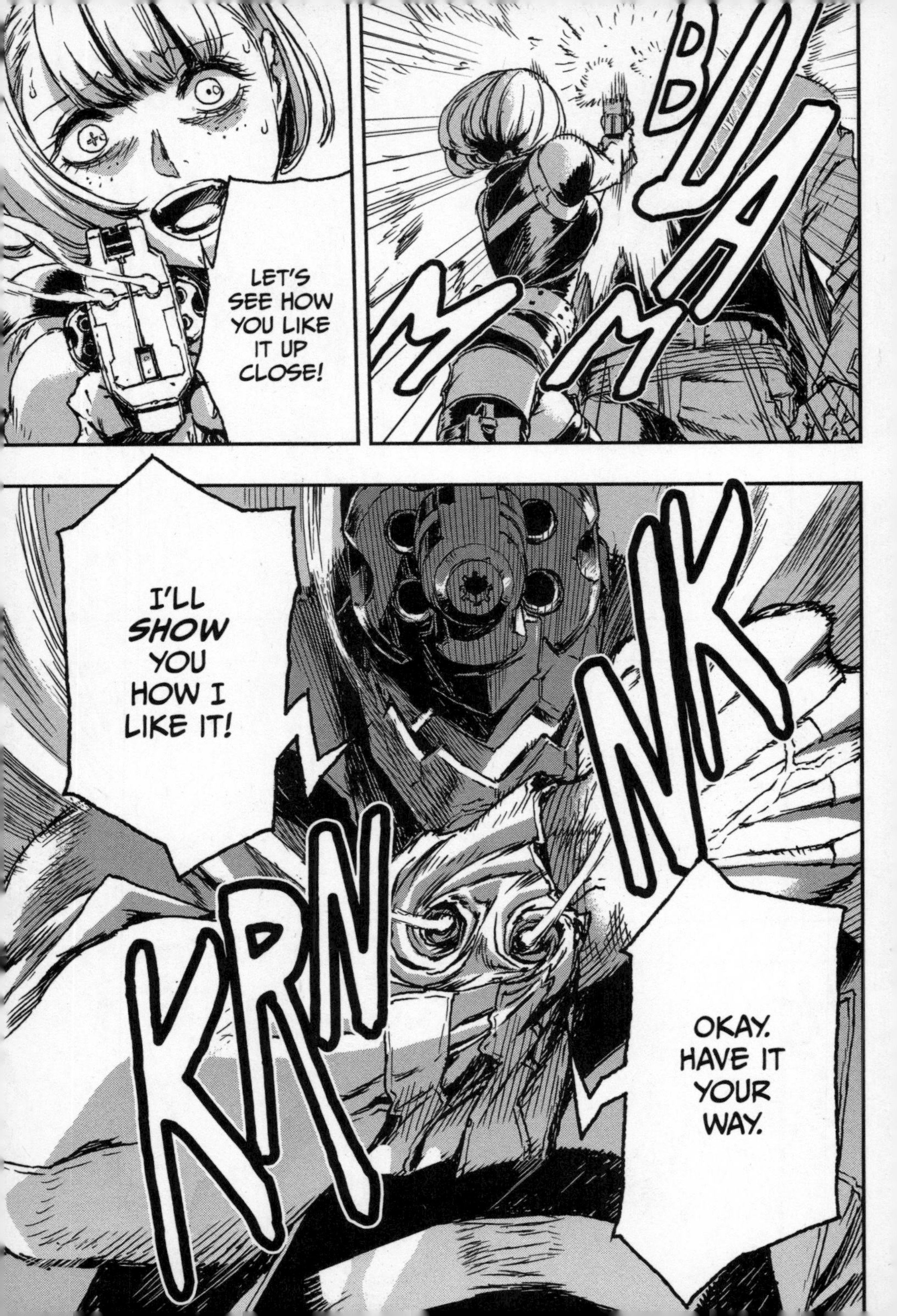
BLAMM
LET'S SEE HOW YOU LIKE IT UP CLOSE!
I'LL *SHOW* YOU HOW I LIKE IT!
KRNNK
OKAY. HAVE IT YOUR WAY.

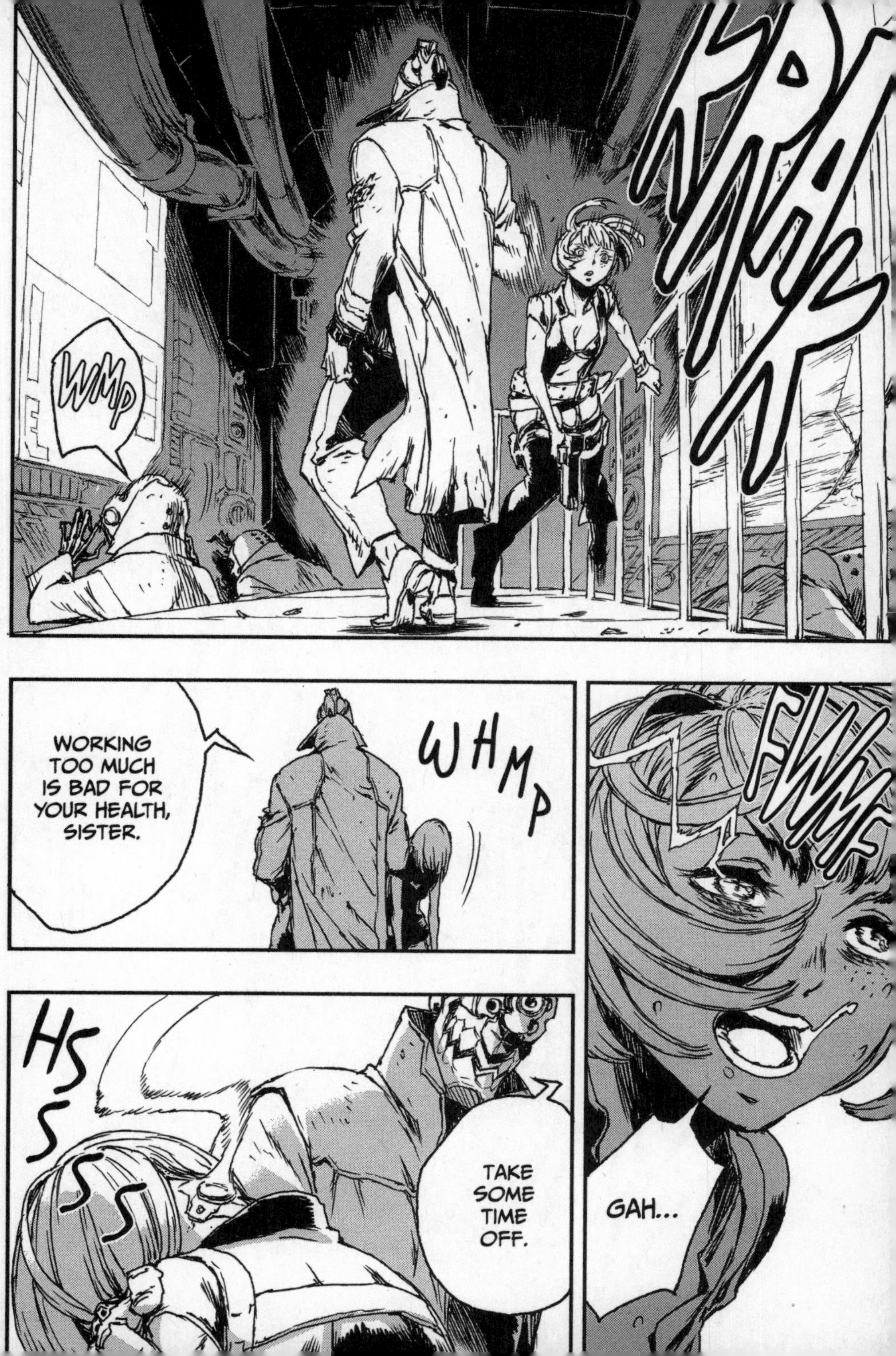
WMP
GAH...
WORKING TOO MUCH IS BAD FOR YOUR HEALTH, SISTER.
WHMP
TAKE SOME TIME OFF.

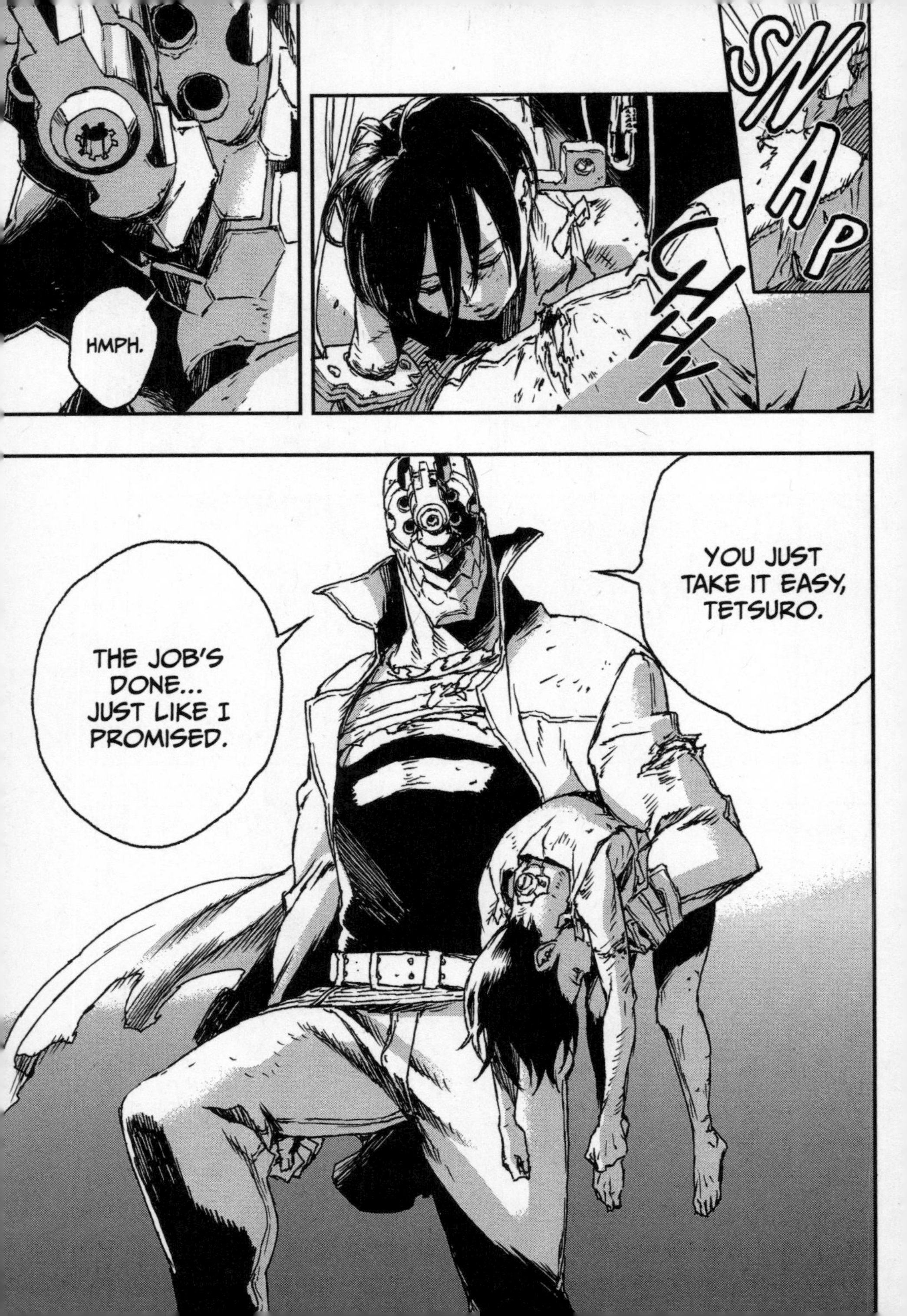
SNAP
CHHK
HMPH.
YOU JUST TAKE IT EASY, TETSURO.
THE JOB'S DONE... JUST LIKE I PROMISED.

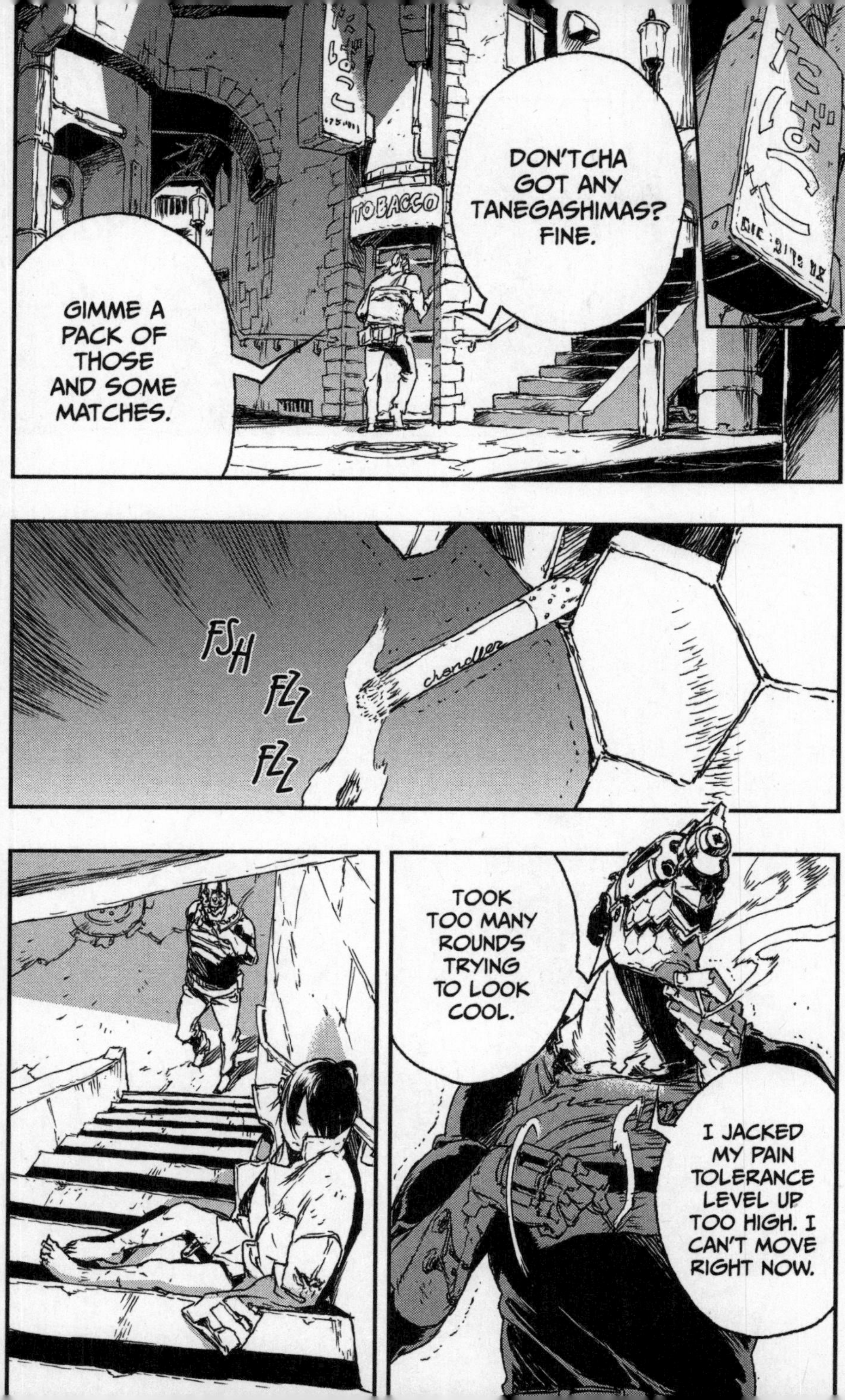
DON'TCHA GOT ANY TANEGASHIMAS? FINE.
TOBACCO
GIMME A PACK OF THOSE AND SOME MATCHES.
FSH
FZZ
FZZ
chandler
TOOK TOO MANY ROUNDS TRYING TO LOOK COOL.
I JACKED MY PAIN TOLERANCE LEVEL UP TOO HIGH. I CAN'T MOVE RIGHT NOW.

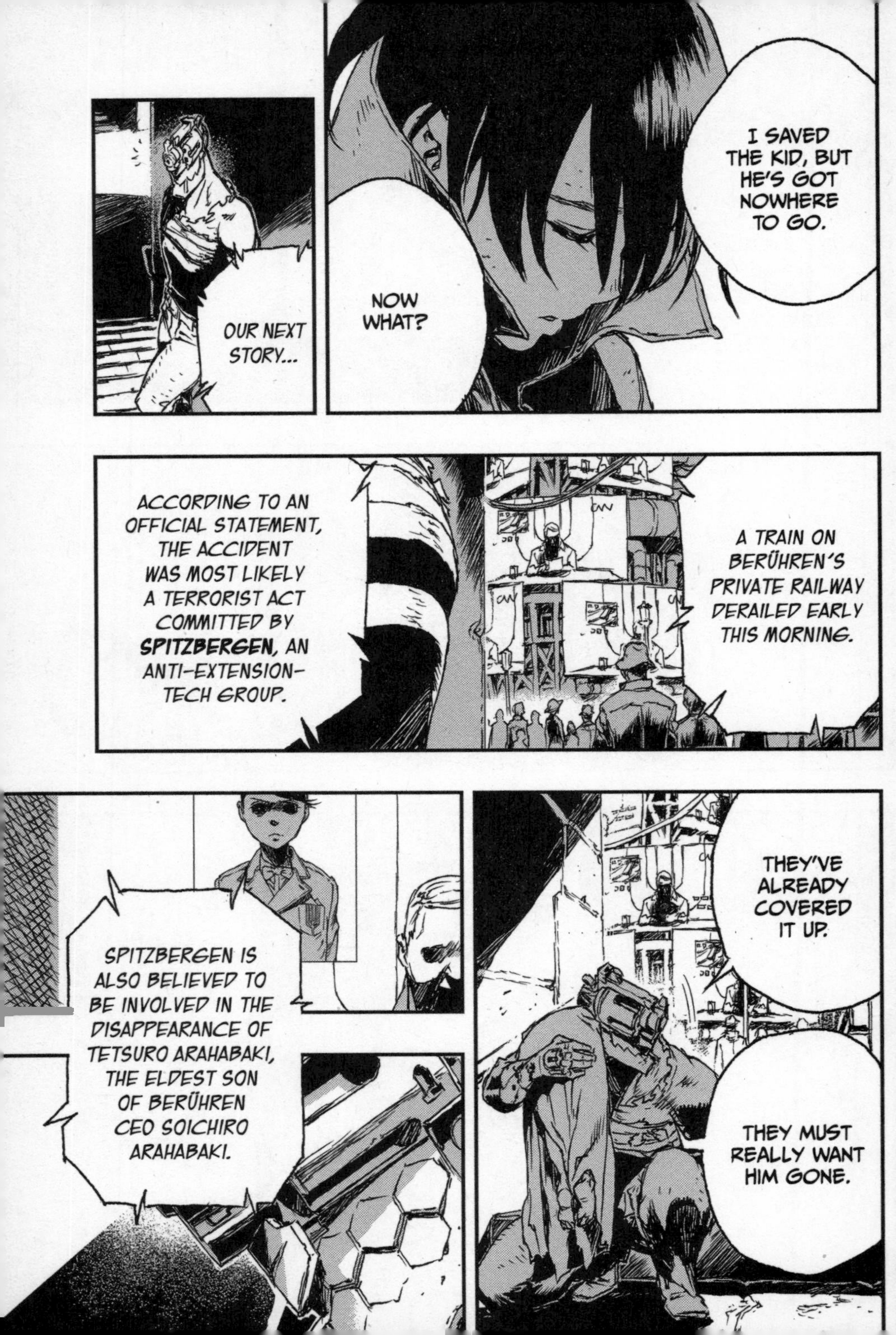
I SAVED THE KID, BUT HE'S GOT NOWHERE TO GO.
NOW WHAT?
OUR NEXT STORY...
A TRAIN ON BERÜHREN'S PRIVATE RAILWAY DERAILED EARLY THIS MORNING.
ACCORDING TO AN OFFICIAL STATEMENT, THE ACCIDENT WAS MOST LIKELY A TERRORIST ACT COMMITTED BY SPITZBERGEN, AN ANTI-EXTENSION-TECH GROUP.
THEY'VE ALREADY COVERED IT UP.
THEY MUST REALLY WANT HIM GONE.
SPITZBERGEN IS ALSO BELIEVED TO BE INVOLVED IN THE DISAPPEARANCE OF TETSURO ARAHABAKI, THE ELDEST SON OF BERÜHREN CEO SOICHIRO ARAHABAKI.

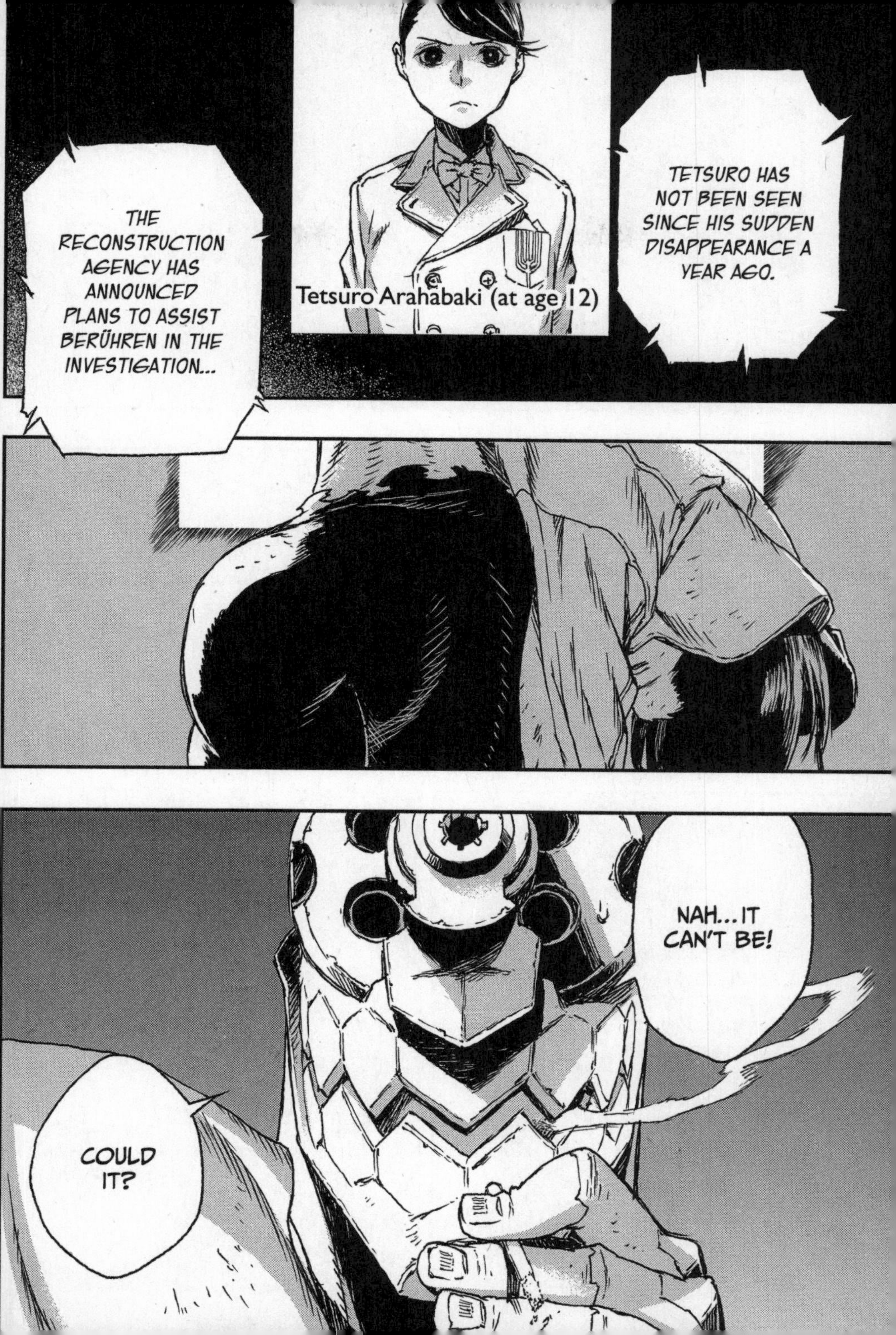
TETSURO HAS NOT BEEN SEEN SINCE HIS SUDDEN DISAPPEARANCE A YEAR AGO.
Tetsuro Arahabaki (at age 12)
THE RECONSTRUCTION AGENCY HAS ANNOUNCED PLANS TO ASSIST BERÜHREN IN THE INVESTIGATION...
NAH... IT CAN'T BE!
COULD IT?

NO GUNS LIFE

The gunsmoke drifts, the muzzle talks

NO
GUNS
LIFE

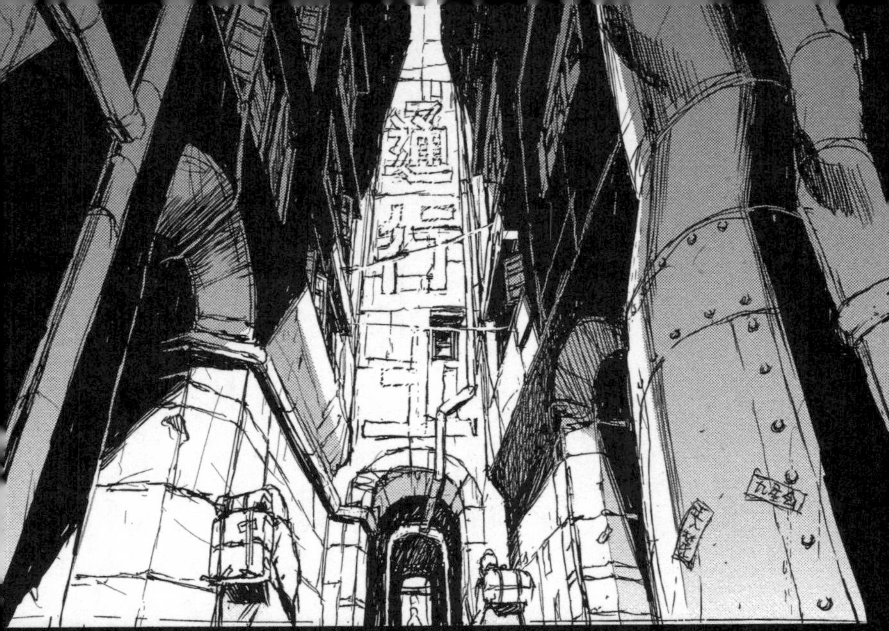

*Closed to Traffic *Kyusei

Chapter 3
Negotiation

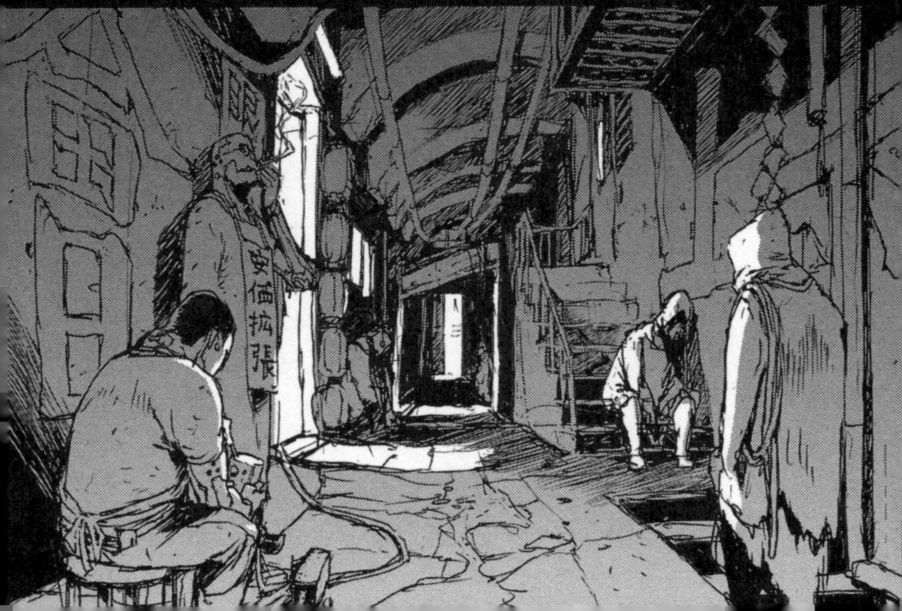
安価拡張

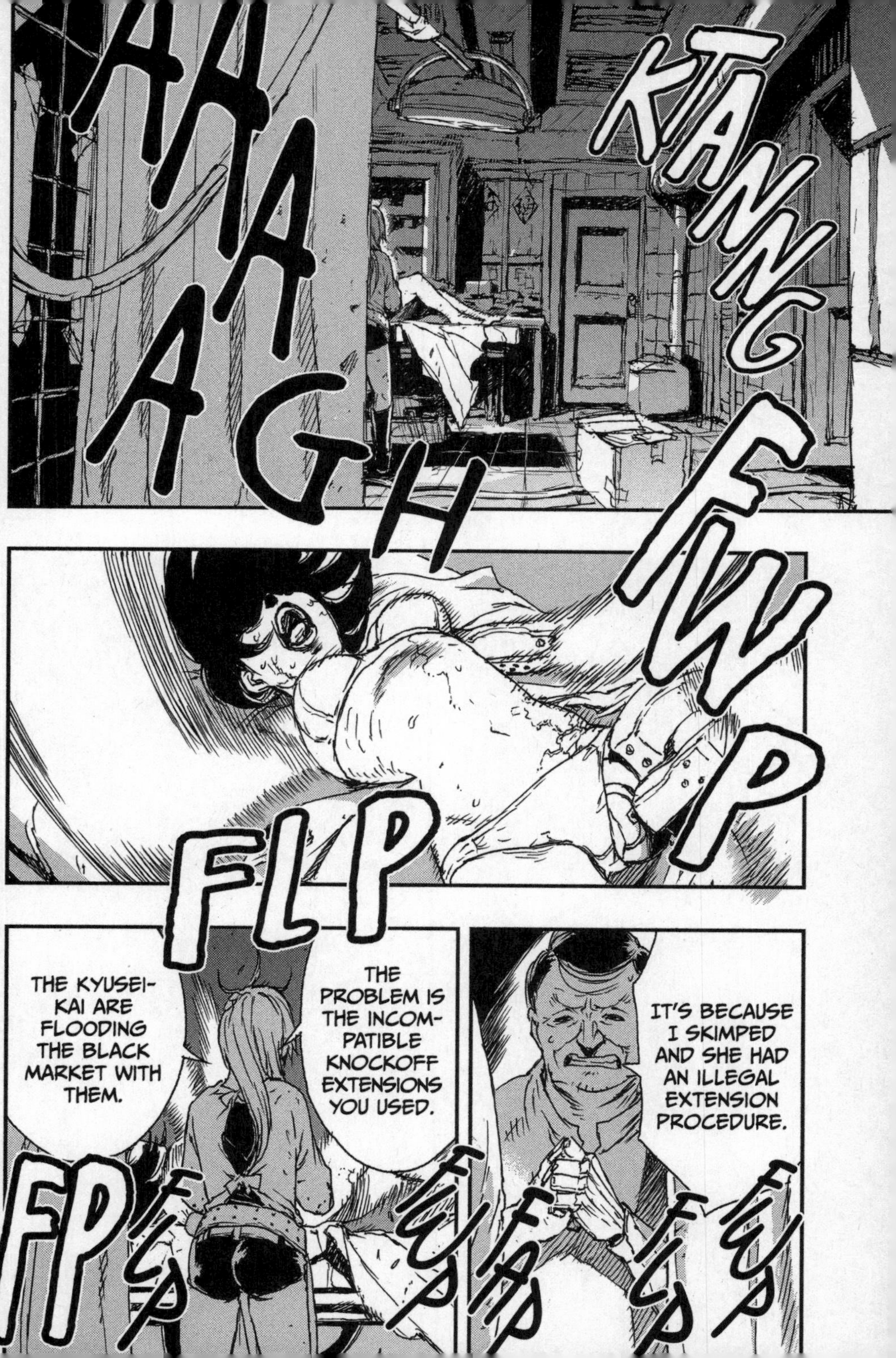
KTANNG
AHAAAGH
FWWP
FLP
IT'S BECAUSE I SKIMPED AND SHE HAD AN ILLEGAL EXTENSION PROCEDURE.
THE PROBLEM IS THE INCOM-PATIBLE KNOCKOFF EXTENSIONS YOU USED.
THE KYUSEI-KAI ARE FLOODING THE BLACK MARKET WITH THEM.
FP

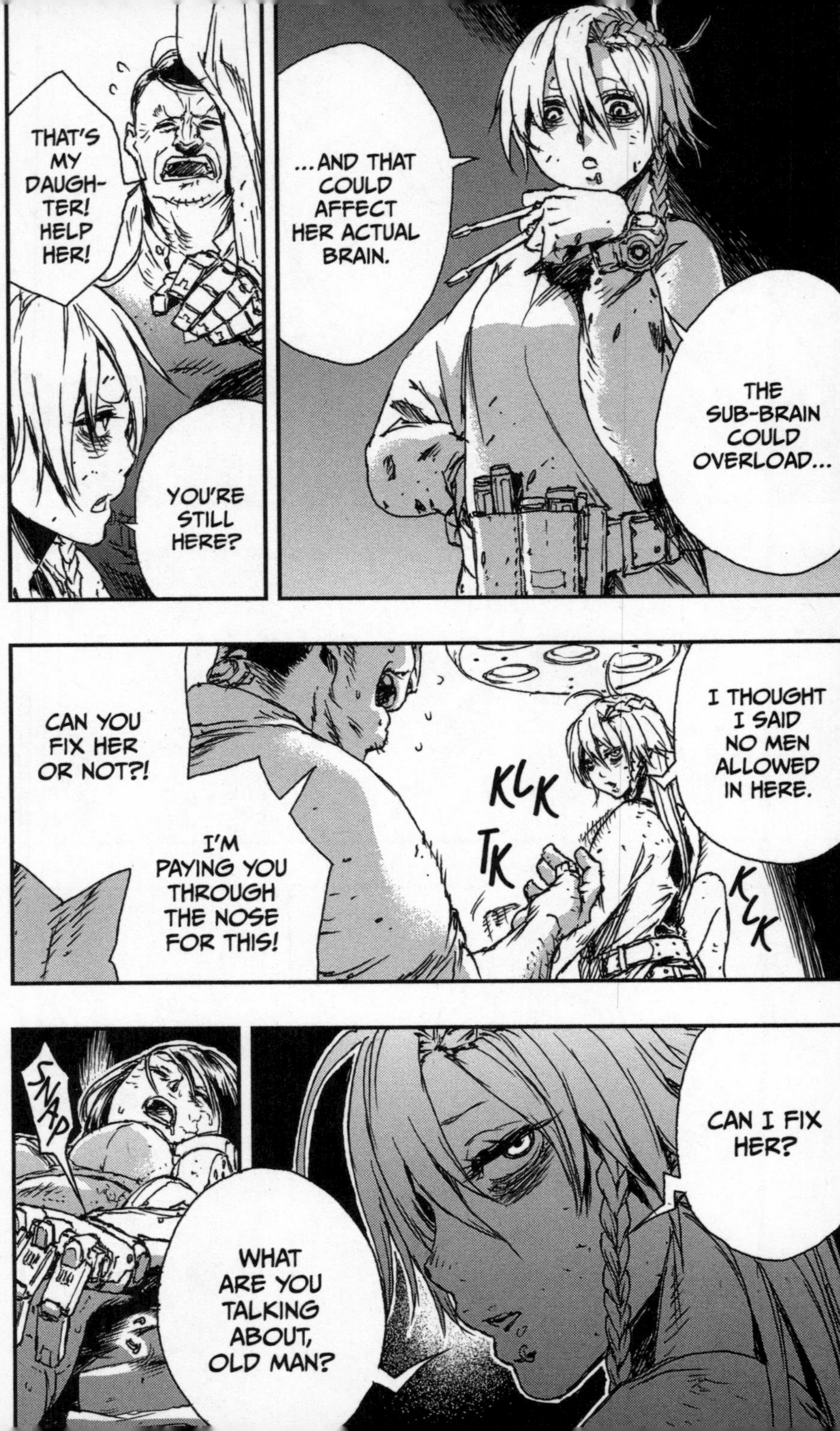
THE SUB-BRAIN COULD OVERLOAD...
...AND THAT COULD AFFECT HER ACTUAL BRAIN.
THAT'S MY DAUGH-TER! HELP HER!
YOU'RE STILL HERE?
I THOUGHT I SAID NO MEN ALLOWED IN HERE.
KLK
KLK
TK
CAN YOU FIX HER OR NOT?!
I'M PAYING YOU THROUGH THE NOSE FOR THIS!
CAN I FIX HER?
WHAT ARE YOU TALKING ABOUT, OLD MAN?
SNAP

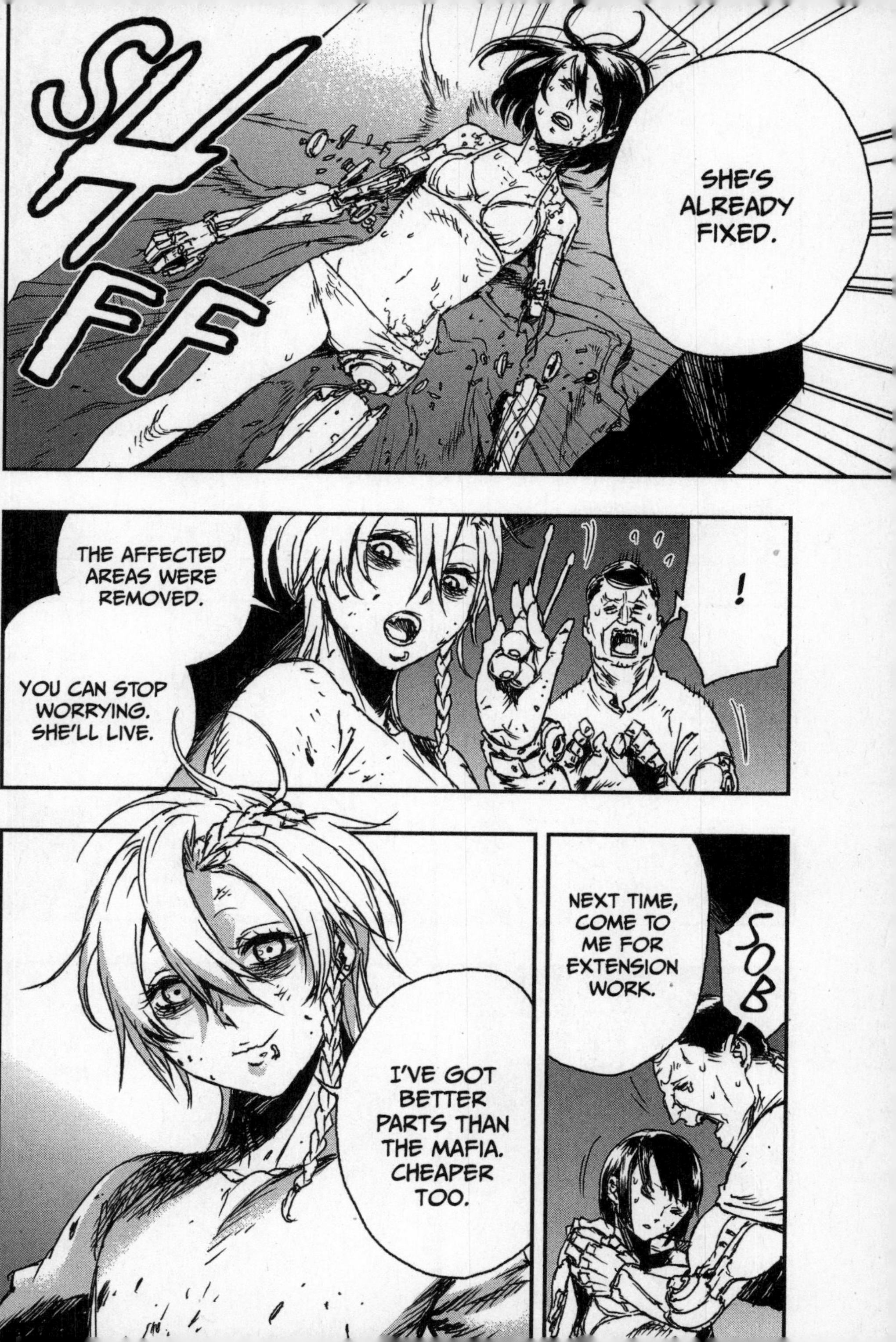
SHE'S ALREADY FIXED.
!
THE AFFECTED AREAS WERE REMOVED.
YOU CAN STOP WORRYING. SHE'LL LIVE.
NEXT TIME, COME TO ME FOR EXTENSION WORK.
SOB
I'VE GOT BETTER PARTS THAN THE MAFIA. CHEAPER TOO.

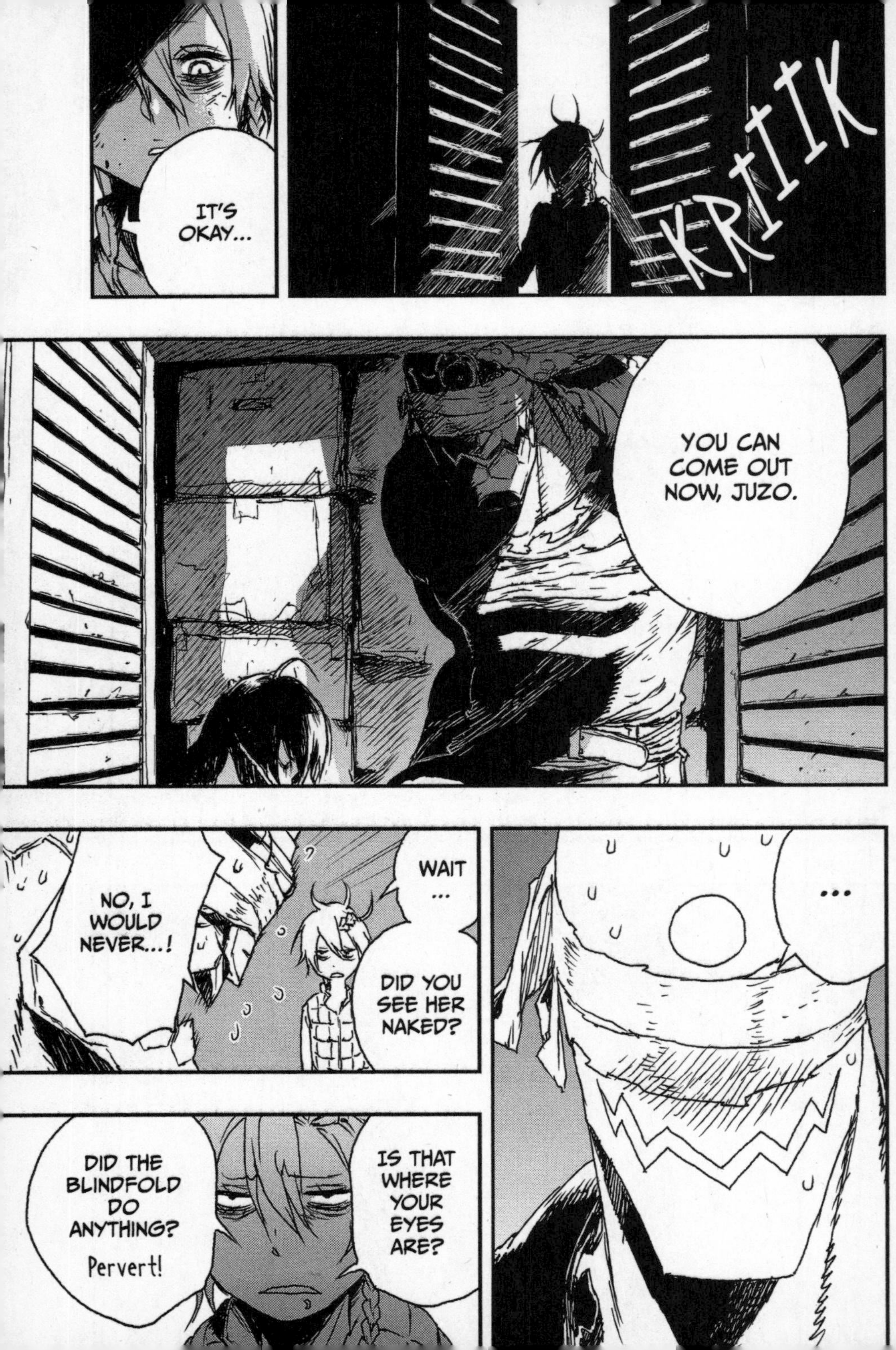
KRTIK
IT'S OKAY...
YOU CAN COME OUT NOW, JUZO.
...
WAIT ...
DID YOU SEE HER NAKED?
NO, I WOULD NEVER...!
IS THAT WHERE YOUR EYES ARE?
DID THE BLINDFOLD DO ANYTHING? Pervert!

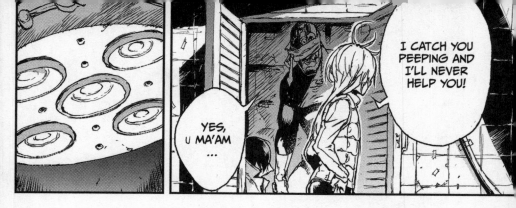

I CATCH YOU PEEPING AND I'LL NEVER HELP YOU!
YES, MA'AM ...
U
SO...
YOU WANT ME TO KEEP THIS KID HIDDEN FROM BERÜHREN...
YEAH.
YOUR ROOM FOR SPECIAL PATIENTS...
I NEED TO BORROW IT FOR A WHILE.
SO HE ACTUALLY HAS A *REASON* TO HIDE FROM THEM.

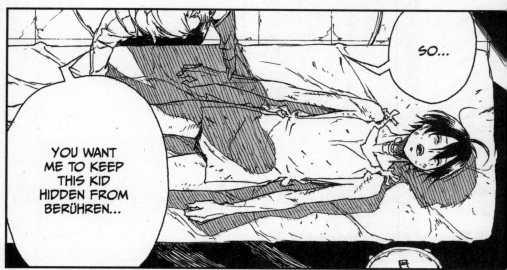

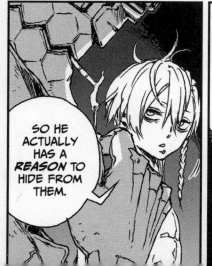

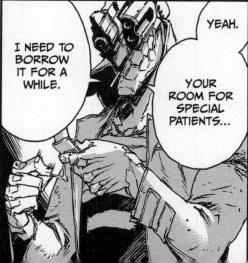

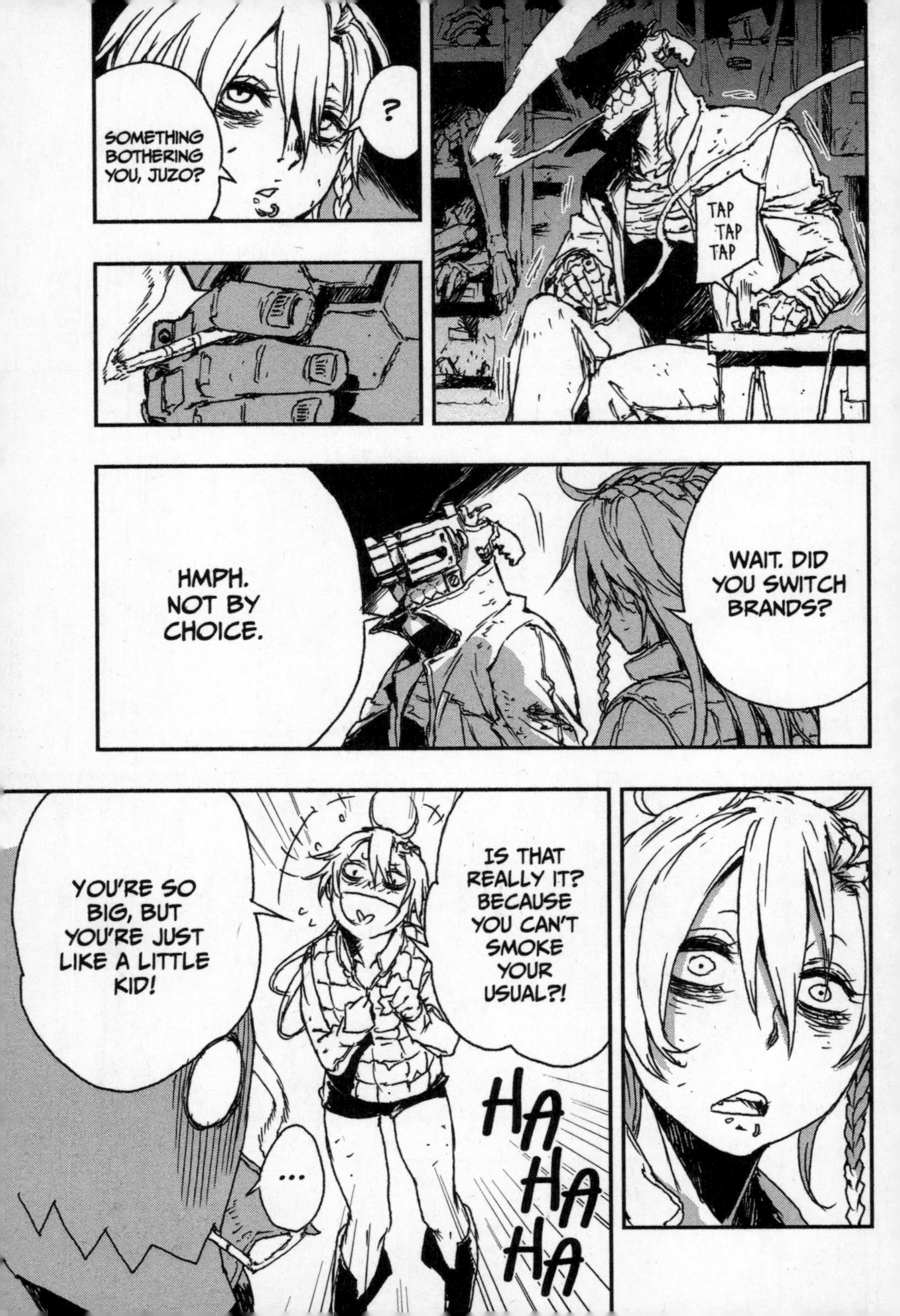
TAP
TAP
TAP
?
SOMETHING BOTHERING YOU, JUZO?
WAIT. DID YOU SWITCH BRANDS?
HMPH. NOT BY CHOICE.
IS THAT REALLY IT? BECAUSE YOU CAN'T SMOKE YOUR USUAL?!
HA HA HA HA
YOU'RE SO BIG, BUT YOU'RE JUST LIKE A LITTLE KID!
...

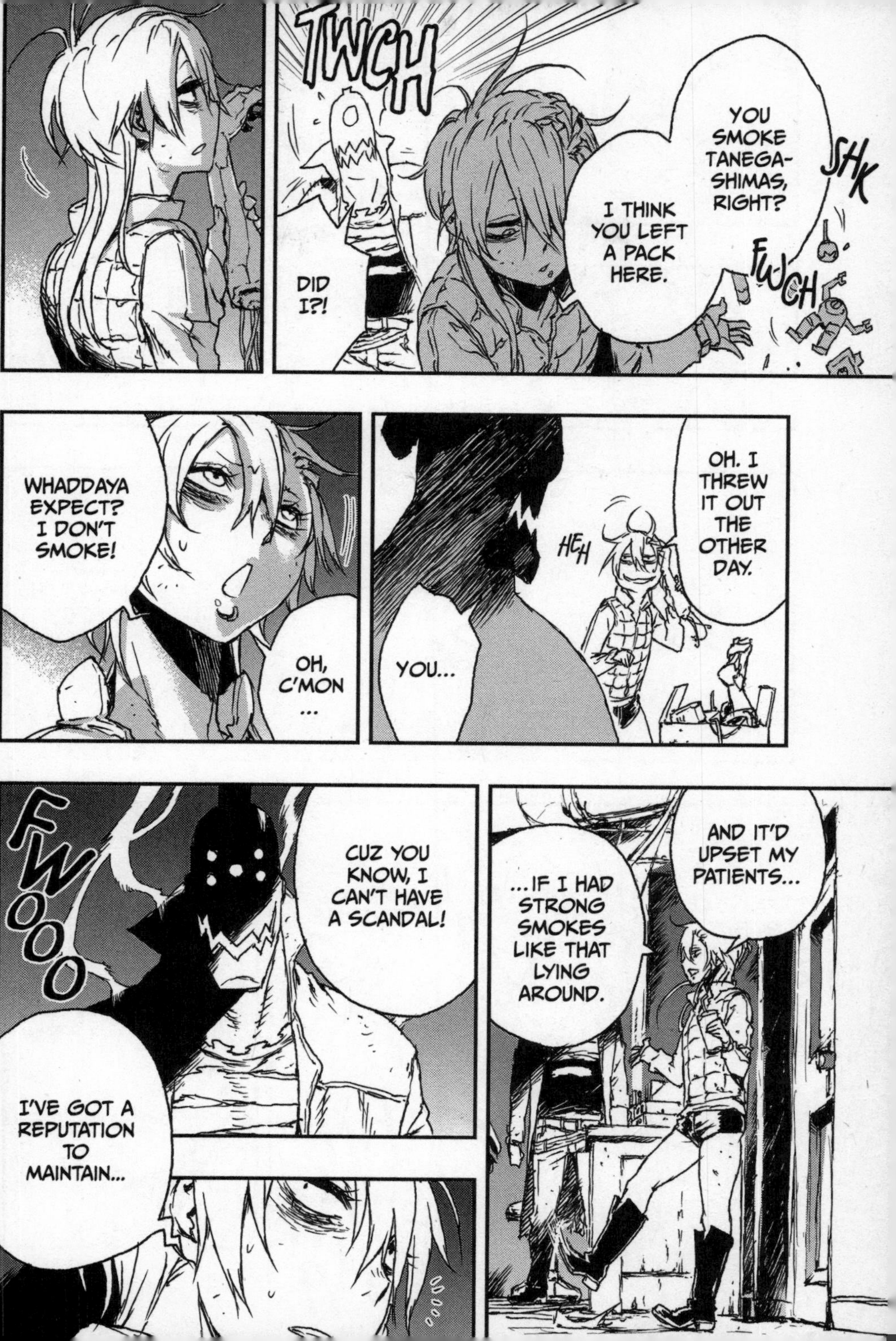
YOU SMOKE TANEGA-SHIMAS, RIGHT?
SHK
TWCH
I THINK YOU LEFT A PACK HERE.
FWCH
DID I?!
OH. I THREW IT OUT THE OTHER DAY.
HEH
YOU...
OH, C'MON...
WHADDAYA EXPECT? I DON'T SMOKE!
AND IT'D UPSET MY PATIENTS...
...IF I HAD STRONG SMOKES LIKE THAT LYING AROUND.
CUZ YOU KNOW, I CAN'T HAVE A SCANDAL!
FWOOO
I'VE GOT A REPUTATION TO MAINTAIN...

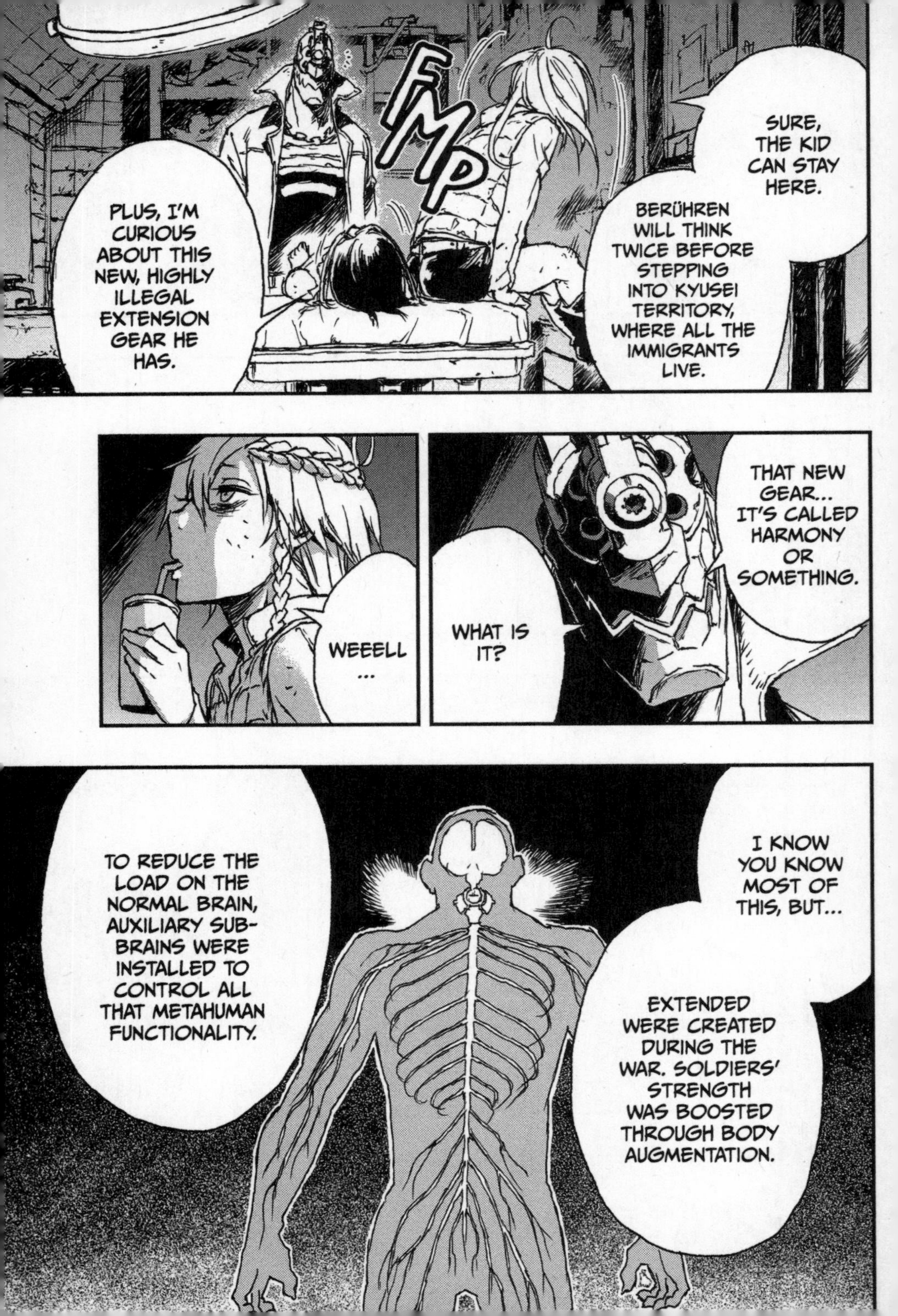
SURE, THE KID CAN STAY HERE.
BERÜHREN WILL THINK TWICE BEFORE STEPPING INTO KYUSEI TERRITORY, WHERE ALL THE IMMIGRANTS LIVE.
FMP
PLUS, I'M CURIOUS ABOUT THIS NEW, HIGHLY ILLEGAL EXTENSION GEAR HE HAS.
THAT NEW GEAR... IT'S CALLED HARMONY OR SOMETHING.
WHAT IS IT?
WEEELL ...
I KNOW YOU KNOW MOST OF THIS, BUT...
EXTENDED WERE CREATED DURING THE WAR. SOLDIERS' STRENGTH WAS BOOSTED THROUGH BODY AUGMENTATION.
TO REDUCE THE LOAD ON THE NORMAL BRAIN, AUXILIARY SUB-BRAINS WERE INSTALLED TO CONTROL ALL THAT METAHUMAN FUNCTIONALITY.

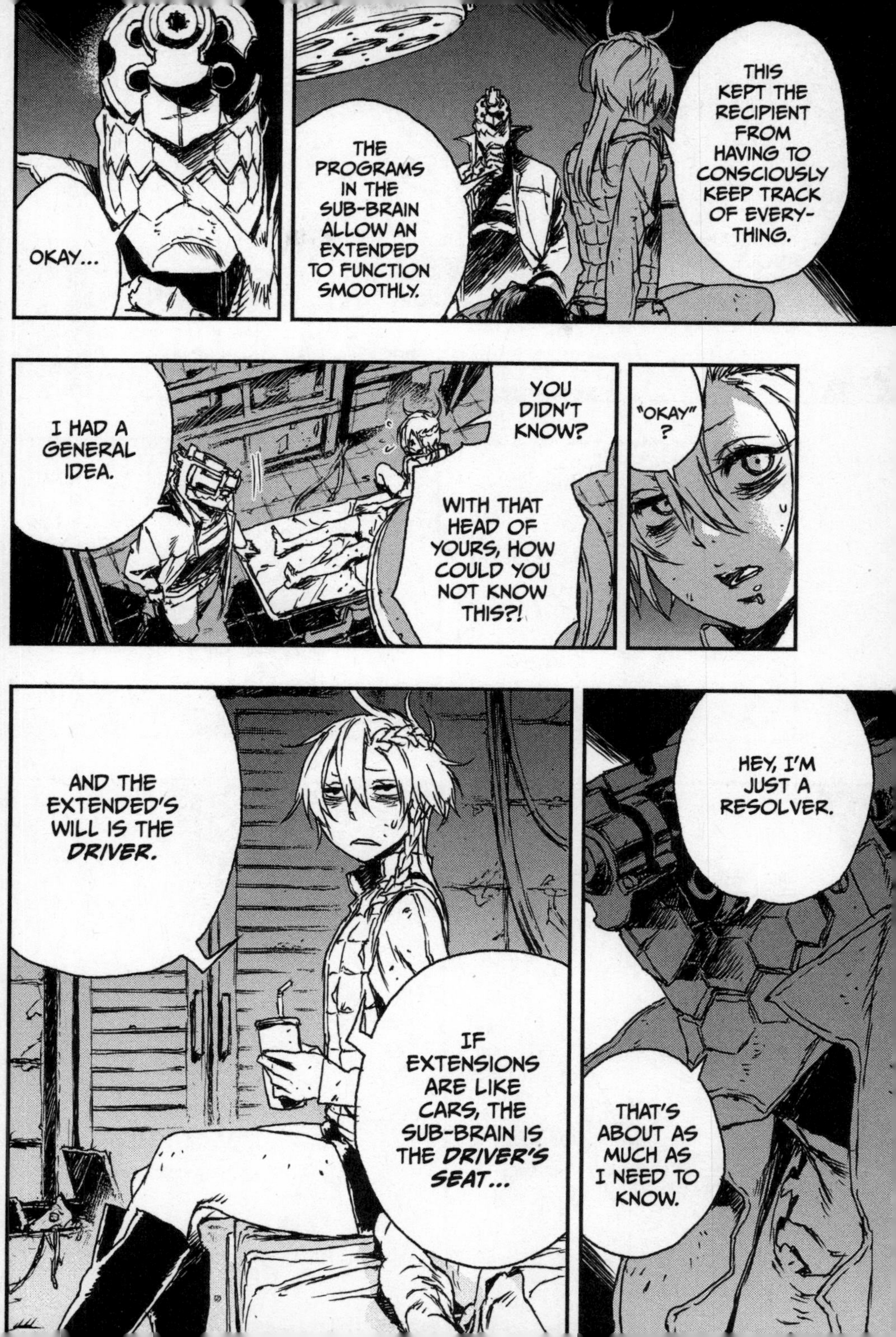
THE PROGRAMS IN THE SUB-BRAIN ALLOW AN EXTENDED TO FUNCTION SMOOTHLY.
THIS KEPT THE RECIPIENT FROM HAVING TO CONSCIOUSLY KEEP TRACK OF EVERY-THING.
OKAY...
"OKAY" ?
YOU DIDN'T KNOW?
WITH THAT HEAD OF YOURS, HOW COULD YOU NOT KNOW THIS?!
I HAD A GENERAL IDEA.
HEY, I'M JUST A RESOLVER.
THAT'S ABOUT AS MUCH AS I NEED TO KNOW.
IF EXTENSIONS ARE LIKE CARS, THE SUB-BRAIN IS THE *DRIVER'S SEAT*...
AND THE EXTENDED'S WILL IS THE *DRIVER*.

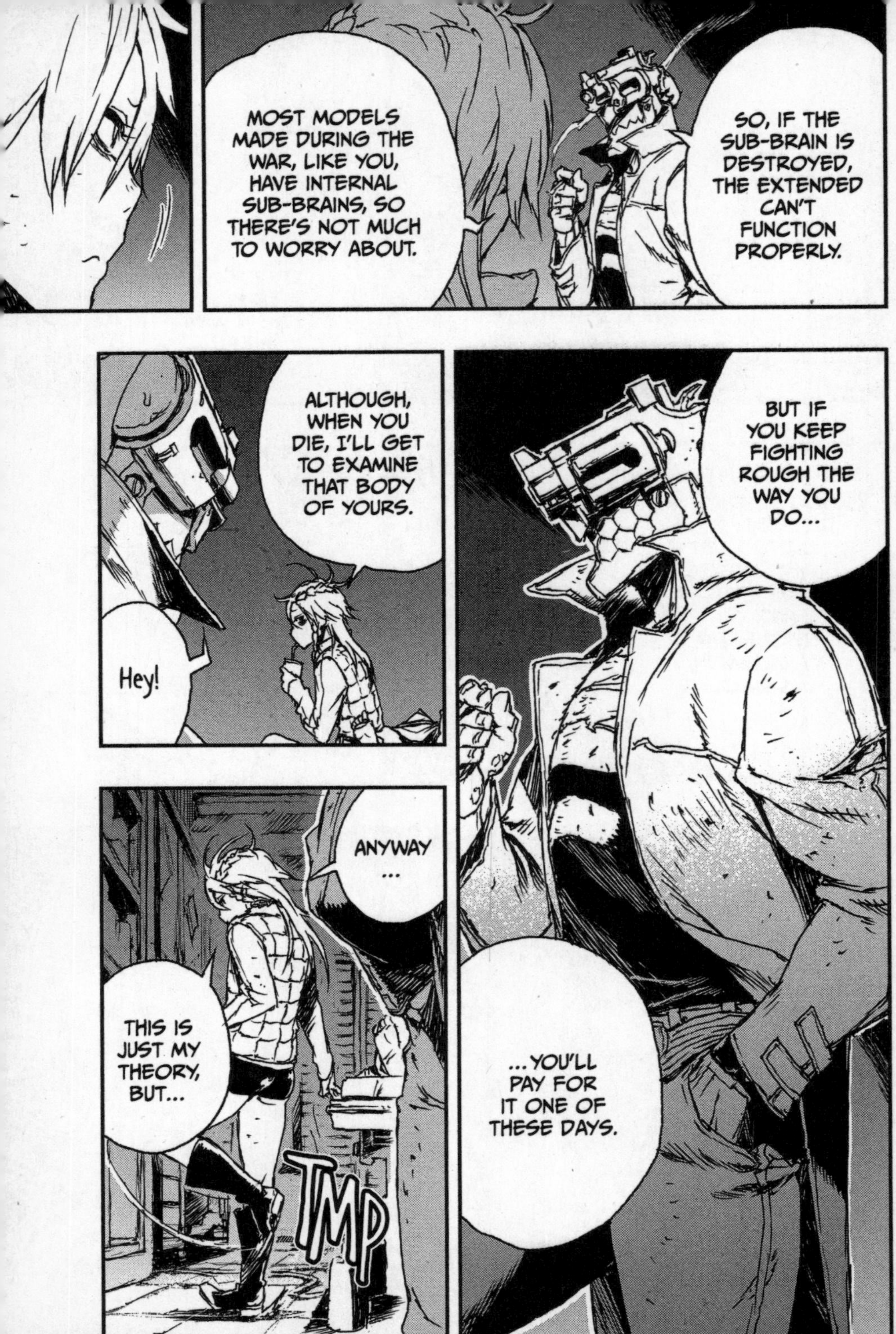
SO, IF THE SUB-BRAIN IS DESTROYED, THE EXTENDED CAN'T FUNCTION PROPERLY.
MOST MODELS MADE DURING THE WAR, LIKE YOU, HAVE INTERNAL SUB-BRAINS, SO THERE'S NOT MUCH TO WORRY ABOUT.
BUT IF YOU KEEP FIGHTING ROUGH THE WAY YOU DO...
...YOU'LL PAY FOR IT ONE OF THESE DAYS.
ALTHOUGH, WHEN YOU DIE, I'LL GET TO EXAMINE THAT BODY OF YOURS.
Hey!
ANYWAY ...
THIS IS JUST MY THEORY, BUT...
TMP

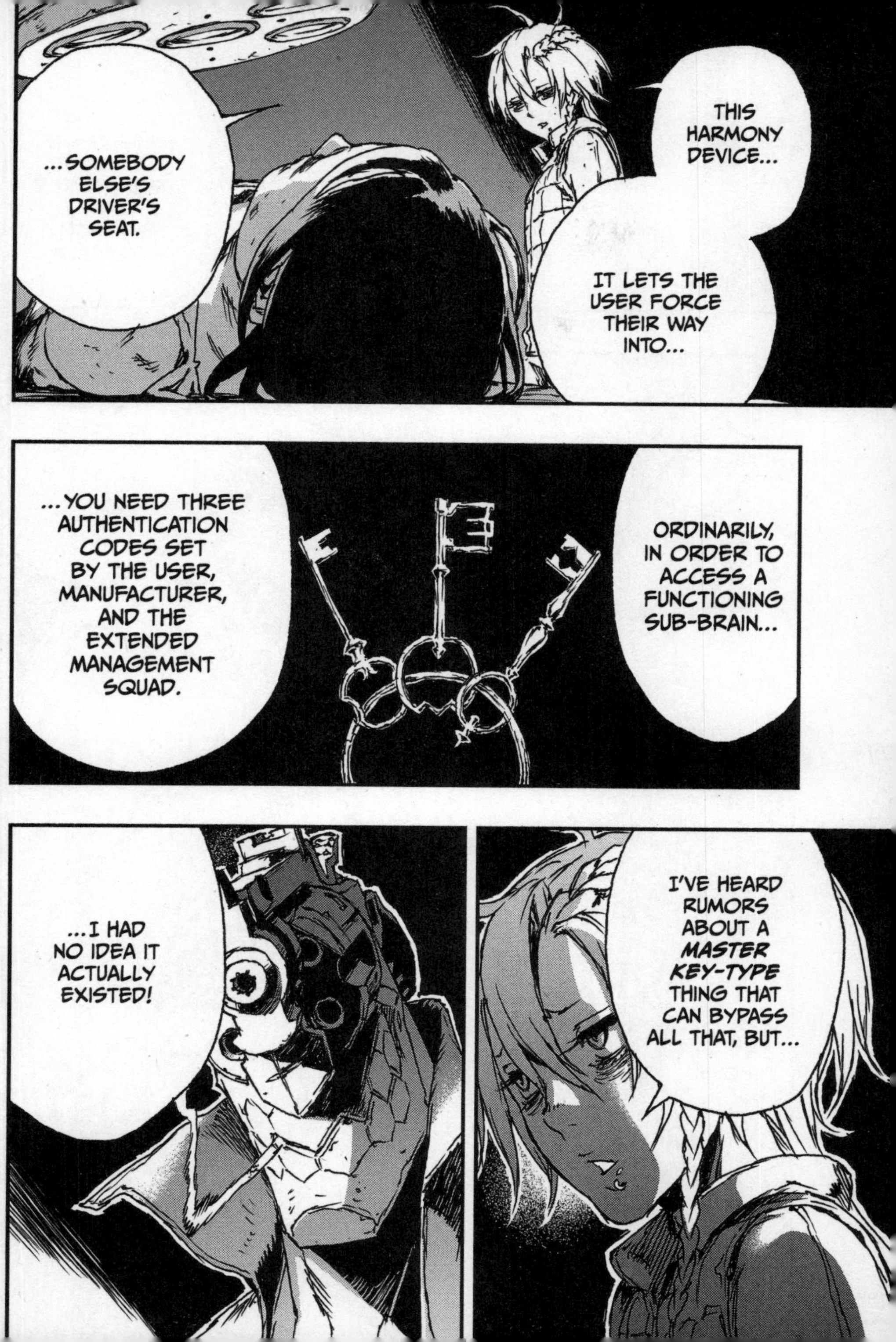
THIS HARMONY DEVICE...
IT LETS THE USER FORCE THEIR WAY INTO...
...SOMEBODY ELSE'S DRIVER'S SEAT.
ORDINARILY, IN ORDER TO ACCESS A FUNCTIONING SUB-BRAIN...
...YOU NEED THREE AUTHENTICATION CODES SET BY THE USER, MANUFACTURER, AND THE EXTENDED MANAGEMENT SQUAD.
I'VE HEARD RUMORS ABOUT A *MASTER KEY-TYPE* THING THAT CAN BYPASS ALL THAT, BUT...
...I HAD NO IDEA IT ACTUALLY EXISTED!

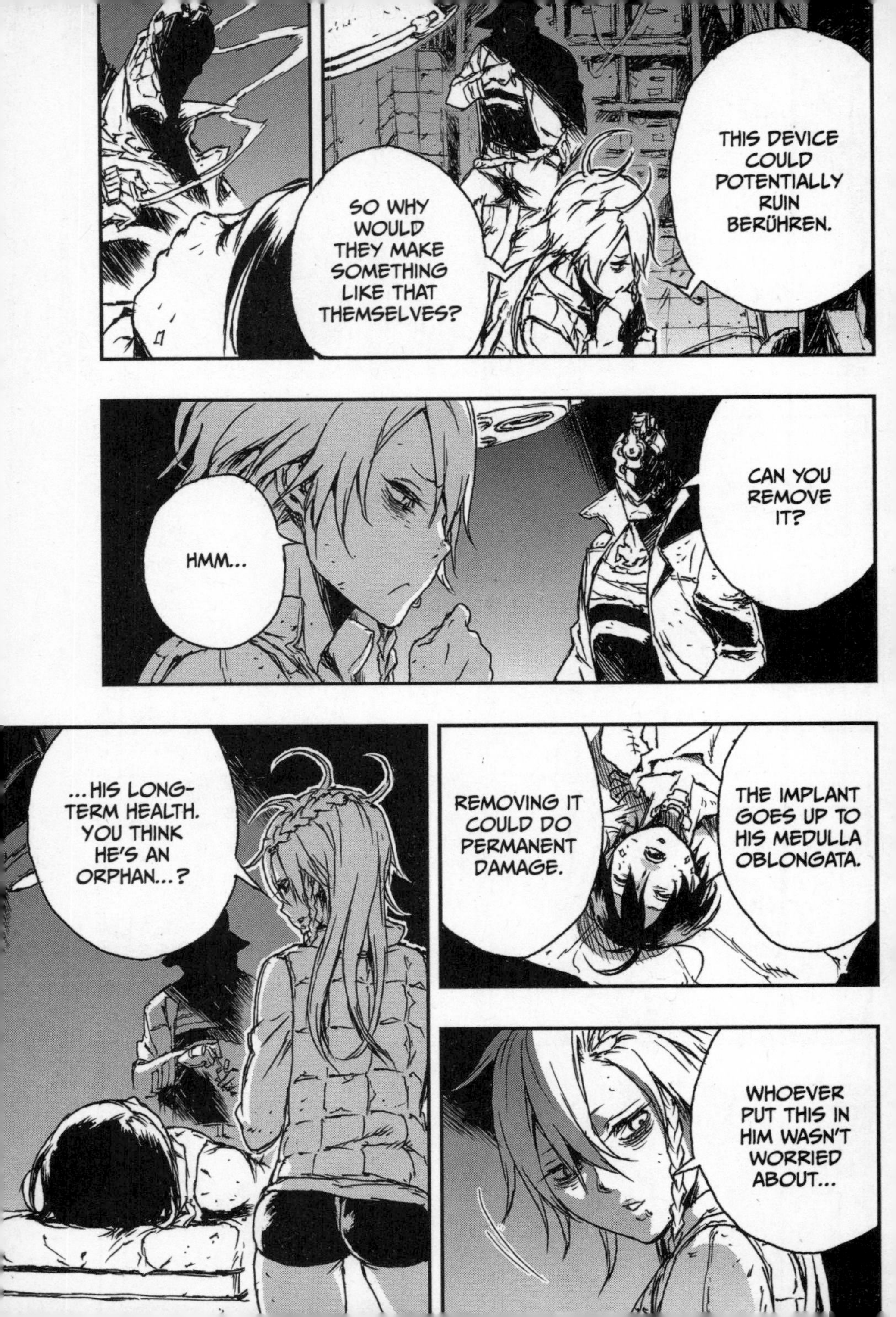
THIS DEVICE COULD POTENTIALLY RUIN BERÜHREN.
SO WHY WOULD THEY MAKE SOMETHING LIKE THAT THEMSELVES?
CAN YOU REMOVE IT?
HMM...
THE IMPLANT GOES UP TO HIS MEDULLA OBLONGATA.
REMOVING IT COULD DO PERMANENT DAMAGE.
WHOEVER PUT THIS IN HIM WASN'T WORRIED ABOUT...
...HIS LONG-TERM HEALTH. YOU THINK HE'S AN ORPHAN...?

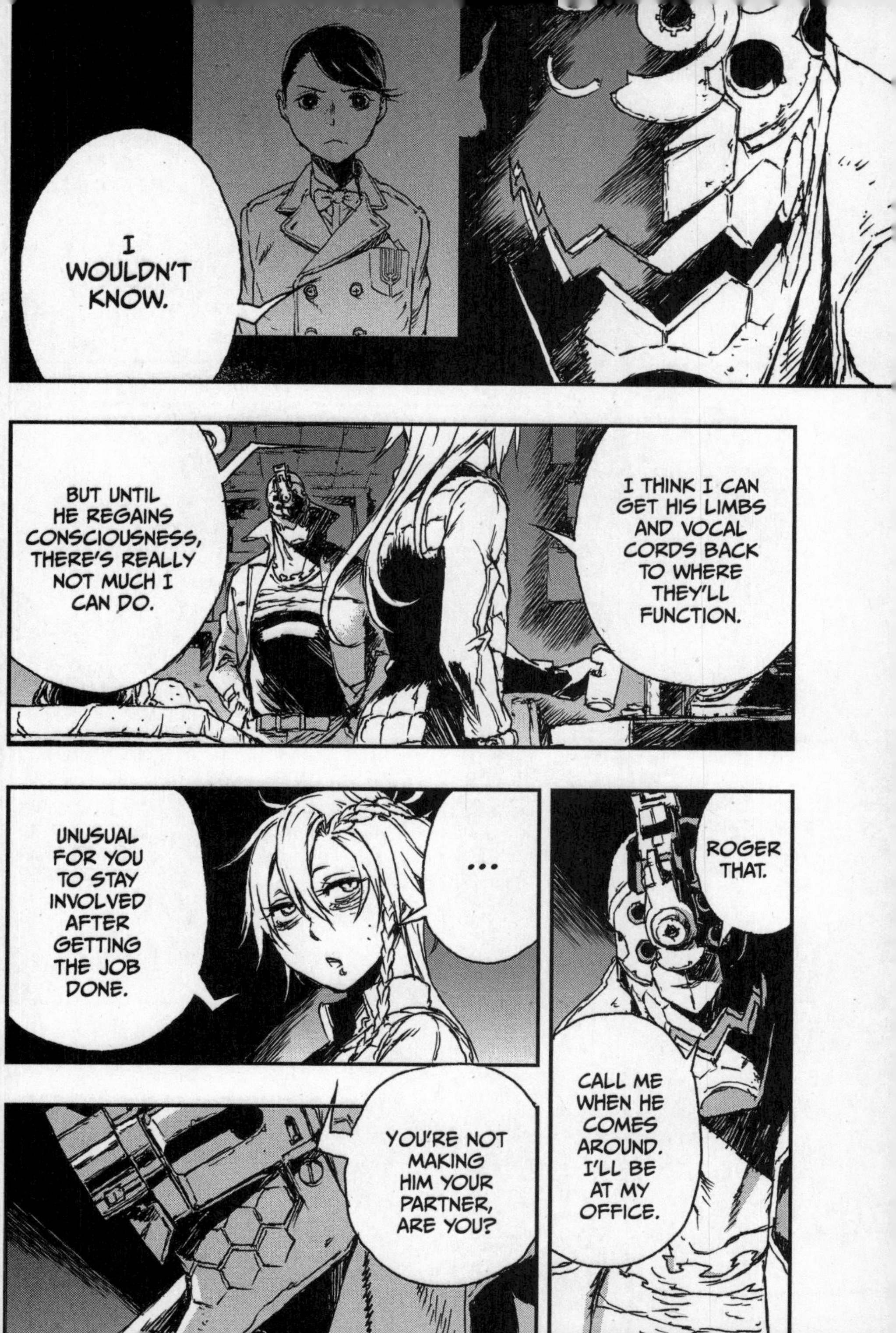

I WOULDN'T KNOW.
I THINK I CAN GET HIS LIMBS AND VOCAL CORDS BACK TO WHERE THEY'LL FUNCTION.
BUT UNTIL HE REGAINS CONSCIOUSNESS, THERE'S REALLY NOT MUCH I CAN DO.
ROGER THAT.
CALL ME WHEN HE COMES AROUND. I'LL BE AT MY OFFICE.
...
UNUSUAL FOR YOU TO STAY INVOLVED AFTER GETTING THE JOB DONE.
YOU'RE NOT MAKING HIM YOUR PARTNER, ARE YOU?

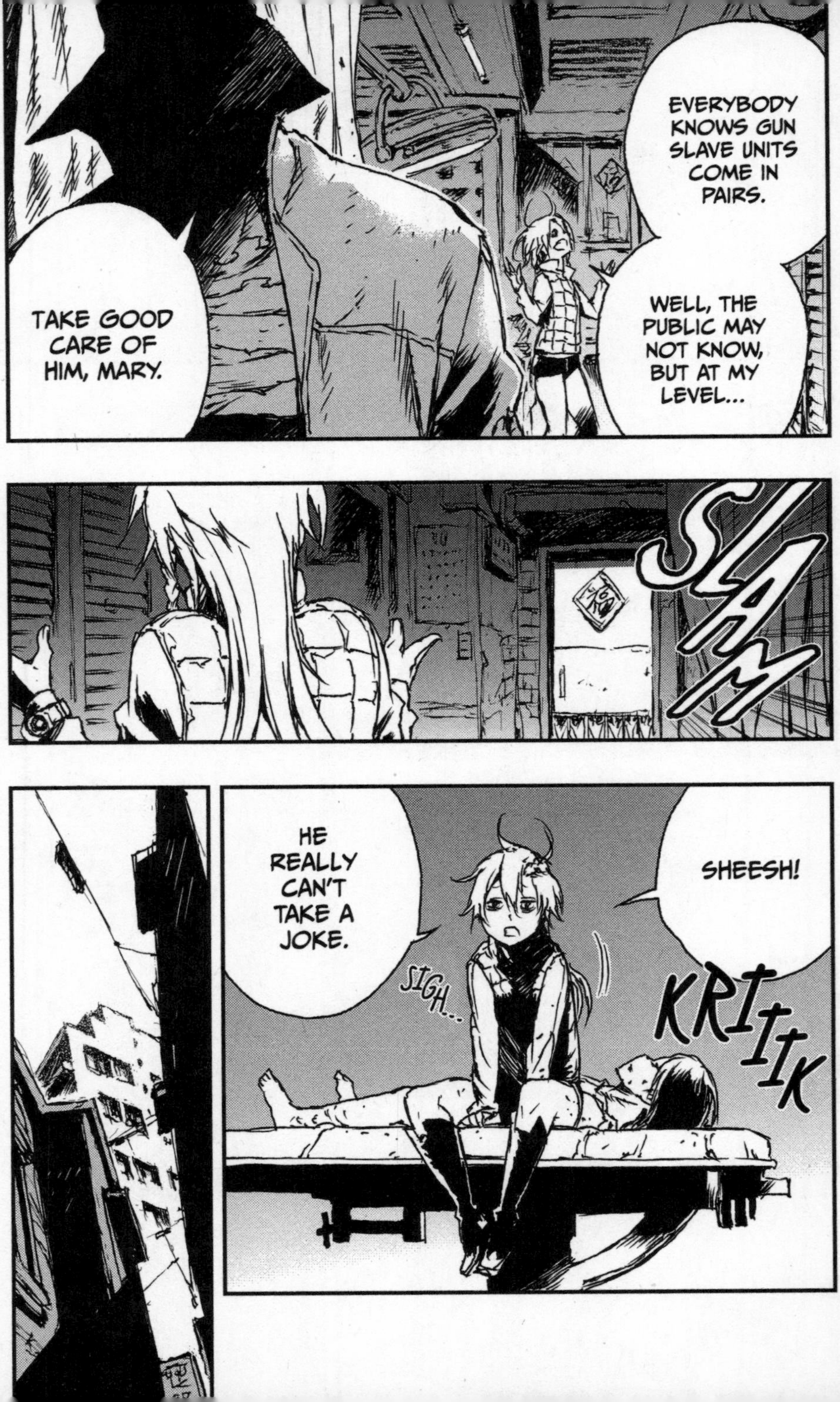
EVERYBODY KNOWS GUN SLAVE UNITS COME IN PAIRS.
WELL, THE PUBLIC MAY NOT KNOW, BUT AT MY LEVEL...
TAKE GOOD CARE OF HIM, MARY.
SLAM
SHEESH!
KRIIIK
HE REALLY CAN'T TAKE A JOKE.
SIGH...

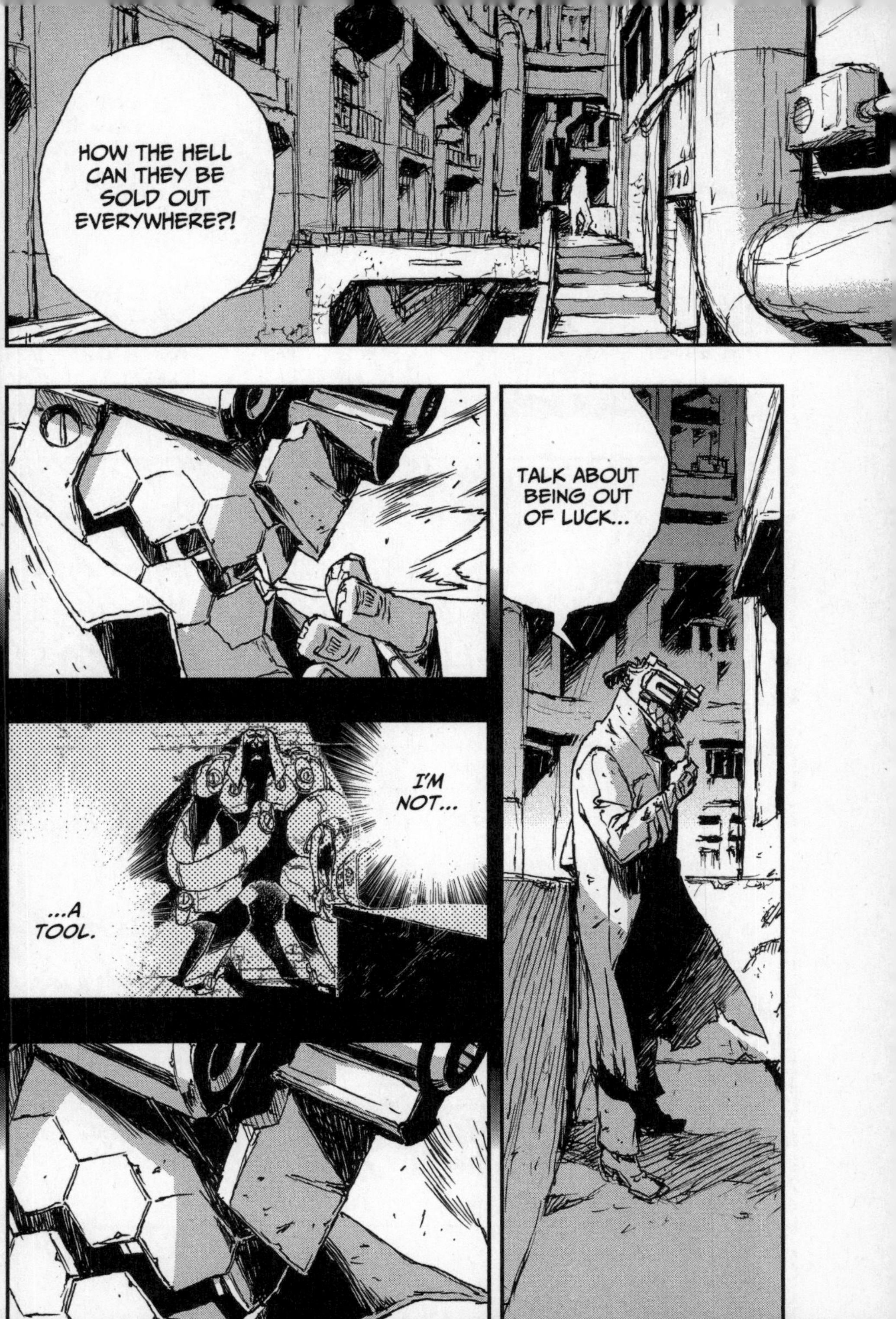
HOW THE HELL CAN THEY BE SOLD OUT EVERYWHERE?!
TALK ABOUT BEING OUT OF LUCK...
I'M NOT...
...A TOOL.

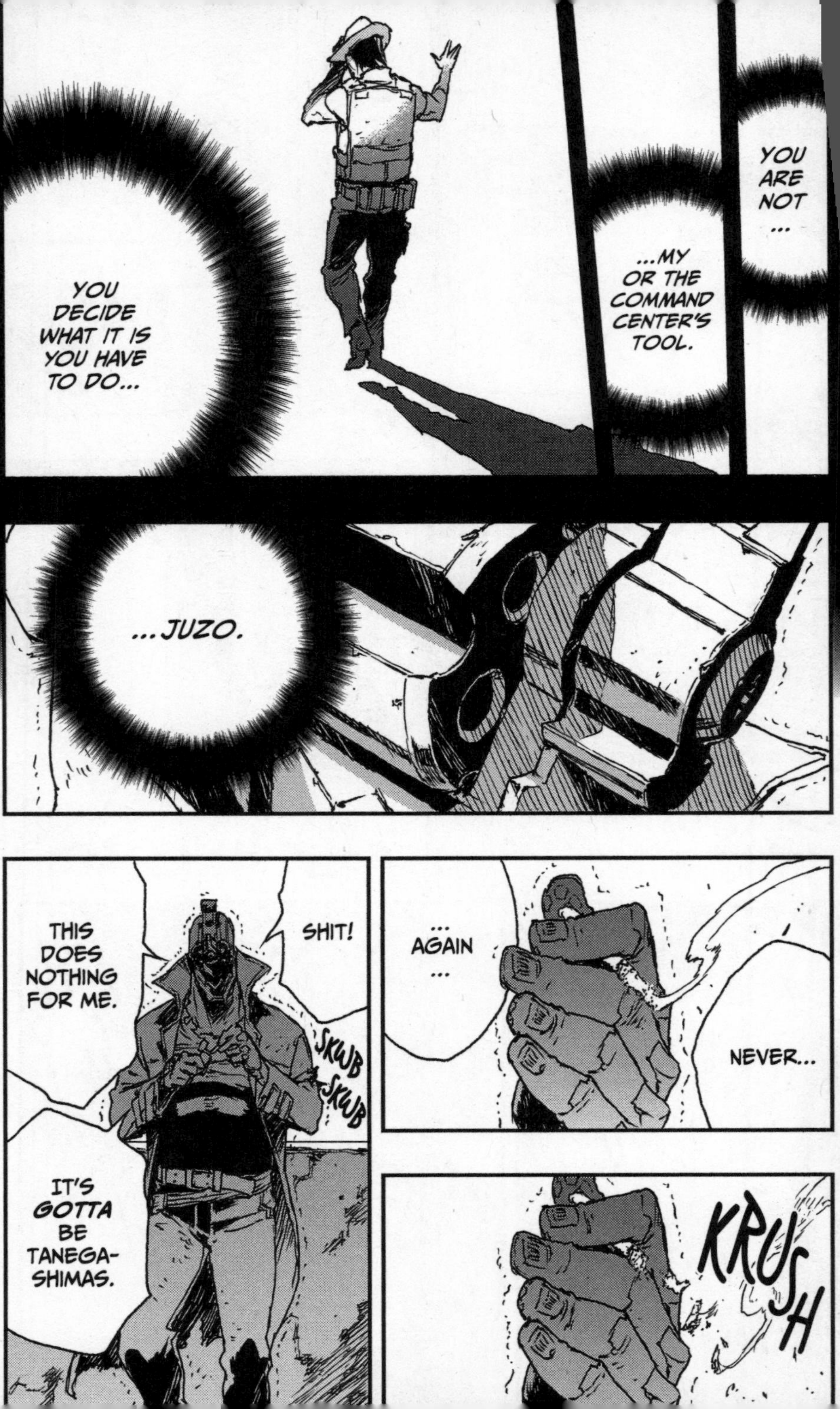
YOU ARE NOT ...
...MY OR THE COMMAND CENTER'S TOOL.
YOU DECIDE WHAT IT IS YOU HAVE TO DO...
...JUZO.
... AGAIN ...
NEVER...
KRUSH
SHIT!
THIS DOES NOTHING FOR ME.
SKWUB SKWUB
IT'S GOTTA BE TANEGA-SHIMAS.

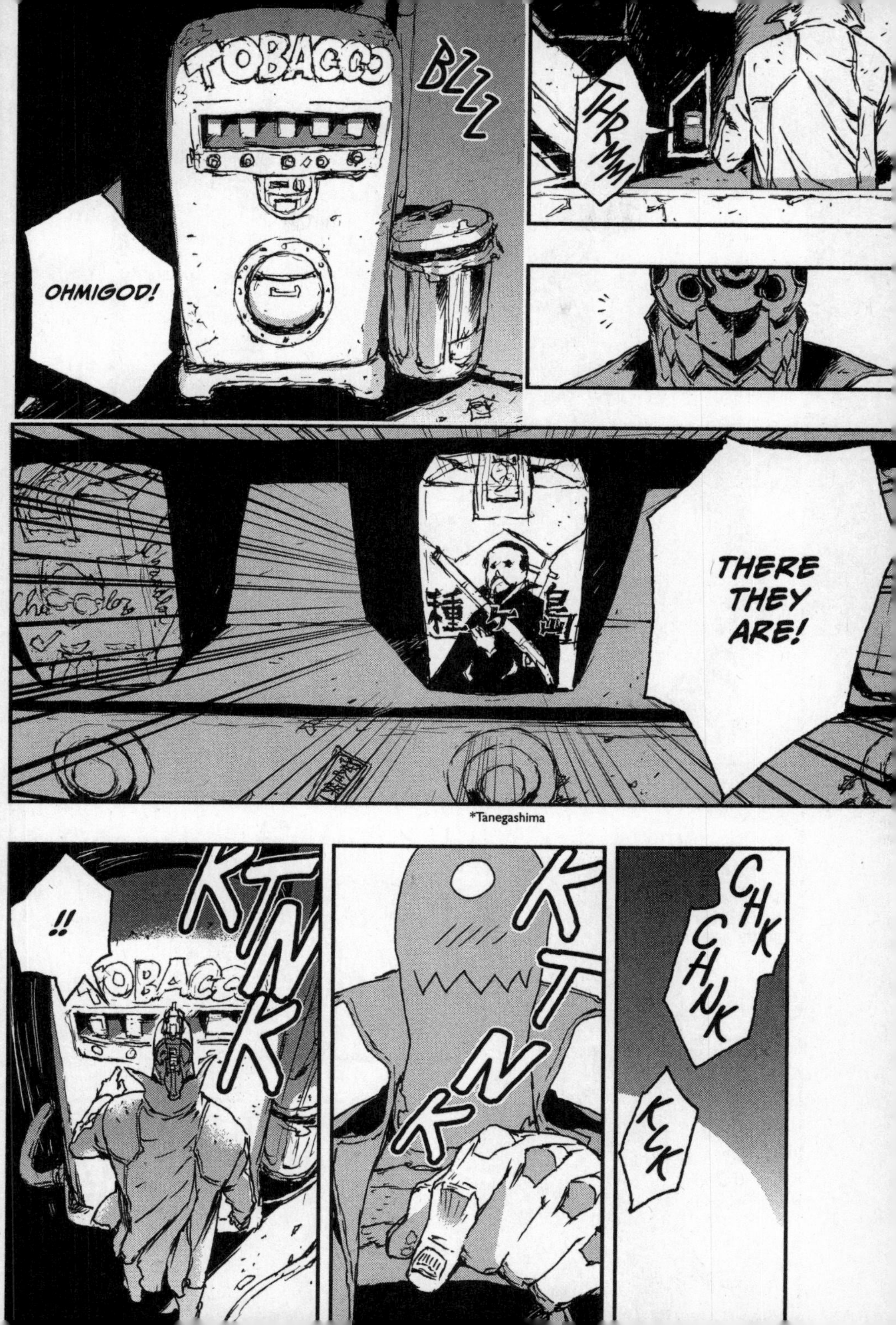
THRMM
TOBACCO
BZZZ
OHMIGOD!
THERE THEY ARE!
種ヶ島
CHK
CHNK
KLK
KTNK
KTNK
!!
TOBACCO
*Tanegashima

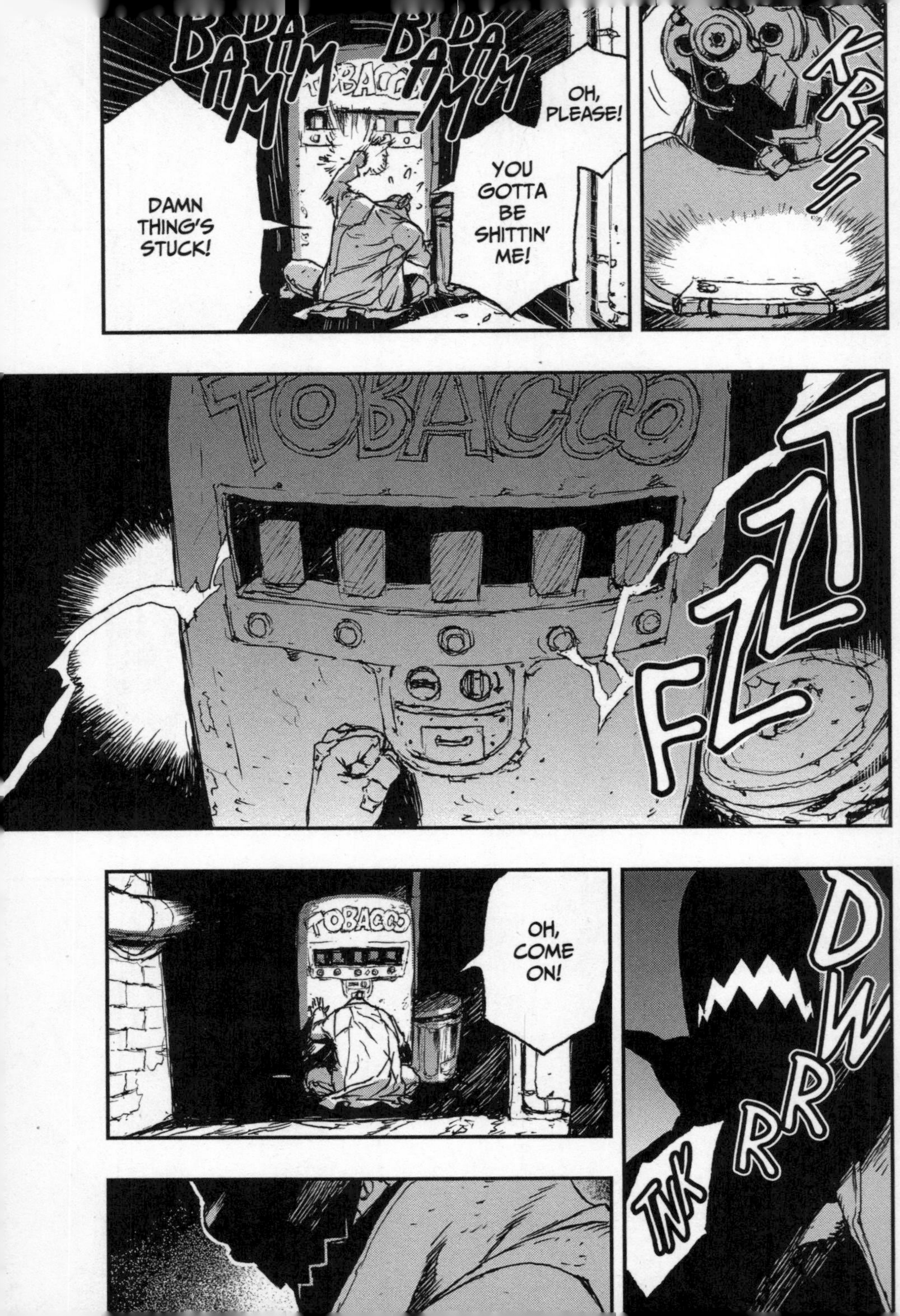
KRIII
BADAMM
OH, PLEASE!
BADAMM
TOBACCO
YOU GOTTA BE SHITTIN' ME!
DAMN THING'S STUCK!
FZZT
TOBACCO
DWRRR
TNK
OH, COME ON!
TOBACCO

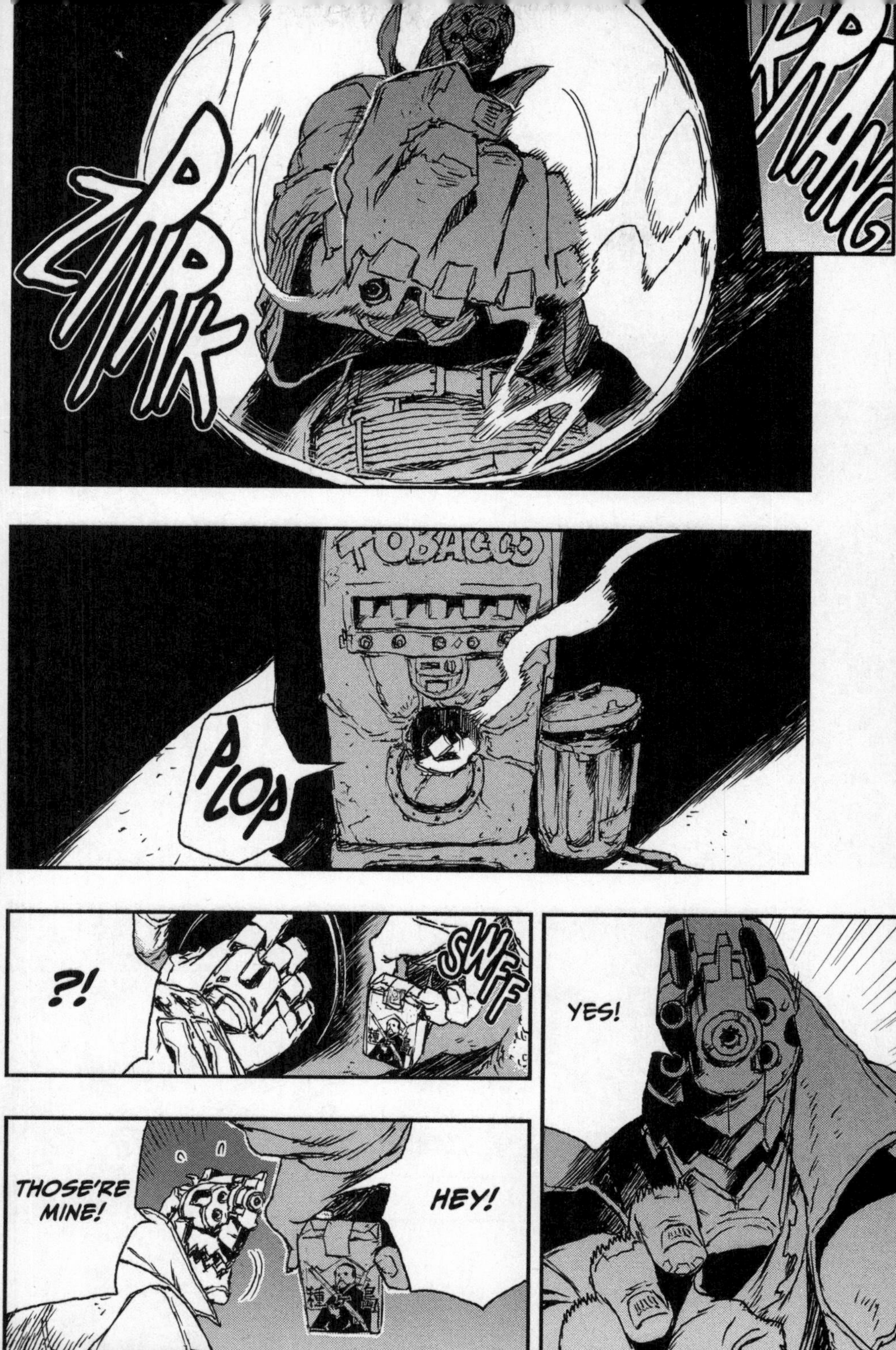
TOBACCO
PLOP
YES!
SWFF
?!
HEY!
THOSE'RE MINE!

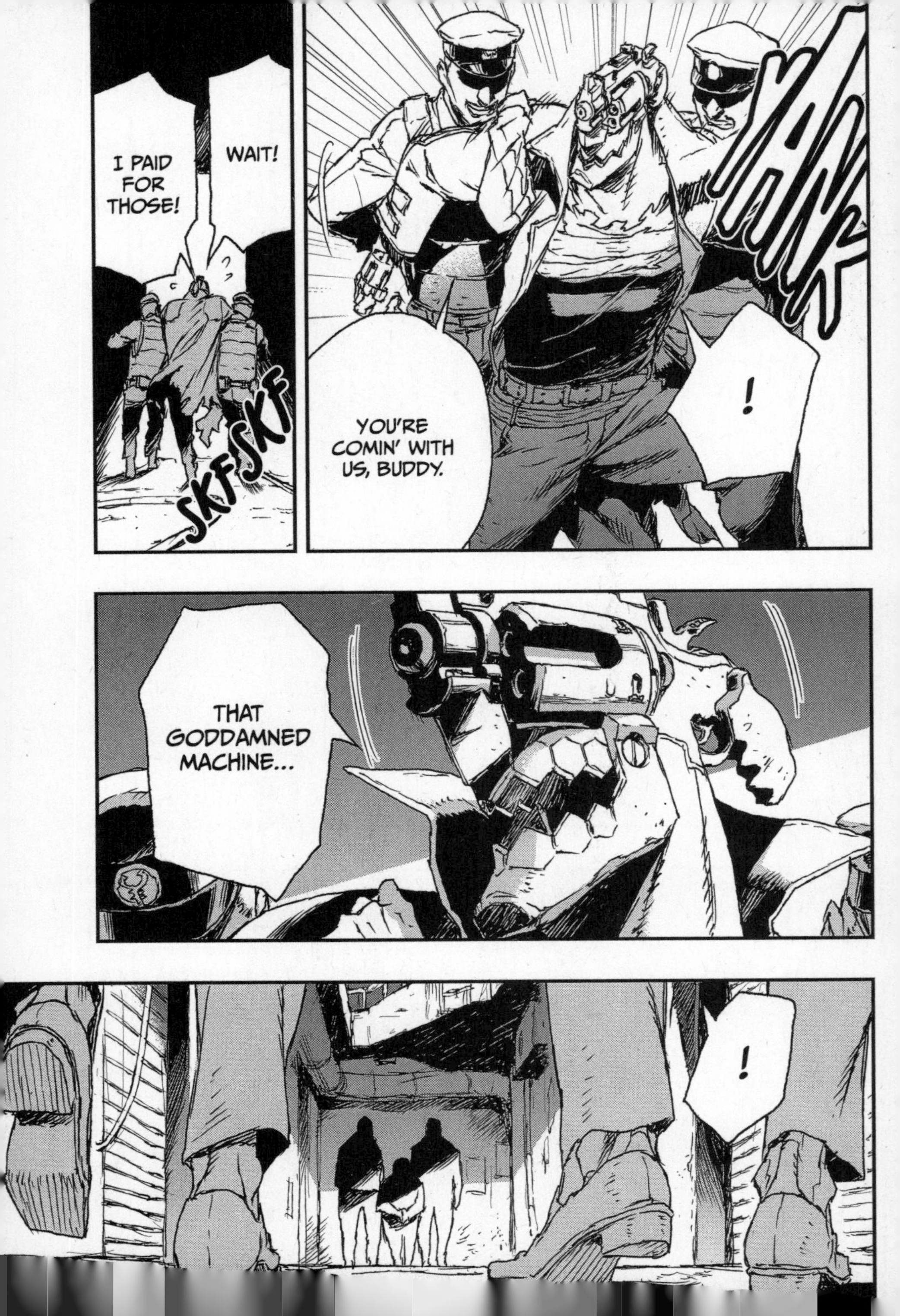
YAK
!
YOU'RE COMIN' WITH US, BUDDY.
WAIT!
I PAID FOR THOSE!
SKFSKF
THAT GODDAMNED MACHINE...
!

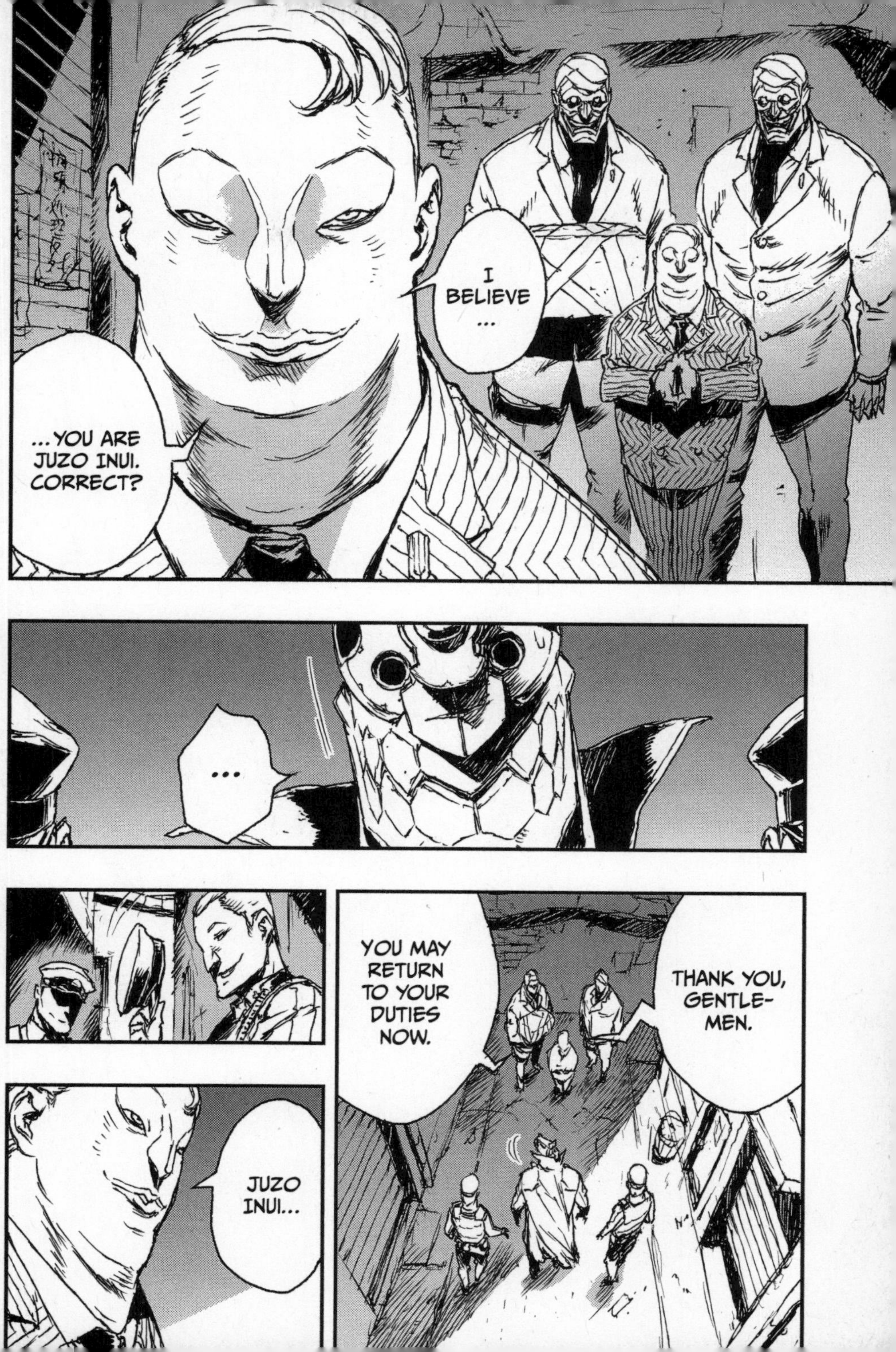
I BELIEVE ...
...YOU ARE JUZO INUI. CORRECT?
...
THANK YOU, GENTLE-MEN.
YOU MAY RETURN TO YOUR DUTIES NOW.
JUZO INUI...

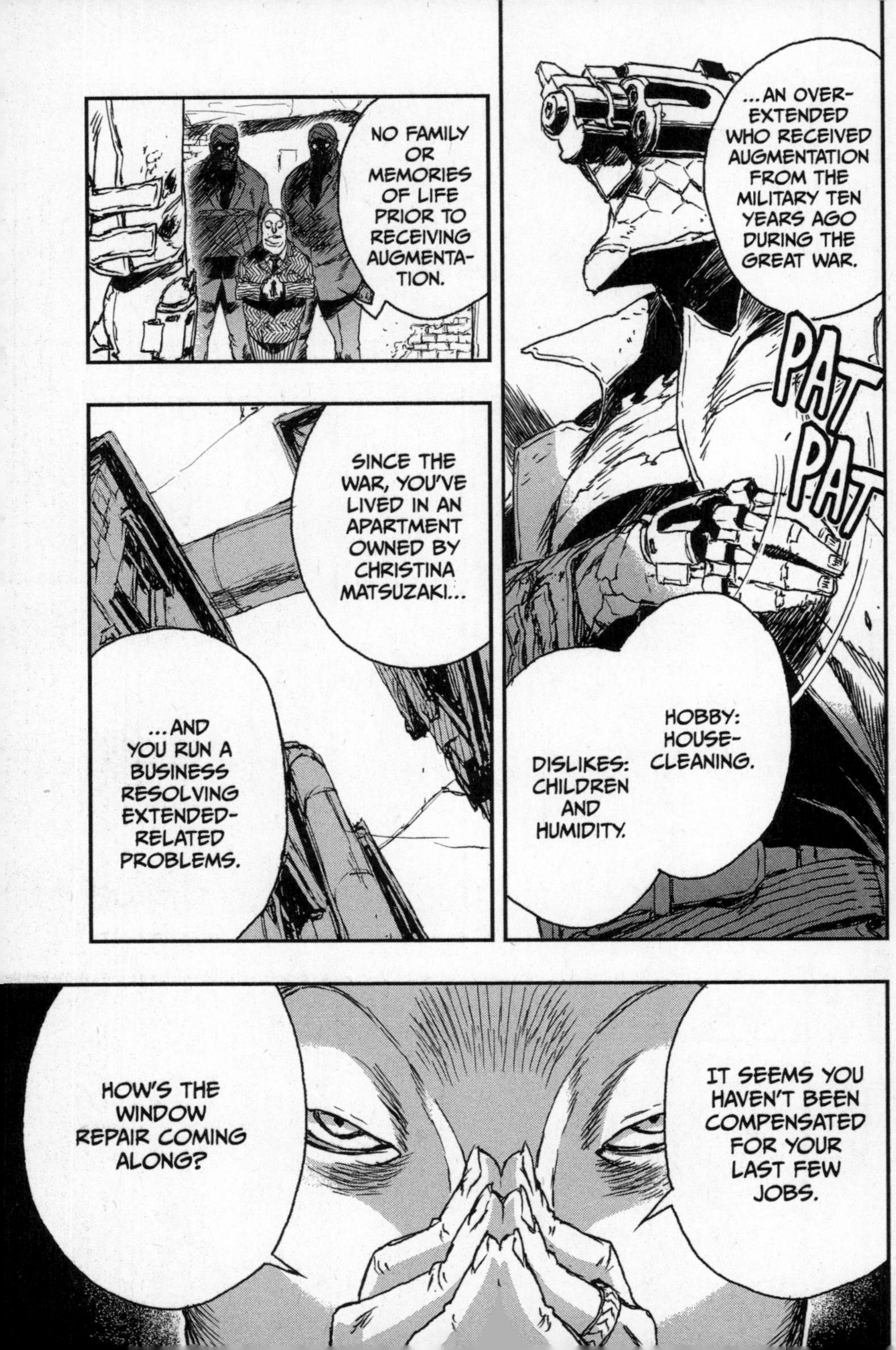
...AN OVER-EXTENDED WHO RECEIVED AUGMENTATION FROM THE MILITARY TEN YEARS AGO DURING THE GREAT WAR.
PAT PAT
HOBBY: HOUSE-CLEANING.
DISLIKES: CHILDREN AND HUMIDITY.
NO FAMILY OR MEMORIES OF LIFE PRIOR TO RECEIVING AUGMENTATION.
SINCE THE WAR, YOU'VE LIVED IN AN APARTMENT OWNED BY CHRISTINA MATSUZAKI...
...AND YOU RUN A BUSINESS RESOLVING EXTENDED-RELATED PROBLEMS.
IT SEEMS YOU HAVEN'T BEEN COMPENSATED FOR YOUR LAST FEW JOBS.
HOW'S THE WINDOW REPAIR COMING ALONG?

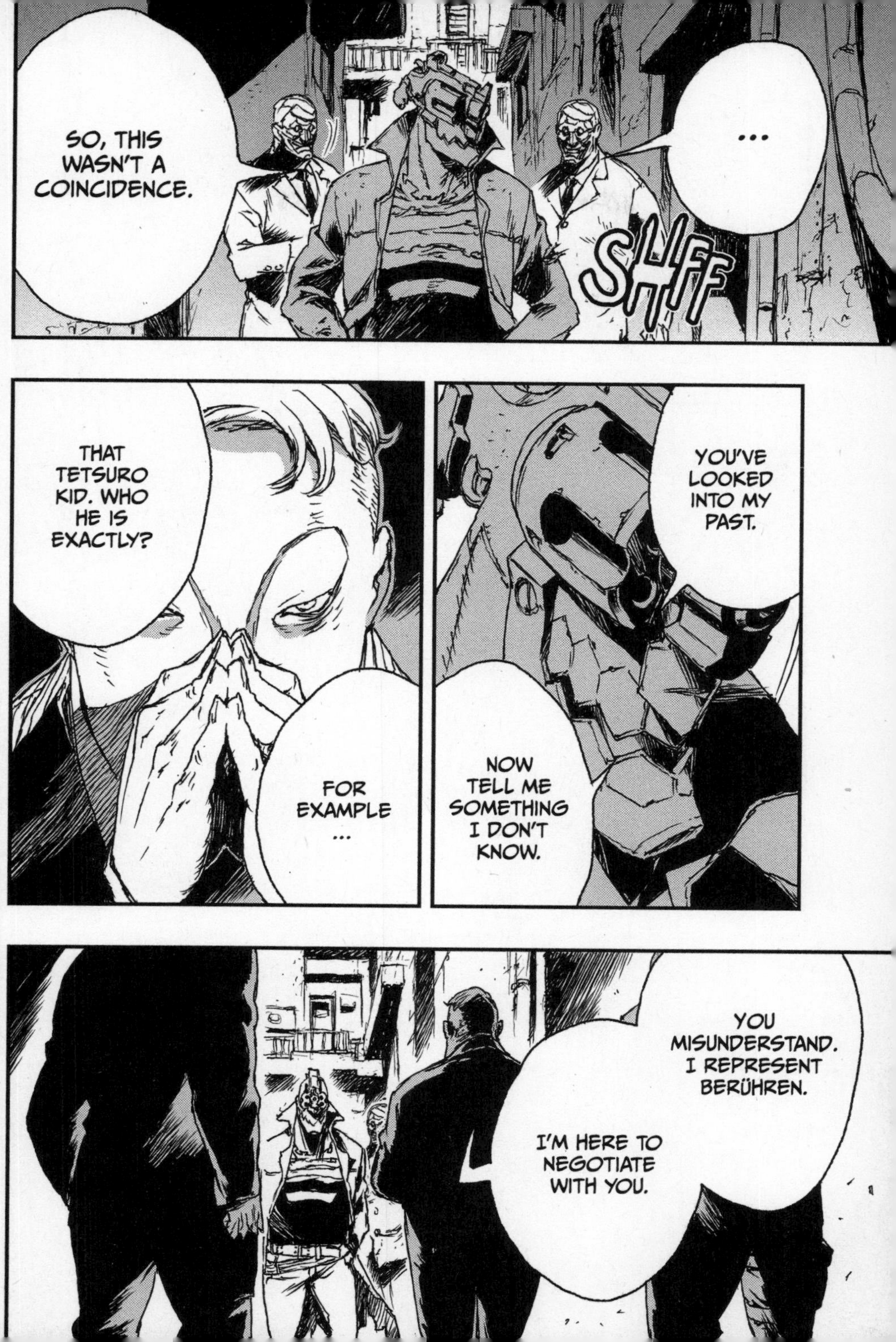
...
SHFF
SO, THIS WASN'T A COINCIDENCE.
YOU'VE LOOKED INTO MY PAST.
NOW TELL ME SOMETHING I DON'T KNOW.
FOR EXAMPLE ...
THAT TETSURO KID. WHO HE IS EXACTLY?
YOU MISUNDERSTAND. I REPRESENT BERÜHREN.
I'M HERE TO NEGOTIATE WITH YOU.

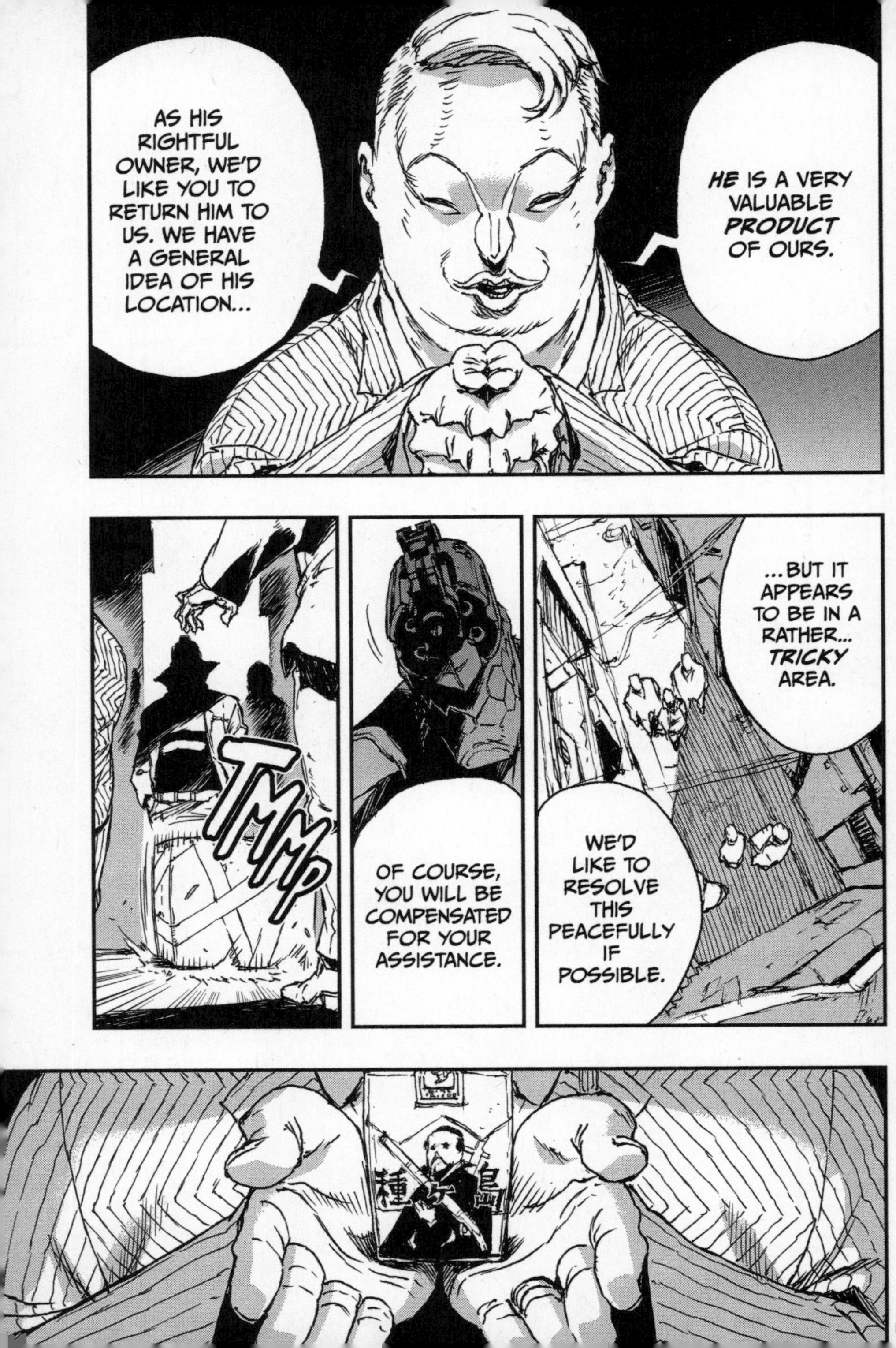
HE IS A VERY VALUABLE PRODUCT OF OURS.
AS HIS RIGHTFUL OWNER, WE'D LIKE YOU TO RETURN HIM TO US. WE HAVE A GENERAL IDEA OF HIS LOCATION...
...BUT IT APPEARS TO BE IN A RATHER... TRICKY AREA.
WE'D LIKE TO RESOLVE THIS PEACEFULLY IF POSSIBLE.
OF COURSE, YOU WILL BE COMPENSATED FOR YOUR ASSISTANCE.
TMMP

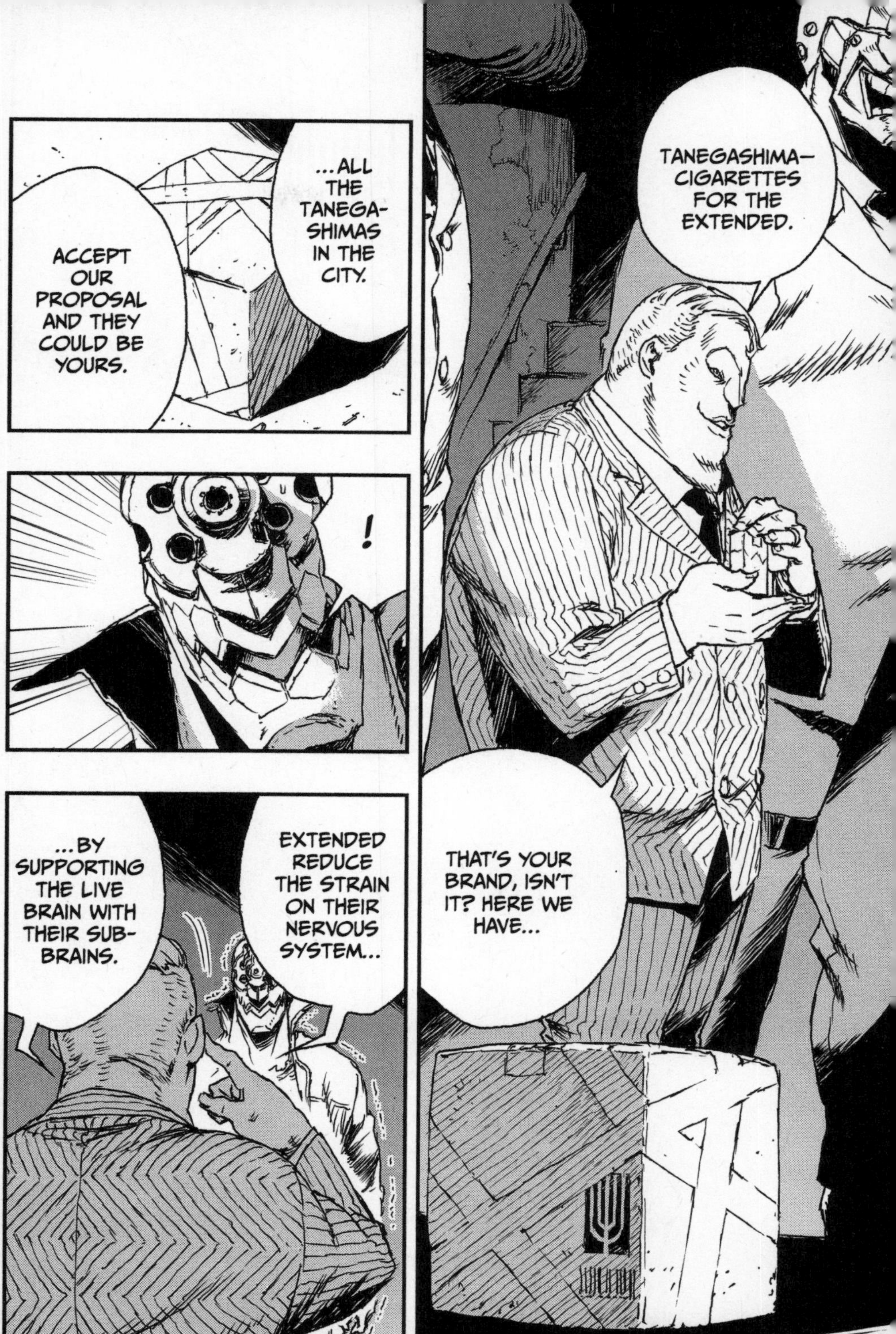
TANEGASHIMA—CIGARETTES FOR THE EXTENDED.
THAT'S YOUR BRAND, ISN'T IT? HERE WE HAVE...
...ALL THE TANEGA-SHIMAS IN THE CITY.
ACCEPT OUR PROPOSAL AND THEY COULD BE YOURS.
!
EXTENDED REDUCE THE STRAIN ON THEIR NERVOUS SYSTEM...
...BY SUPPORTING THE LIVE BRAIN WITH THEIR SUB-BRAINS.

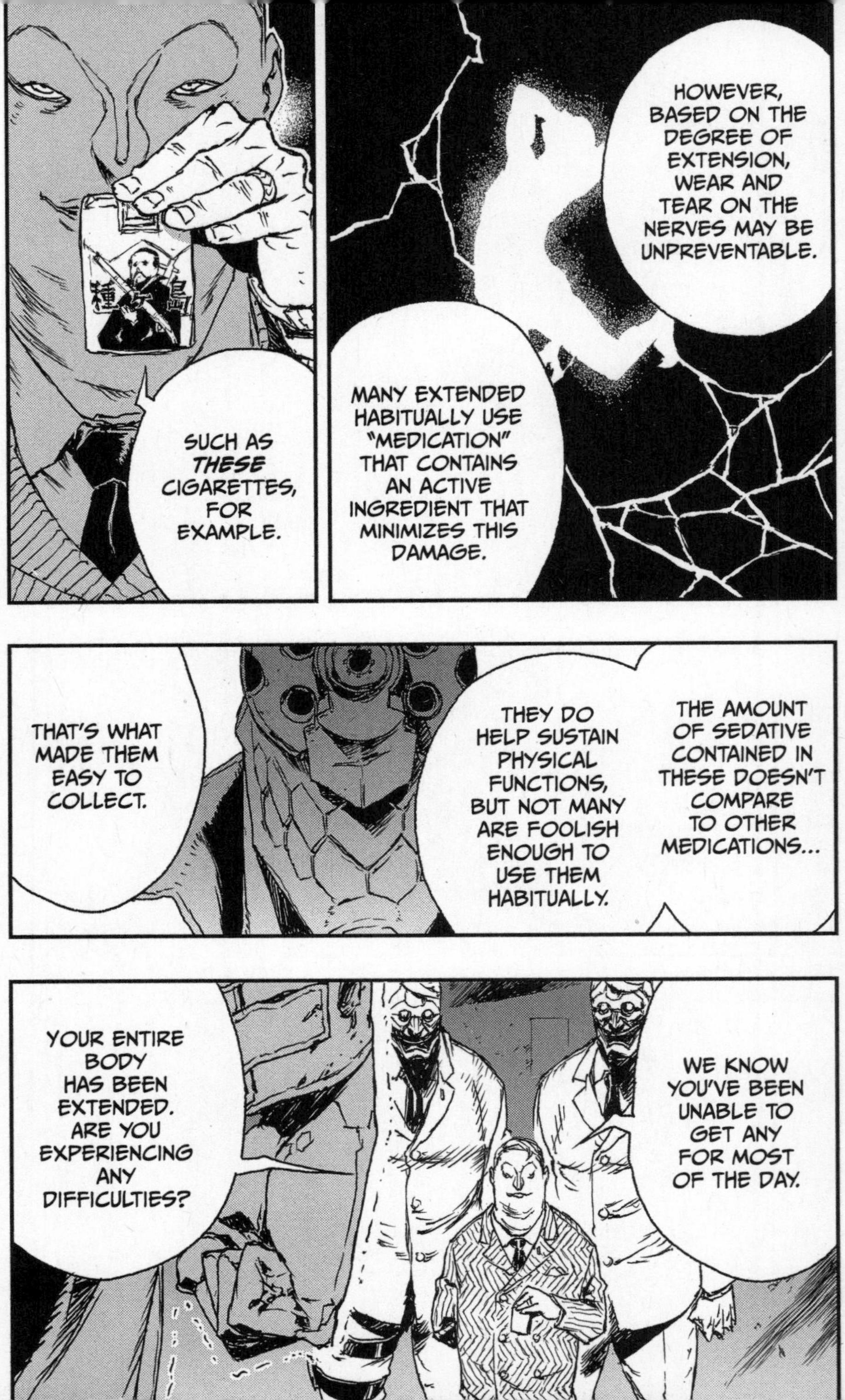
HOWEVER, BASED ON THE DEGREE OF EXTENSION, WEAR AND TEAR ON THE NERVES MAY BE UNPREVENTABLE.
MANY EXTENDED HABITUALLY USE "MEDICATION" THAT CONTAINS AN ACTIVE INGREDIENT THAT MINIMIZES THIS DAMAGE.
SUCH AS *THESE* CIGARETTES, FOR EXAMPLE.
THE AMOUNT OF SEDATIVE CONTAINED IN THESE DOESN'T COMPARE TO OTHER MEDICATIONS...
THEY DO HELP SUSTAIN PHYSICAL FUNCTIONS, BUT NOT MANY ARE FOOLISH ENOUGH TO USE THEM HABITUALLY.
THAT'S WHAT MADE THEM EASY TO COLLECT.
WE KNOW YOU'VE BEEN UNABLE TO GET ANY FOR MOST OF THE DAY.
YOUR ENTIRE BODY HAS BEEN EXTENDED. ARE YOU EXPERIENCING ANY DIFFICULTIES?

THAT WAS A DUMB THING TO DO...

HEH...

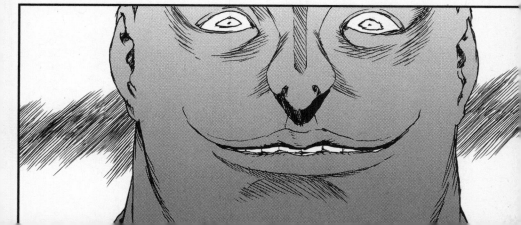

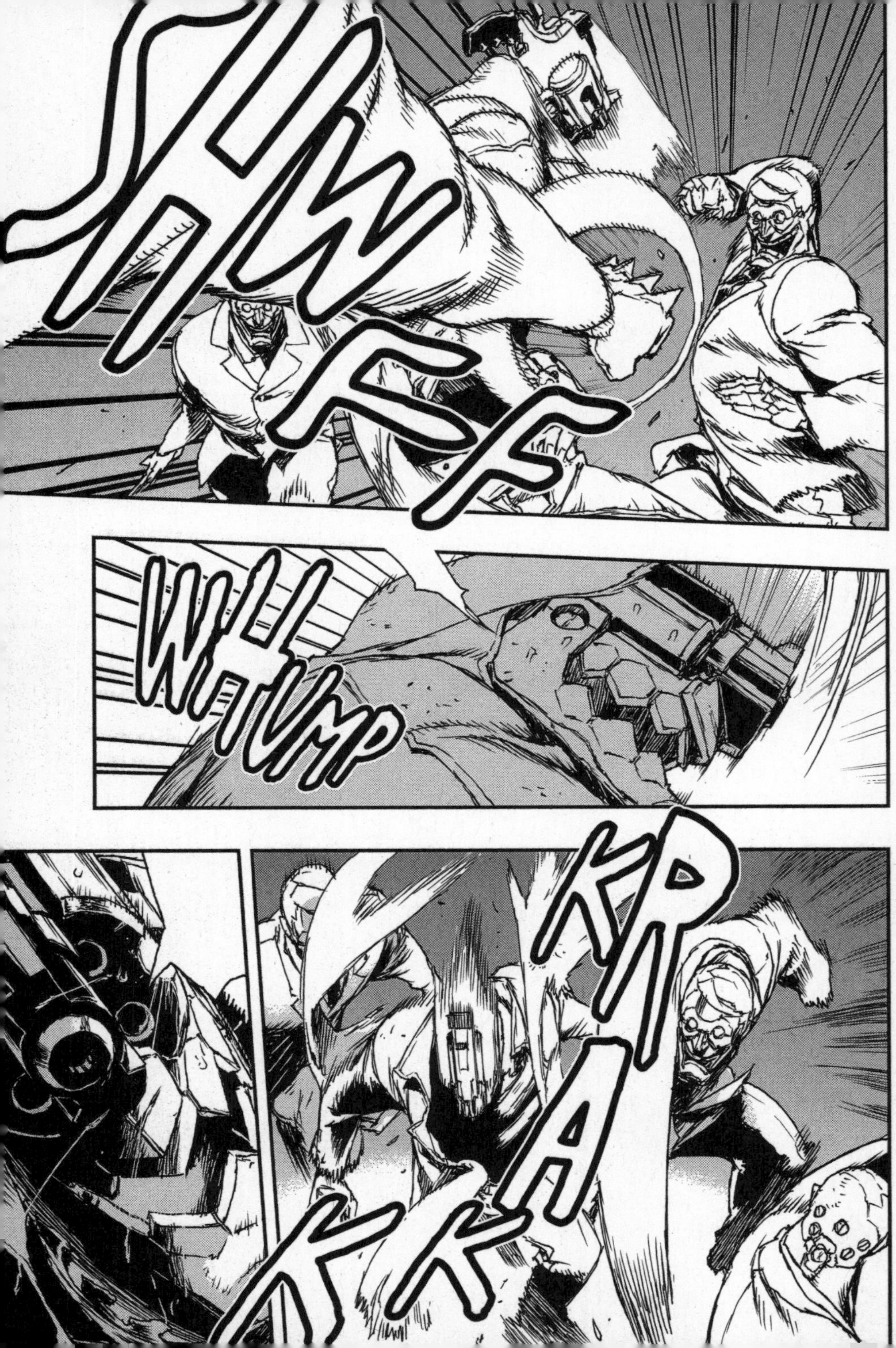
SHWFF
WHUMP
KRAKK

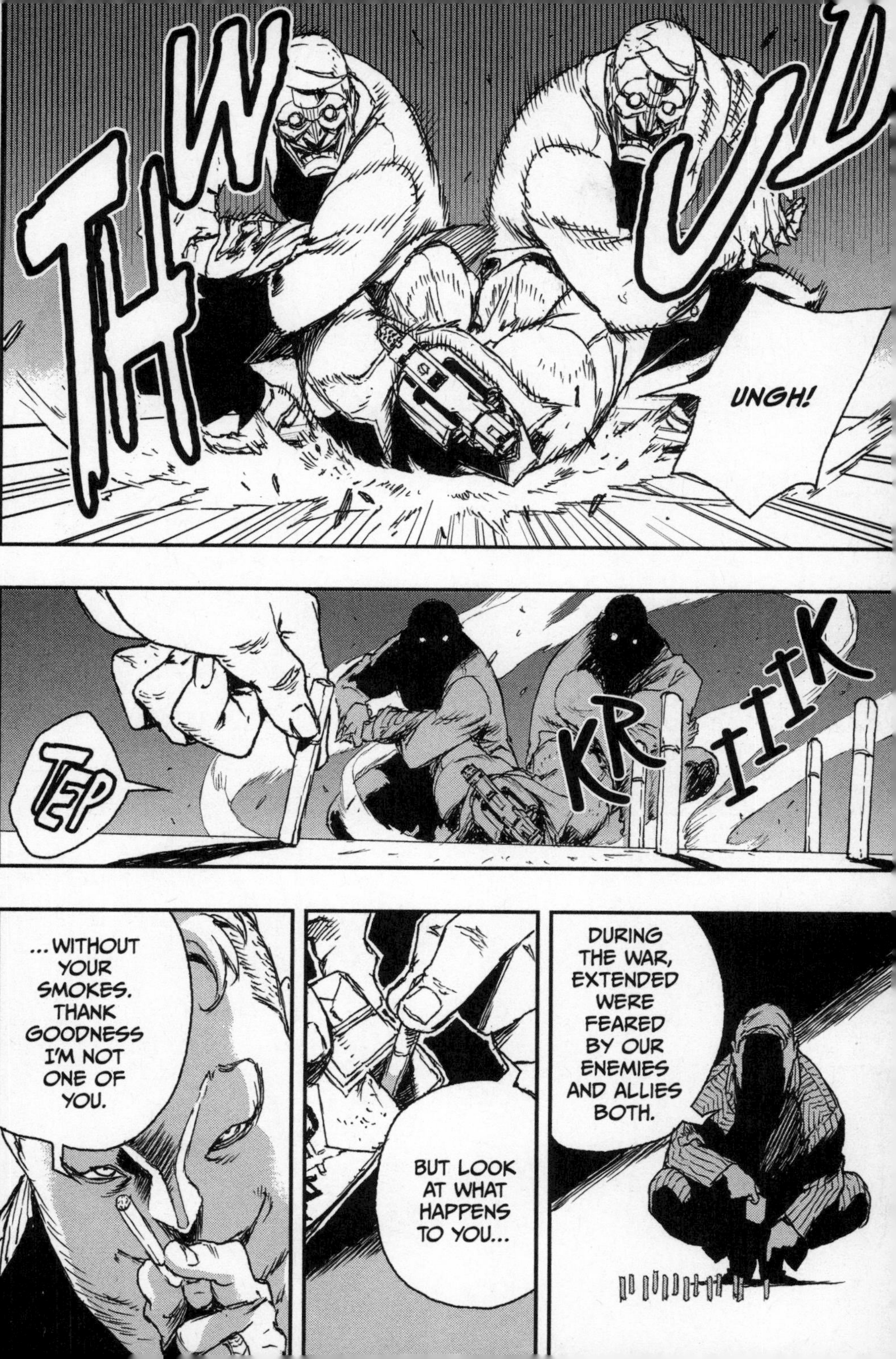
THWU
UNGH!
KRIIIK
TEP
DURING THE WAR, EXTENDED WERE FEARED BY OUR ENEMIES AND ALLIES BOTH.
BUT LOOK AT WHAT HAPPENS TO YOU...
...WITHOUT YOUR SMOKES. THANK GOODNESS I'M NOT ONE OF YOU.

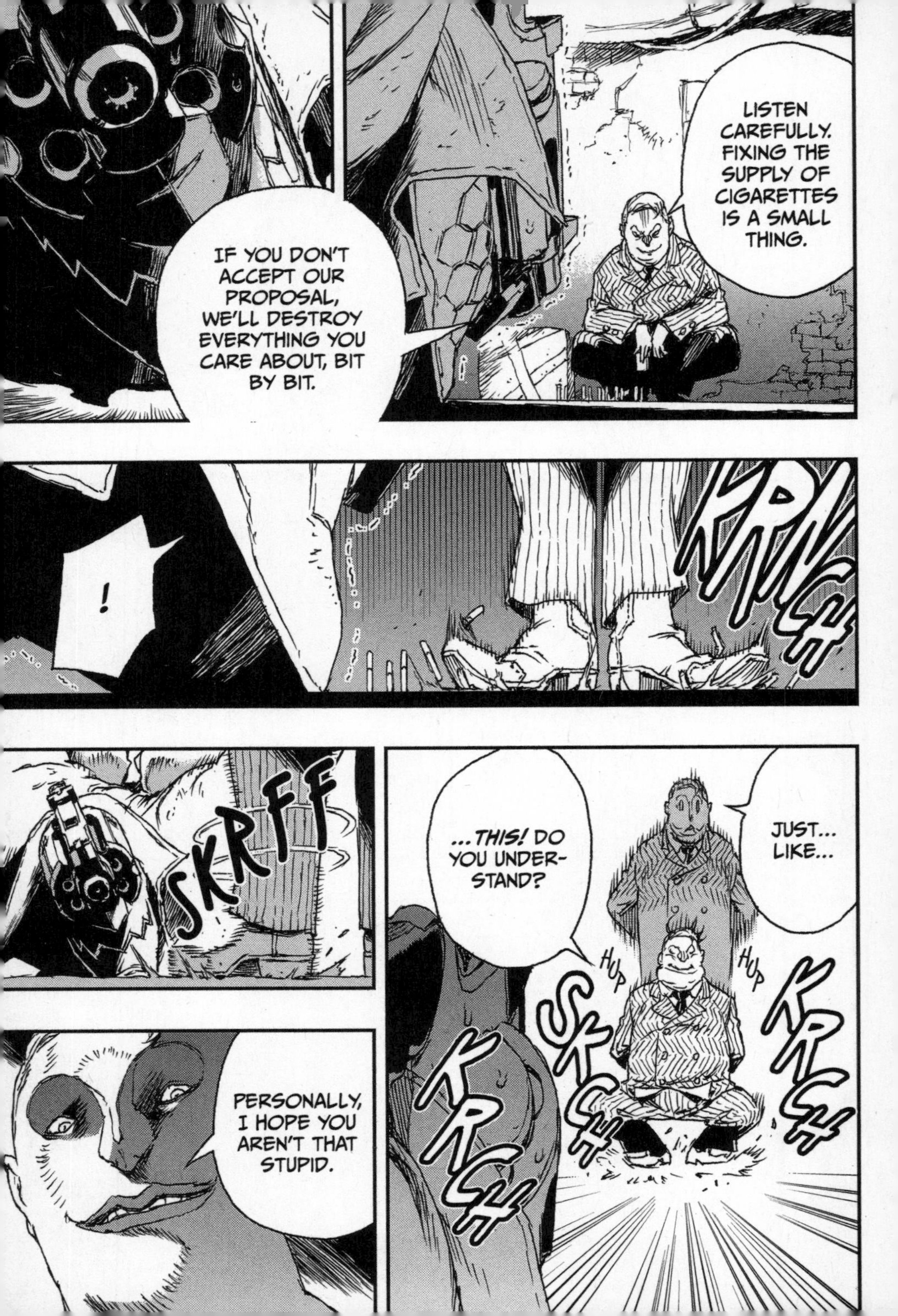
LISTEN CAREFULLY. FIXING THE SUPPLY OF CIGARETTES IS A SMALL THING.
IF YOU DON'T ACCEPT OUR PROPOSAL, WE'LL DESTROY EVERYTHING YOU CARE ABOUT, BIT BY BIT.
KRNCH
!
JUST... LIKE...
...THIS! DO YOU UNDER-STAND?
HUP
HUP
KRCH
SKRCH
KRCH
SKRFF
PERSONALLY, I HOPE YOU AREN'T THAT STUPID.

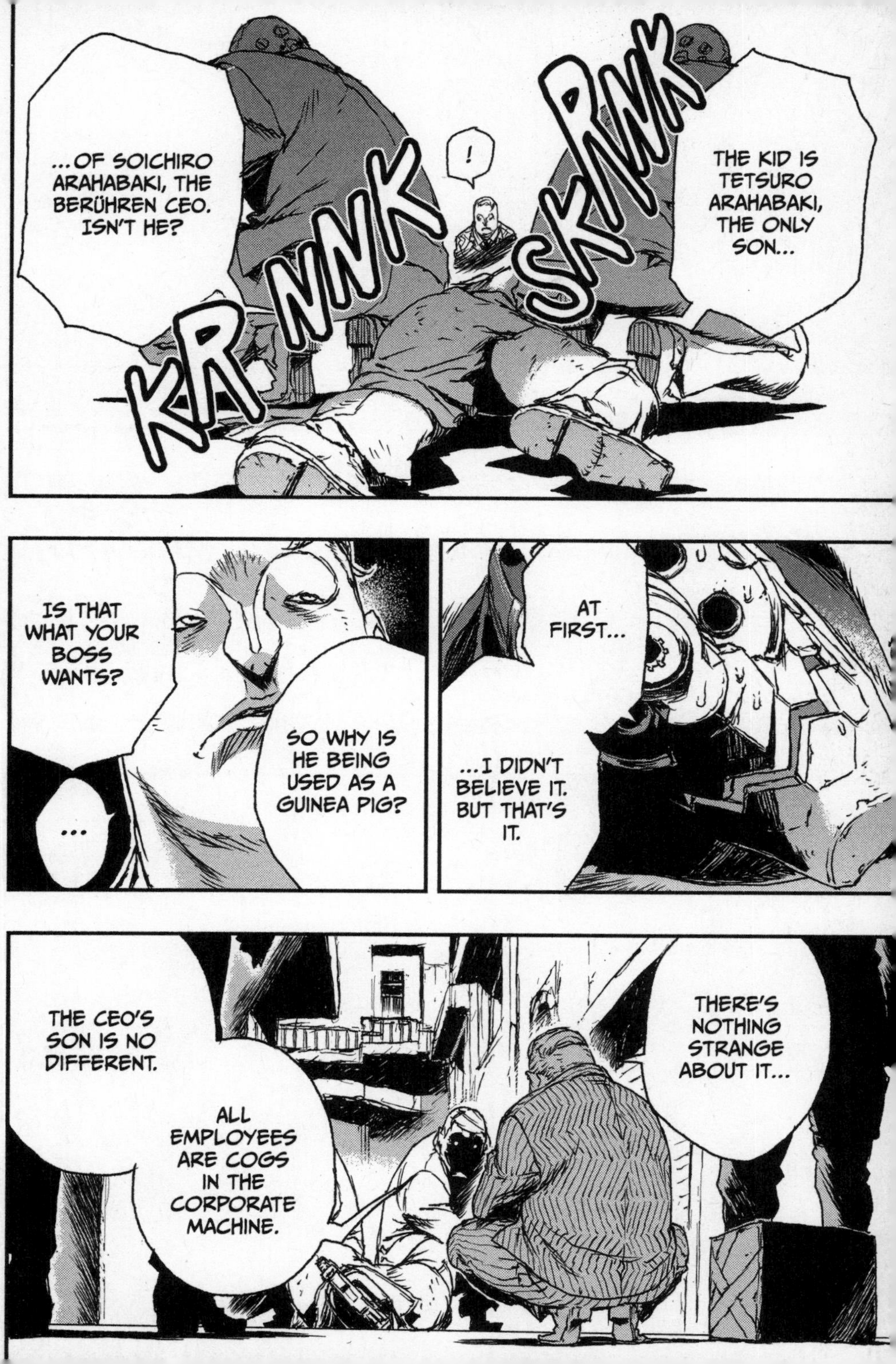
THE KID IS TETSURO ARAHABAKI, THE ONLY SON...
!
SKRNK
KRNNK
...OF SOICHIRO ARAHABAKI, THE BERÜHREN CEO. ISN'T HE?
AT FIRST...
...I DIDN'T BELIEVE IT. BUT THAT'S IT.
SO WHY IS HE BEING USED AS A GUINEA PIG?
IS THAT WHAT YOUR BOSS WANTS?
...
THERE'S NOTHING STRANGE ABOUT IT...
ALL EMPLOYEES ARE COGS IN THE CORPORATE MACHINE.
THE CEO'S SON IS NO DIFFERENT.

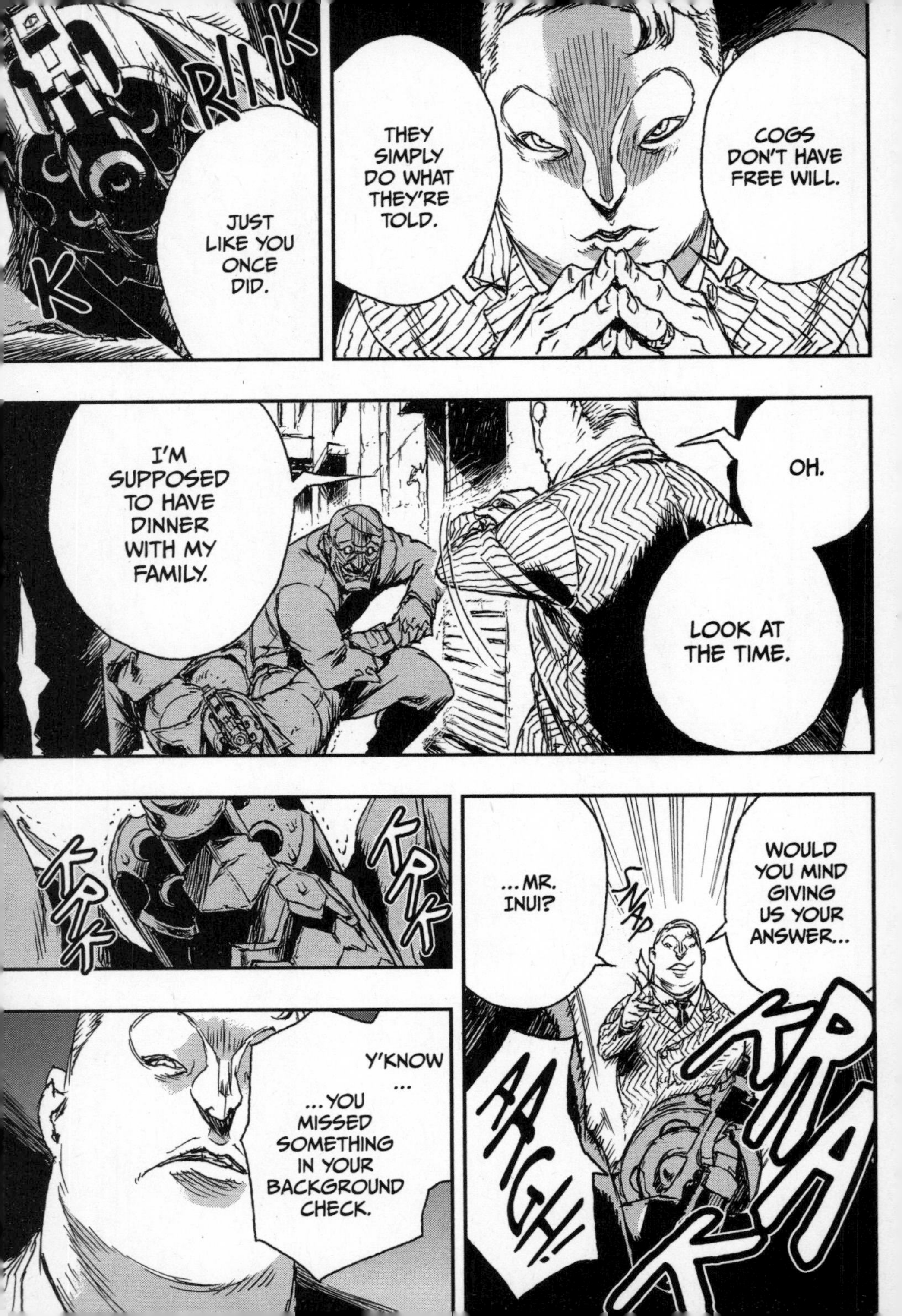
COGS DON'T HAVE FREE WILL.
THEY SIMPLY DO WHAT THEY'RE TOLD.
RIIK
K
JUST LIKE YOU ONCE DID.
OH.
LOOK AT THE TIME.
I'M SUPPOSED TO HAVE DINNER WITH MY FAMILY.
WOULD YOU MIND GIVING US YOUR ANSWER...
SNAP
...MR. INUI?
KRAAK
AAGH!
KRK
KRK
Y'KNOW ...
...YOU MISSED SOMETHING IN YOUR BACKGROUND CHECK.

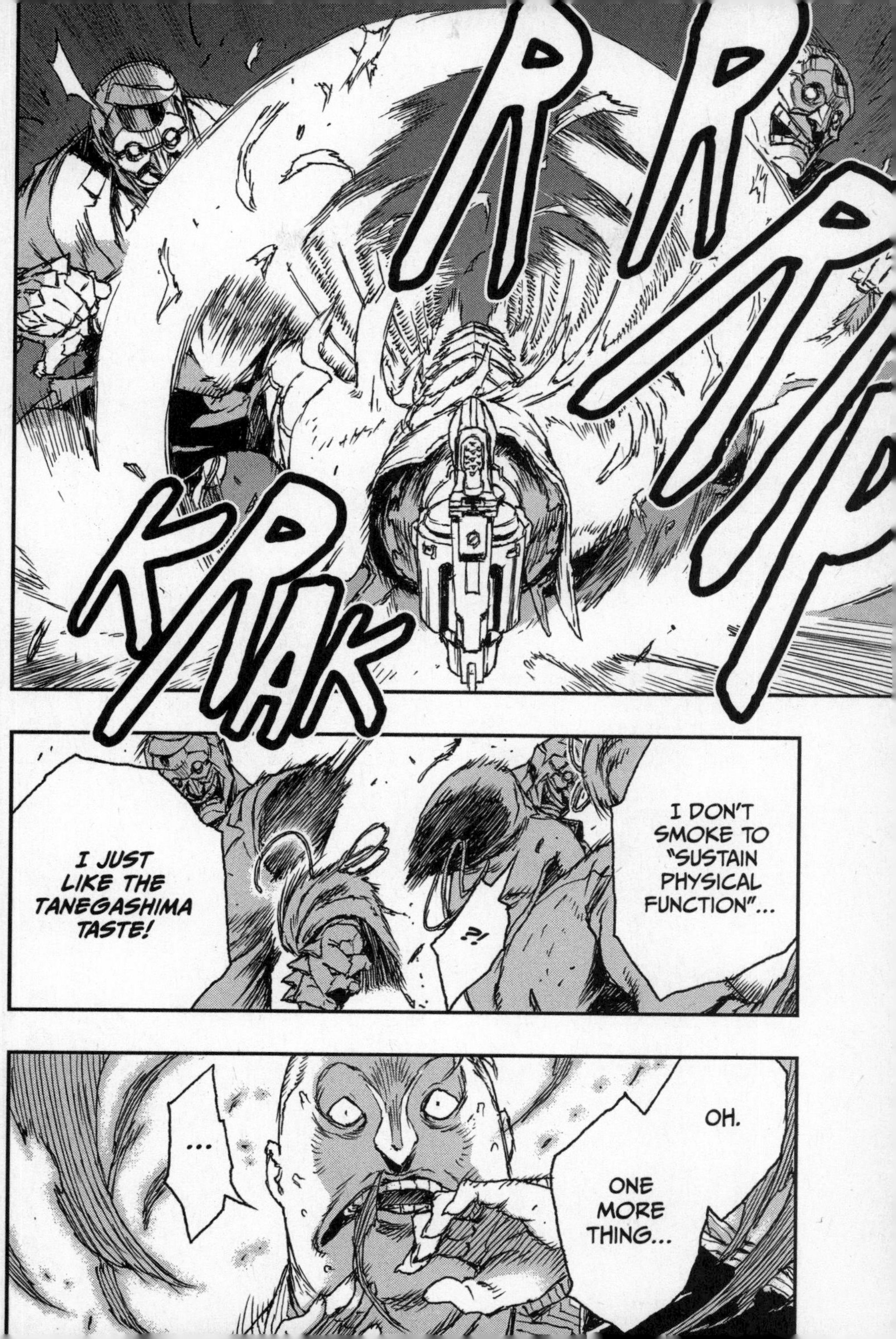
KRAK
I DON'T SMOKE TO "SUSTAIN PHYSICAL FUNCTION"...
?!
I JUST LIKE THE TANEGASHIMA TASTE!
OH.
ONE MORE THING...
...

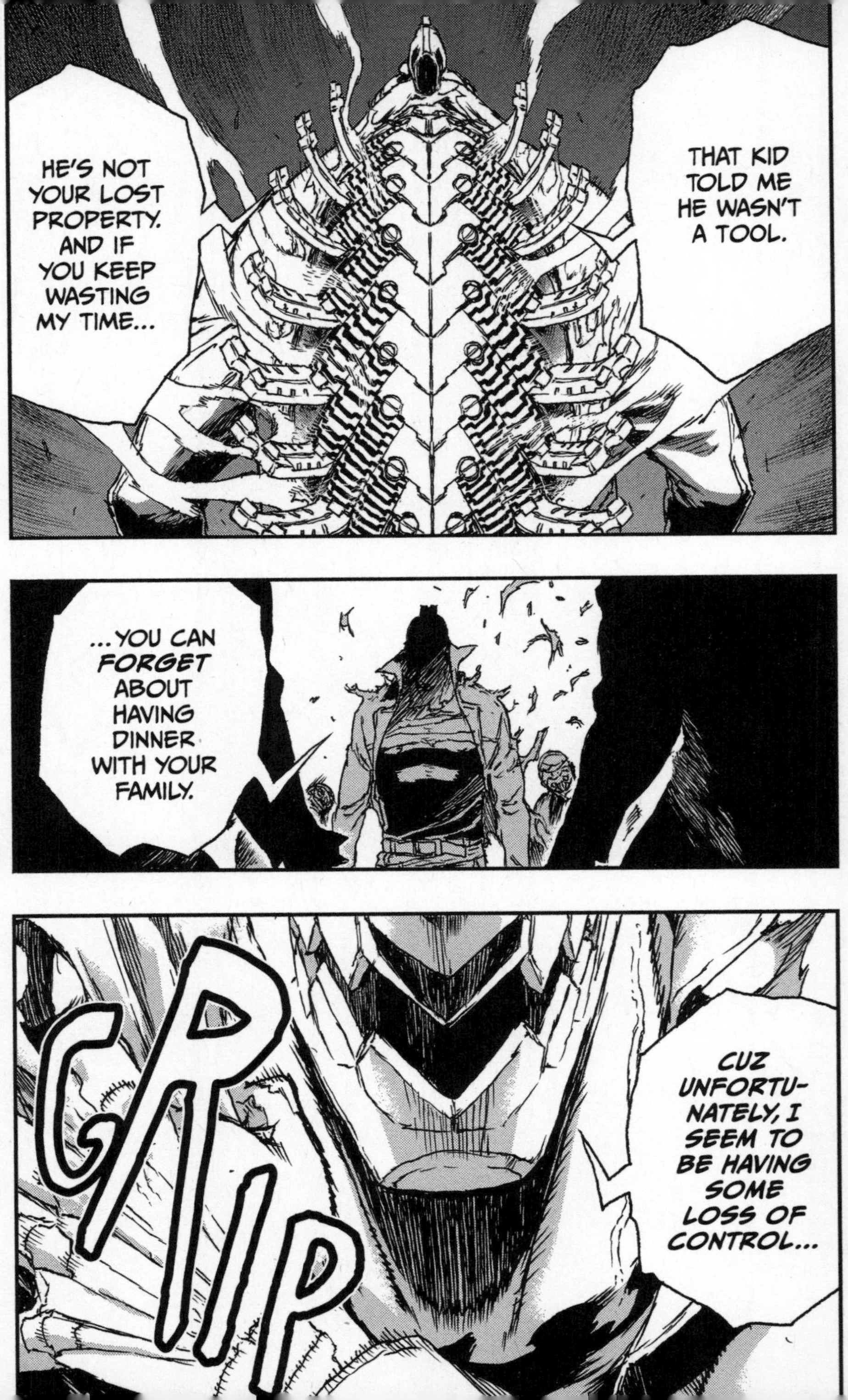
THAT KID TOLD ME HE WASN'T A TOOL.
HE'S NOT YOUR LOST PROPERTY. AND IF YOU KEEP WASTING MY TIME...
...YOU CAN *FORGET* ABOUT HAVING DINNER WITH YOUR FAMILY.
CUZ UNFORTU-NATELY, I SEEM TO BE HAVING SOME LOSS OF CONTROL...
GRIP

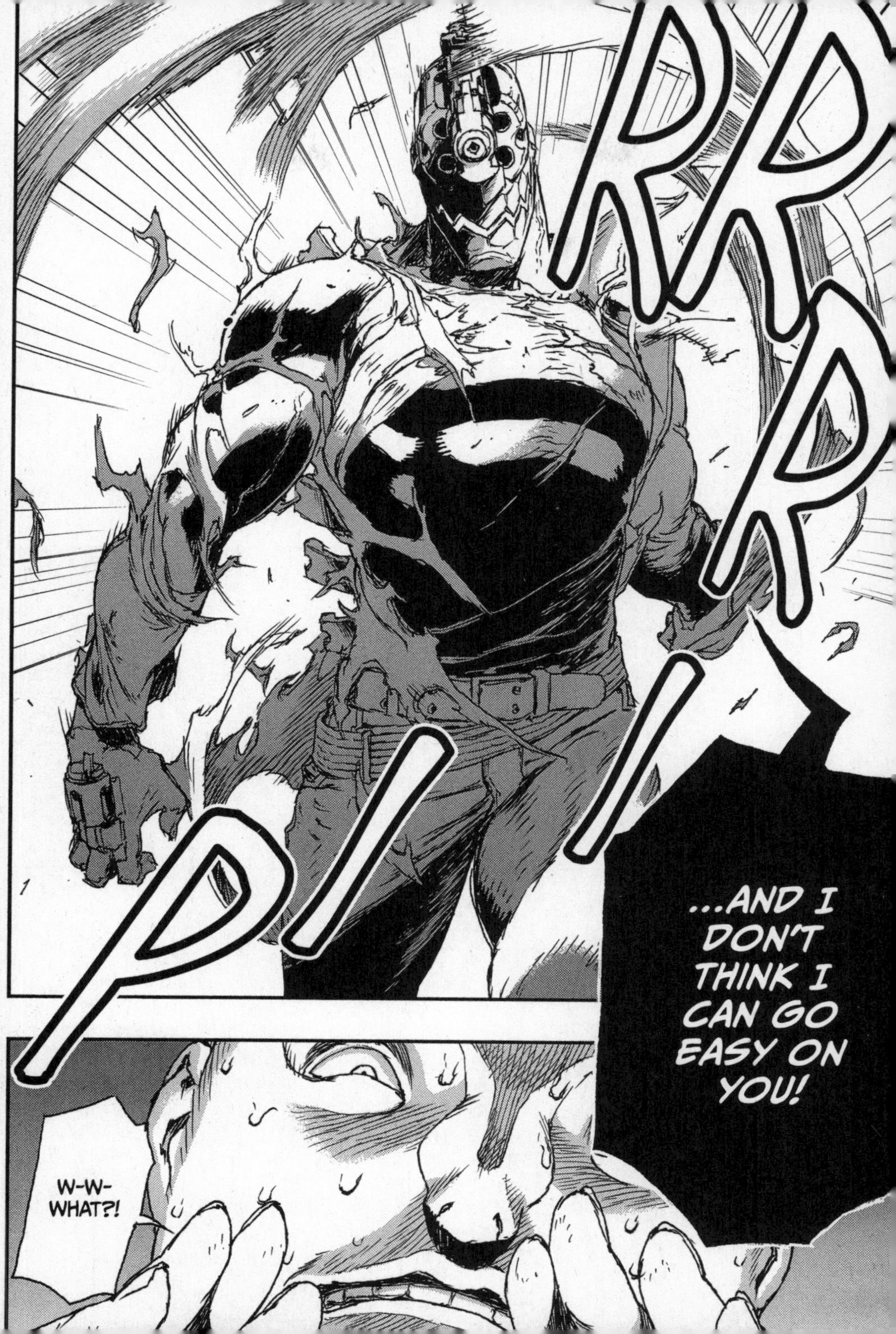
RRRRIIIIP
...AND I DON'T THINK I CAN GO EASY ON YOU!
W-W-WHAT?!

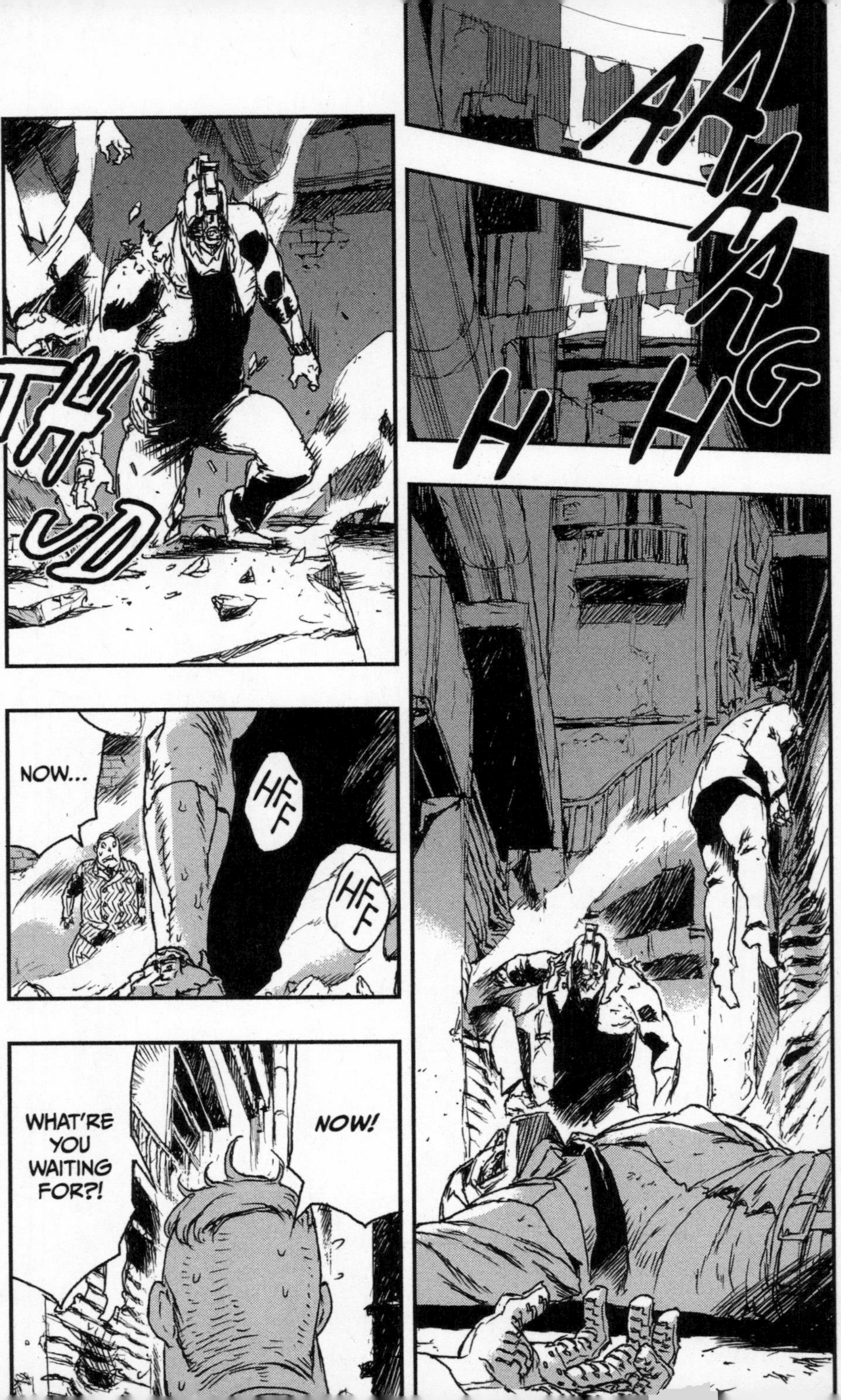
AAAAAGHH
THUD
NOW...
HFF
HFF
NOW!
WHAT'RE YOU WAITING FOR?!

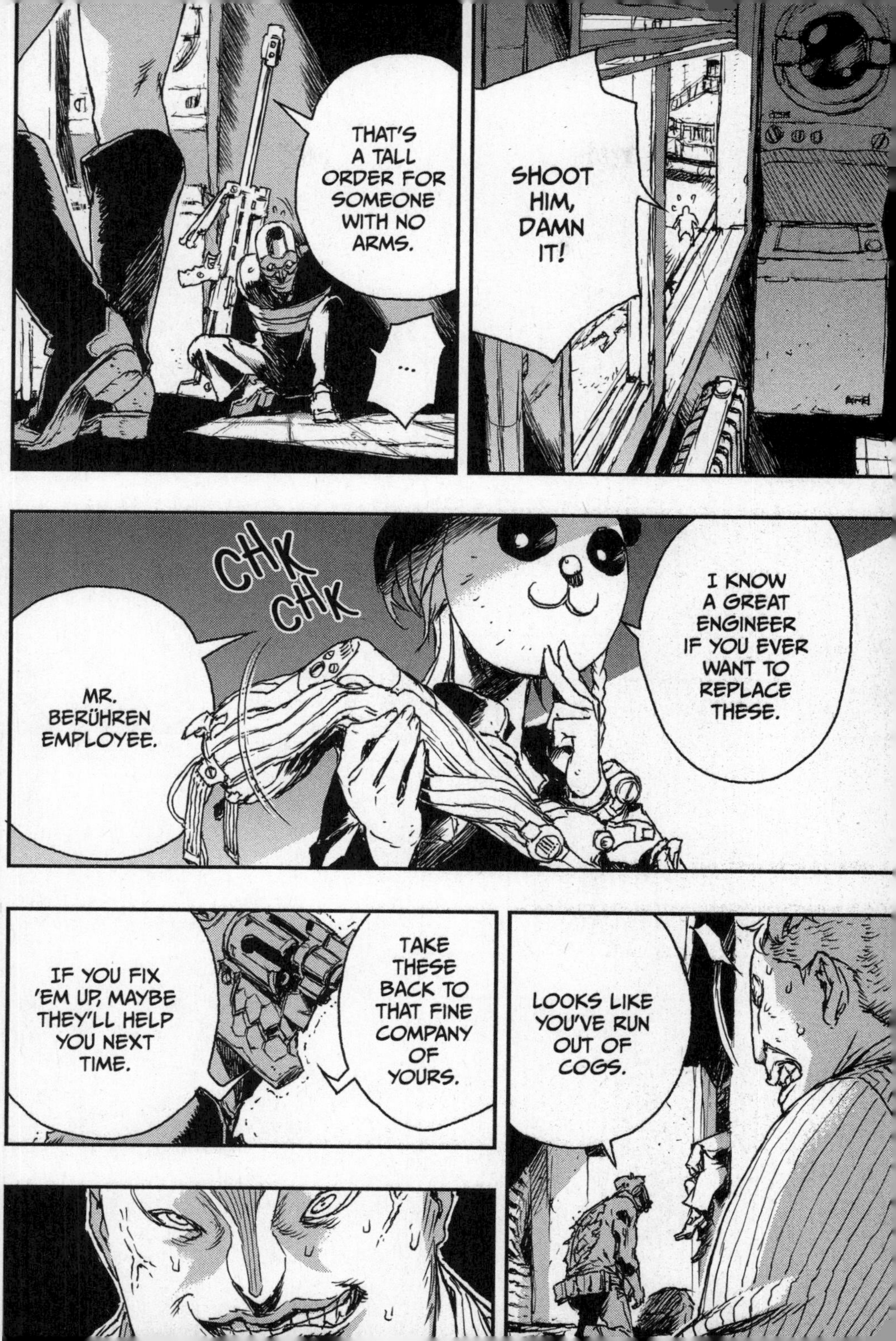
SHOOT HIM, DAMN IT!
THAT'S A TALL ORDER FOR SOMEONE WITH NO ARMS.
...
I KNOW A GREAT ENGINEER IF YOU EVER WANT TO REPLACE THESE.
CHK CHK
MR. BERÜHREN EMPLOYEE.
LOOKS LIKE YOU'VE RUN OUT OF COGS.
TAKE THESE BACK TO THAT FINE COMPANY OF YOURS.
IF YOU FIX 'EM UP, MAYBE THEY'LL HELP YOU NEXT TIME.

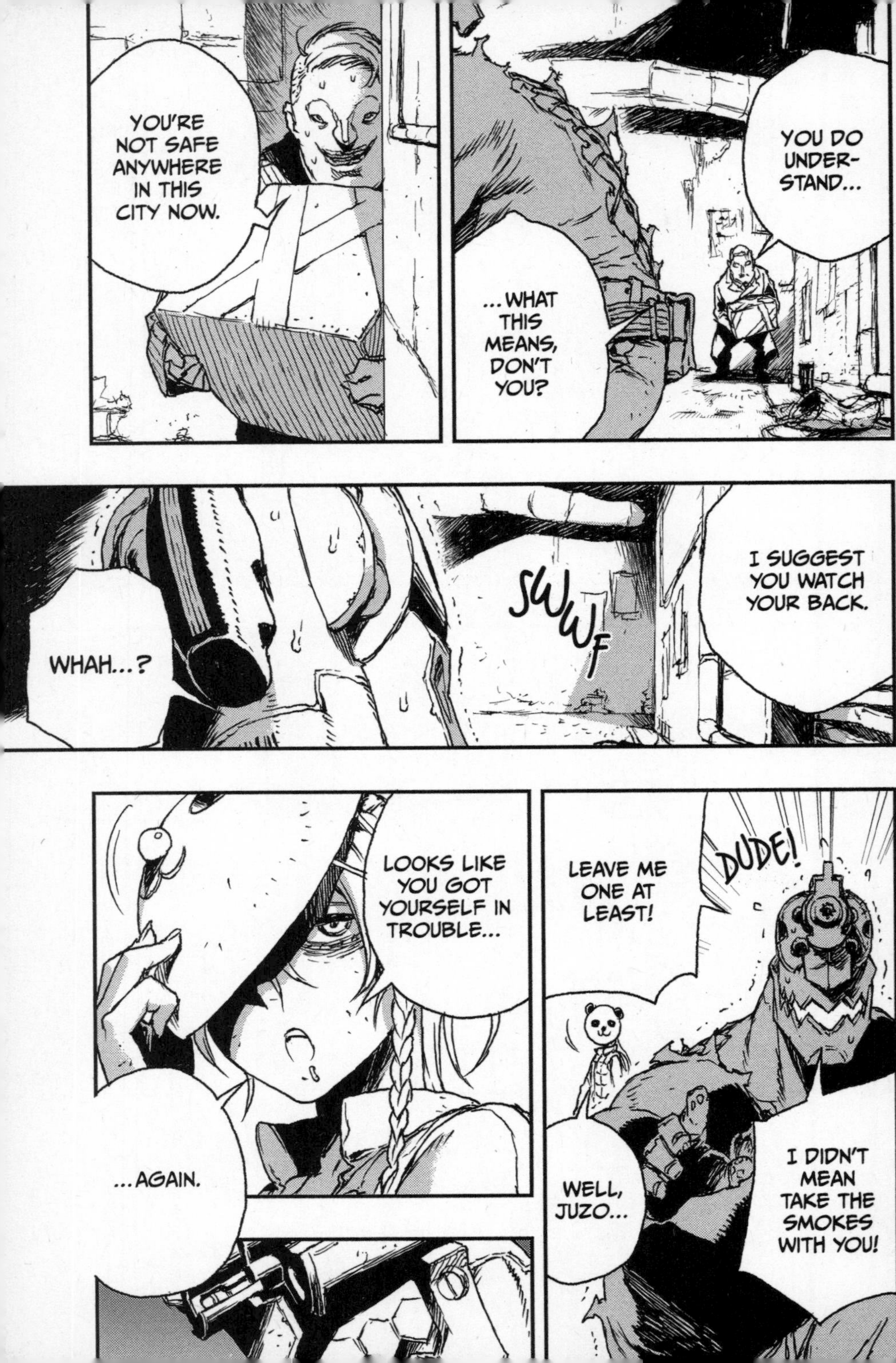
YOU DO UNDER-STAND...
...WHAT THIS MEANS, DON'T YOU?
YOU'RE NOT SAFE ANYWHERE IN THIS CITY NOW.
I SUGGEST YOU WATCH YOUR BACK.
SWWF
WHAH...?
DUDE!
LEAVE ME ONE AT LEAST!
I DIDN'T MEAN TAKE THE SMOKES WITH YOU!
WELL, JUZO...
LOOKS LIKE YOU GOT YOURSELF IN TROUBLE...
...AGAIN.

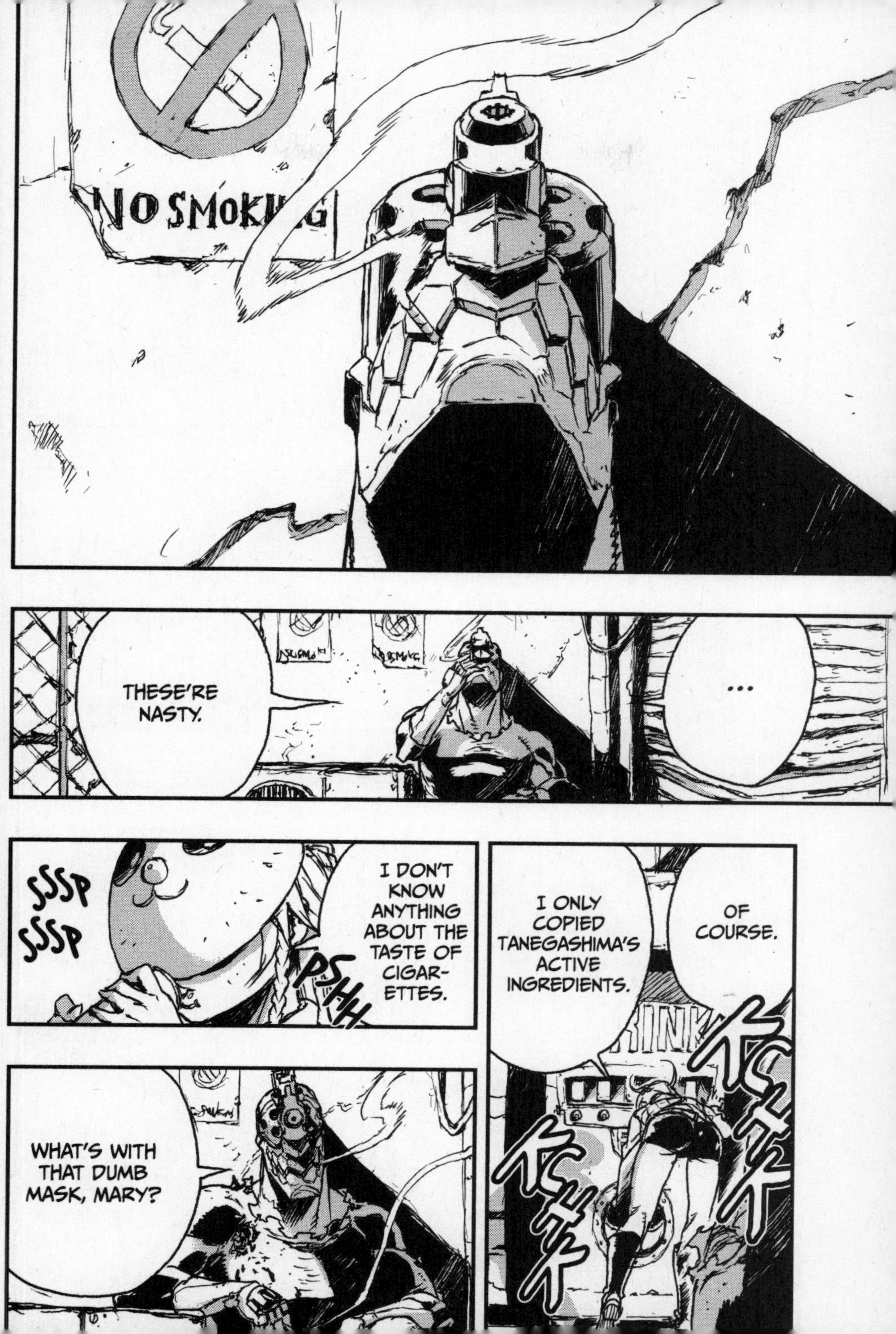
NO SMOKING
...
THESE'RE NASTY.
OF COURSE.
I ONLY COPIED TANEGASHIMA'S ACTIVE INGREDIENTS.
KCHK
KCHK
I DON'T KNOW ANYTHING ABOUT THE TASTE OF CIGAR-ETTES.
SSSP SSSP
PSHH
WHAT'S WITH THAT DUMB MASK, MARY?

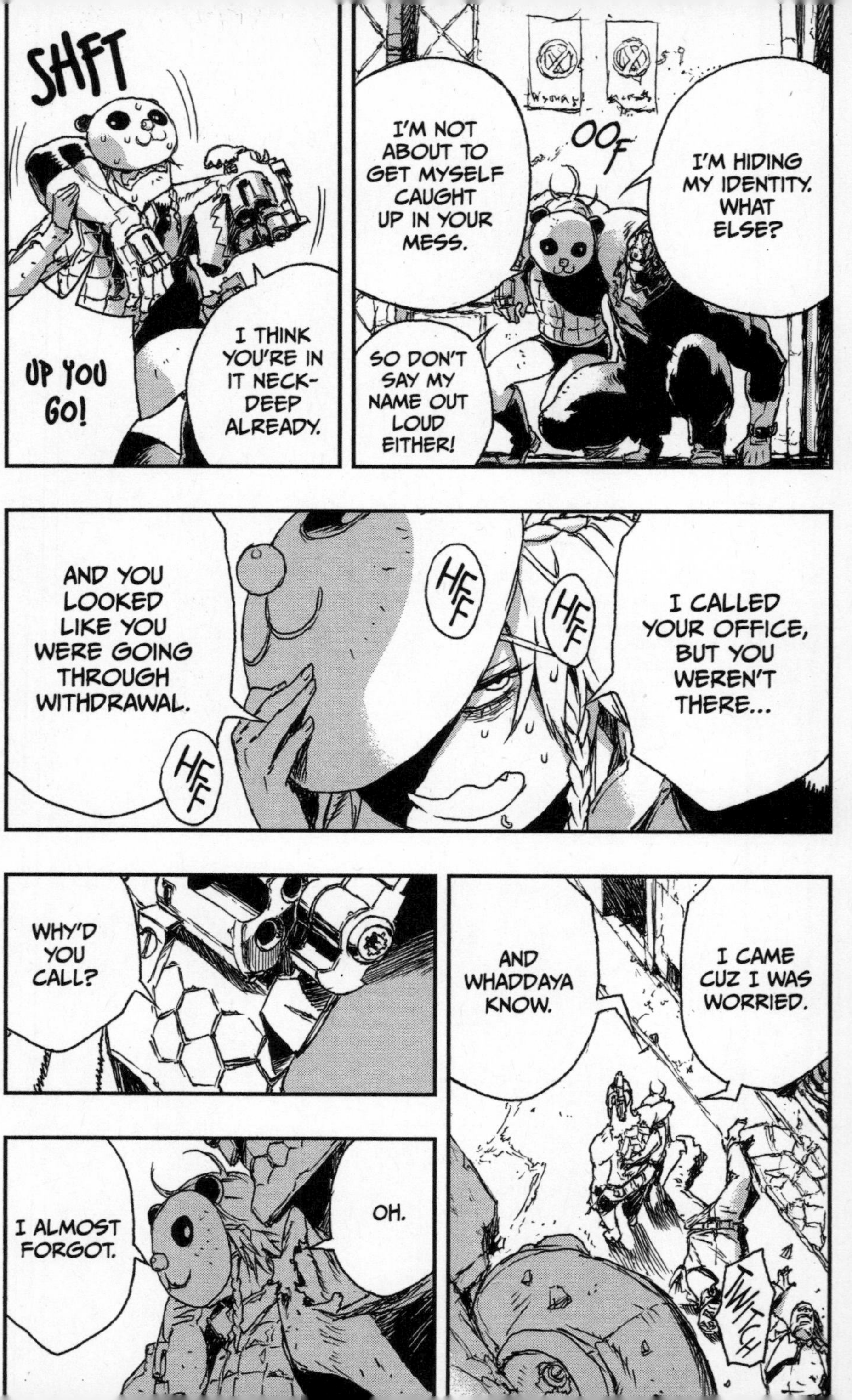
I'M HIDING MY IDENTITY. WHAT ELSE?
OOF
I'M NOT ABOUT TO GET MYSELF CAUGHT UP IN YOUR MESS.
SO DON'T SAY MY NAME OUT LOUD EITHER!
SHFT
I THINK YOU'RE IN IT NECK-DEEP ALREADY.
UP YOU GO!
HEFF
HEFF
I CALLED YOUR OFFICE, BUT YOU WEREN'T THERE...
HEFF
AND YOU LOOKED LIKE YOU WERE GOING THROUGH WITHDRAWAL.
I CAME CUZ I WAS WORRIED.
AND WHADDAYA KNOW.
TWITCH
WHY'D YOU CALL?
OH.
I ALMOST FORGOT.

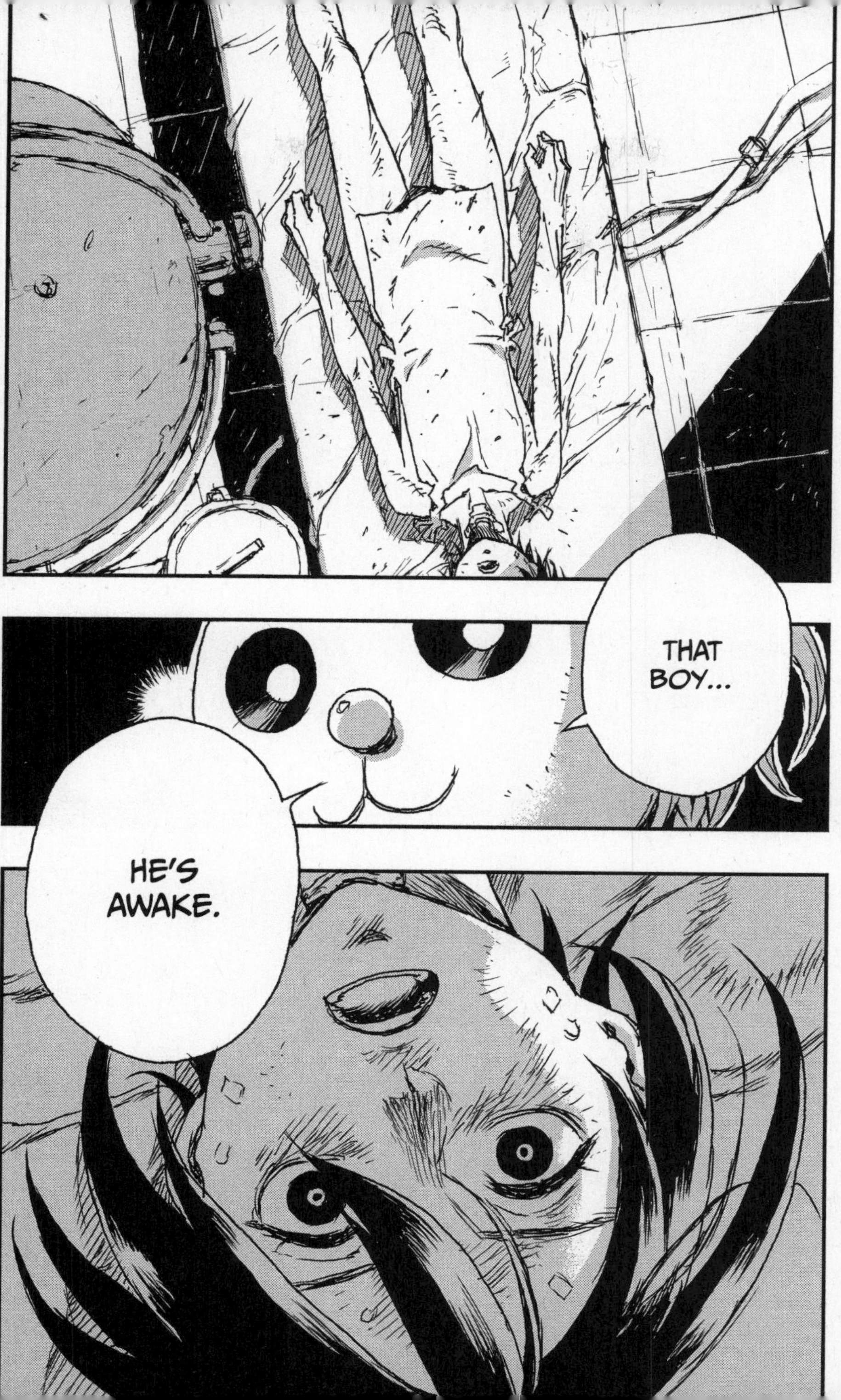
THAT BOY...
HE'S AWAKE.

NO GUNS LIFE

The gunsmoke drifts, the muzzle talks

NO

GUNS

LIFE

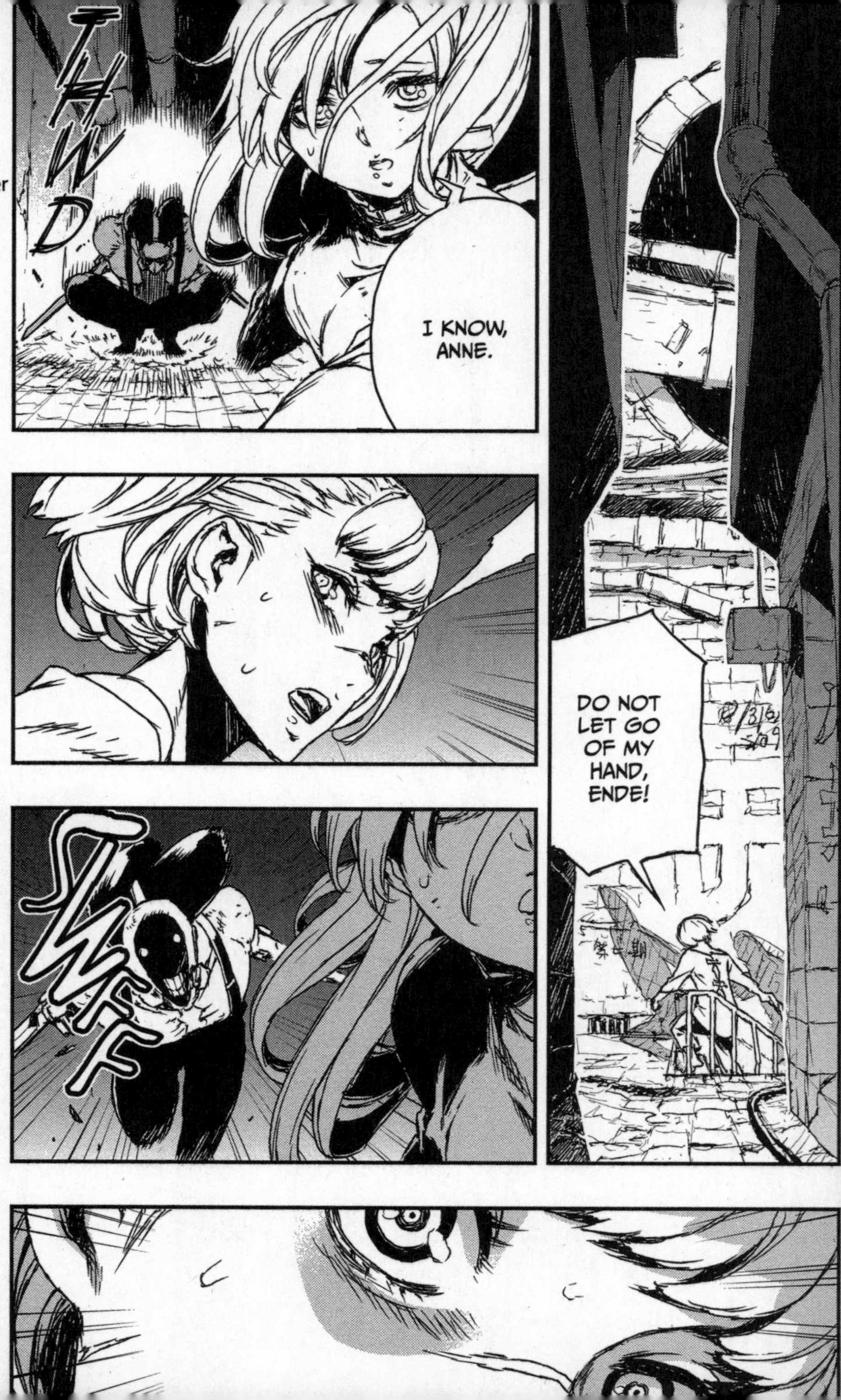
DO NOT LET GO OF MY HAND, ENDE!
THWD
I KNOW, ANNE.
SWFF

Chapter 4
Puppet

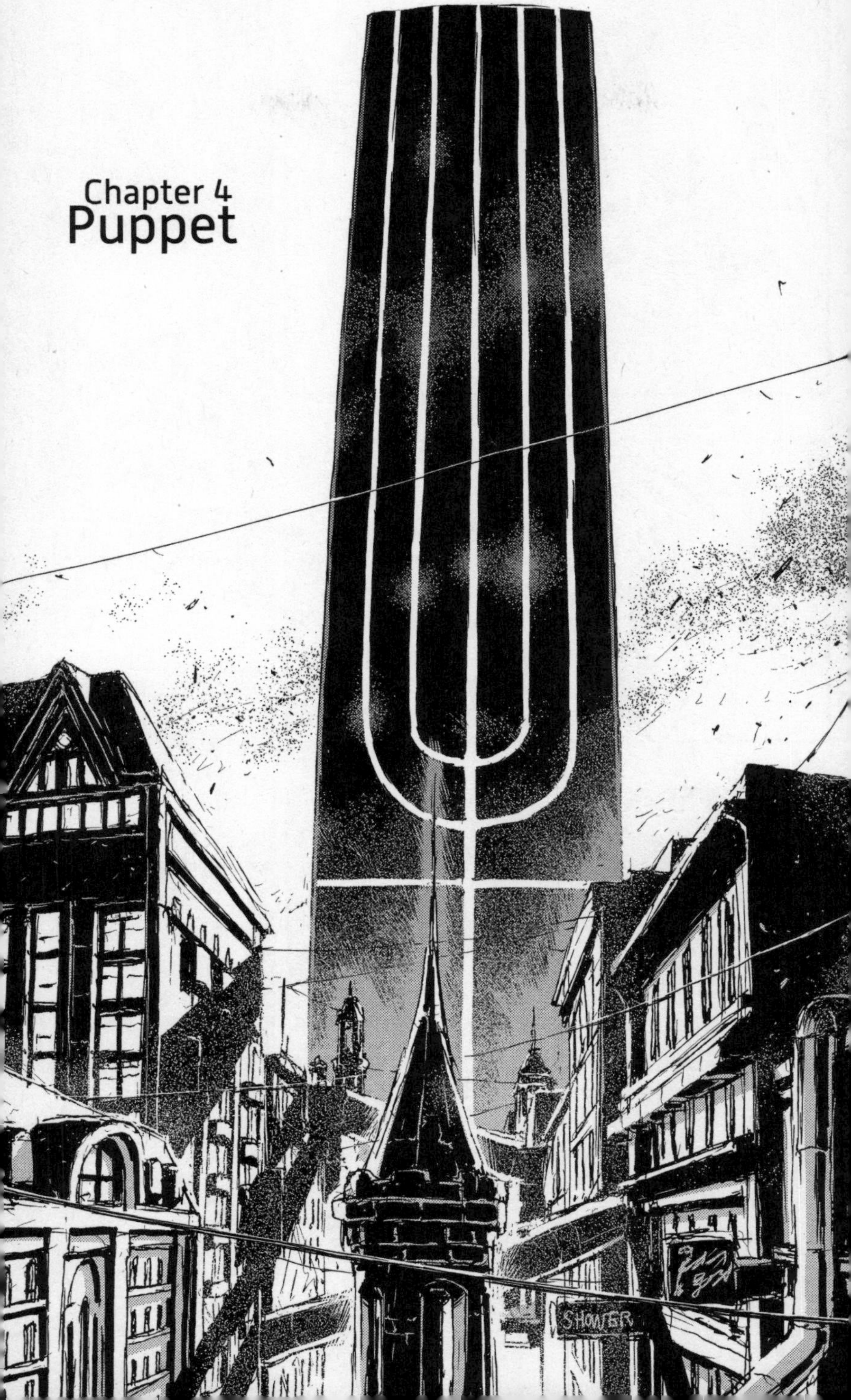
SHOWER

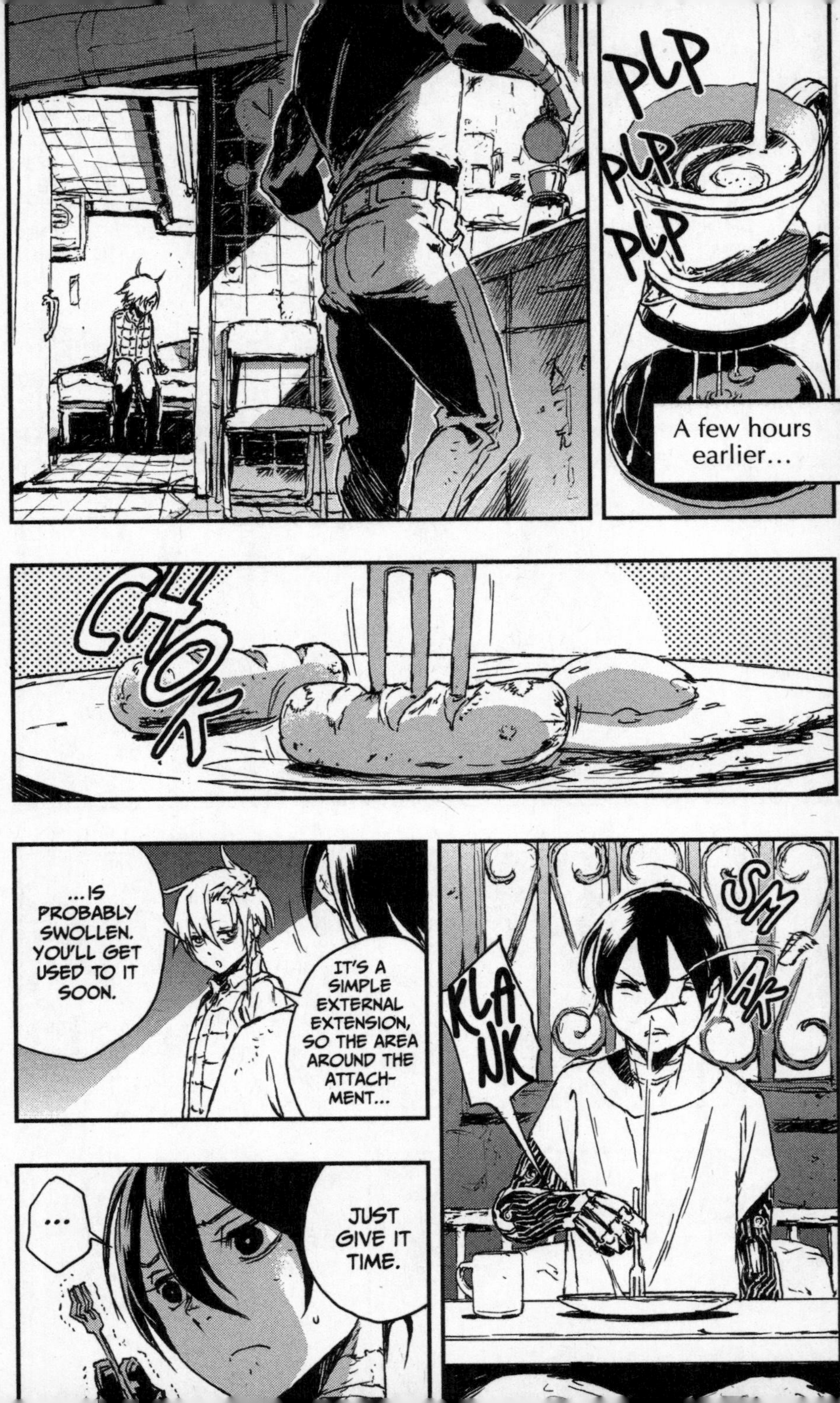
PLP
PLP
PLP
A few hours earlier…
CHOK
SMAK
KLANK
IT'S A SIMPLE EXTERNAL EXTENSION, SO THE AREA AROUND THE ATTACH-MENT…
…IS PROBABLY SWOLLEN. YOU'LL GET USED TO IT SOON.
JUST GIVE IT TIME.
…

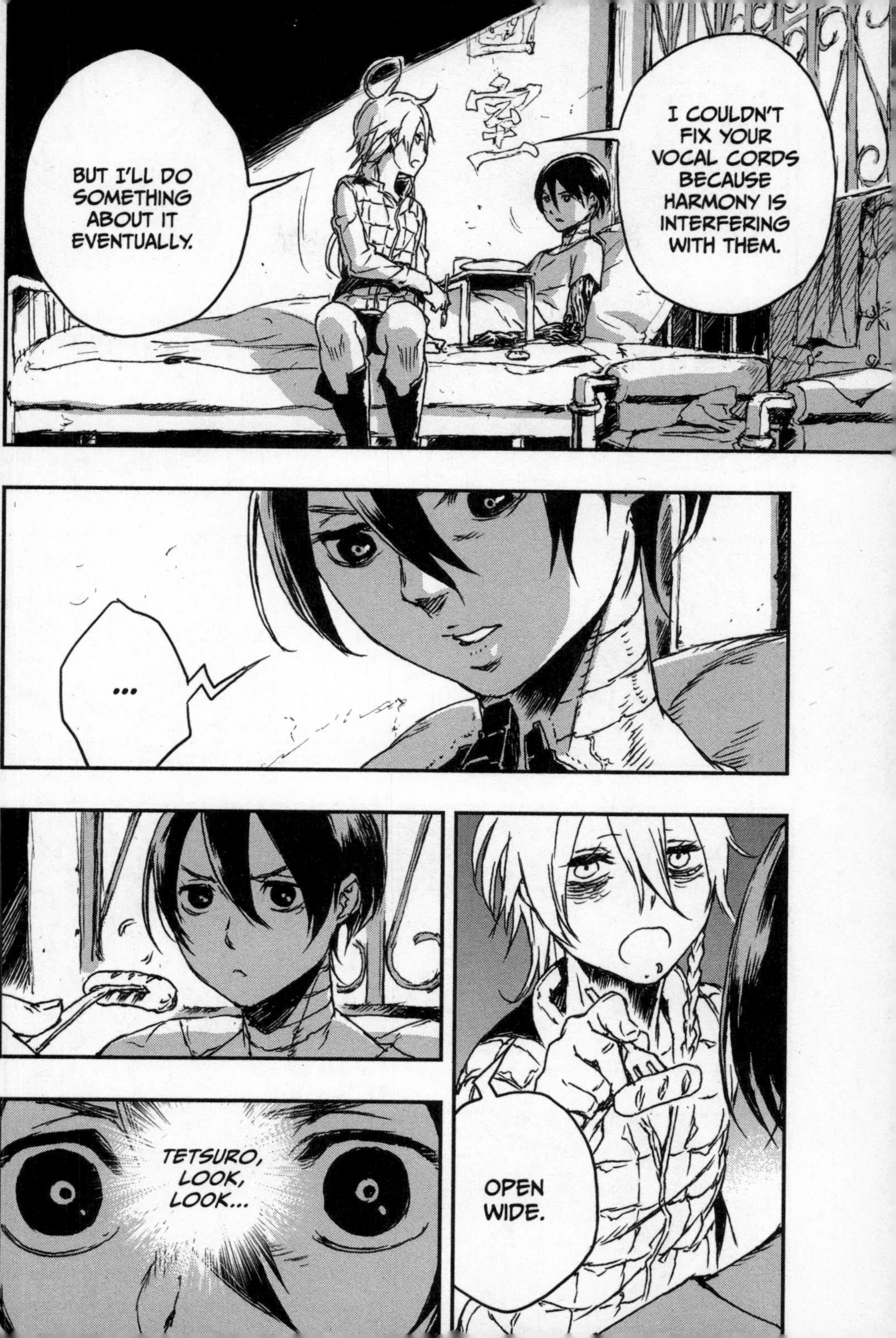
I COULDN'T FIX YOUR VOCAL CORDS BECAUSE HARMONY IS INTERFERING WITH THEM.
BUT I'LL DO SOMETHING ABOUT IT EVENTUALLY.
...
OPEN WIDE.
TETSURO, LOOK, LOOK...

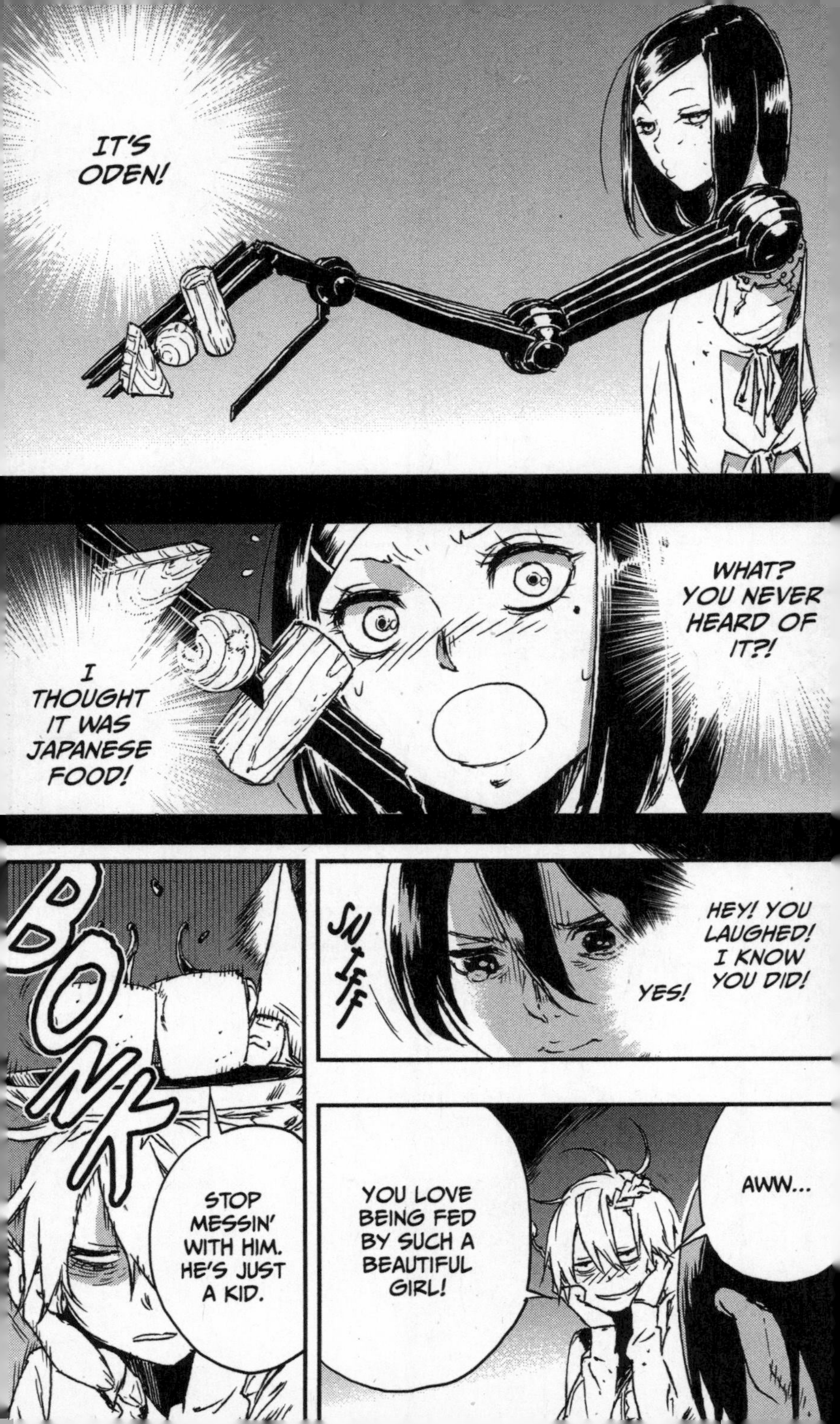
IT'S ODEN!
WHAT? YOU NEVER HEARD OF IT?!
I THOUGHT IT WAS JAPANESE FOOD!
HEY! YOU LAUGHED! I KNOW YOU DID!
YES!
SNIFF
AWW...
YOU LOVE BEING FED BY SUCH A BEAUTIFUL GIRL!
BONK
STOP MESSIN' WITH HIM. HE'S JUST A KID.

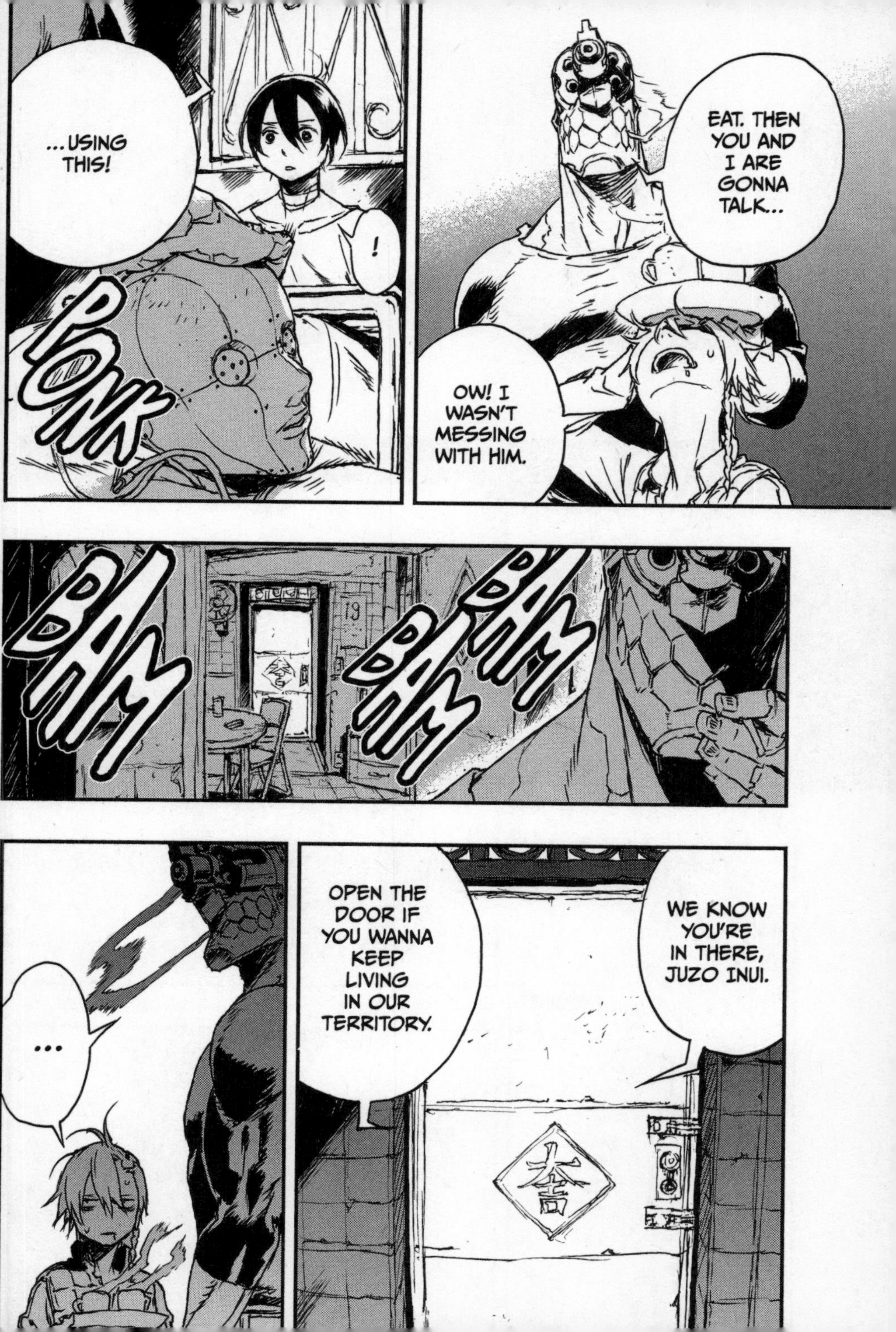
EAT. THEN YOU AND I ARE GONNA TALK...
OW! I WASN'T MESSING WITH HIM.
...USING THIS!
!
PONK
BHM BHM
BHM BHM
WE KNOW YOU'RE IN THERE, JUZO INUI.
OPEN THE DOOR IF YOU WANNA KEEP LIVING IN OUR TERRITORY.
...

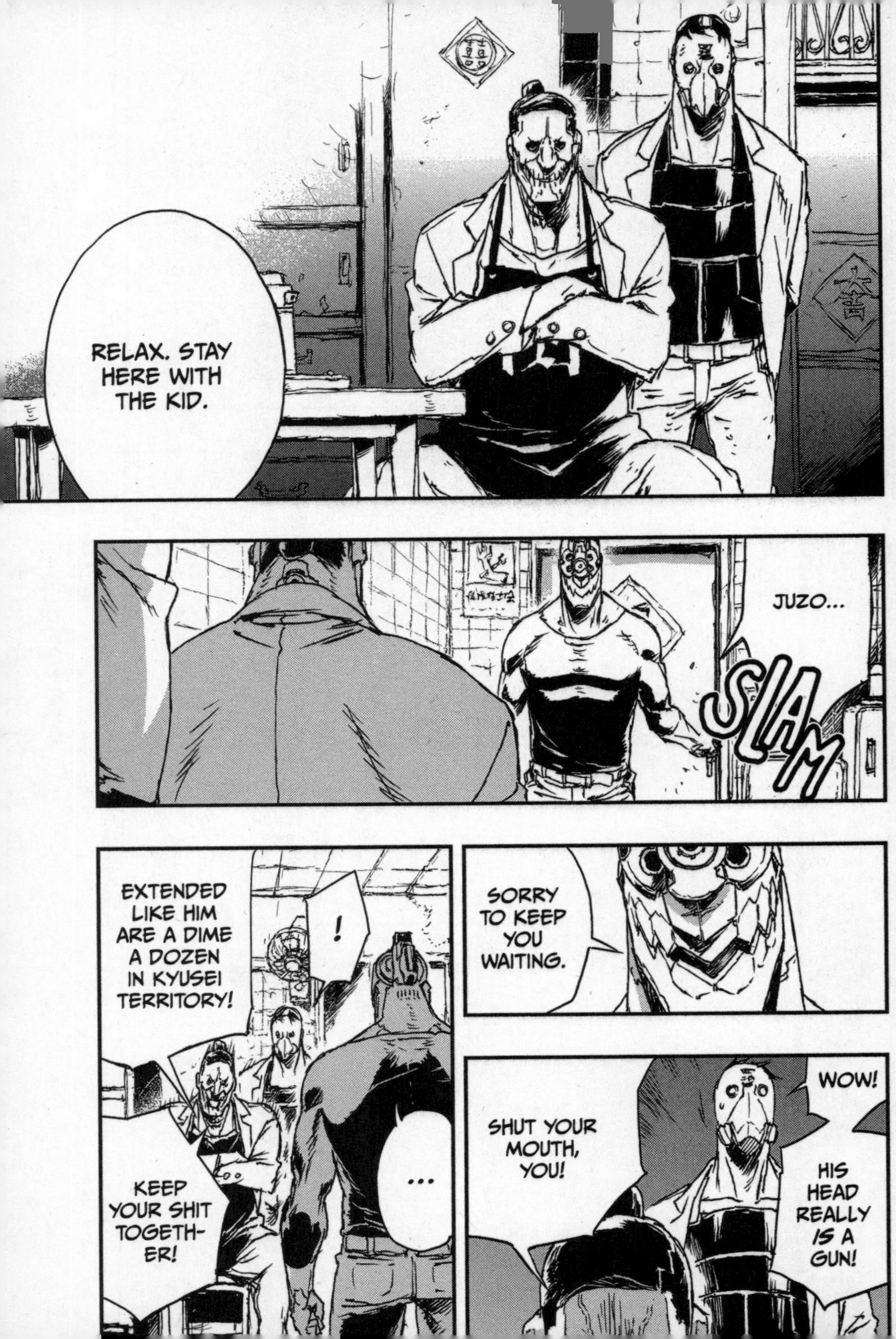
RELAX. STAY HERE WITH THE KID.
JUZO...
SLAM
SORRY TO KEEP YOU WAITING.
WOW!
HIS HEAD REALLY IS A GUN!
SHUT YOUR MOUTH, YOU!
!
EXTENDED LIKE HIM ARE A DIME A DOZEN IN KYUSEI TERRITORY!
...
KEEP YOUR SHIT TOGETH-ER!

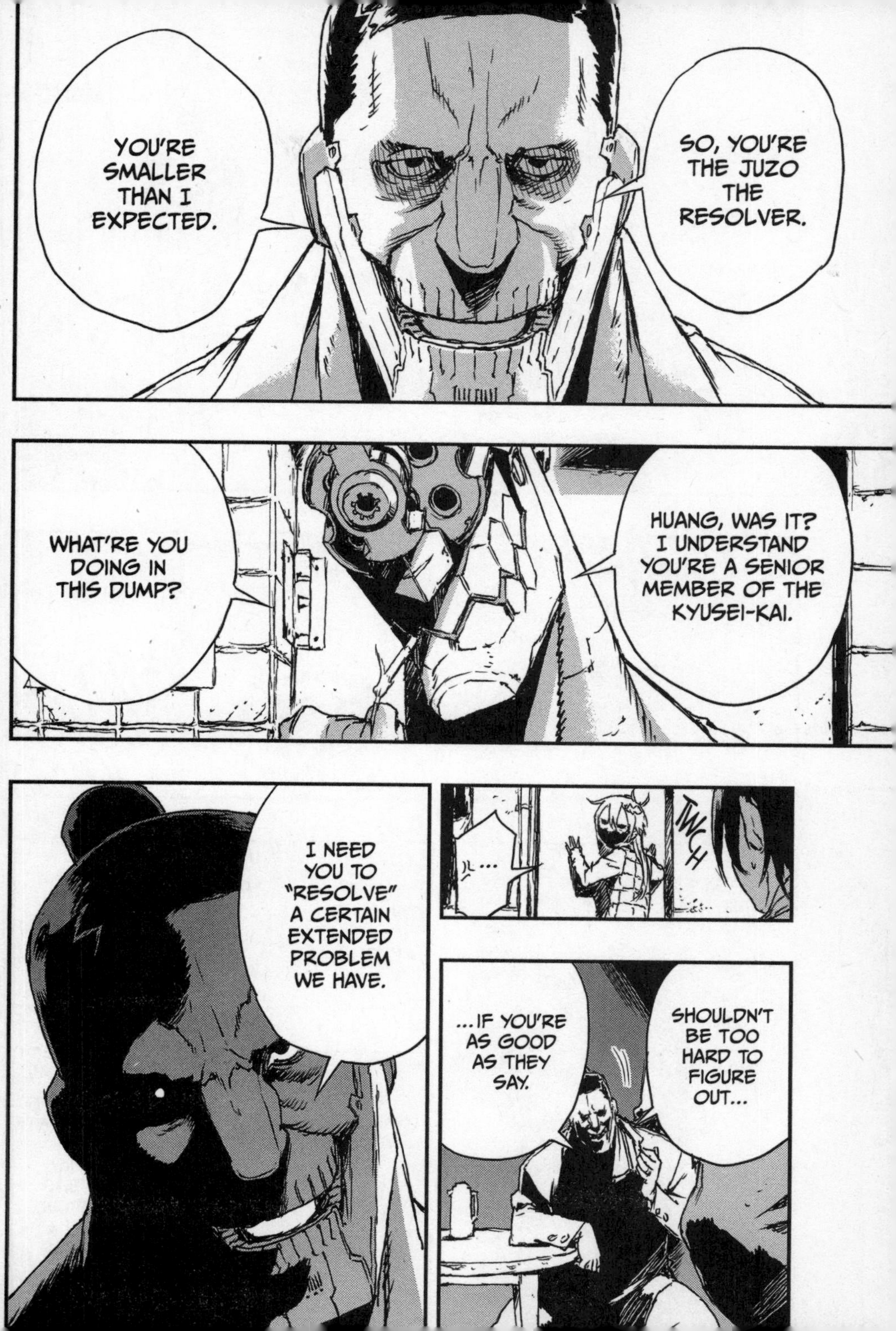
SO, YOU'RE THE JUZO THE RESOLVER.
YOU'RE SMALLER THAN I EXPECTED.
HUANG, WAS IT? I UNDERSTAND YOU'RE A SENIOR MEMBER OF THE KYUSEI-KAI.
WHAT'RE YOU DOING IN THIS DUMP?
TWCH
...
SHOULDN'T BE TOO HARD TO FIGURE OUT...
...IF YOU'RE AS GOOD AS THEY SAY.
I NEED YOU TO "RESOLVE" A CERTAIN EXTENDED PROBLEM WE HAVE.

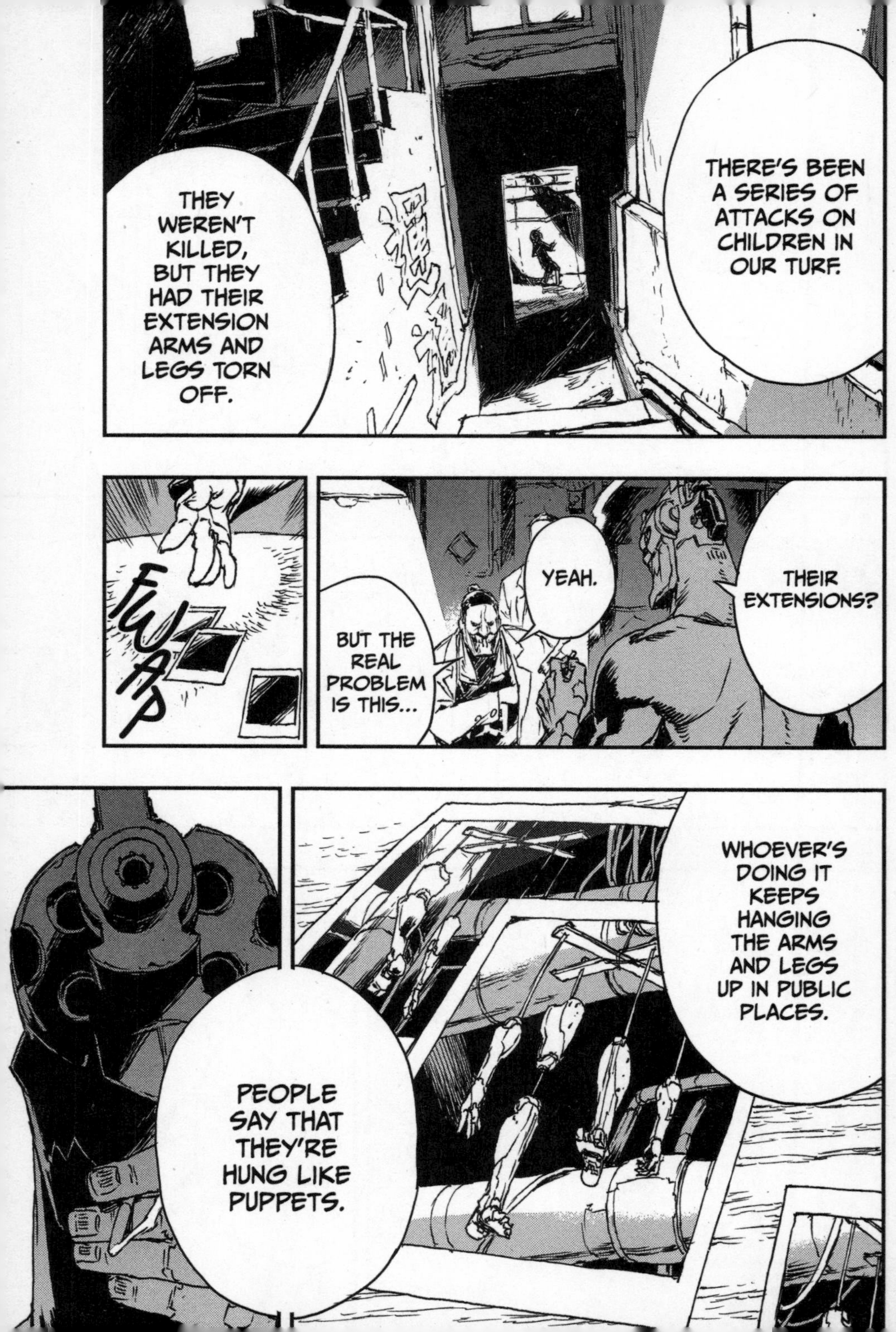
THERE'S BEEN A SERIES OF ATTACKS ON CHILDREN IN OUR TURF.
THEY WEREN'T KILLED, BUT THEY HAD THEIR EXTENSION ARMS AND LEGS TORN OFF.
THEIR EXTENSIONS?
YEAH.
BUT THE REAL PROBLEM IS THIS...
FWAP
WHOEVER'S DOING IT KEEPS HANGING THE ARMS AND LEGS UP IN PUBLIC PLACES.
PEOPLE SAY THAT THEY'RE HUNG LIKE PUPPETS.

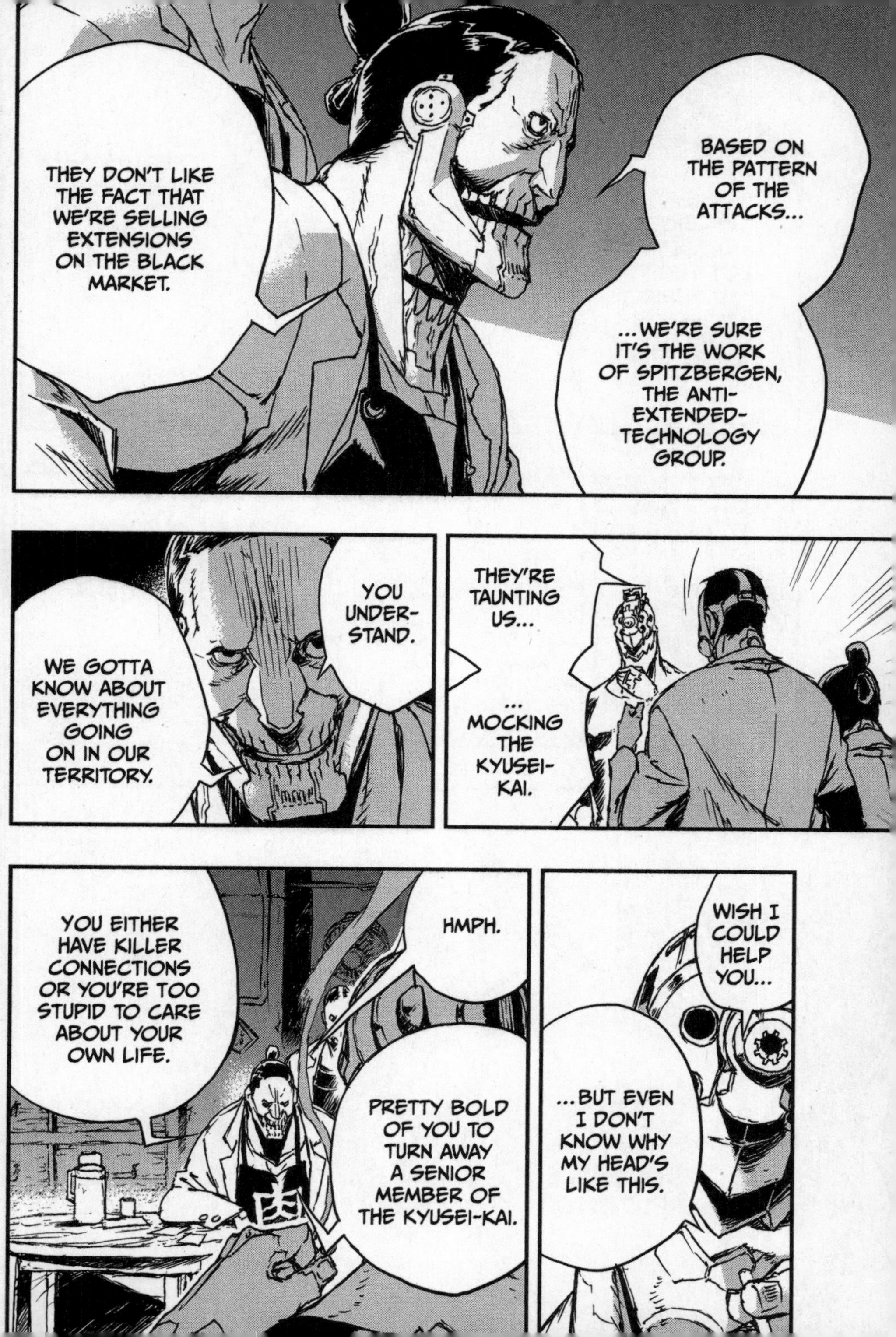
BASED ON THE PATTERN OF THE ATTACKS...
...WE'RE SURE IT'S THE WORK OF SPITZBERGEN, THE ANTI-EXTENDED-TECHNOLOGY GROUP.
THEY DON'T LIKE THE FACT THAT WE'RE SELLING EXTENSIONS ON THE BLACK MARKET.
THEY'RE TAUNTING US...
...MOCKING THE KYUSEI-KAI.
YOU UNDER-STAND.
WE GOTTA KNOW ABOUT EVERYTHING GOING ON IN OUR TERRITORY.
WISH I COULD HELP YOU...
...BUT EVEN I DON'T KNOW WHY MY HEAD'S LIKE THIS.
HMPH.
PRETTY BOLD OF YOU TO TURN AWAY A SENIOR MEMBER OF THE KYUSEI-KAI.
YOU EITHER HAVE KILLER CONNECTIONS OR YOU'RE TOO STUPID TO CARE ABOUT YOUR OWN LIFE.

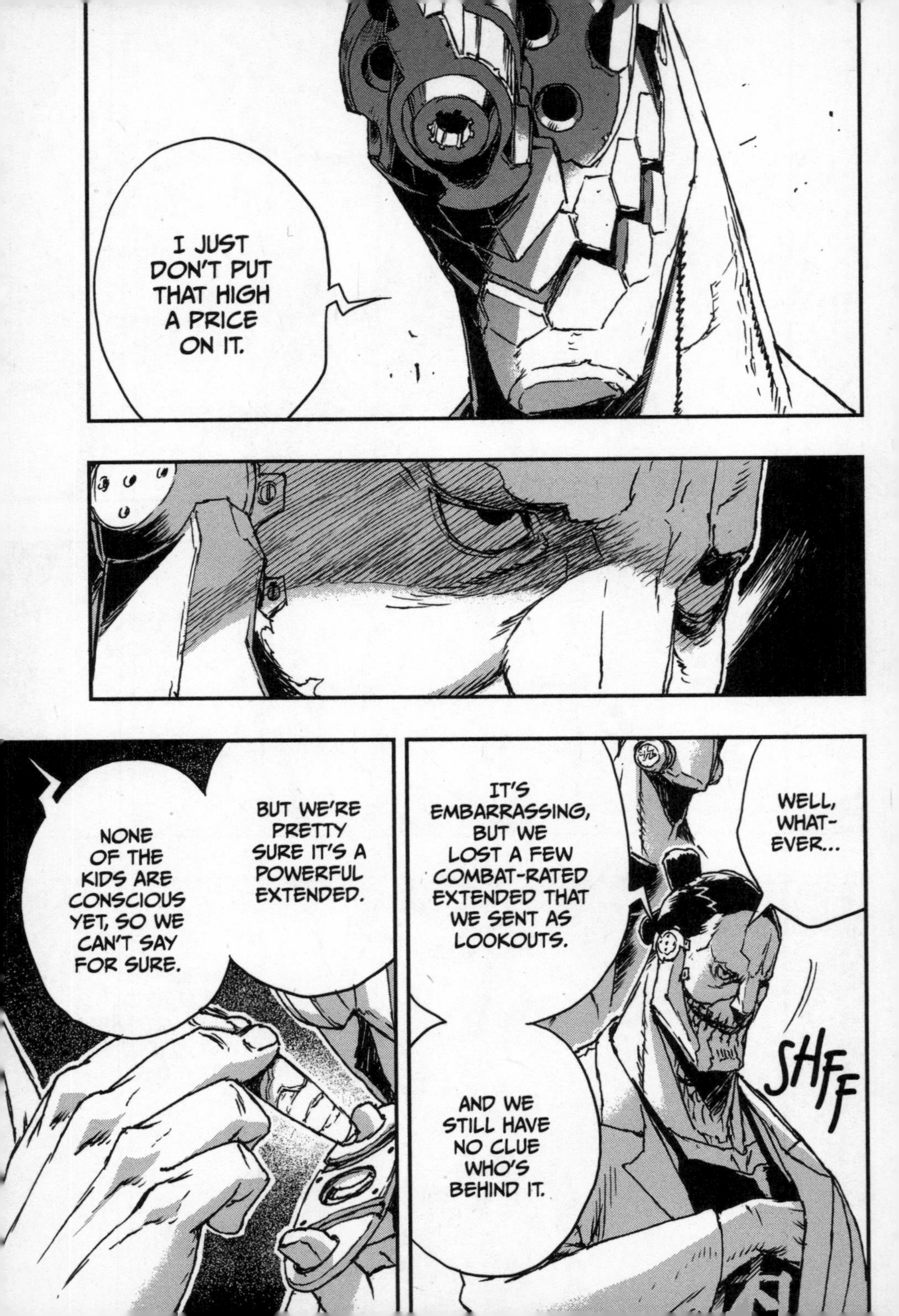
I JUST DON'T PUT THAT HIGH A PRICE ON IT.
WELL, WHAT-EVER...
IT'S EMBARRASSING, BUT WE LOST A FEW COMBAT-RATED EXTENDED THAT WE SENT AS LOOKOUTS.
AND WE STILL HAVE NO CLUE WHO'S BEHIND IT.
SHFF
NONE OF THE KIDS ARE CONSCIOUS YET, SO WE CAN'T SAY FOR SURE.
BUT WE'RE PRETTY SURE IT'S A POWERFUL EXTENDED.

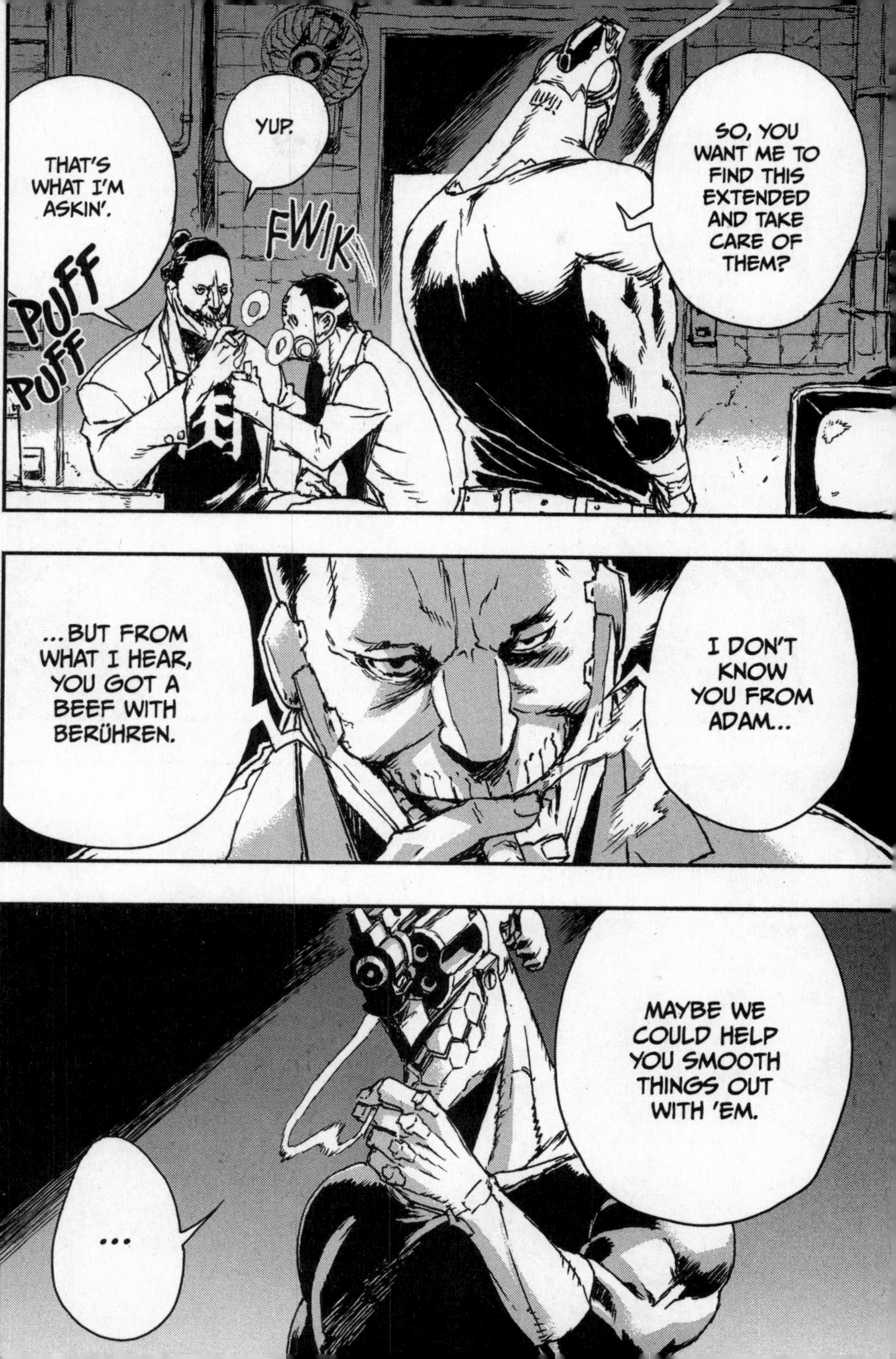
SO, YOU WANT ME TO FIND THIS EXTENDED AND TAKE CARE OF THEM?
FWIK
YUP.
THAT'S WHAT I'M ASKIN'.
PUFF PUFF
I DON'T KNOW YOU FROM ADAM...
...BUT FROM WHAT I HEAR, YOU GOT A BEEF WITH BERÜHREN.
MAYBE WE COULD HELP YOU SMOOTH THINGS OUT WITH 'EM.
...

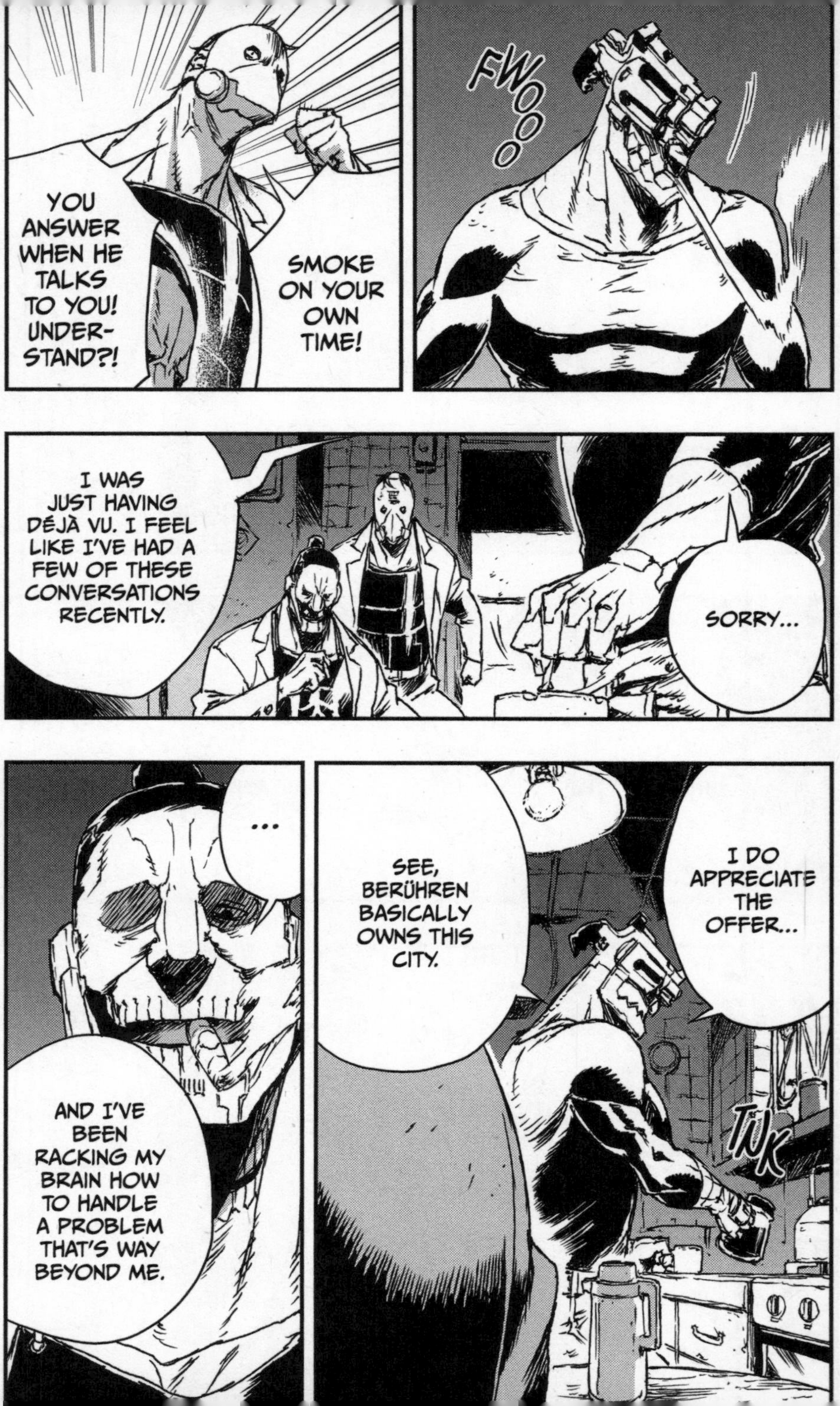
FWOOOOO
YOU ANSWER WHEN HE TALKS TO YOU! UNDER-STAND?!
SMOKE ON YOUR OWN TIME!
SORRY...
I WAS JUST HAVING DÉJÀ VU. I FEEL LIKE I'VE HAD A FEW OF THESE CONVERSATIONS RECENTLY.
I DO APPRECIATE THE OFFER...
SEE, BERÜHREN BASICALLY OWNS THIS CITY.
TUNK
...
AND I'VE BEEN RACKING MY BRAIN HOW TO HANDLE A PROBLEM THAT'S WAY BEYOND ME.

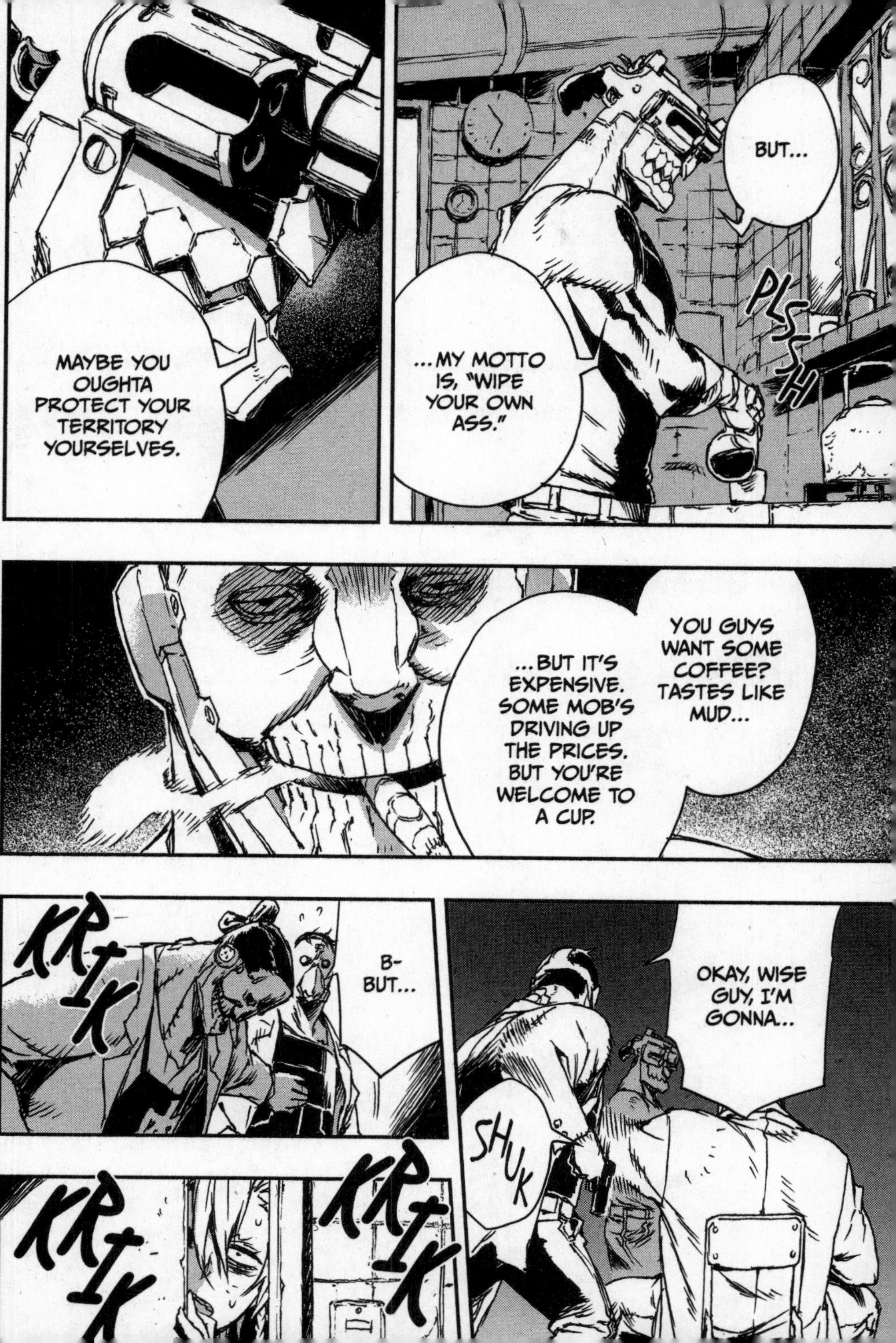
BUT...
PLSSH
...MY MOTTO IS, "WIPE YOUR OWN ASS."
MAYBE YOU OUGHTA PROTECT YOUR TERRITORY YOURSELVES.
YOU GUYS WANT SOME COFFEE? TASTES LIKE MUD...
...BUT IT'S EXPENSIVE. SOME MOB'S DRIVING UP THE PRICES. BUT YOU'RE WELCOME TO A CUP.
OKAY, WISE GUY, I'M GONNA...
SHUK
KRIK
B- BUT...
KRIK
KRIK

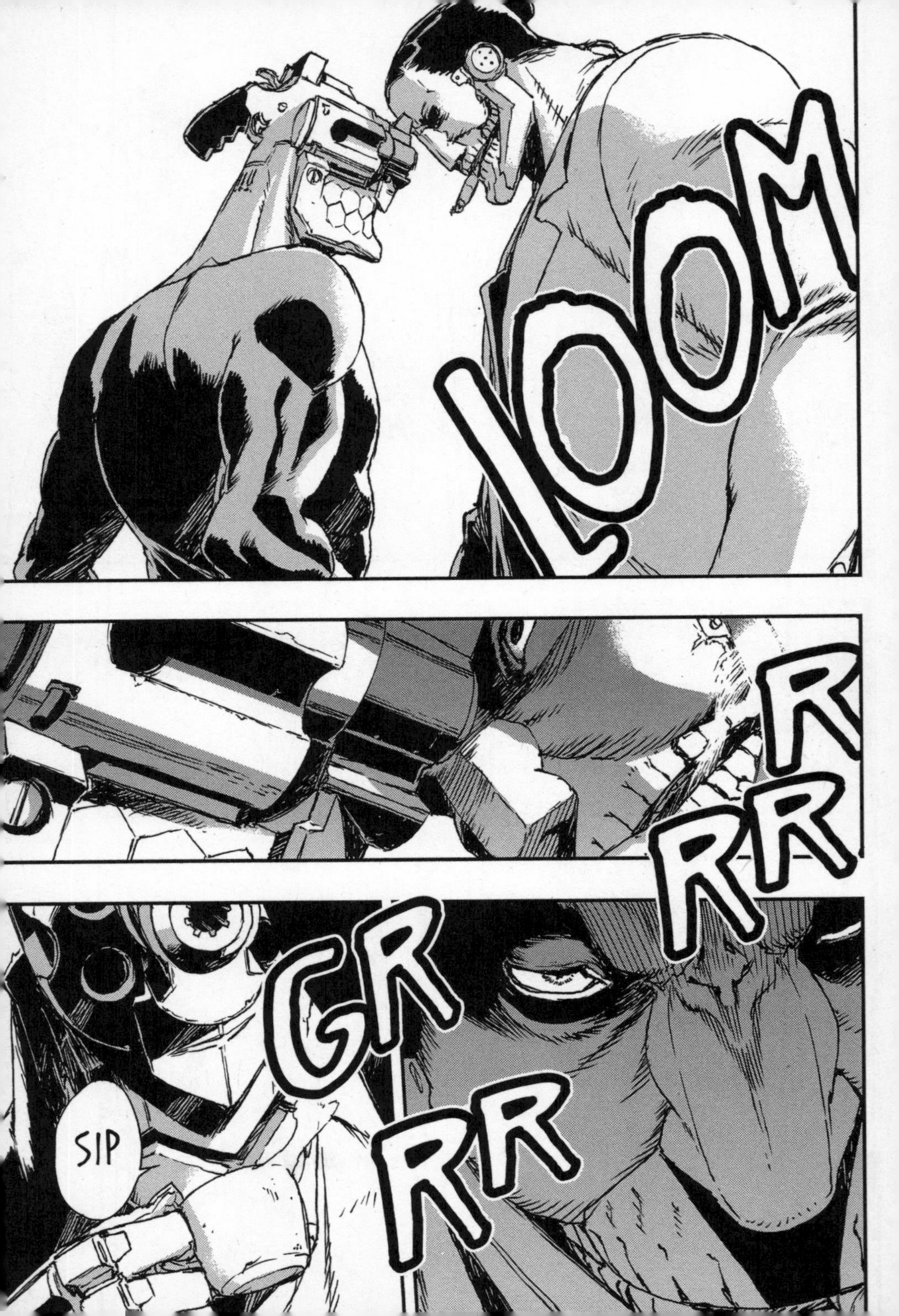
LOOM
R
RR
GR
RR
SIP

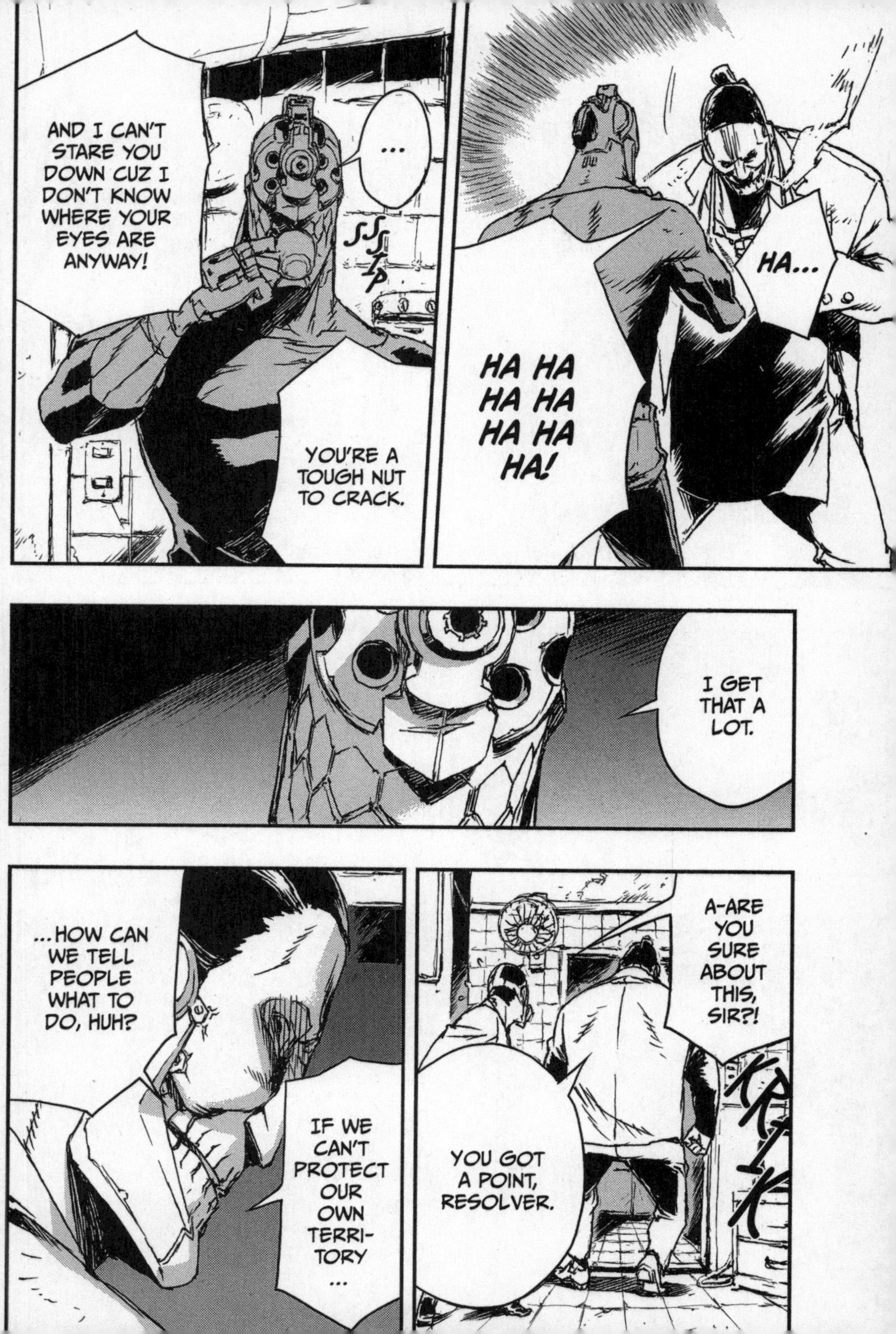
HA...
HA HA HA HA HA HA HA!
...
AND I CAN'T STARE YOU DOWN CUZ I DON'T KNOW WHERE YOUR EYES ARE ANYWAY!
SSSTP
YOU'RE A TOUGH NUT TO CRACK.
I GET THAT A LOT.
A-ARE YOU SURE ABOUT THIS, SIR?!
KRTIK
YOU GOT A POINT, RESOLVER.
IF WE CAN'T PROTECT OUR OWN TERRITORY...
...HOW CAN WE TELL PEOPLE WHAT TO DO, HUH?

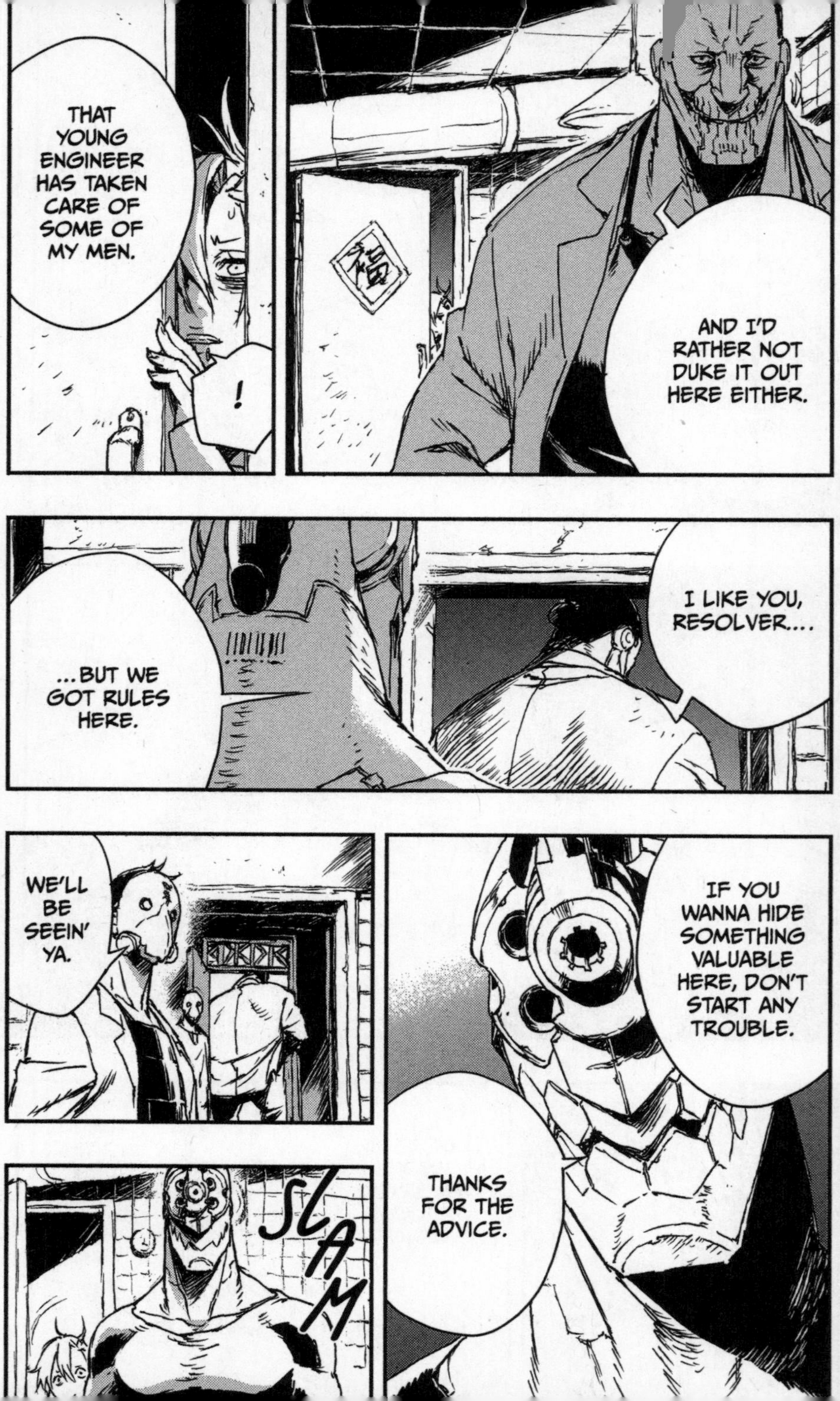
AND I'D RATHER NOT DUKE IT OUT HERE EITHER.
THAT YOUNG ENGINEER HAS TAKEN CARE OF SOME OF MY MEN.
!
I LIKE YOU, RESOLVER....
...BUT WE GOT RULES HERE.
IF YOU WANNA HIDE SOMETHING VALUABLE HERE, DON'T START ANY TROUBLE.
THANKS FOR THE ADVICE.
WE'LL BE SEEIN' YA.
SLAM

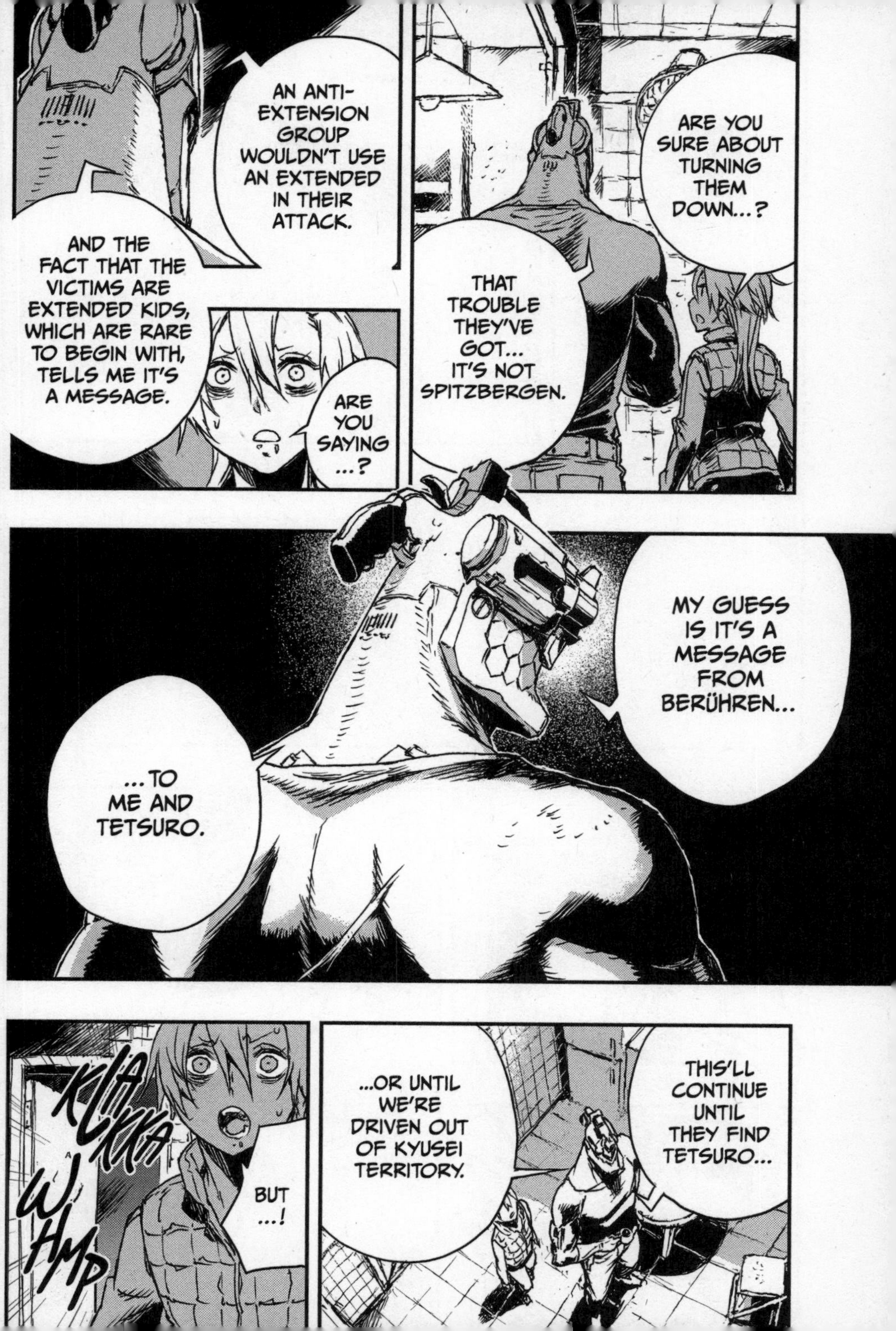
ARE YOU SURE ABOUT TURNING THEM DOWN...?
THAT TROUBLE THEY'VE GOT... IT'S NOT SPITZBERGEN.
AN ANTI-EXTENSION GROUP WOULDN'T USE AN EXTENDED IN THEIR ATTACK.
AND THE FACT THAT THE VICTIMS ARE EXTENDED KIDS, WHICH ARE RARE TO BEGIN WITH, TELLS ME IT'S A MESSAGE.
ARE YOU SAYING...?
MY GUESS IS IT'S A MESSAGE FROM BERÜHREN...
...TO ME AND TETSURO.
THIS'LL CONTINUE UNTIL THEY FIND TETSURO...
...OR UNTIL WE'RE DRIVEN OUT OF KYUSEI TERRITORY.
BUT...!
KLAKKA
WHMP

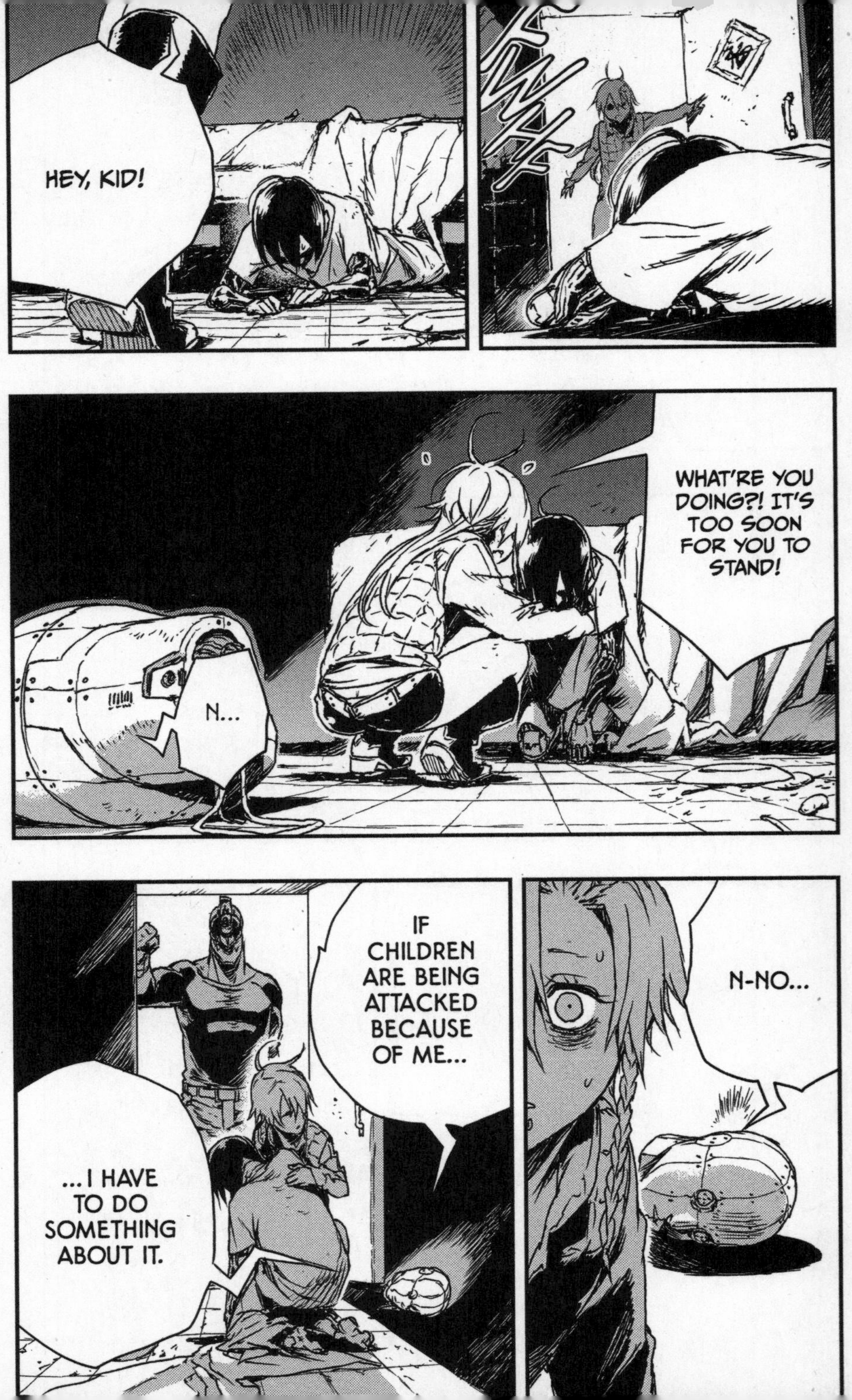
HEY, KID!
WHAT'RE YOU DOING?! IT'S TOO SOON FOR YOU TO STAND!
N...
N-NO...
IF CHILDREN ARE BEING ATTACKED BECAUSE OF ME...
...I HAVE TO DO SOMETHING ABOUT IT.

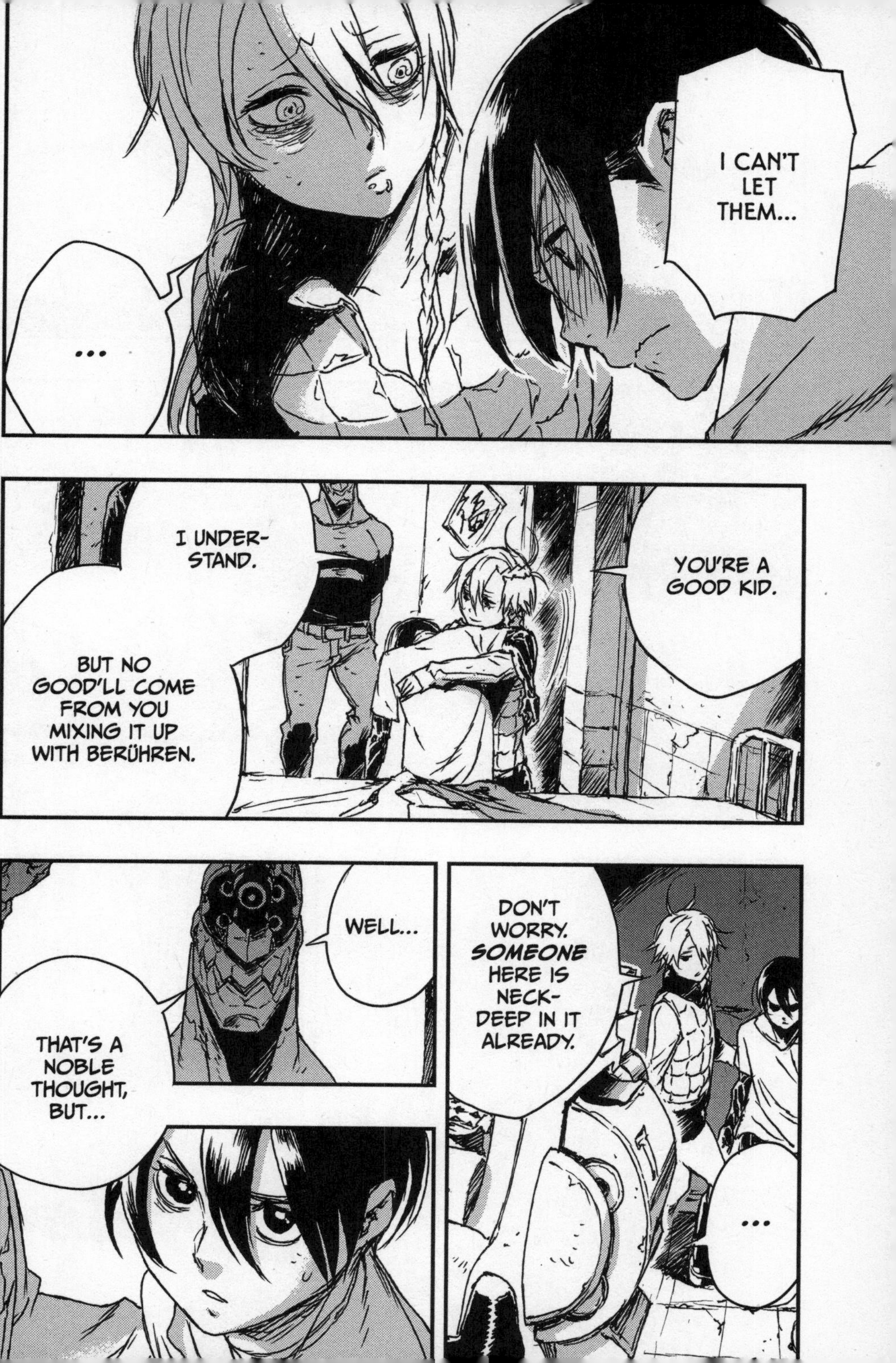
I CAN'T LET THEM...
...
YOU'RE A GOOD KID.
I UNDER-STAND.
BUT NO GOOD'LL COME FROM YOU MIXING IT UP WITH BERÜHREN.
DON'T WORRY. ***SOMEONE*** HERE IS NECK-DEEP IN IT ALREADY.
...
WELL...
THAT'S A NOBLE THOUGHT, BUT...

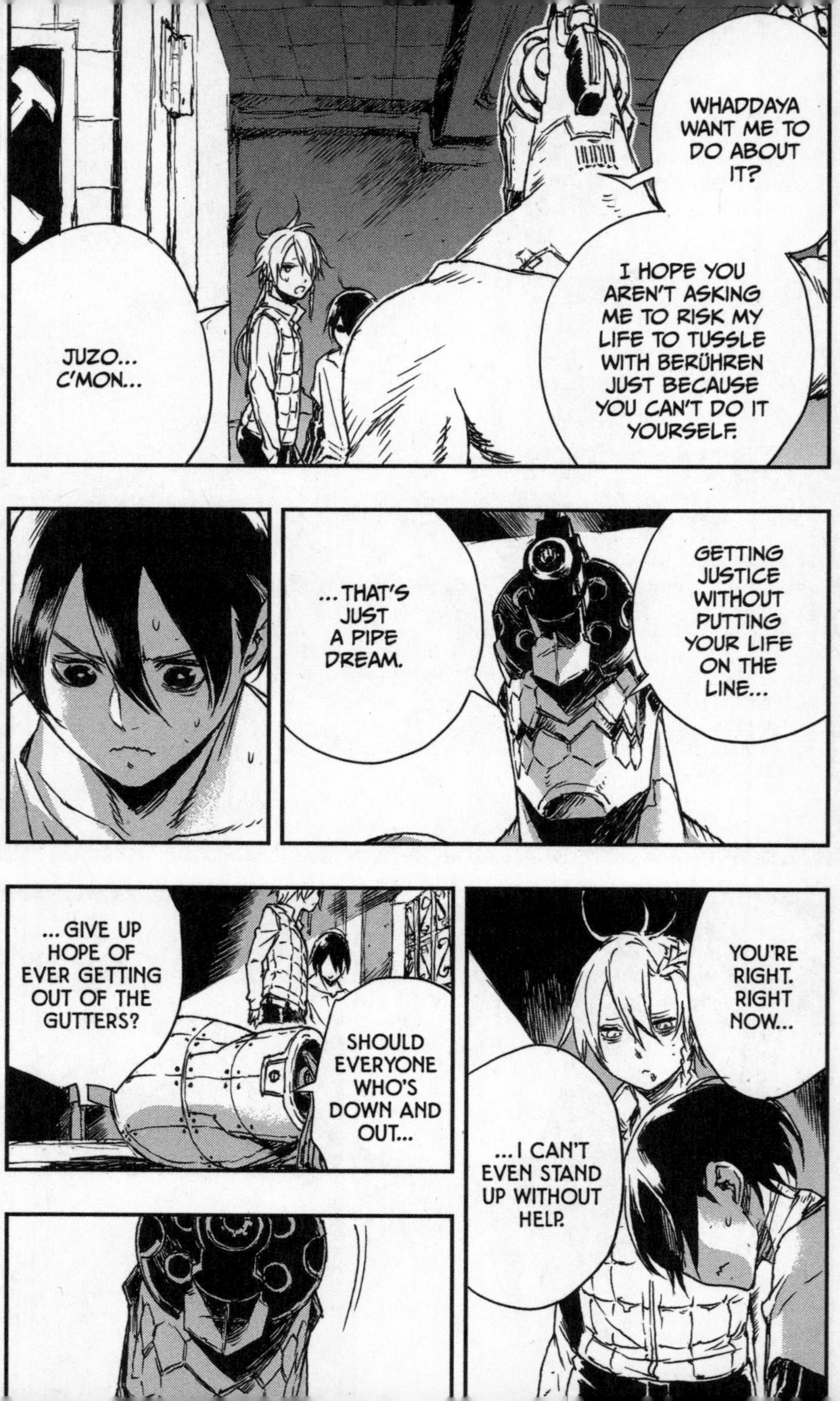
WHADDAYA WANT ME TO DO ABOUT IT?
I HOPE YOU AREN'T ASKING ME TO RISK MY LIFE TO TUSSLE WITH BERÜHREN JUST BECAUSE YOU CAN'T DO IT YOURSELF.
JUZO... C'MON...
GETTING JUSTICE WITHOUT PUTTING YOUR LIFE ON THE LINE...
...THAT'S JUST A PIPE DREAM.
YOU'RE RIGHT. RIGHT NOW...
...I CAN'T EVEN STAND UP WITHOUT HELP.
SHOULD EVERYONE WHO'S DOWN AND OUT...
...GIVE UP HOPE OF EVER GETTING OUT OF THE GUTTERS?

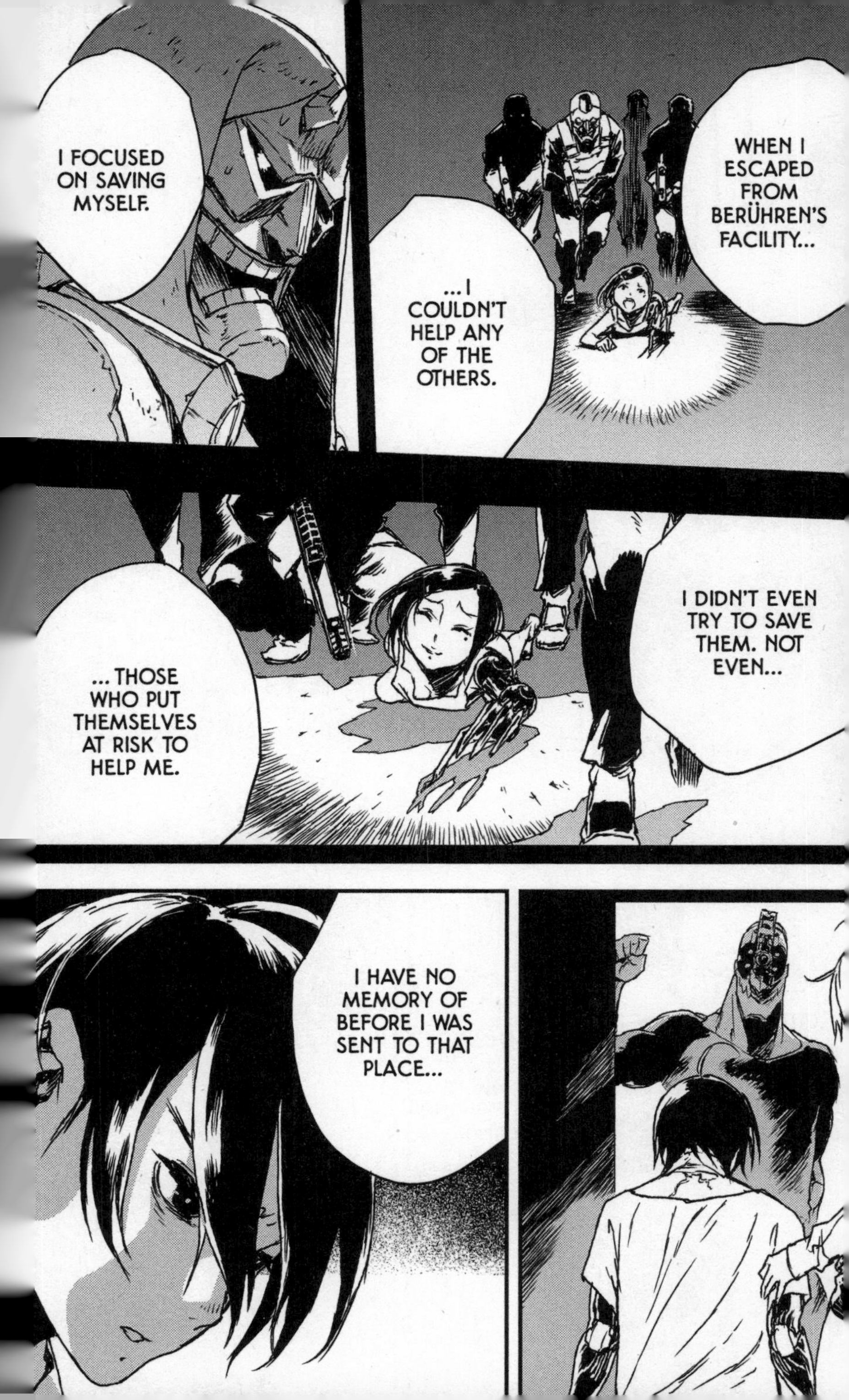
WHEN I ESCAPED FROM BERÜHREN'S FACILITY...
...I COULDN'T HELP ANY OF THE OTHERS.
I FOCUSED ON SAVING MYSELF.
I DIDN'T EVEN TRY TO SAVE THEM. NOT EVEN...
...THOSE WHO PUT THEMSELVES AT RISK TO HELP ME.
I HAVE NO MEMORY OF BEFORE I WAS SENT TO THAT PLACE...

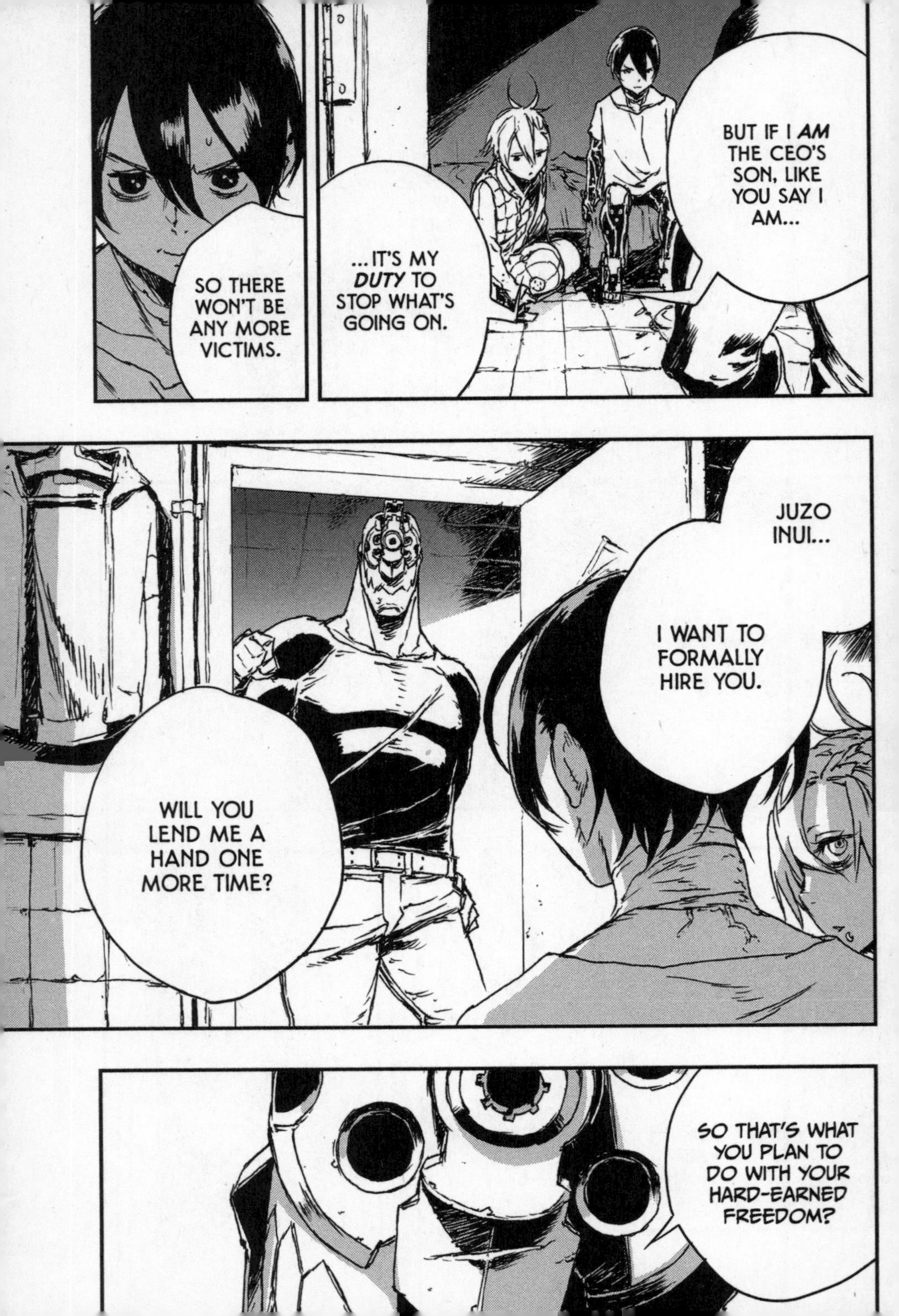
BUT IF I *AM* THE CEO'S SON, LIKE YOU SAY I AM...
...IT'S MY *DUTY* TO STOP WHAT'S GOING ON.
SO THERE WON'T BE ANY MORE VICTIMS.
JUZO INUI...
I WANT TO FORMALLY HIRE YOU.
WILL YOU LEND ME A HAND ONE MORE TIME?
SO THAT'S WHAT YOU PLAN TO DO WITH YOUR HARD-EARNED FREEDOM?

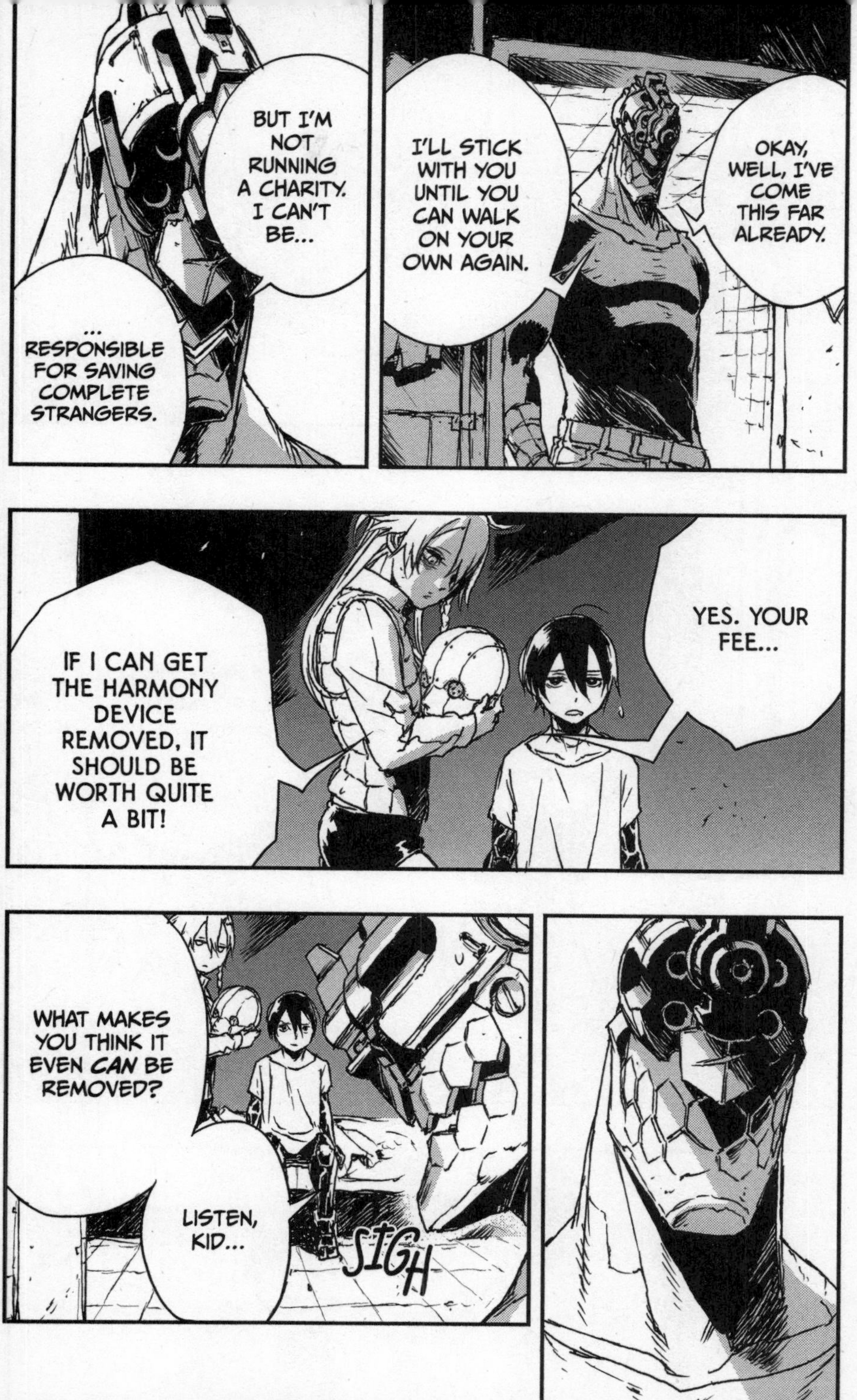
OKAY, WELL, I'VE COME THIS FAR ALREADY.
I'LL STICK WITH YOU UNTIL YOU CAN WALK ON YOUR OWN AGAIN.
BUT I'M NOT RUNNING A CHARITY. I CAN'T BE...
...RESPONSIBLE FOR SAVING COMPLETE STRANGERS.
YES. YOUR FEE...
IF I CAN GET THE HARMONY DEVICE REMOVED, IT SHOULD BE WORTH QUITE A BIT!
WHAT MAKES YOU THINK IT EVEN *CAN* BE REMOVED?
SIGH
LISTEN, KID...

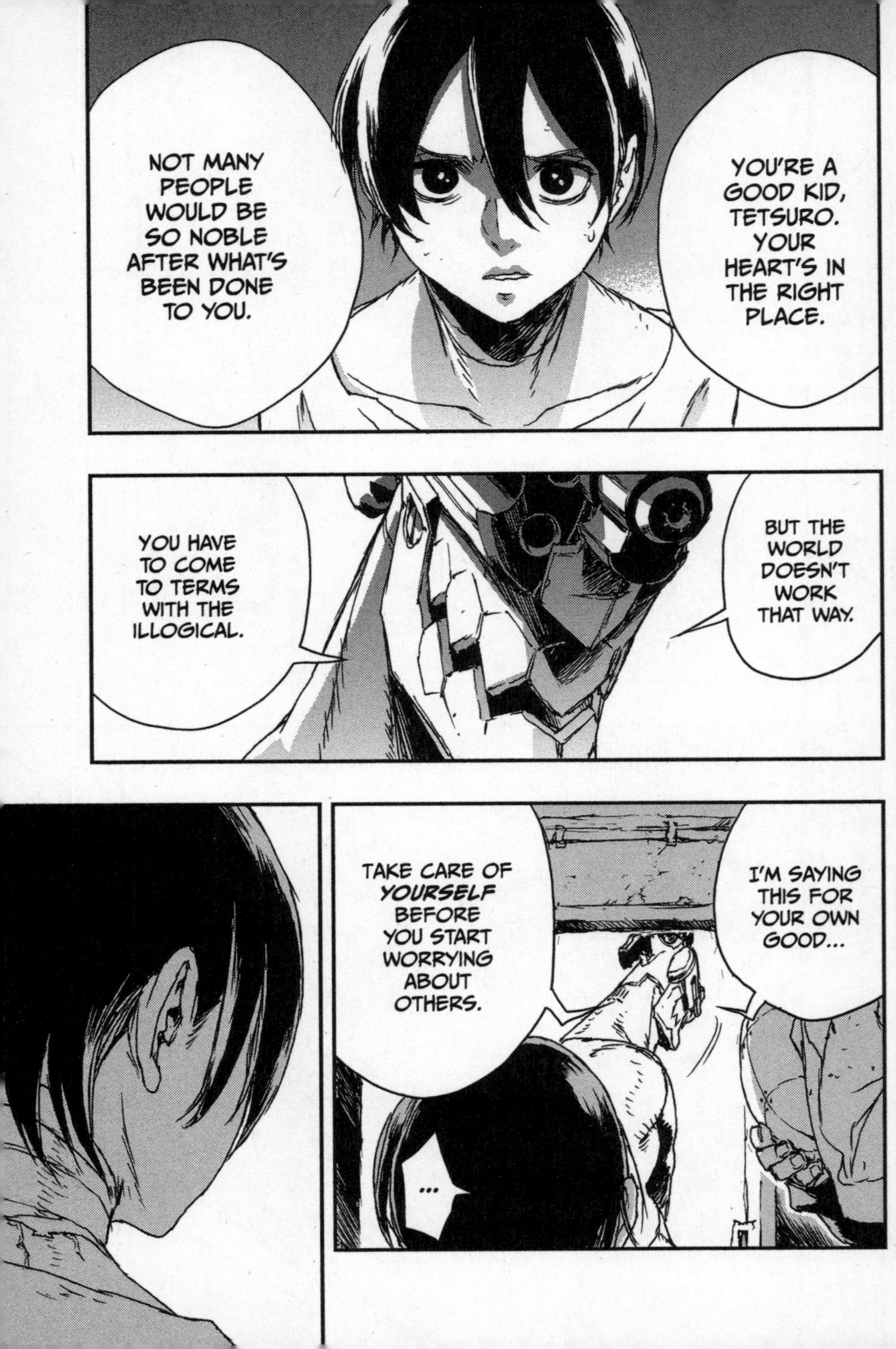
YOU'RE A GOOD KID, TETSURO. YOUR HEART'S IN THE RIGHT PLACE.
NOT MANY PEOPLE WOULD BE SO NOBLE AFTER WHAT'S BEEN DONE TO YOU.
BUT THE WORLD DOESN'T WORK THAT WAY.
YOU HAVE TO COME TO TERMS WITH THE ILLOGICAL.
I'M SAYING THIS FOR YOUR OWN GOOD...
TAKE CARE OF *YOURSELF* BEFORE YOU START WORRYING ABOUT OTHERS.
...

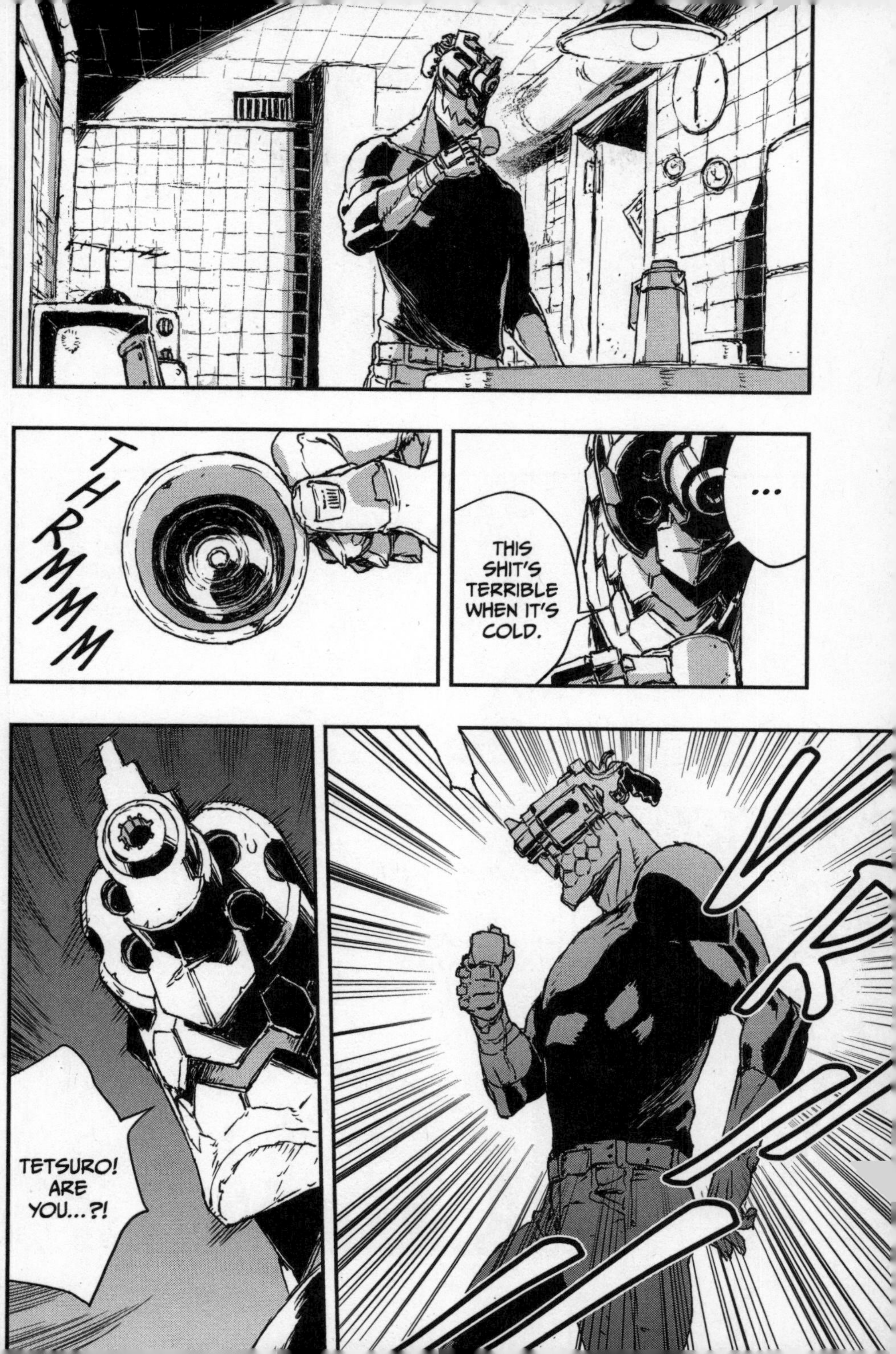
...
THIS SHIT'S TERRIBLE WHEN IT'S COLD.
THRMMMM
TETSURO! ARE YOU...?!

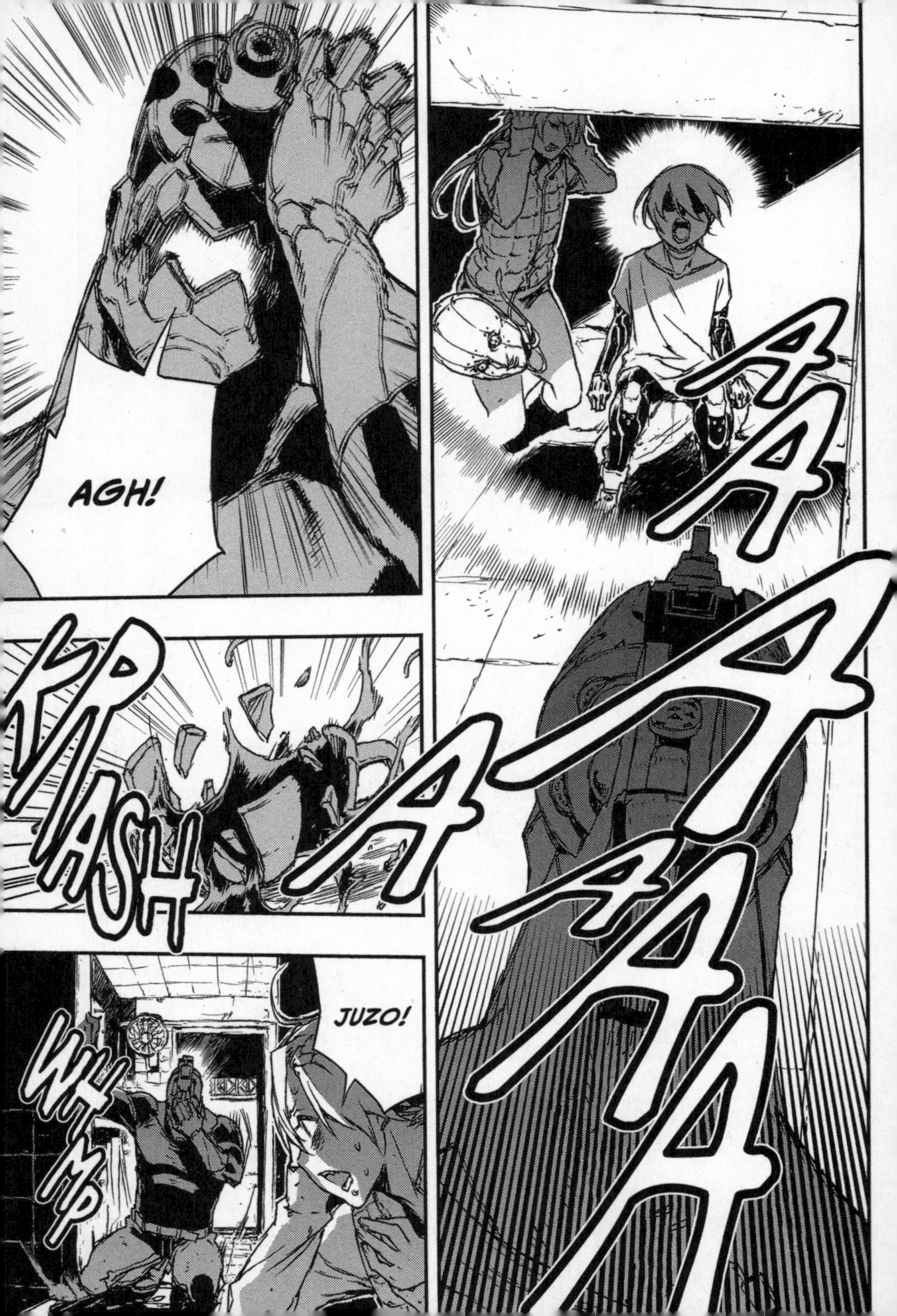
AAAAAAAAAA
AGH!
KRASH
JUZO!
WHUMP

JUZO!
ARE YOU
OKAY?

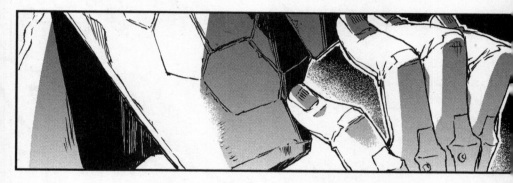

JUZO
....?

SNFF

HOLD
ON. WAIT.
WHAT?!

UH...

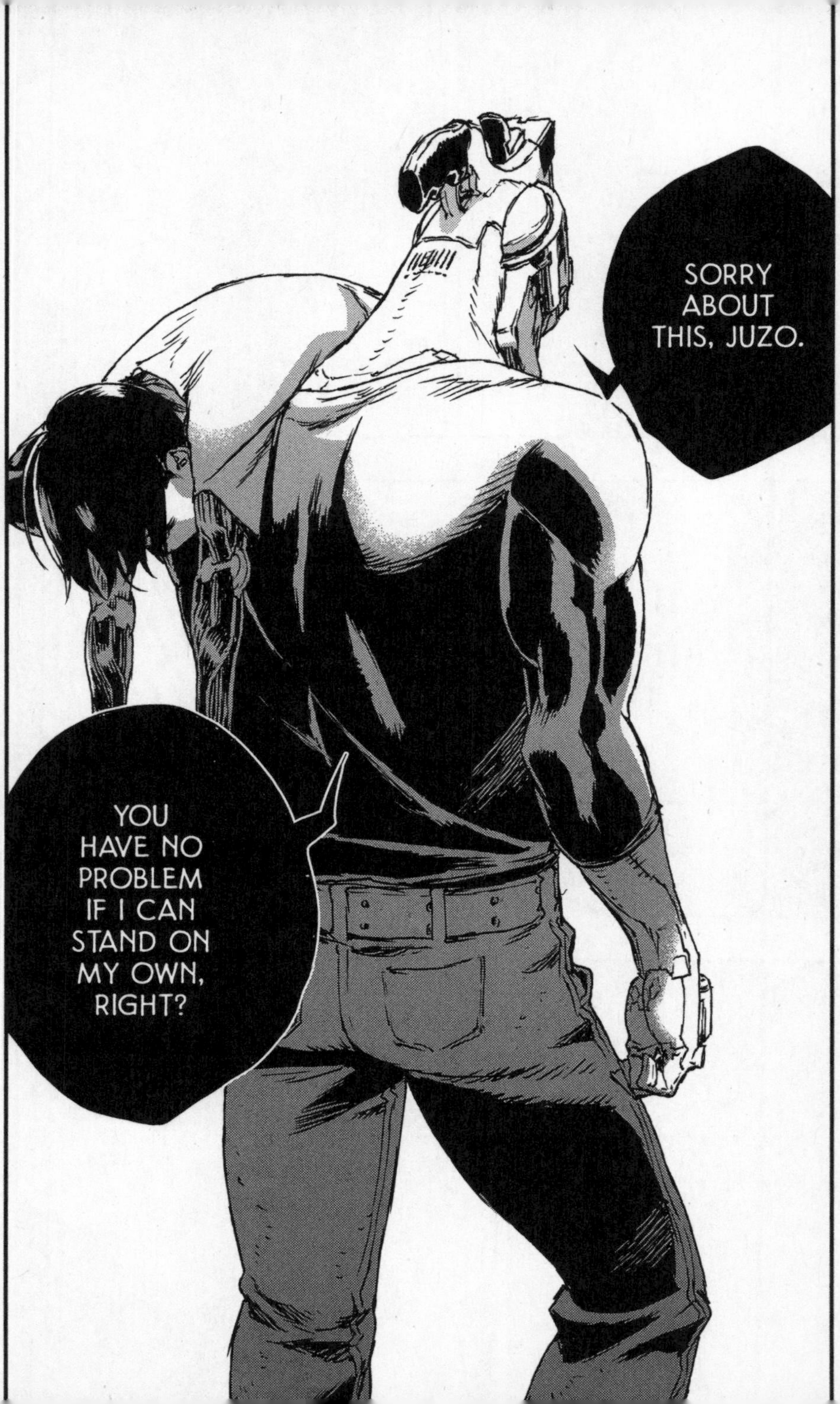
SORRY ABOUT THIS, JUZO.
YOU HAVE NO PROBLEM IF I CAN STAND ON MY OWN, RIGHT?

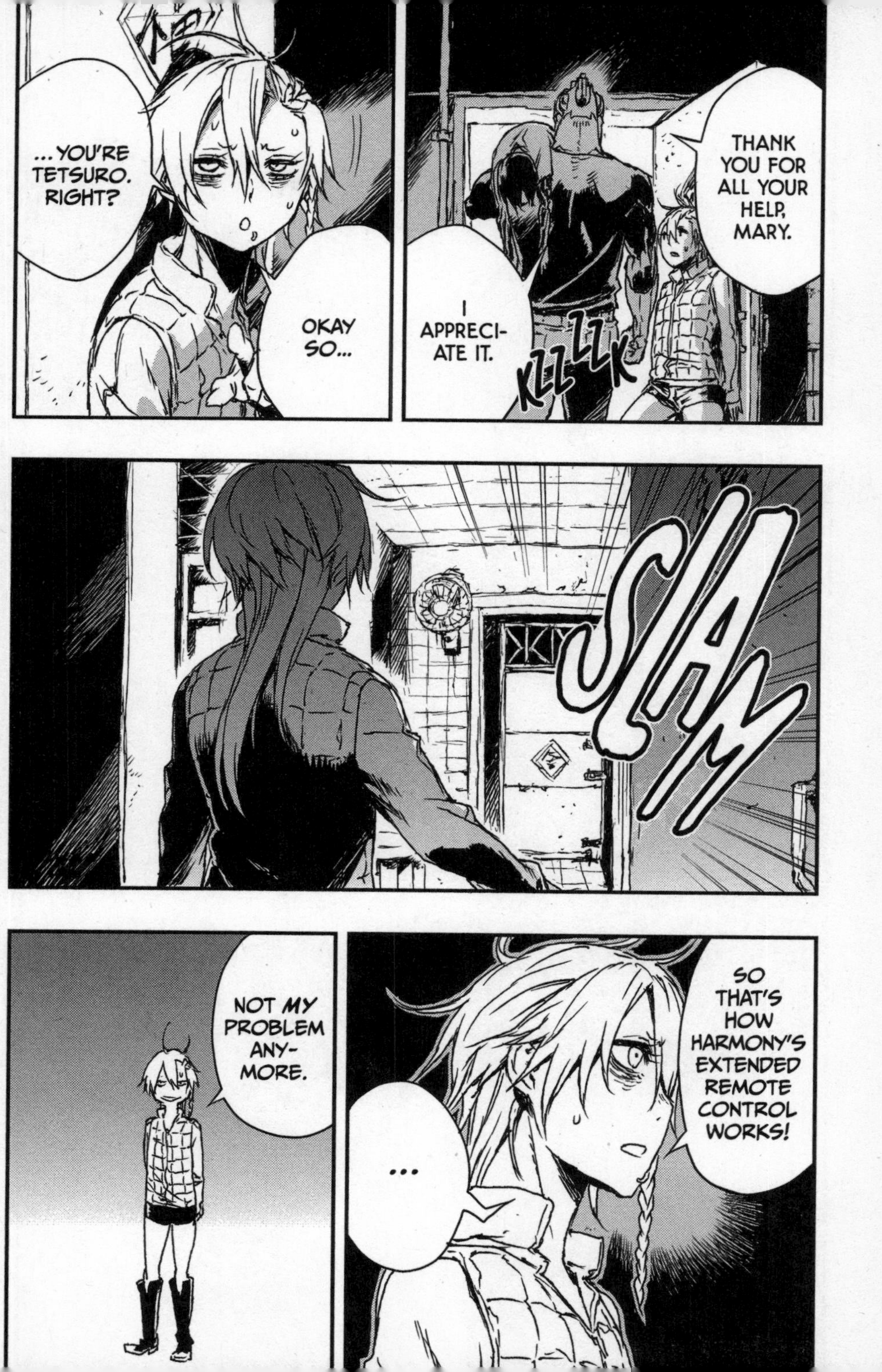
THANK YOU FOR ALL YOUR HELP, MARY.
I APPRECIATE IT.
KZZZZK
...YOU'RE TETSURO. RIGHT?
OKAY SO...
SLAM
SO THAT'S HOW HARMONY'S EXTENDED REMOTE CONTROL WORKS!
...
NOT MY PROBLEM ANYMORE.

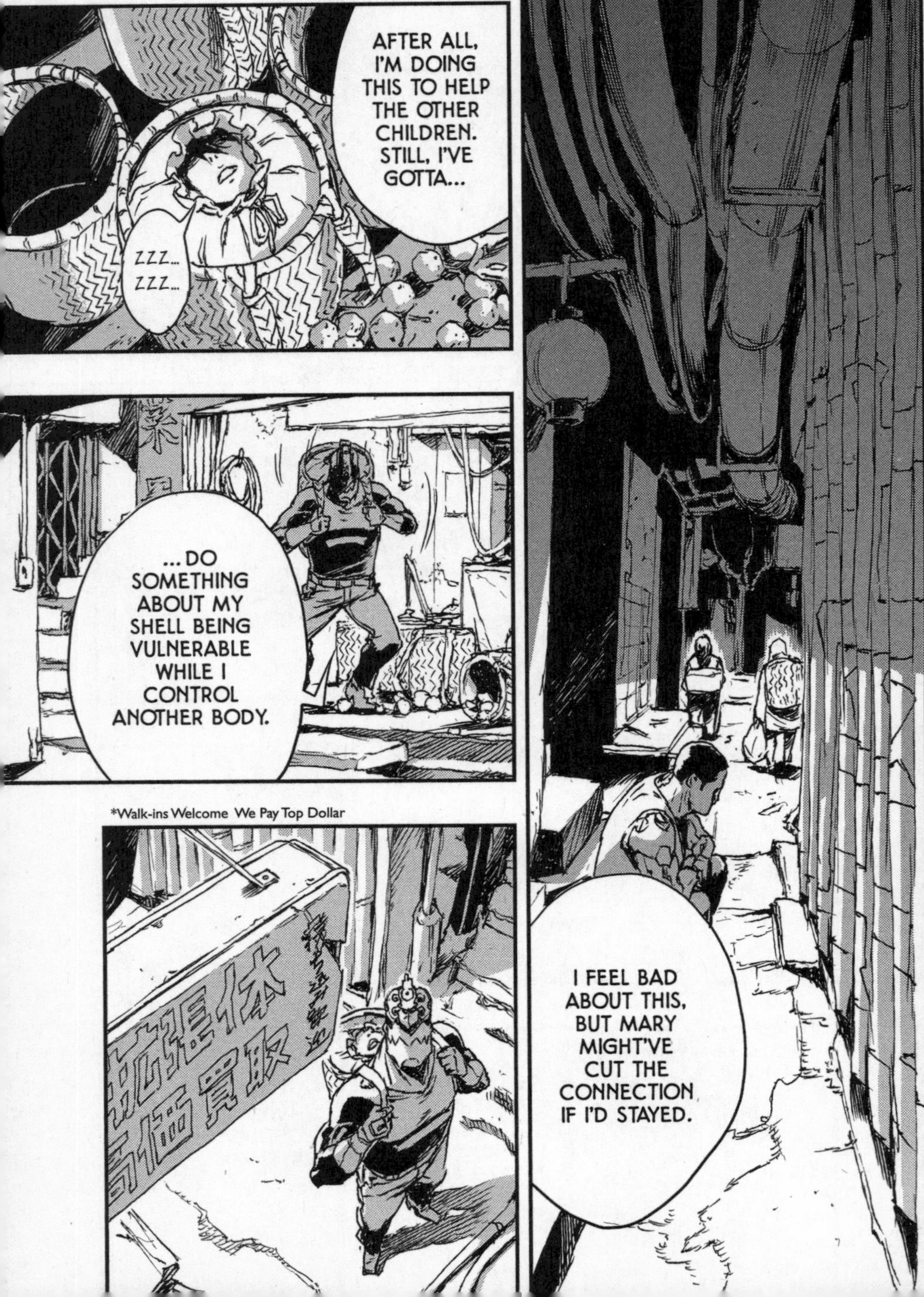
I FEEL BAD ABOUT THIS, BUT MARY MIGHT'VE CUT THE CONNECTION IF I'D STAYED.
AFTER ALL, I'M DOING THIS TO HELP THE OTHER CHILDREN. STILL, I'VE GOTTA...
ZZZ... ZZZ...
...DO SOMETHING ABOUT MY SHELL BEING VULNERABLE WHILE I CONTROL ANOTHER BODY.
*Walk-ins Welcome We Pay Top Dollar

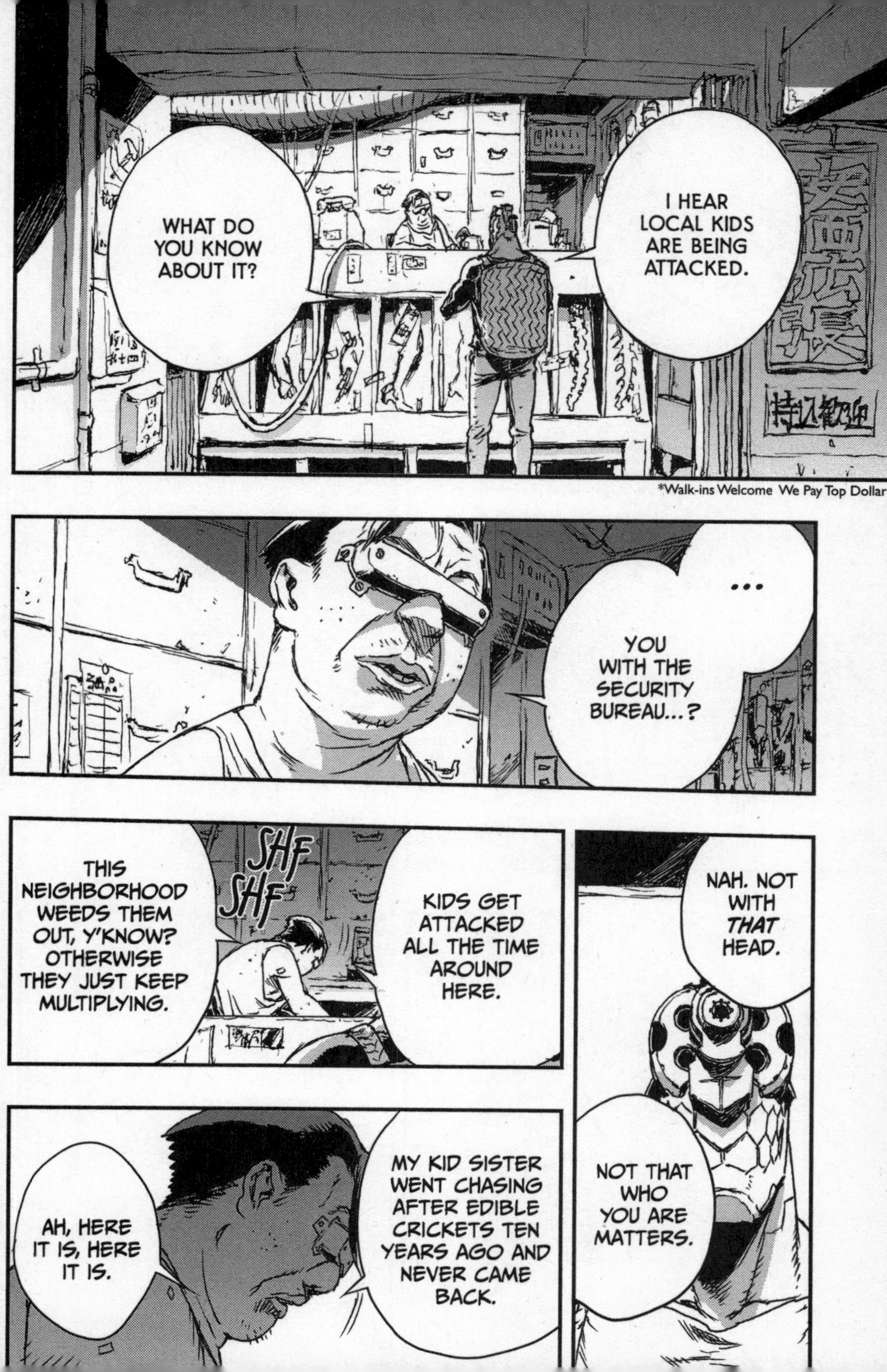
I HEAR LOCAL KIDS ARE BEING ATTACKED.
WHAT DO YOU KNOW ABOUT IT?
...
YOU WITH THE SECURITY BUREAU...?
NAH. NOT WITH *THAT* HEAD.
NOT THAT WHO YOU ARE MATTERS.
KIDS GET ATTACKED ALL THE TIME AROUND HERE.
SHF SHF
THIS NEIGHBORHOOD WEEDS THEM OUT, Y'KNOW? OTHERWISE THEY JUST KEEP MULTIPLYING.
MY KID SISTER WENT CHASING AFTER EDIBLE CRICKETS TEN YEARS AGO AND NEVER CAME BACK.
AH, HERE IT IS, HERE IT IS.
*Walk-ins Welcome We Pay Top Dollar

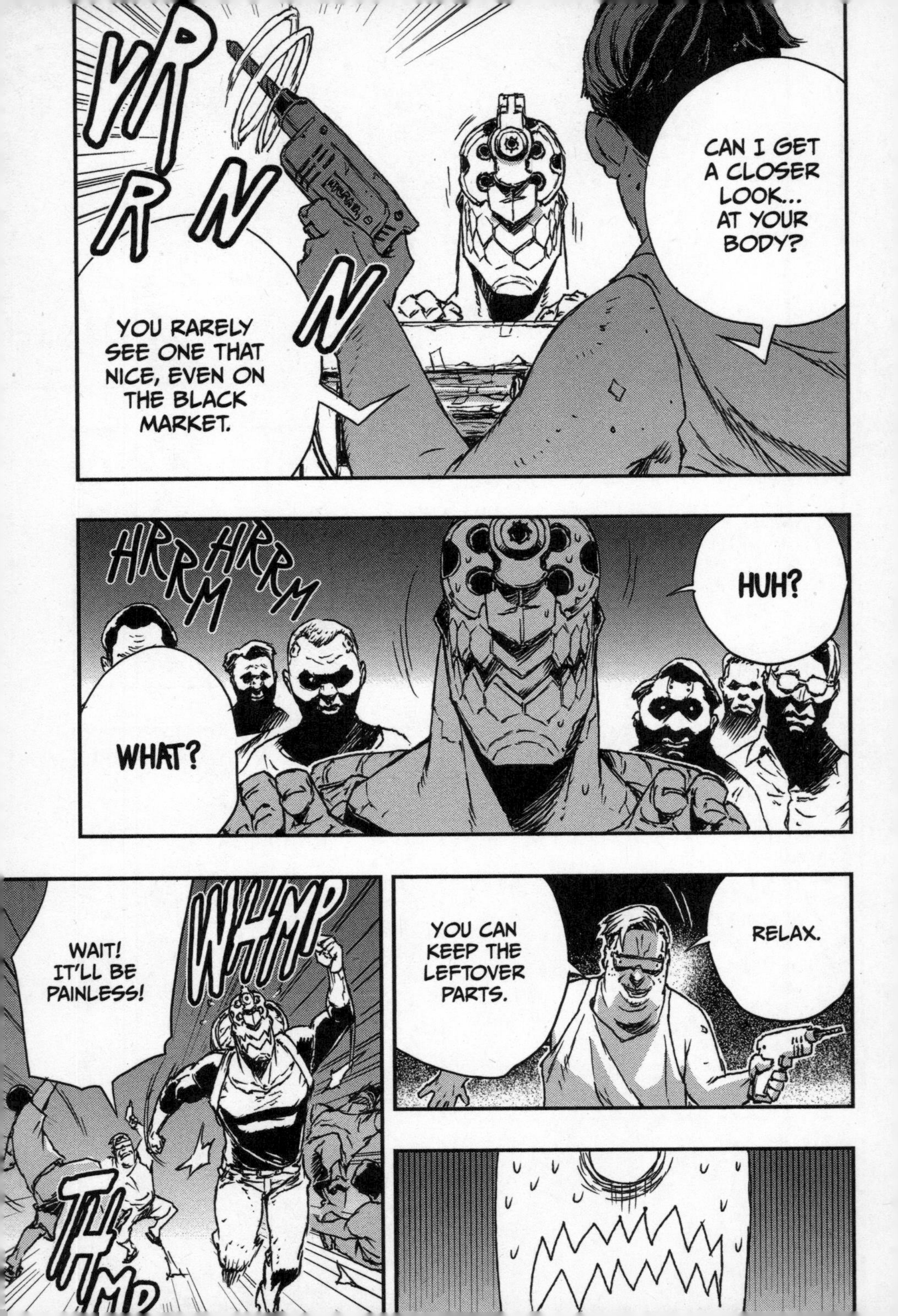
CAN I GET A CLOSER LOOK... AT YOUR BODY?
VRRNNN
YOU RARELY SEE ONE THAT NICE, EVEN ON THE BLACK MARKET.
HUH?
HRRRM HRRRM
WHAT?
RELAX.
YOU CAN KEEP THE LEFTOVER PARTS.
WHUMP
WAIT! IT'LL BE PAINLESS!
THMP

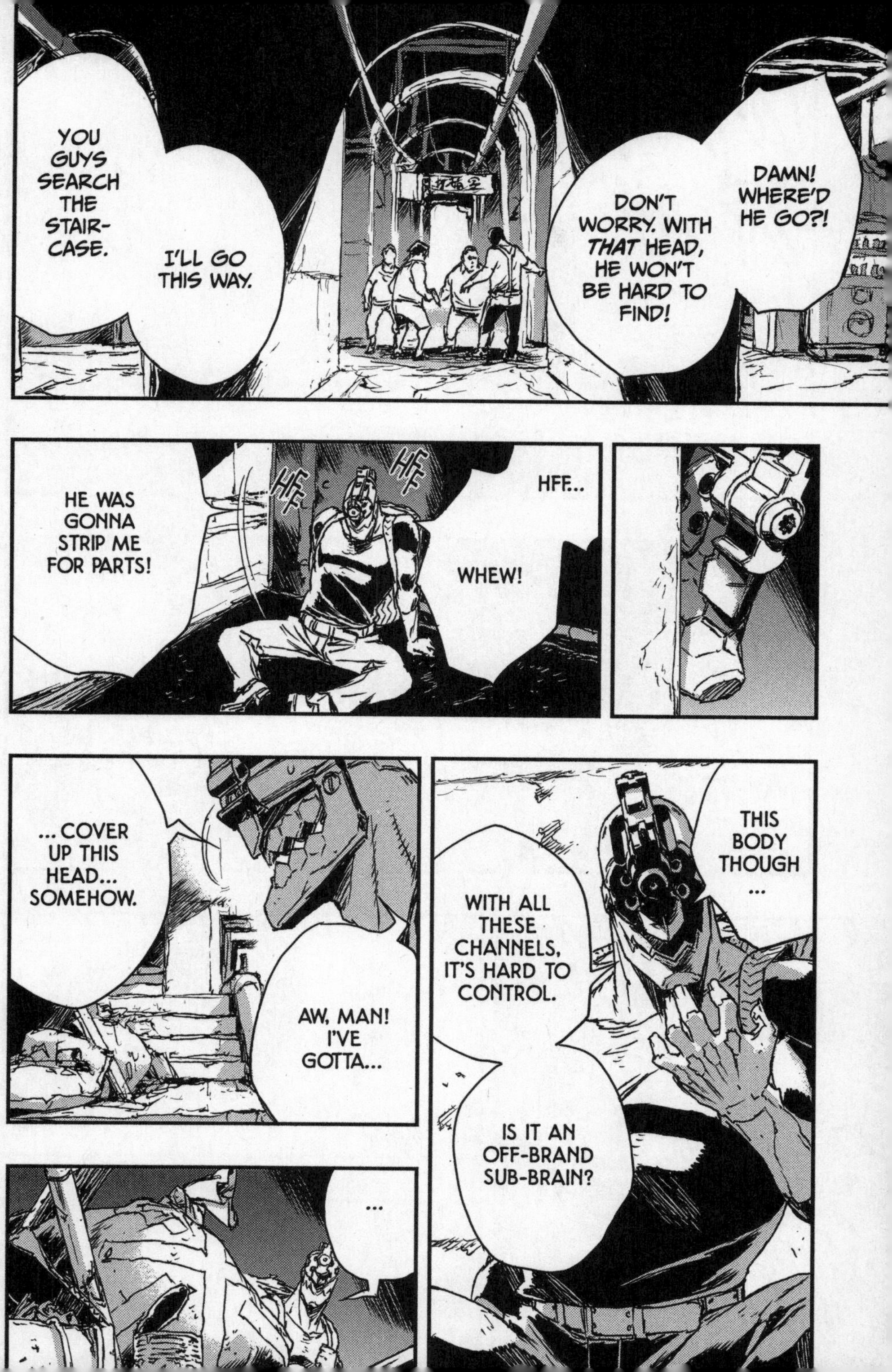
DAMN! WHERE'D HE GO?!
DON'T WORRY. WITH *THAT* HEAD, HE WON'T BE HARD TO FIND!
YOU GUYS SEARCH THE STAIR-CASE.
I'LL GO THIS WAY.
HFF...
WHEW!
HFF HFF
HE WAS GONNA STRIP ME FOR PARTS!
THIS BODY THOUGH...
WITH ALL THESE CHANNELS, IT'S HARD TO CONTROL.
IS IT AN OFF-BRAND SUB-BRAIN?
AW, MAN! I'VE GOTTA...
...COVER UP THIS HEAD... SOMEHOW.
...

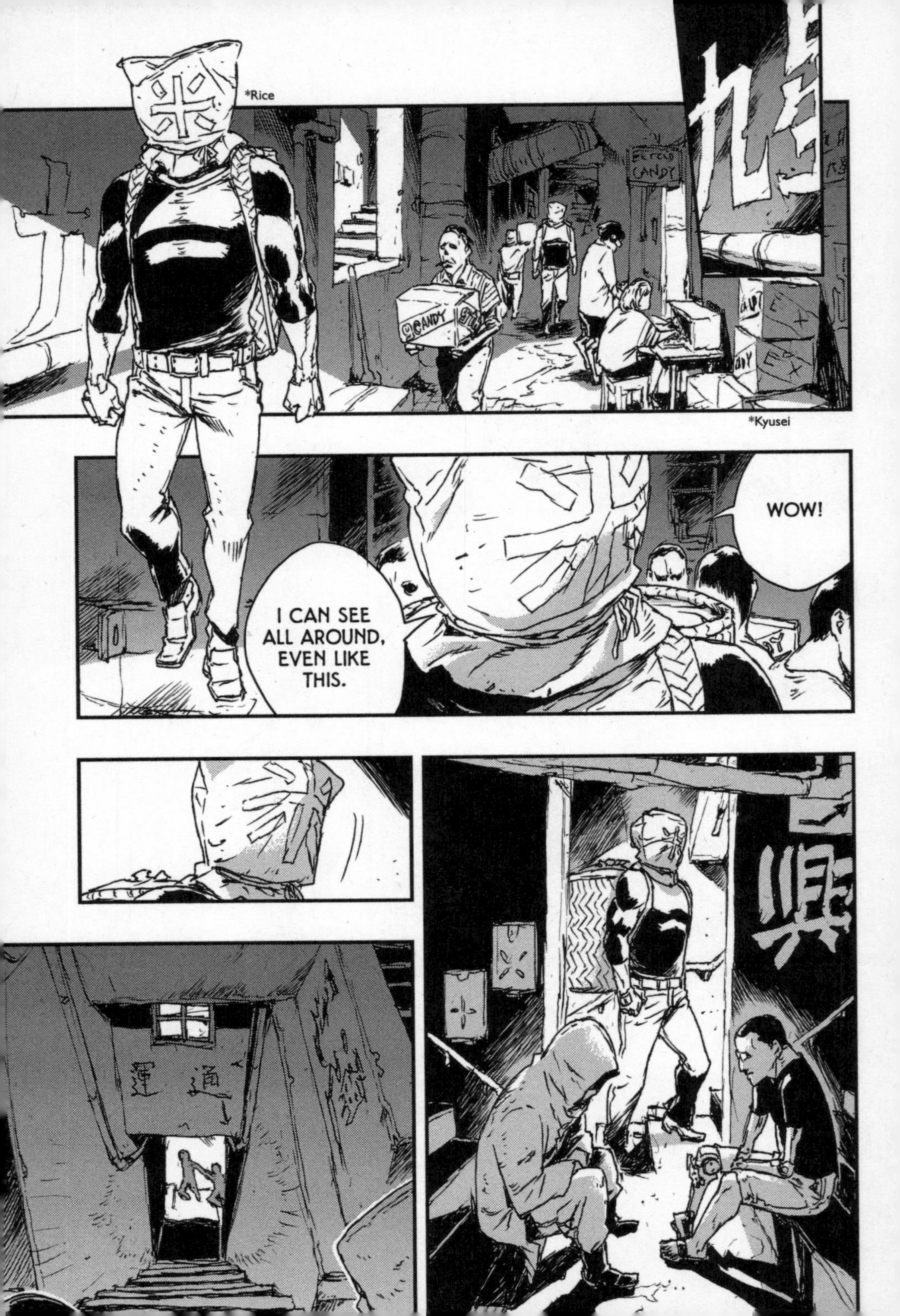
*Rice
*Kyusei
WOW!
I CAN SEE ALL AROUND, EVEN LIKE THIS.

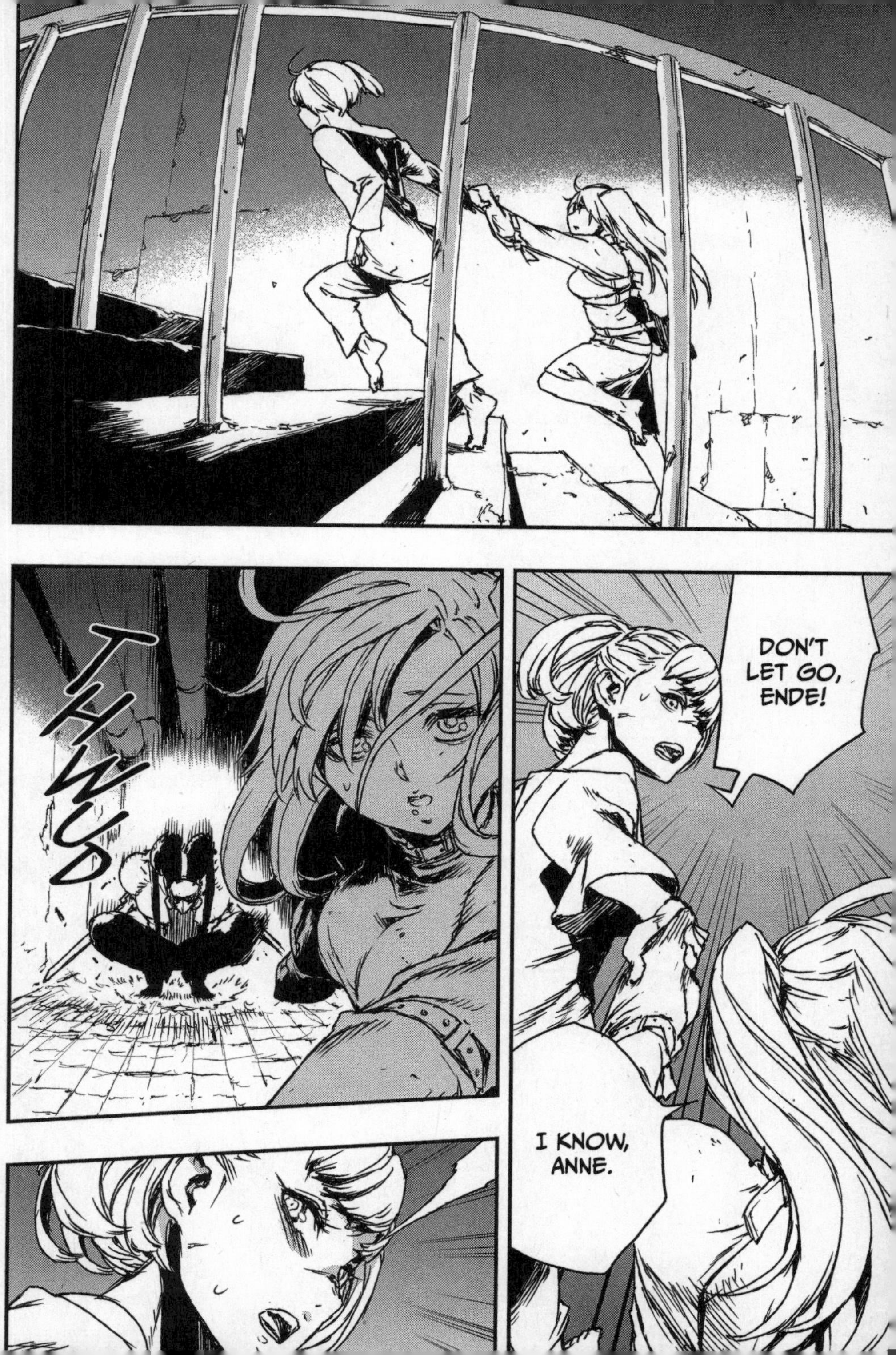
DON'T LET GO, ENDE!
I KNOW, ANNE.
THWUD

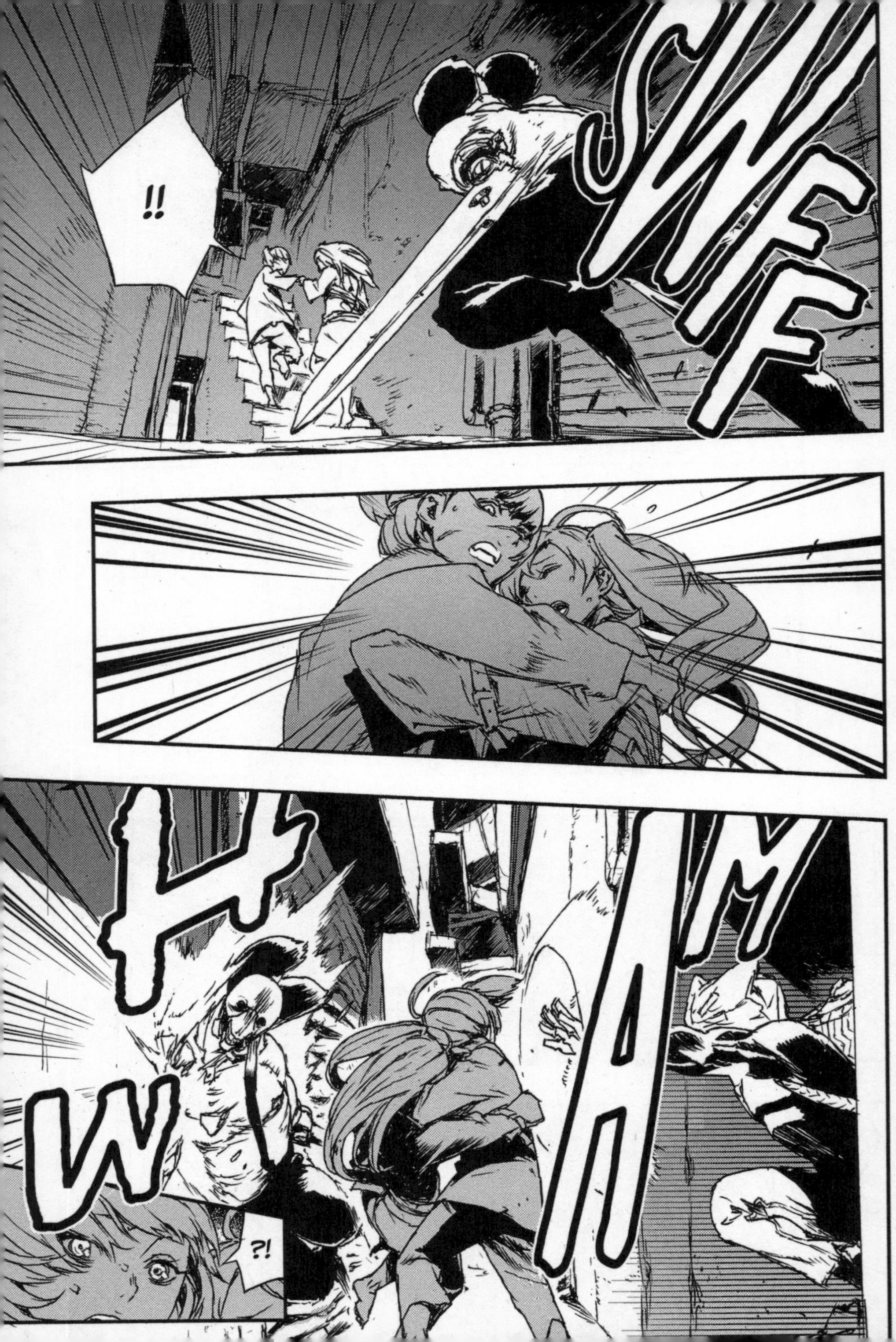
SWFF
!!
WHAM
?!

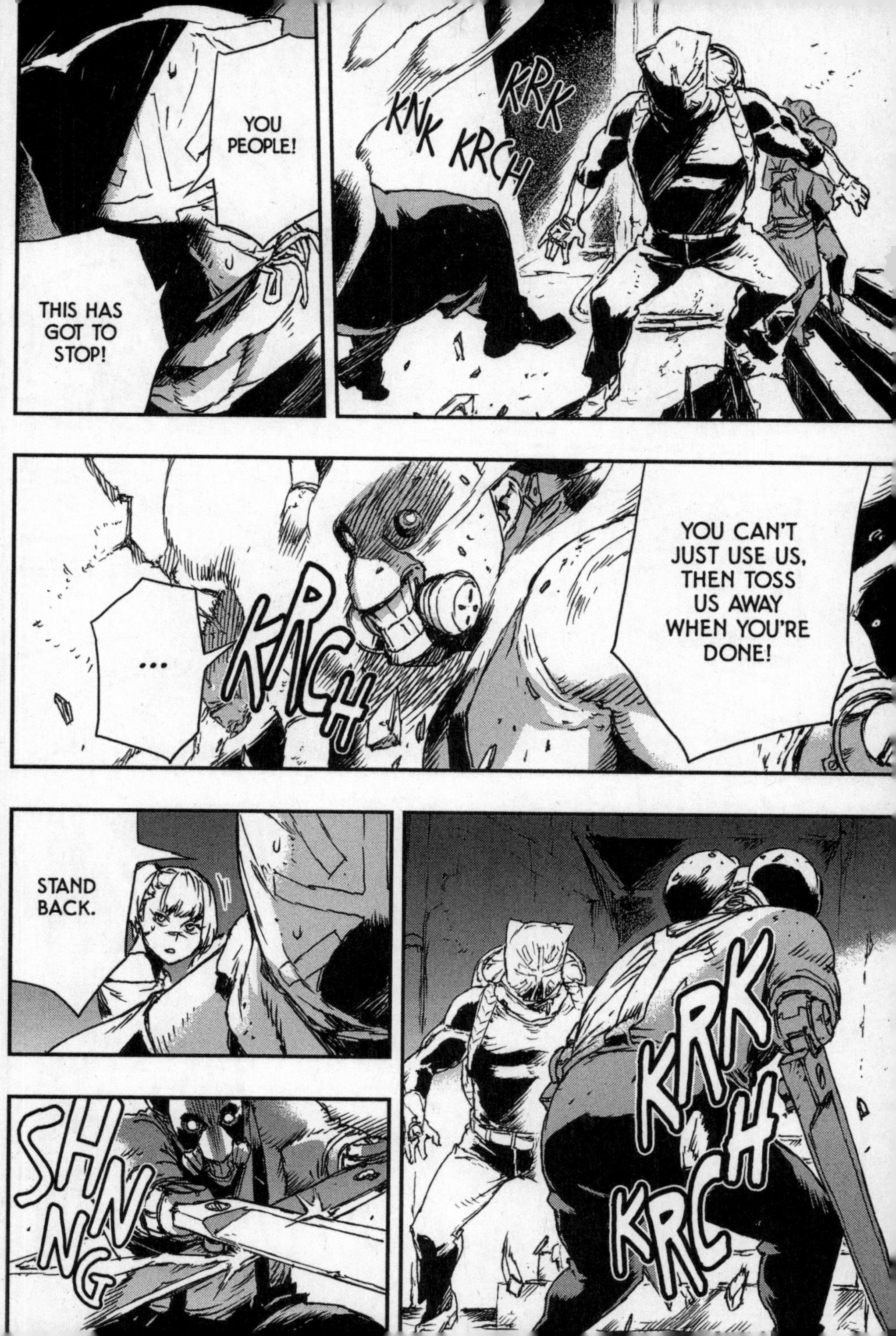
KRK
KNK KRCH
YOU PEOPLE!
THIS HAS GOT TO STOP!
YOU CAN'T JUST USE US, THEN TOSS US AWAY WHEN YOU'RE DONE!
KRCH
...
KRK KRCH
KRCH
STAND BACK.
SHNNG

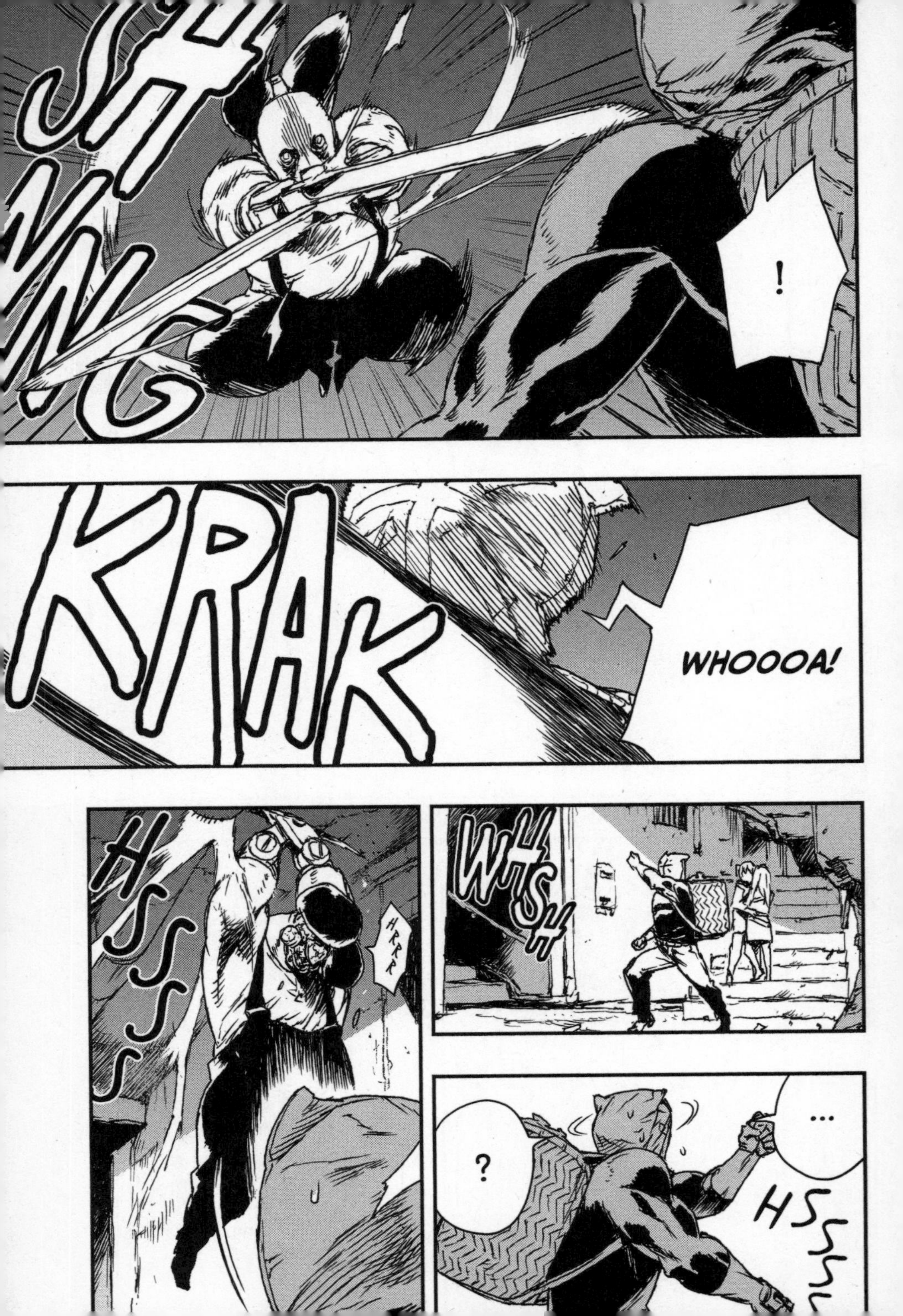
!
SHING
WHOOOA!
KRAK
WHSH
...
?
HSSS
HSSSSS
HRRRR

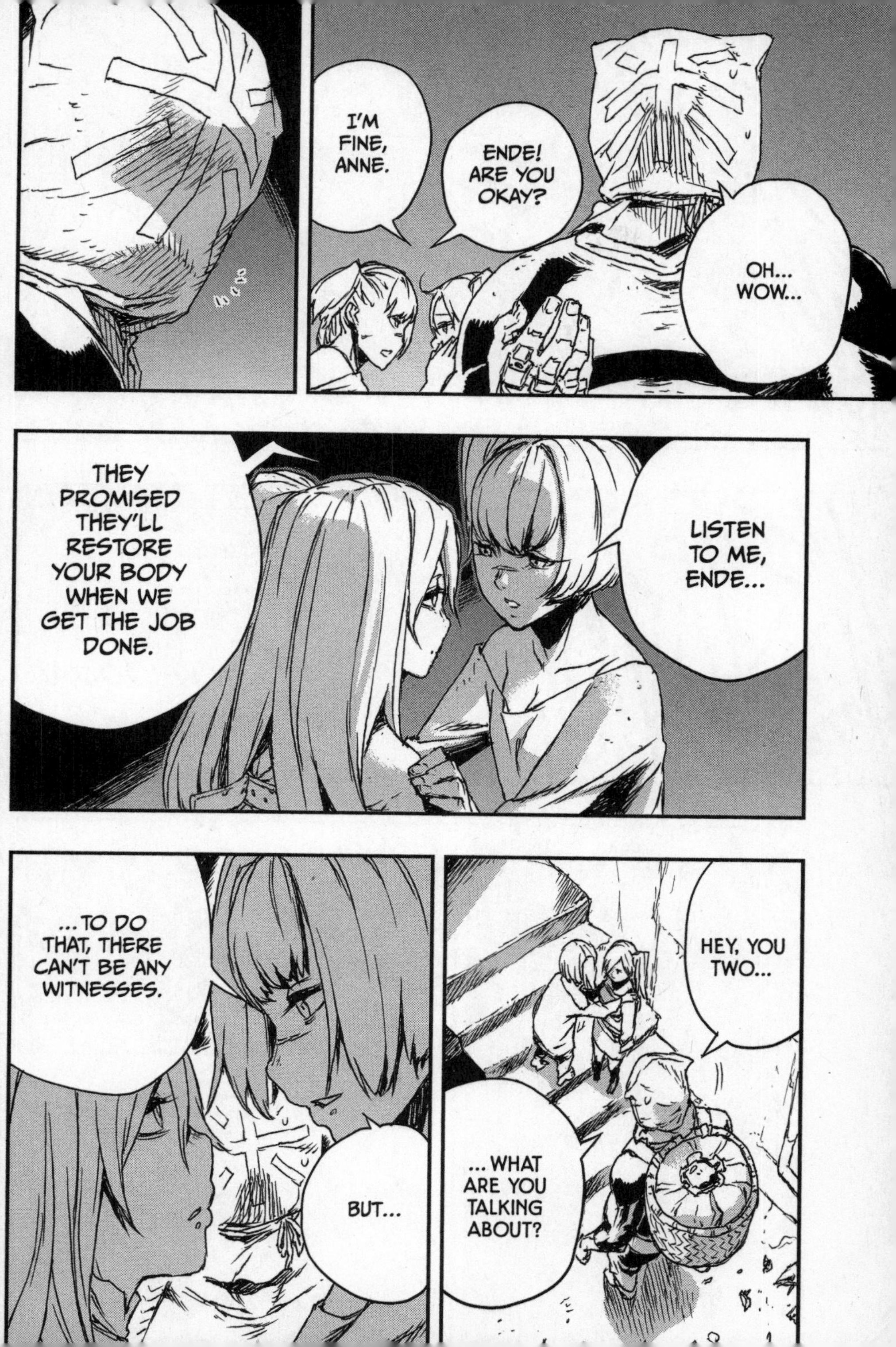

ENDE! ARE YOU OKAY?
I'M FINE, ANNE.
OH... WOW...
LISTEN TO ME, ENDE...
THEY PROMISED THEY'LL RESTORE YOUR BODY WHEN WE GET THE JOB DONE.
HEY, YOU TWO...
...WHAT ARE YOU TALKING ABOUT?
...TO DO THAT, THERE CAN'T BE ANY WITNESSES.
BUT...

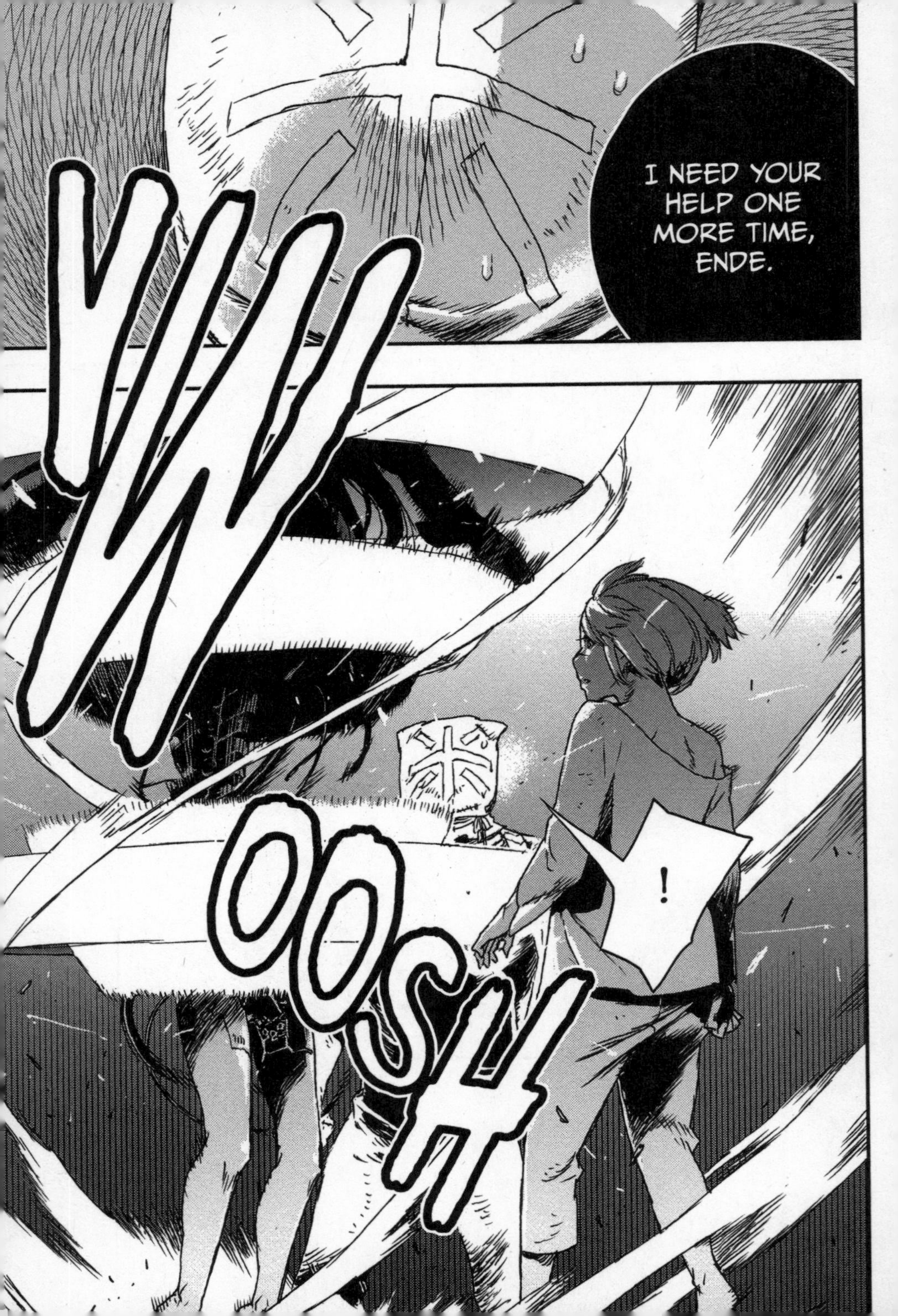
I NEED YOUR HELP ONE MORE TIME, ENDE.
WHOOSH
!

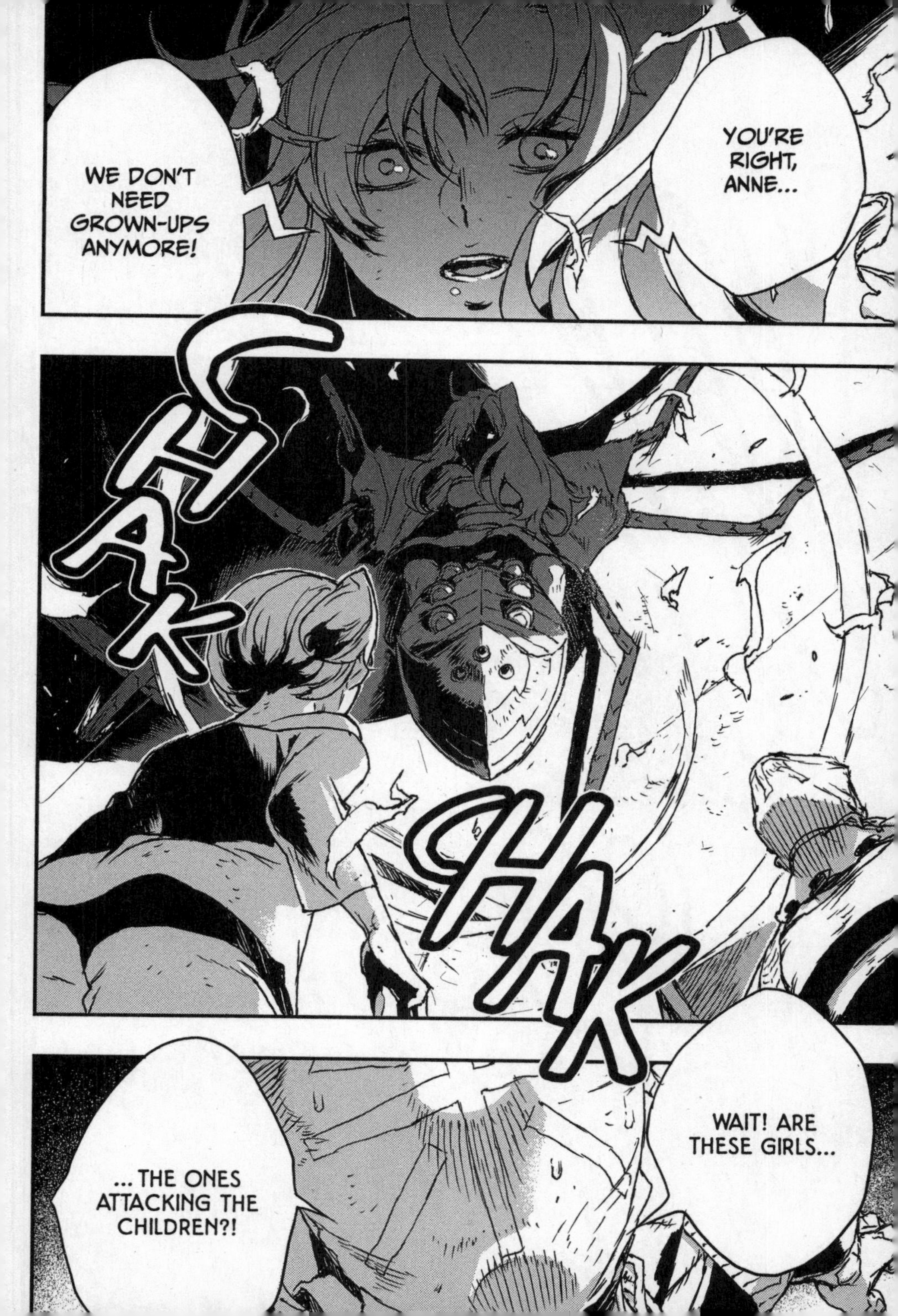
YOU'RE RIGHT, ANNE...
WE DON'T NEED GROWN-UPS ANYMORE!
CHAK
CHAK
WAIT! ARE THESE GIRLS...
...THE ONES ATTACKING THE CHILDREN?!

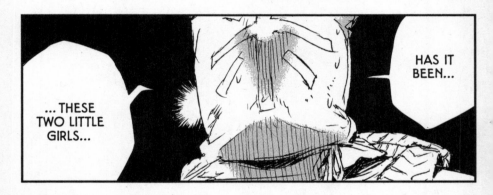

HAS IT BEEN...

...THESE TWO LITTLE GIRLS...

...ATTACKING THE LOCAL CHILDREN?!

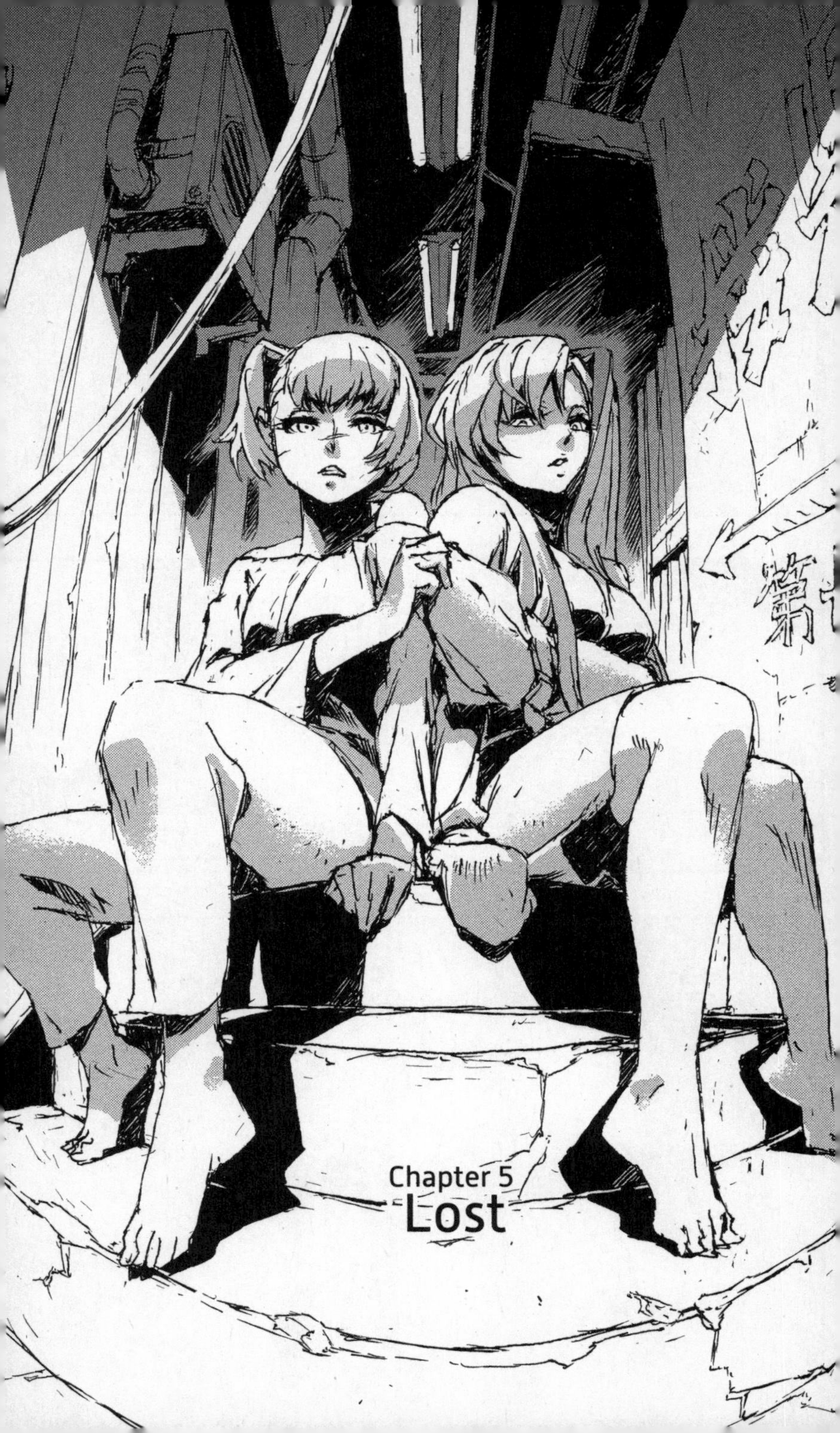
Chapter 5
Lost

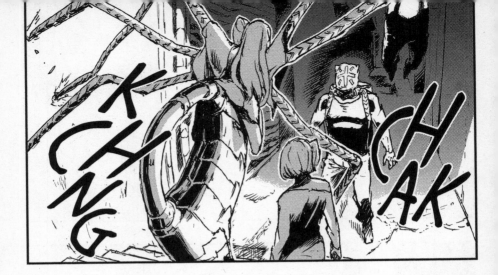

CHAK
KCHING
WAIT!
YOU GUYS ARE EXTENDED, RIGHT?
THAT BODY...
YOU WERE TEST SUBJECTS AT THE FACILITY TOO, WEREN'T YOU?
WHO... WHO *ARE* YOU?
HOW DO YOU KNOW ABOUT THAT?
I WAS HELD THERE TOO.
BUT WITH SOME HELP, I WAS ABLE TO ESCAPE!
AND NOW...
...IT'S MY TURN TO HELP YOU!

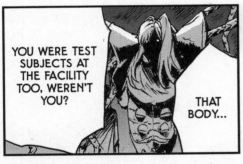

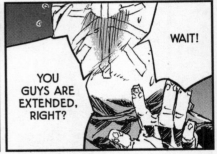

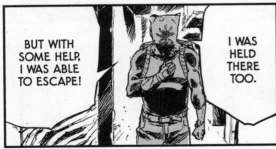

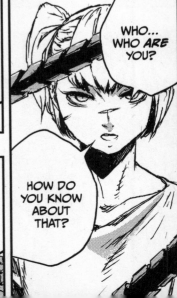

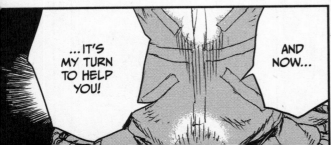

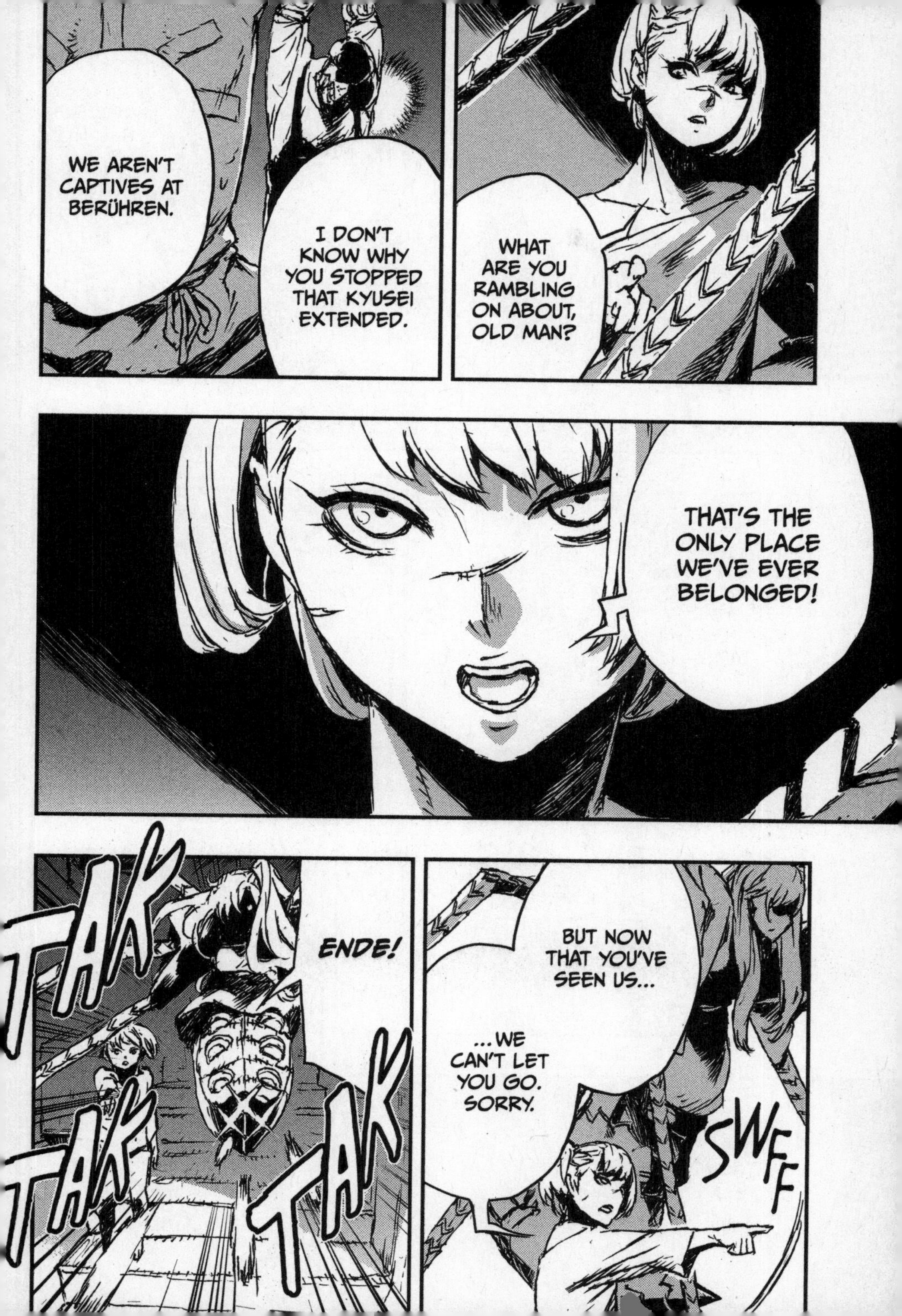
WHAT ARE YOU RAMBLING ON ABOUT, OLD MAN?
I DON'T KNOW WHY YOU STOPPED THAT KYUSEI EXTENDED.
WE AREN'T CAPTIVES AT BERÜHREN.
THAT'S THE ONLY PLACE WE'VE EVER BELONGED!
BUT NOW THAT YOU'VE SEEN US...
...WE CAN'T LET YOU GO. SORRY.
SWFF
ENDE!
TAK
TAK
TAK

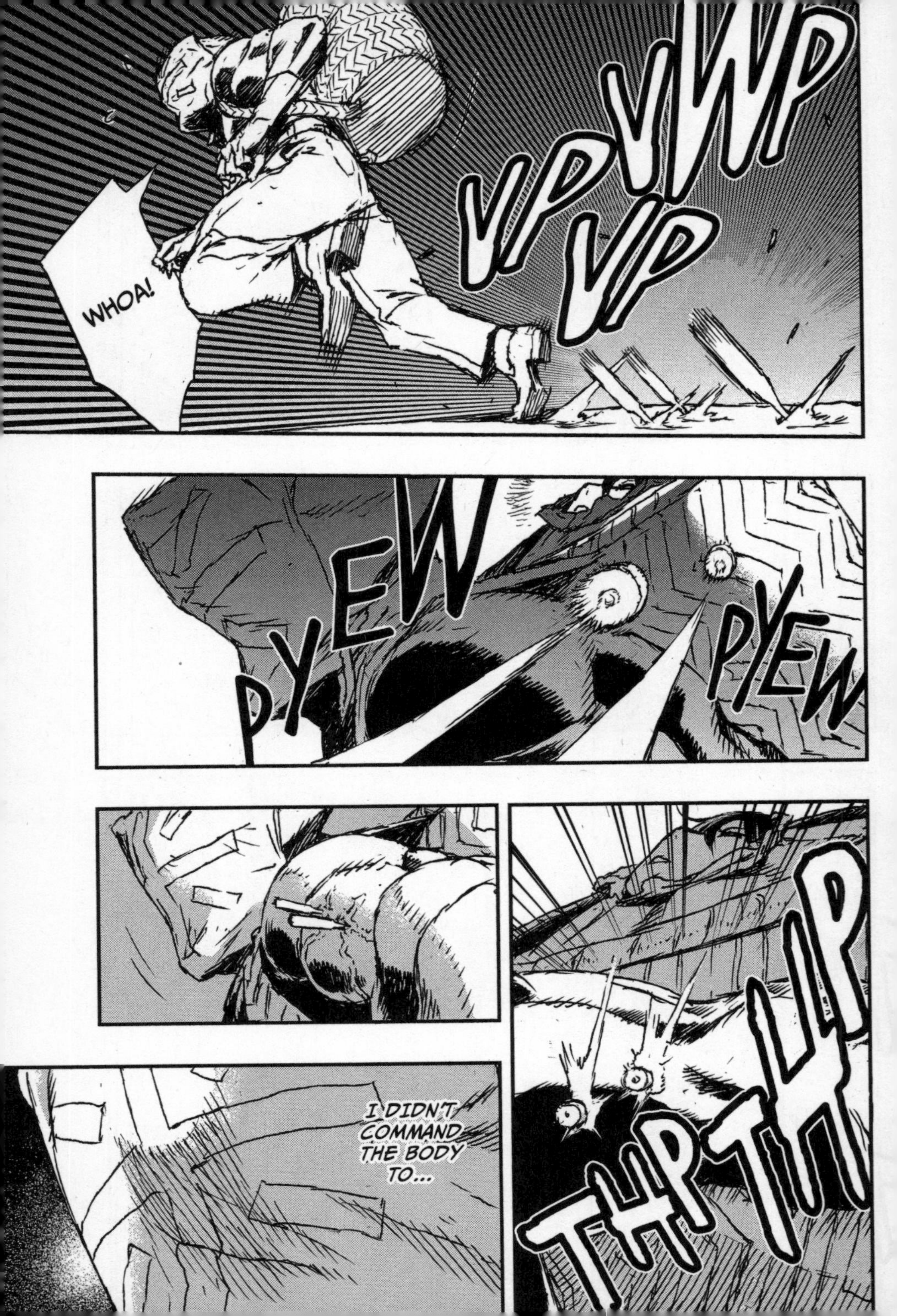
WHOA!
PYEW
PYEW
THP THP
I DIDN'T COMMAND THE BODY TO...

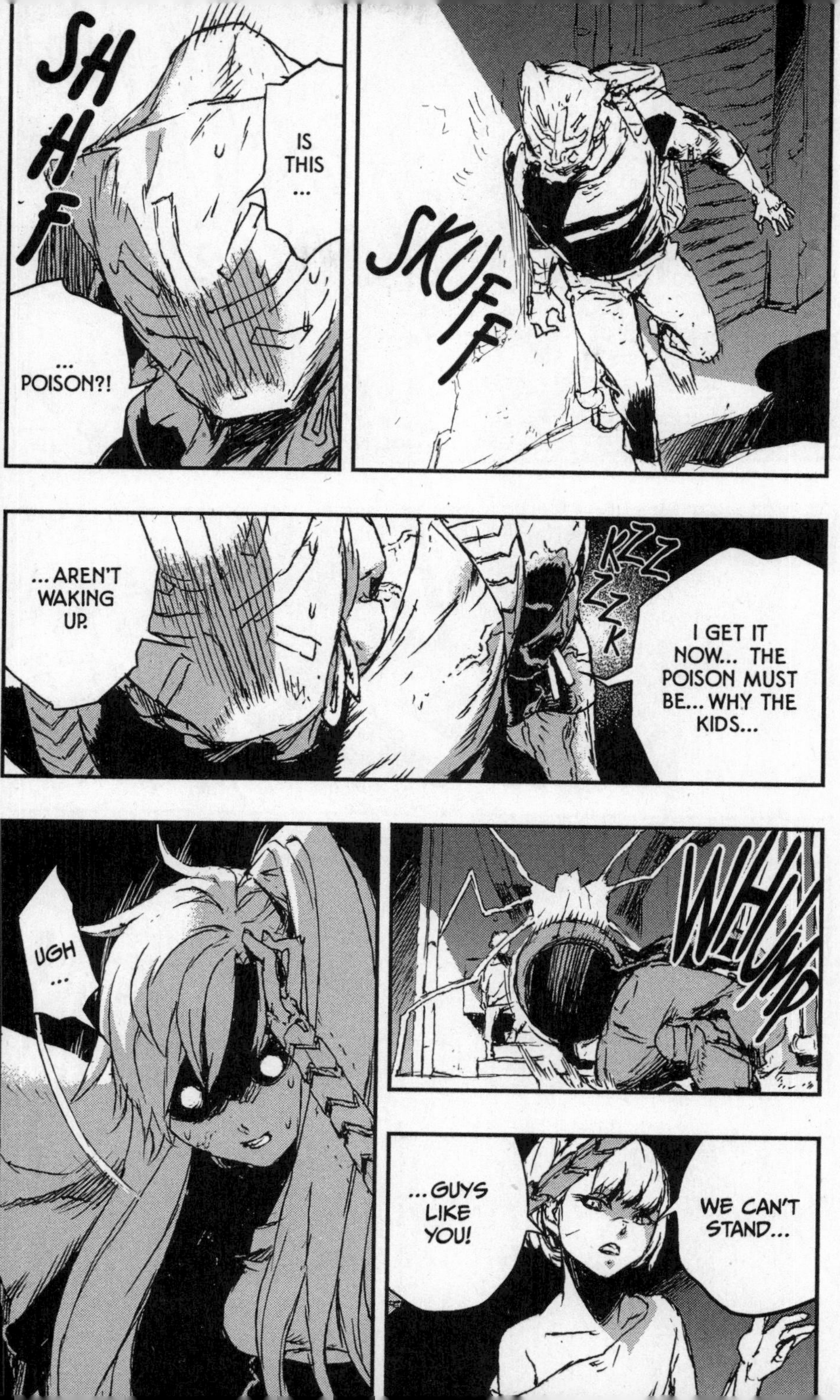
SKUFF
SHHF
IS THIS ...
... POISON?!
KZZZZZK
I GET IT NOW... THE POISON MUST BE... WHY THE KIDS...
...AREN'T WAKING UP.
WHUMP
WE CAN'T STAND...
...GUYS LIKE YOU!
UGH ...

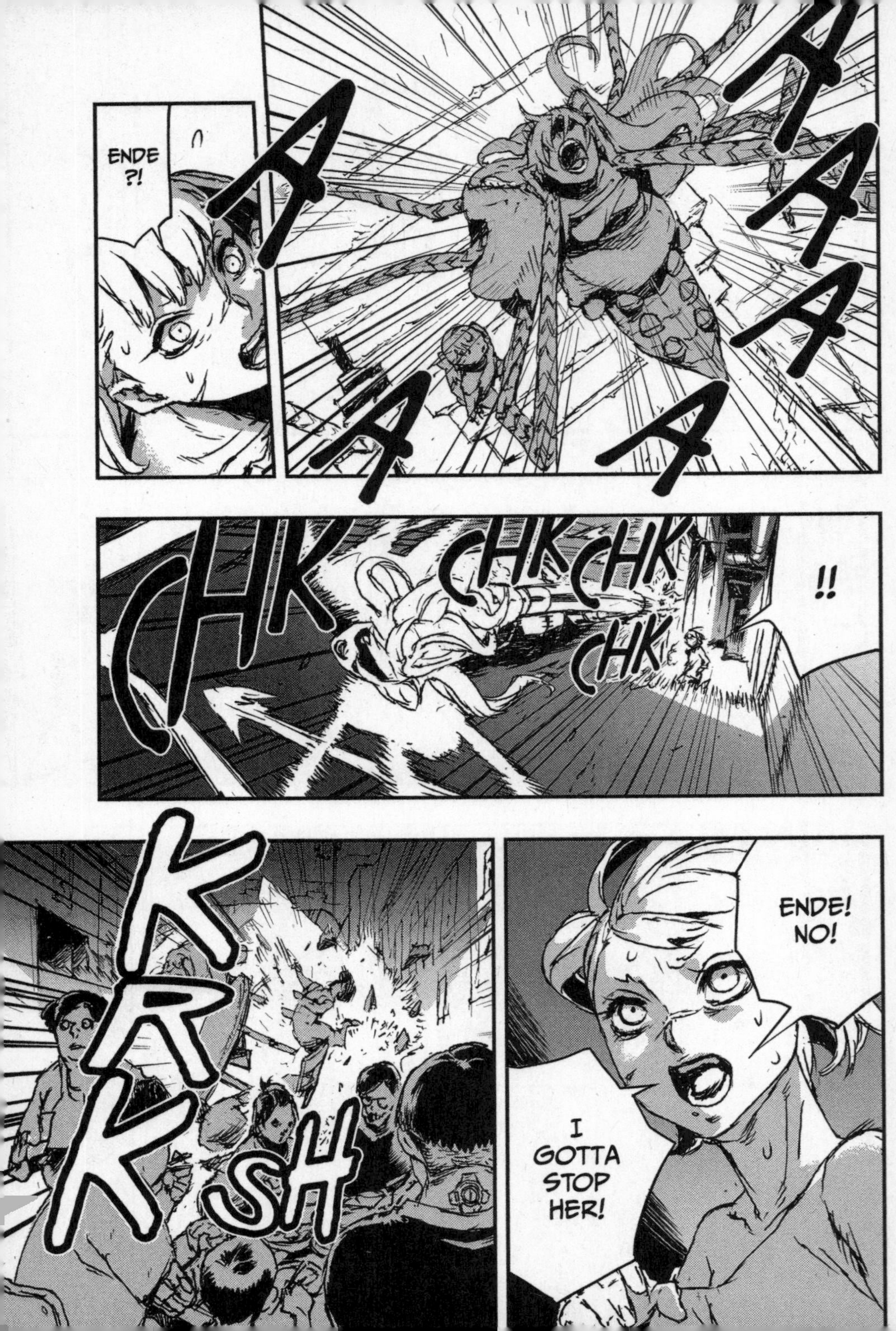
AAAAAAAA
ENDE ?!
CHK CHKCHK CHK
!!
ENDE! NO!
I GOTTA STOP HER!
KRKSH

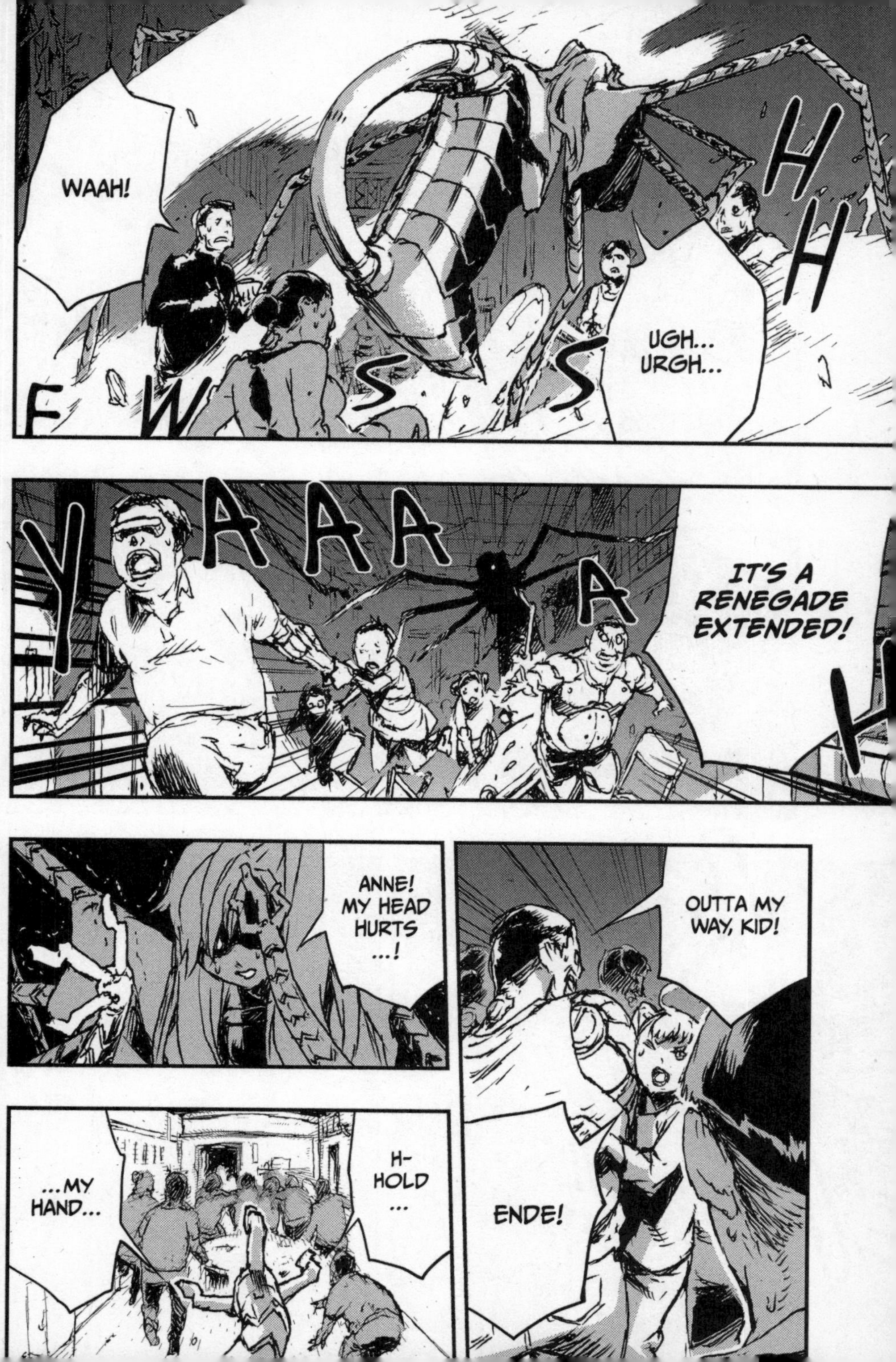
HHH
UGH... URGH...
WAAH!
FWSS
K
IT'S A RENEGADE EXTENDED!
YAAAA
OUTTA MY WAY, KID!
ENDE!
ANNE! MY HEAD HURTS ...!
H- HOLD ...
...MY HAND...

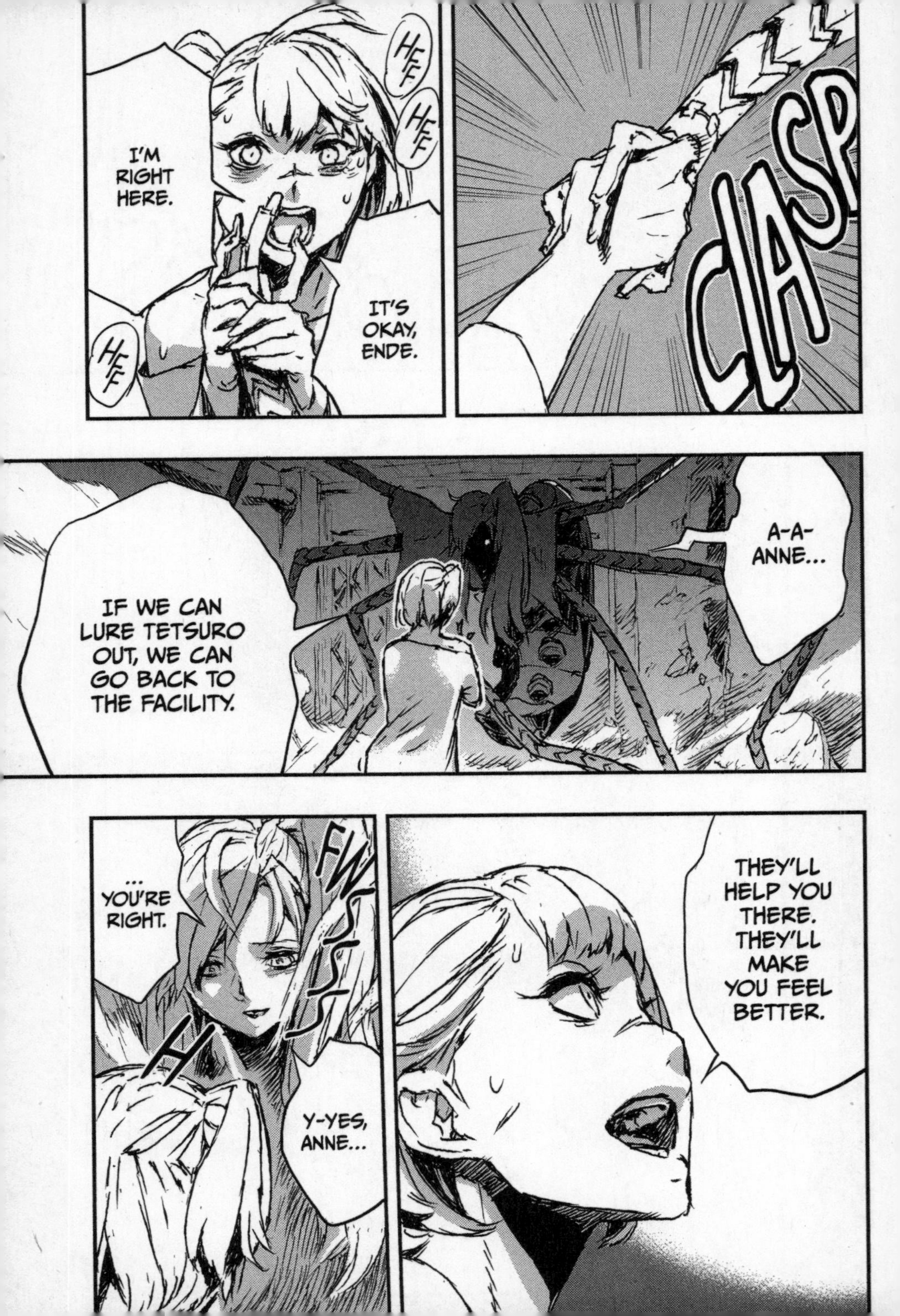
CLASP
HEF
HEF
I'M RIGHT HERE.
IT'S OKAY, ENDE.
HEF
A-A-ANNE...
IF WE CAN LURE TETSURO OUT, WE CAN GO BACK TO THE FACILITY.
THEY'LL HELP YOU THERE. THEY'LL MAKE YOU FEEL BETTER.
... YOU'RE RIGHT.
Y-YES, ANNE...

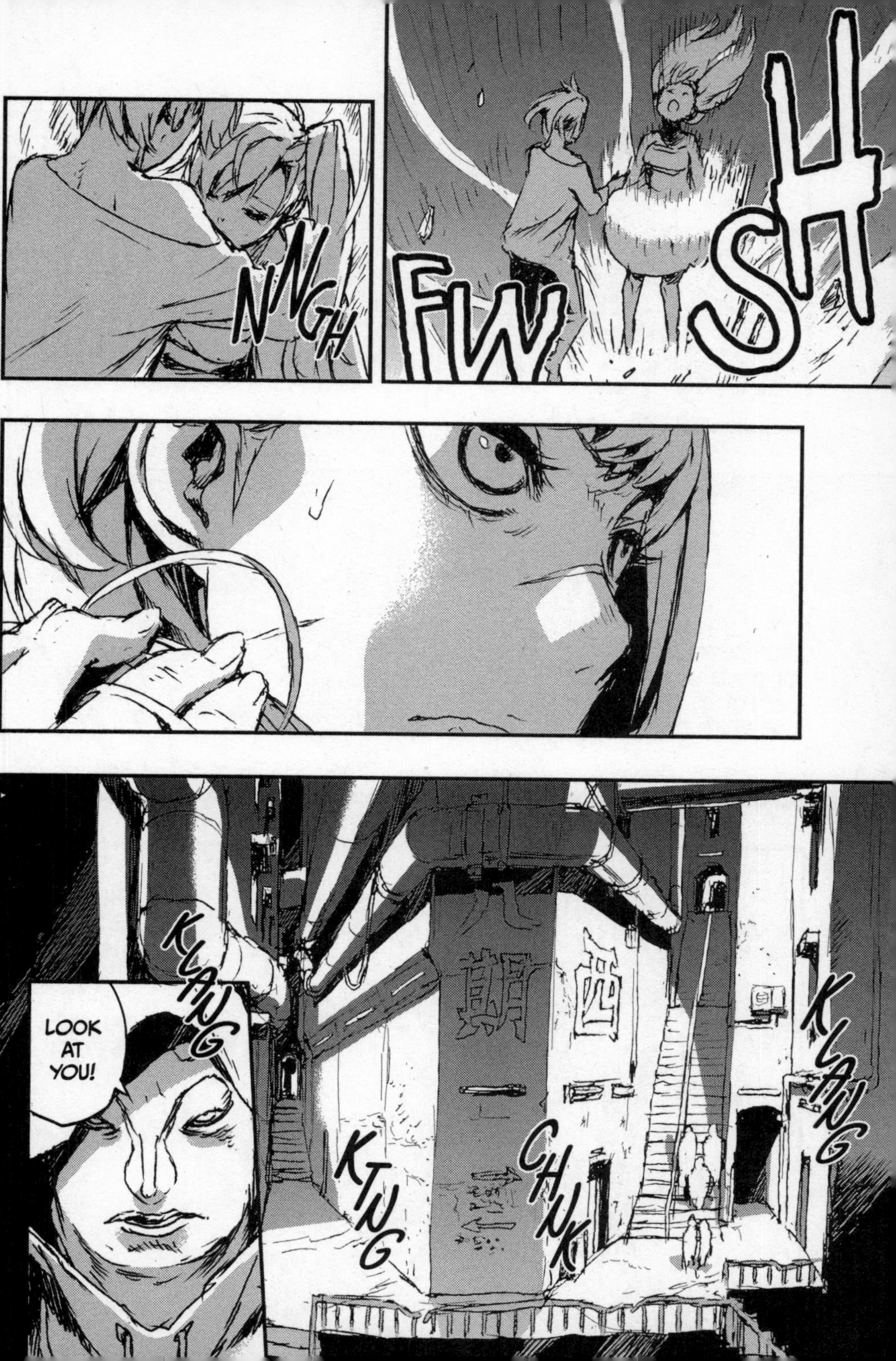
FWSH
NNNGH
KLANG
CHUNK
KTING
KLANG
LOOK AT YOU!

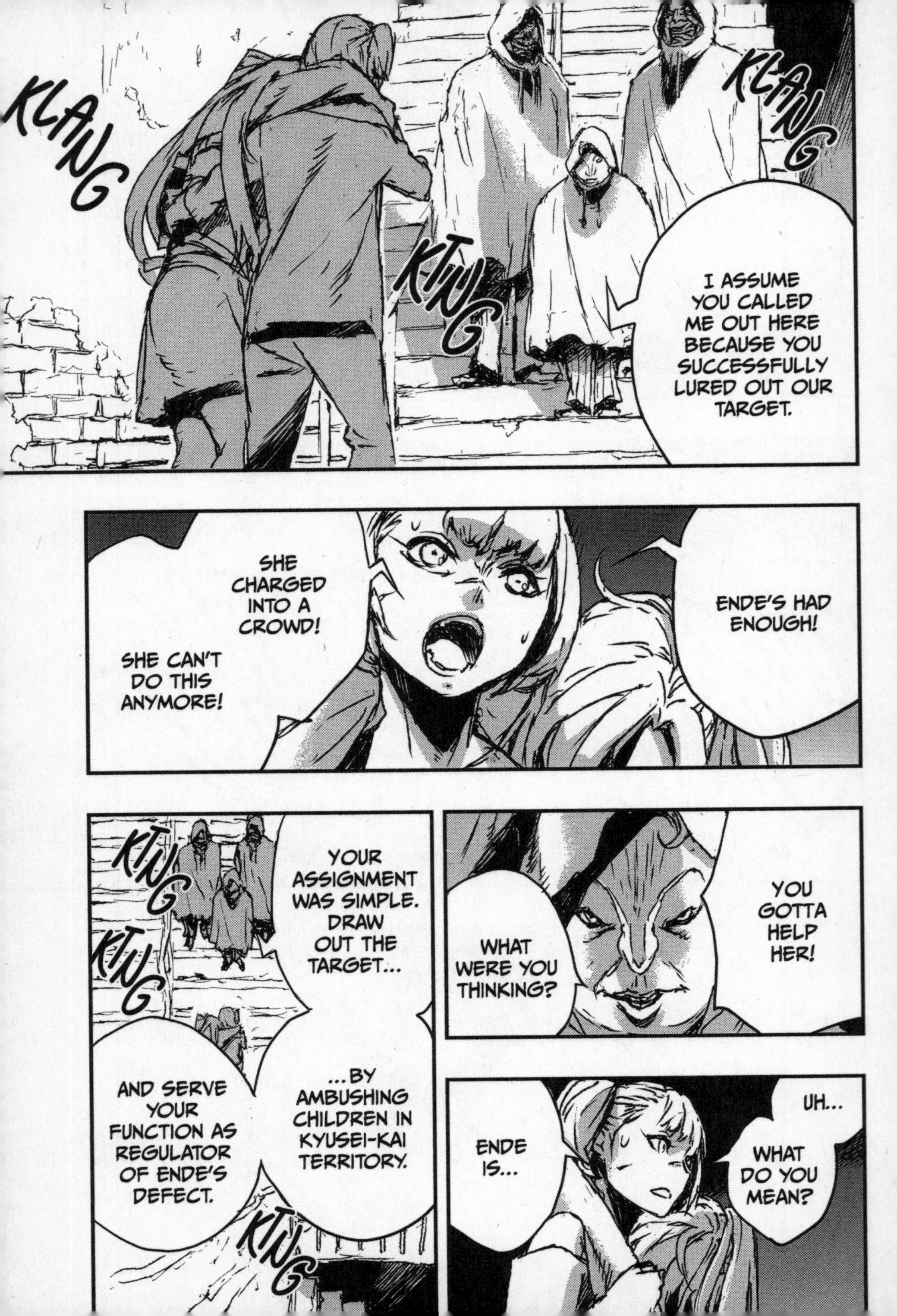
KLANG
I ASSUME YOU CALLED ME OUT HERE BECAUSE YOU SUCCESSFULLY LURED OUT OUR TARGET.
KTING
KLANG
ENDE'S HAD ENOUGH!
SHE CHARGED INTO A CROWD!
SHE CAN'T DO THIS ANYMORE!
YOU GOTTA HELP HER!
WHAT WERE YOU THINKING?
UH... WHAT DO YOU MEAN?
ENDE IS...
KTING
KTING
YOUR ASSIGNMENT WAS SIMPLE. DRAW OUT THE TARGET...
...BY AMBUSHING CHILDREN IN KYUSEI-KAI TERRITORY.
AND SERVE YOUR FUNCTION AS REGULATOR OF ENDE'S DEFECT.
KTING

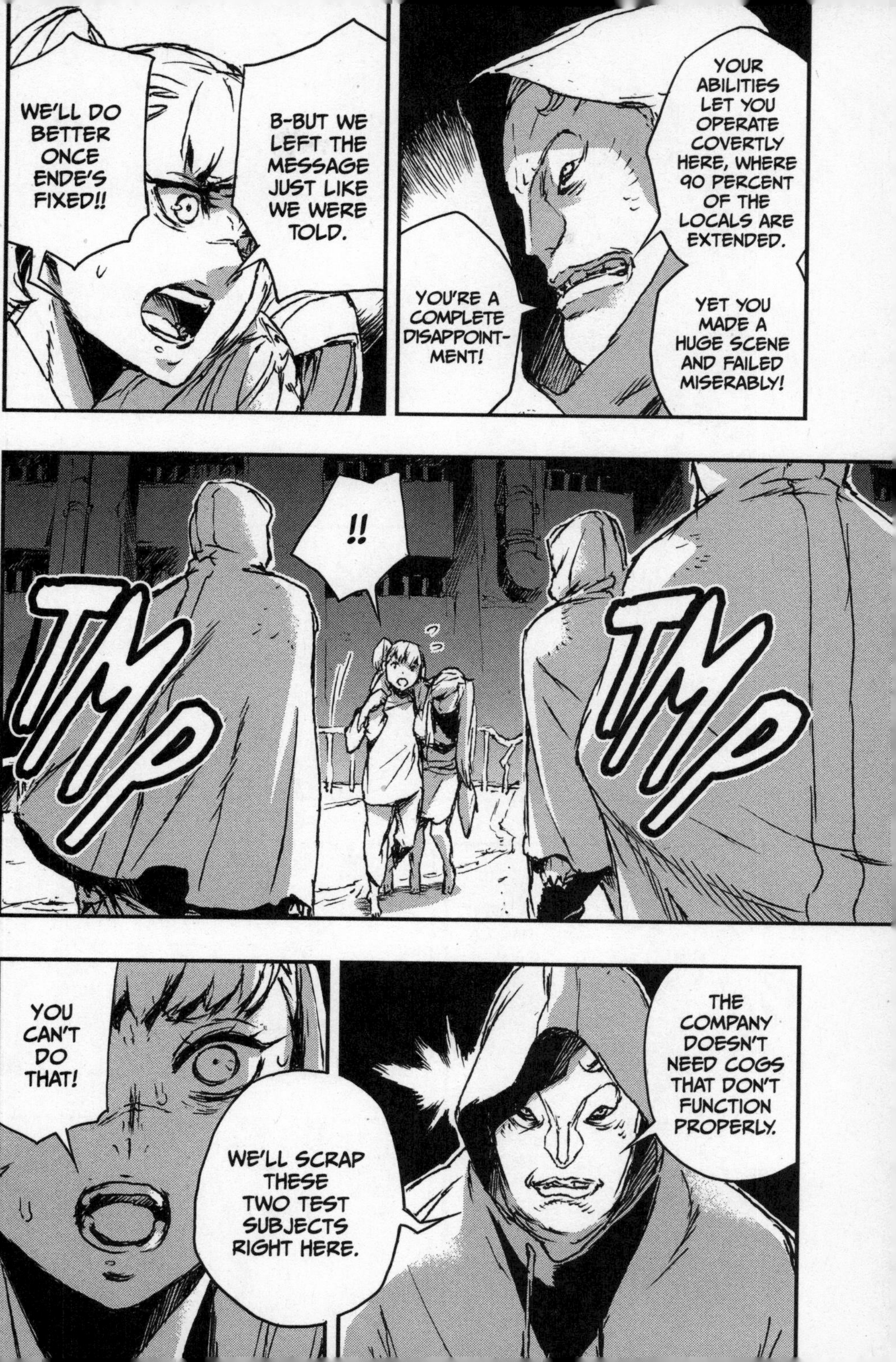
YOUR ABILITIES LET YOU OPERATE COVERTLY HERE, WHERE 90 PERCENT OF THE LOCALS ARE EXTENDED.
YET YOU MADE A HUGE SCENE AND FAILED MISERABLY!
YOU'RE A COMPLETE DISAPPOINTMENT!
B-BUT WE LEFT THE MESSAGE JUST LIKE WE WERE TOLD.
WE'LL DO BETTER ONCE ENDE'S FIXED!!
TMP
!!
TMP
THE COMPANY DOESN'T NEED COGS THAT DON'T FUNCTION PROPERLY.
WE'LL SCRAP THESE TWO TEST SUBJECTS RIGHT HERE.
YOU CAN'T DO THAT!

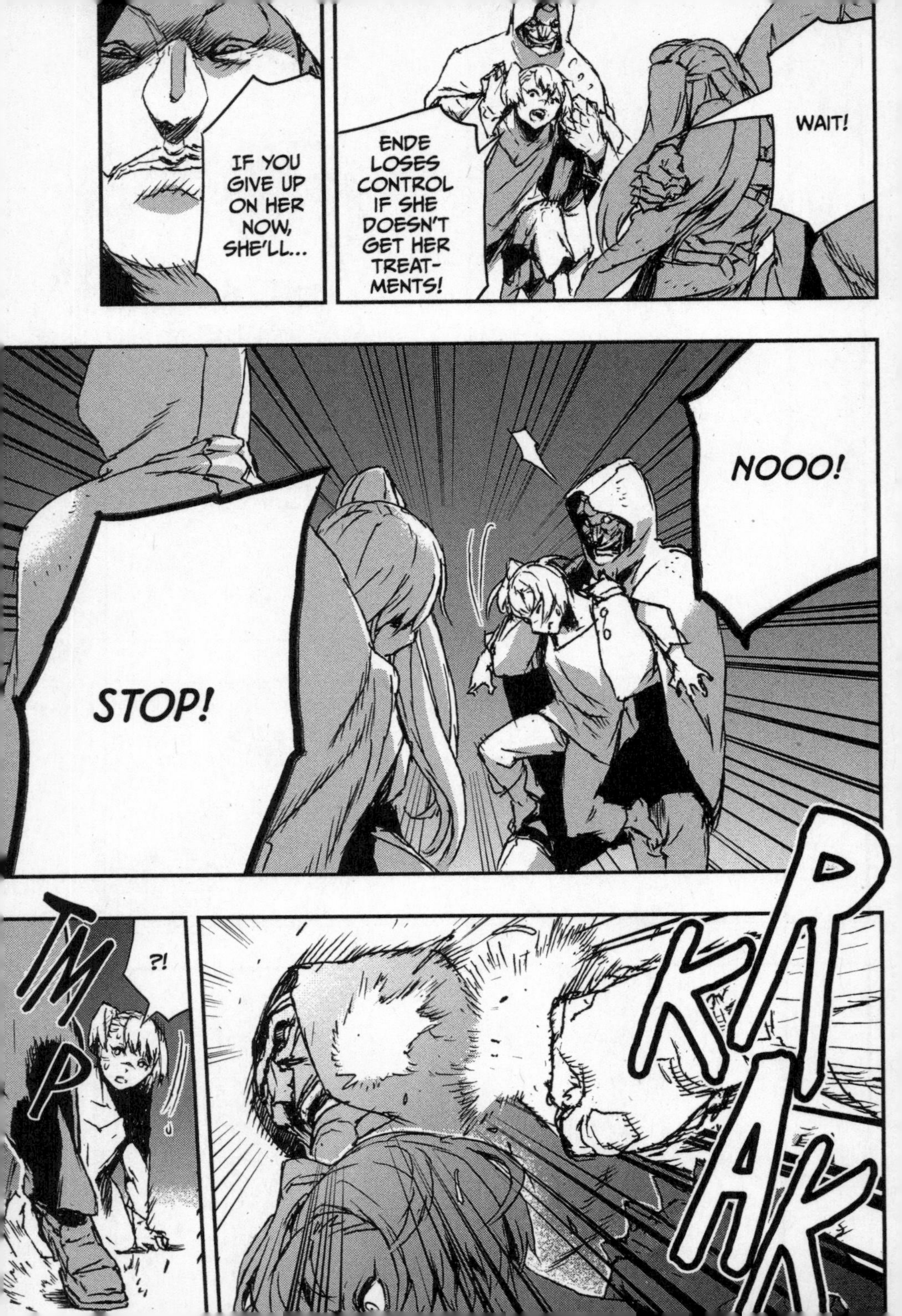
WAIT!
ENDE LOSES CONTROL IF SHE DOESN'T GET HER TREAT-MENTS!
IF YOU GIVE UP ON HER NOW, SHE'LL...
NOOO!
STOP!
KRAK
?!
TMP

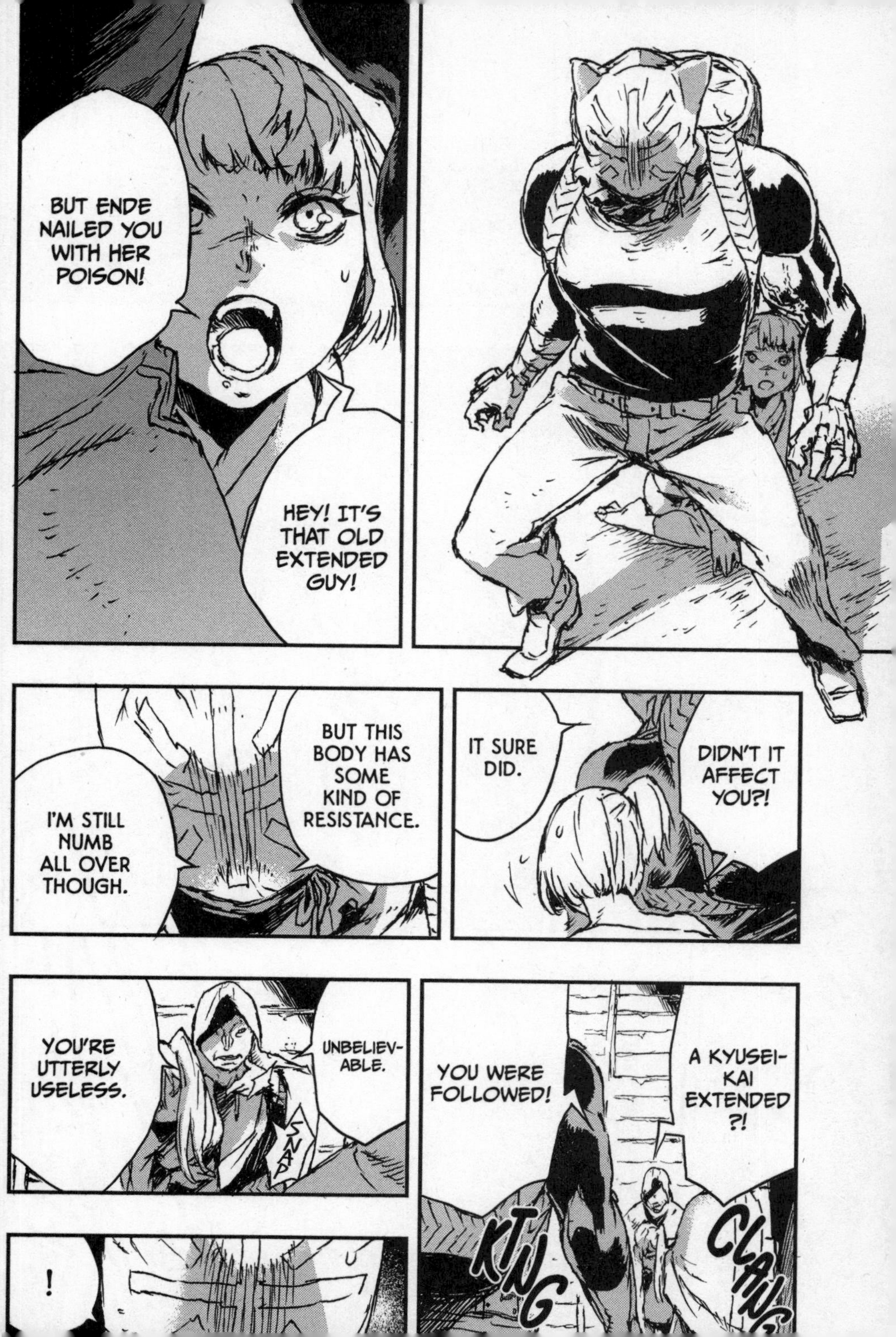
HEY! IT'S THAT OLD EXTENDED GUY!
BUT ENDE NAILED YOU WITH HER POISON!
DIDN'T IT AFFECT YOU?!
IT SURE DID.
BUT THIS BODY HAS SOME KIND OF RESISTANCE.
I'M STILL NUMB ALL OVER THOUGH.
A KYUSEI-KAI EXTENDED ?!
YOU WERE FOLLOWED!
UNBELIEV-ABLE.
YOU'RE UTTERLY USELESS.
SNAP
CLANG
KTING
!

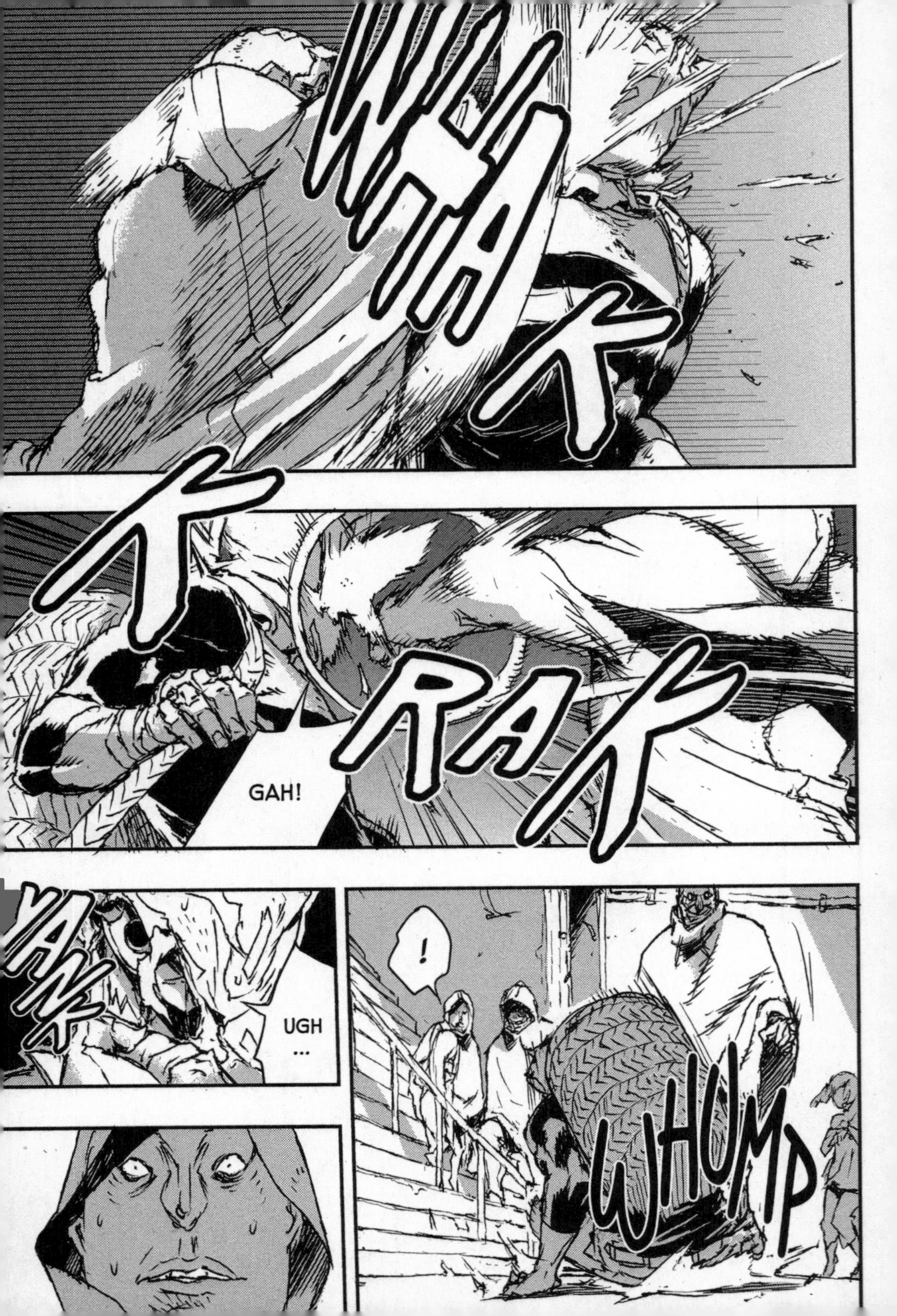

WHAK
K
RAK
GAH!
!
WHUMP
YANK
UGH
...

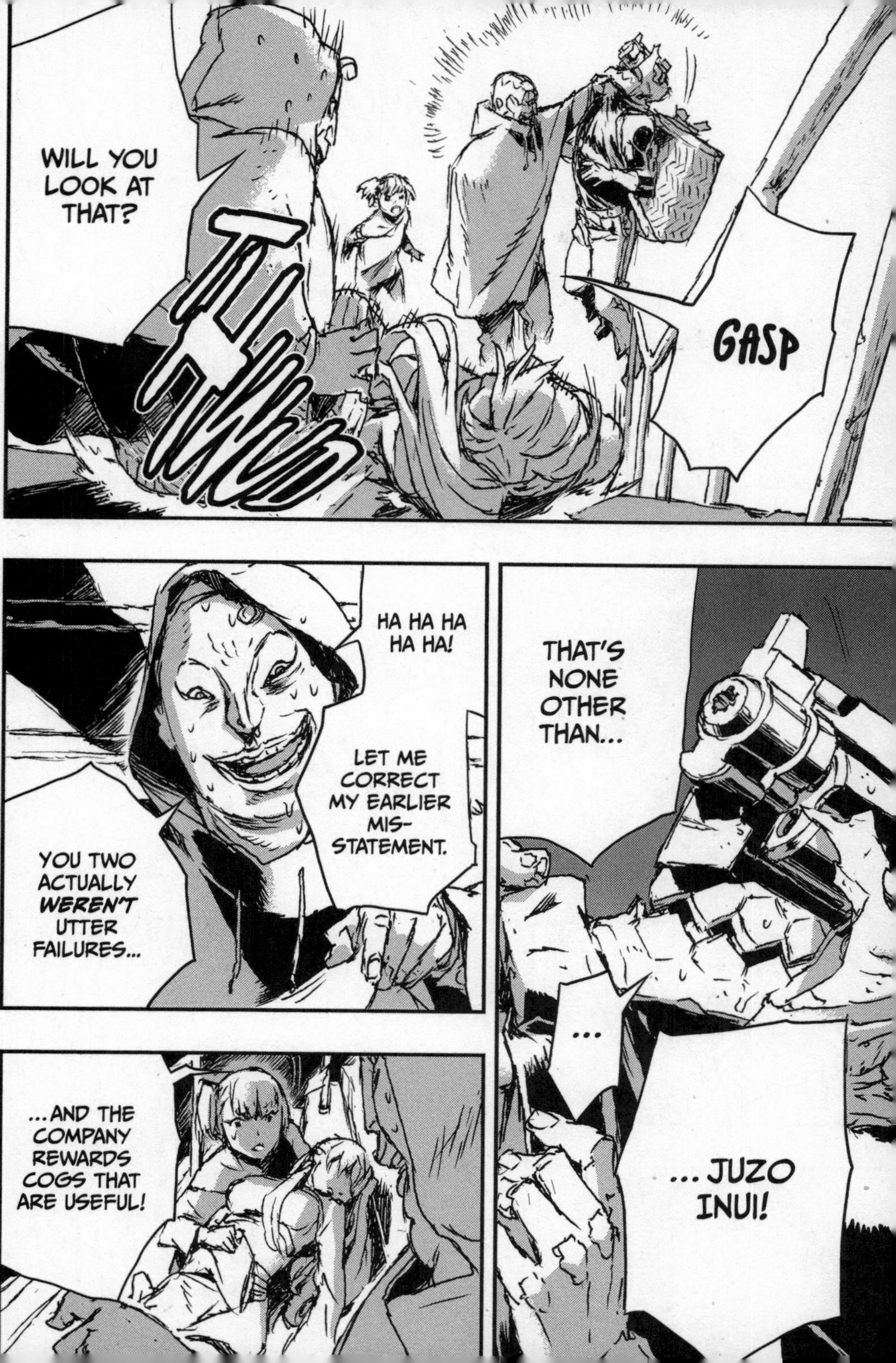
GASP
WILL YOU LOOK AT THAT?
THAT'S NONE OTHER THAN...
...
...JUZO INUI!
HA HA HA HA HA!
LET ME CORRECT MY EARLIER MIS-STATEMENT.
YOU TWO ACTUALLY *WEREN'T* UTTER FAILURES...
...AND THE COMPANY REWARDS COGS THAT ARE USEFUL!

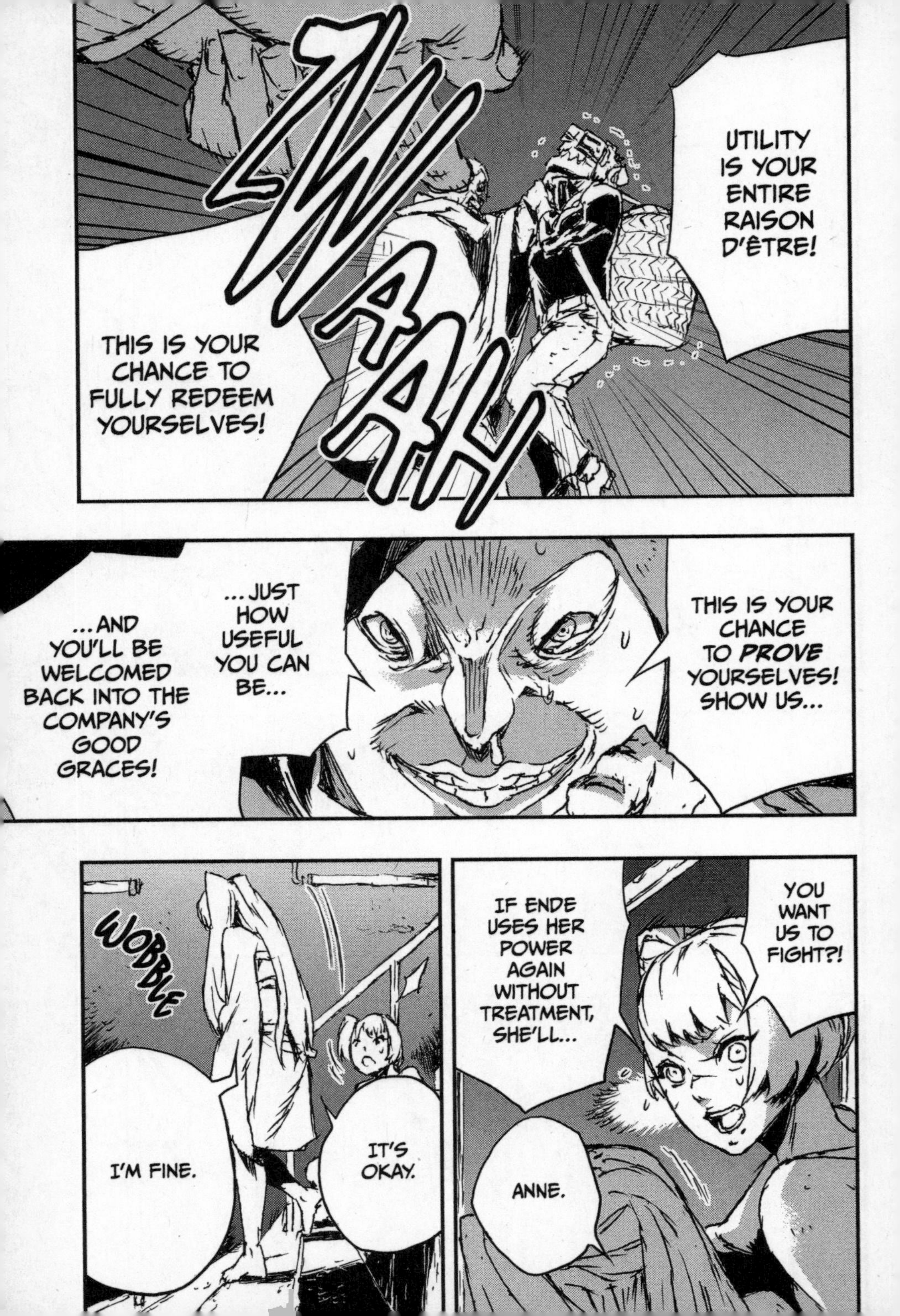
UTILITY IS YOUR ENTIRE RAISON D'ÊTRE!
WAAH
THIS IS YOUR CHANCE TO FULLY REDEEM YOURSELVES!
THIS IS YOUR CHANCE TO *PROVE* YOURSELVES! SHOW US...
...JUST HOW USEFUL YOU CAN BE...
...AND YOU'LL BE WELCOMED BACK INTO THE COMPANY'S GOOD GRACES!
YOU WANT US TO FIGHT?!
IF ENDE USES HER POWER AGAIN WITHOUT TREATMENT, SHE'LL...
ANNE.
WOBBLE
IT'S OKAY.
I'M FINE.

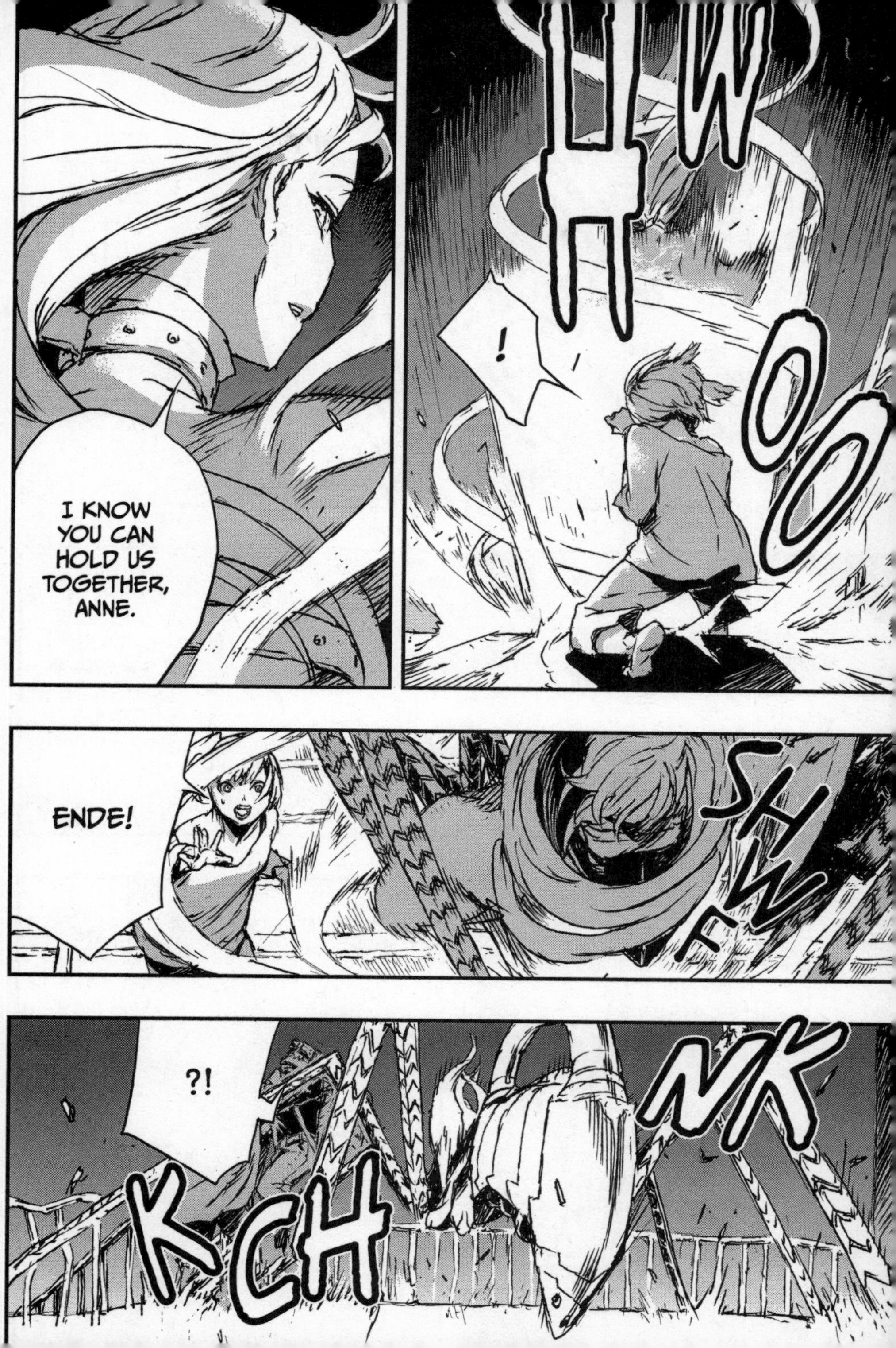
WHOOO
!
I KNOW YOU CAN HOLD US TOGETHER, ANNE.
SHWF
ENDE!
?!
KCHNK

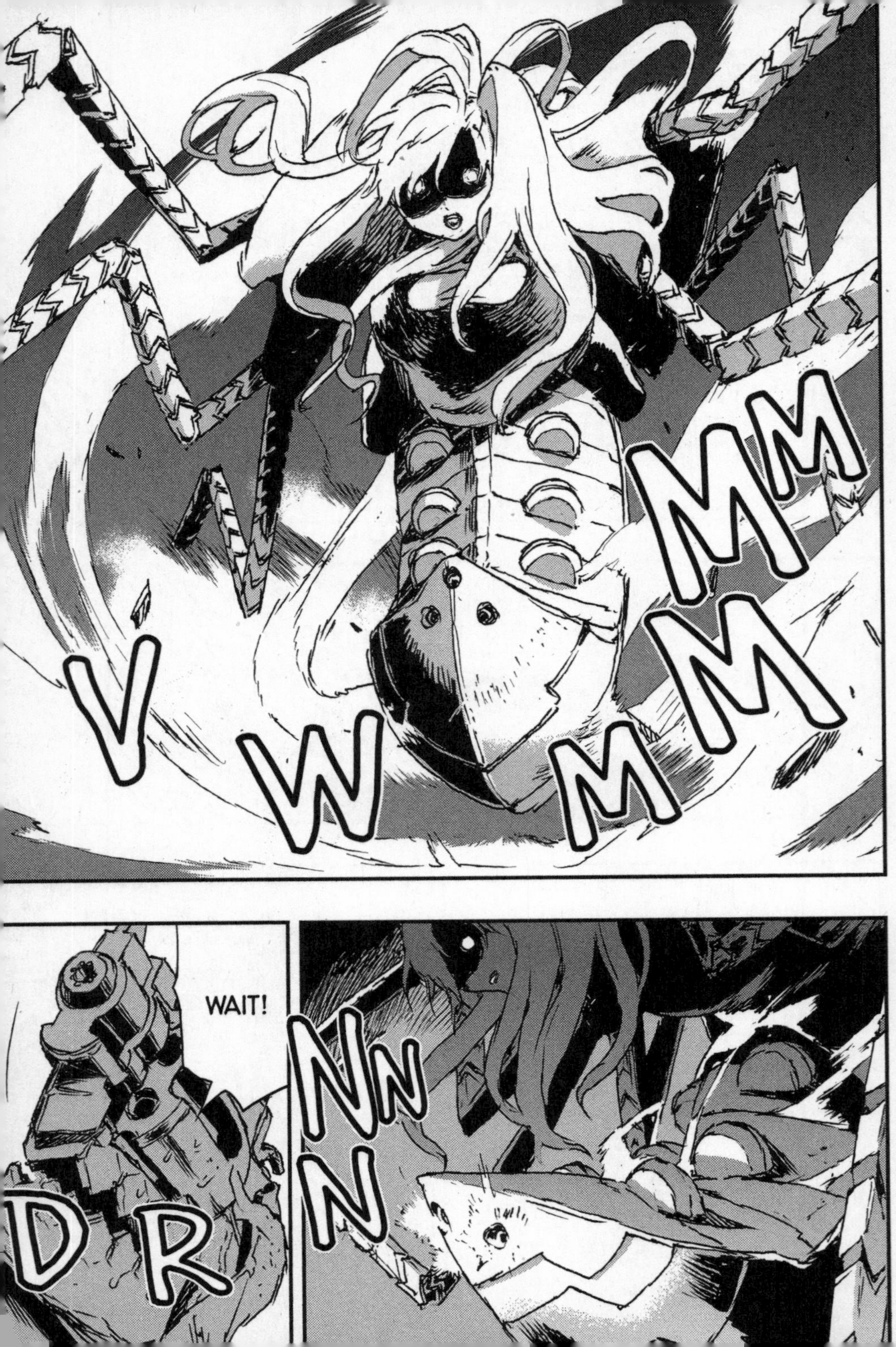
VWMMMMM
WAIT!
DRNNNN

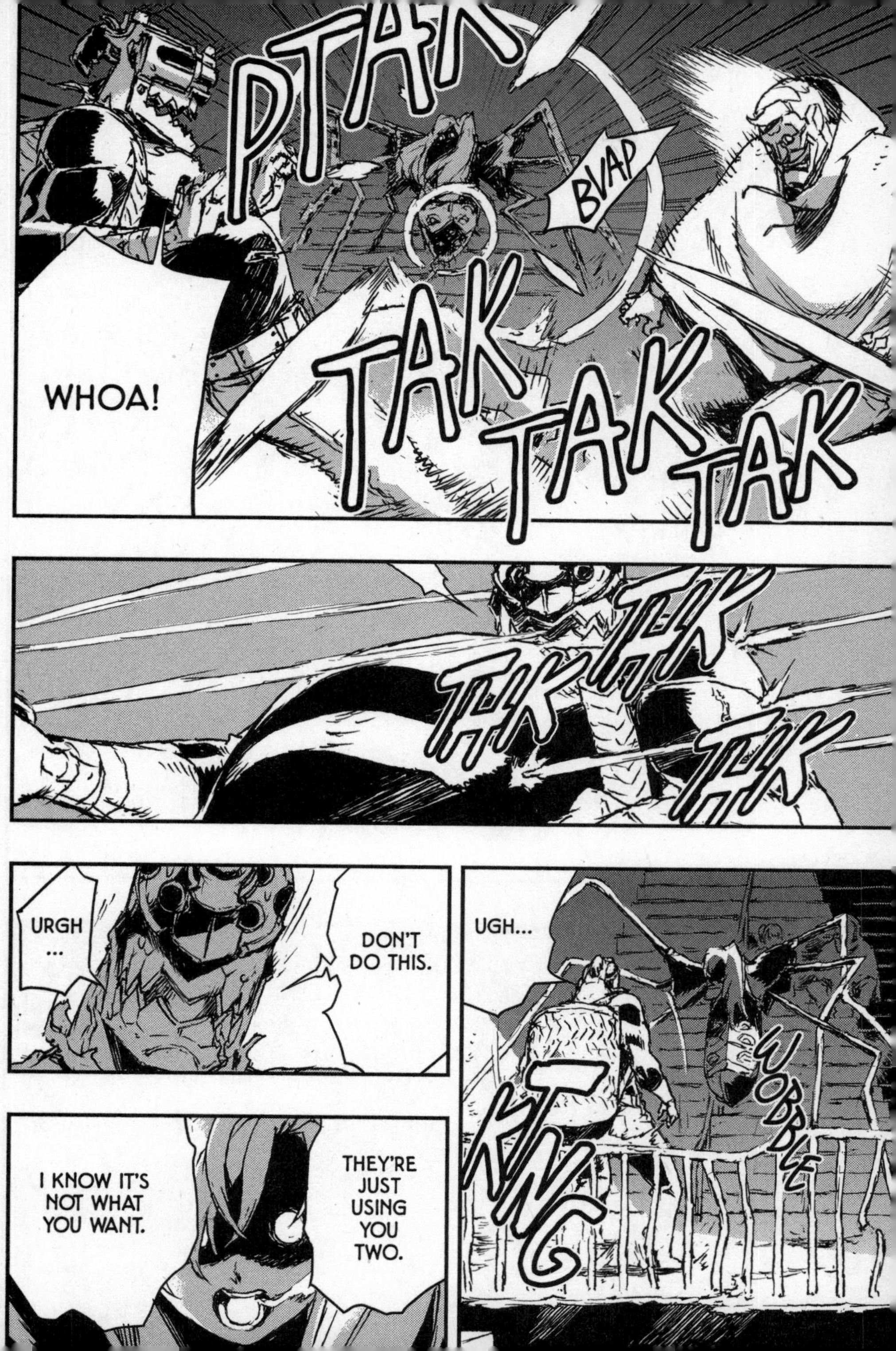
PTAK
BVAP
TAK TAK TAK
WHOA!
TAK TAK TAK TAK
UGH...
WOBBLE
URGH ...
DON'T DO THIS.
THEY'RE JUST USING YOU TWO.
I KNOW IT'S NOT WHAT YOU WANT.

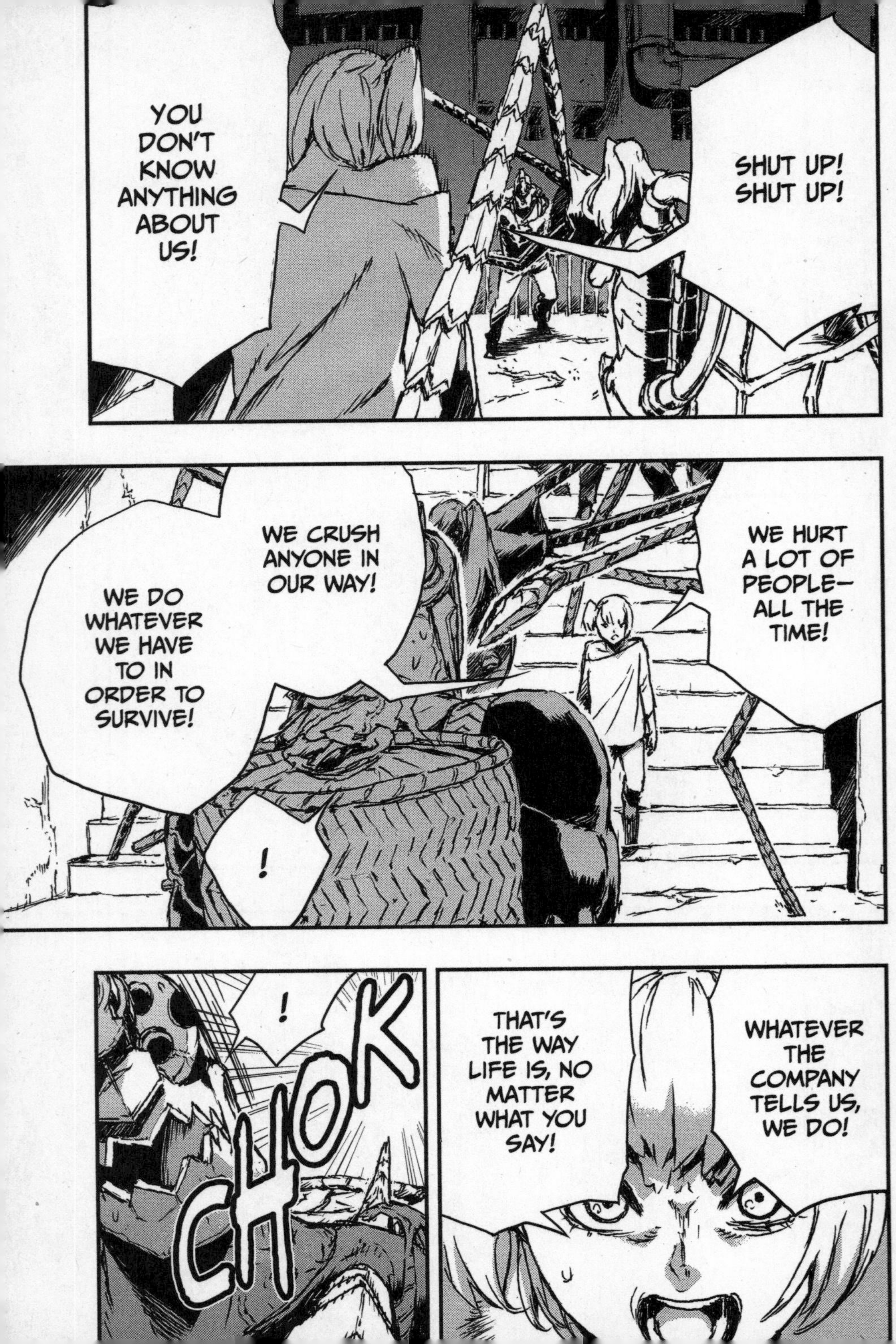
SHUT UP! SHUT UP!
YOU DON'T KNOW ANYTHING ABOUT US!
WE HURT A LOT OF PEOPLE— ALL THE TIME!
WE CRUSH ANYONE IN OUR WAY!
WE DO WHATEVER WE HAVE TO IN ORDER TO SURVIVE!
!
WHATEVER THE COMPANY TELLS US, WE DO!
THAT'S THE WAY LIFE IS, NO MATTER WHAT YOU SAY!
!
CHOK

AAAGH!

THWUMP

VWNN

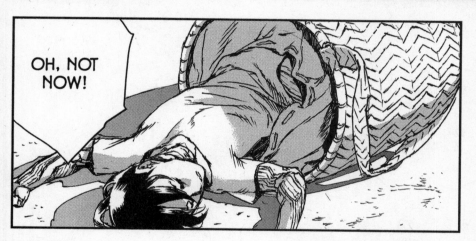

OH, NOT NOW!

TETSURO ARAHABAKI...

I FIGURED YOU'D KEEP HIM CLOSE BY.

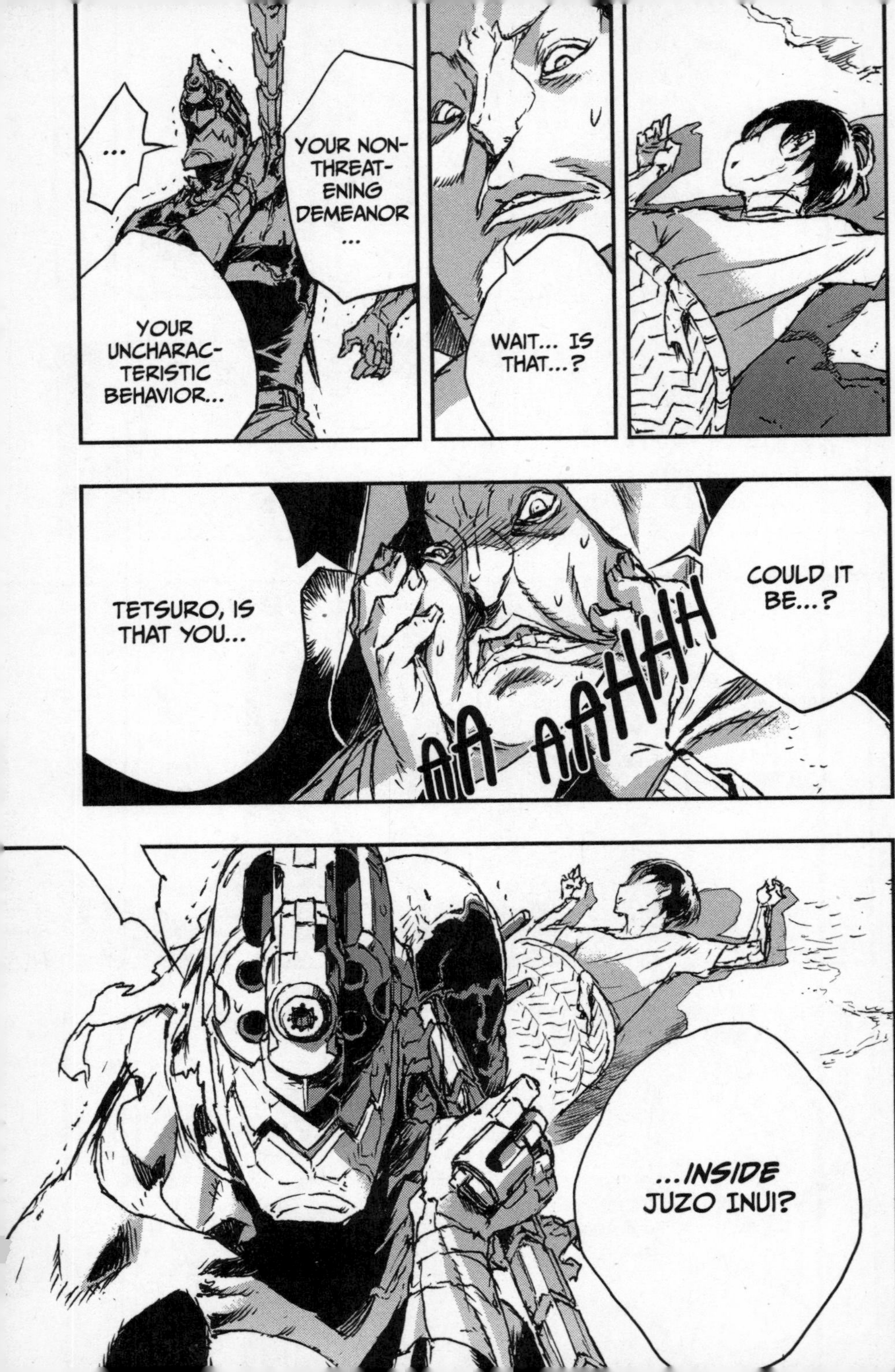
WAIT... IS THAT...?
YOUR NON-THREAT-ENING DEMEANOR ...
...
YOUR UNCHARAC-TERISTIC BEHAVIOR...
COULD IT BE...?
AA AAHHH
TETSURO, IS THAT YOU...
...INSIDE JUZO INUI?

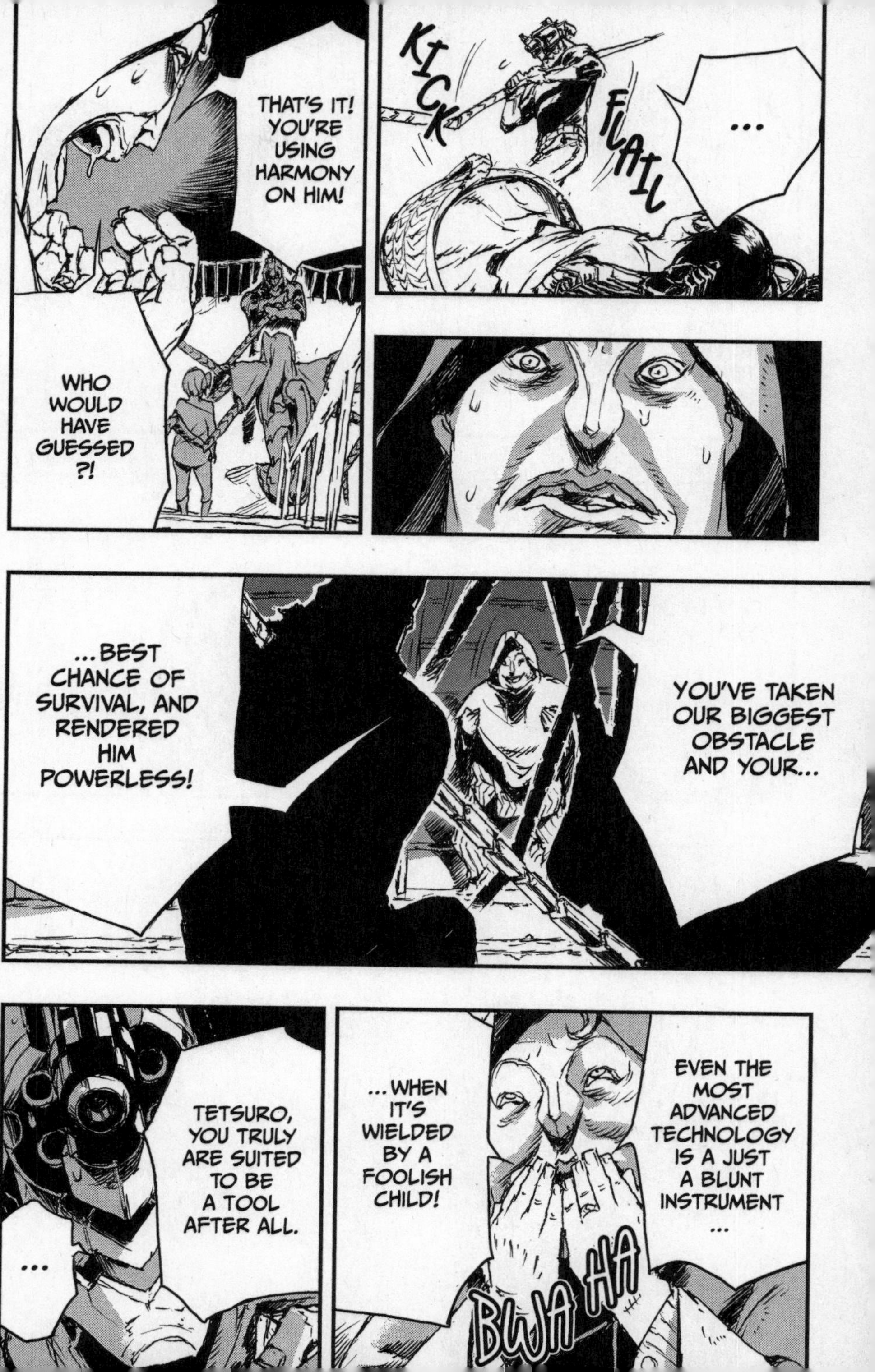
...
KICK
FLAIL
THAT'S IT! YOU'RE USING HARMONY ON HIM!
WHO WOULD HAVE GUESSED?!
YOU'VE TAKEN OUR BIGGEST OBSTACLE AND YOUR...
...BEST CHANCE OF SURVIVAL, AND RENDERED HIM POWERLESS!
EVEN THE MOST ADVANCED TECHNOLOGY IS A JUST A BLUNT INSTRUMENT ...
...WHEN IT'S WIELDED BY A FOOLISH CHILD!
BWA HA
TETSURO, YOU TRULY ARE SUITED TO BE A TOOL AFTER ALL.
...

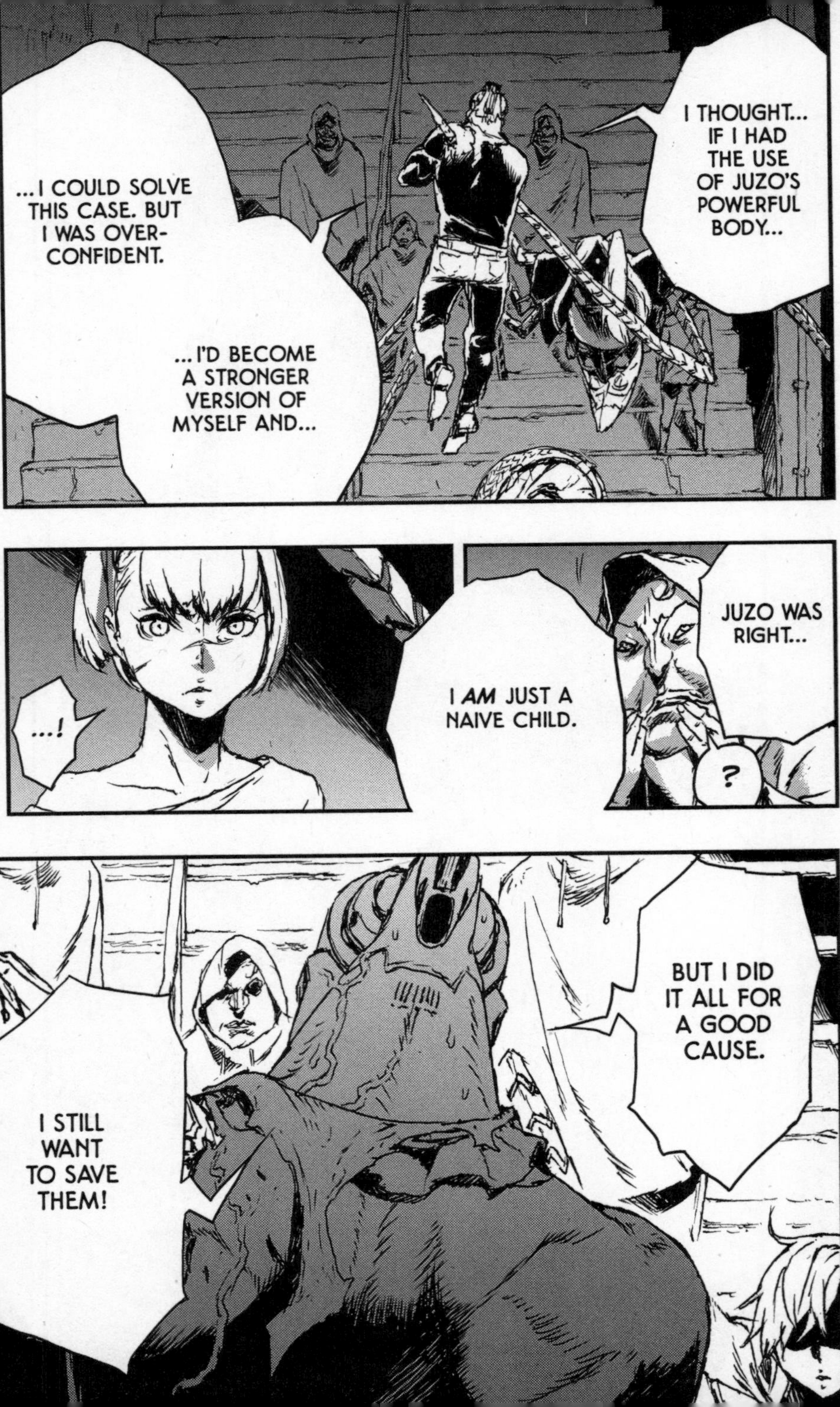
I THOUGHT... IF I HAD THE USE OF JUZO'S POWERFUL BODY...
...I'D BECOME A STRONGER VERSION OF MYSELF AND...
...I COULD SOLVE THIS CASE. BUT I WAS OVER-CONFIDENT.
JUZO WAS RIGHT...
I *AM* JUST A NAIVE CHILD.
?
...!
BUT I DID IT ALL FOR A GOOD CAUSE.
I STILL WANT TO SAVE THEM!

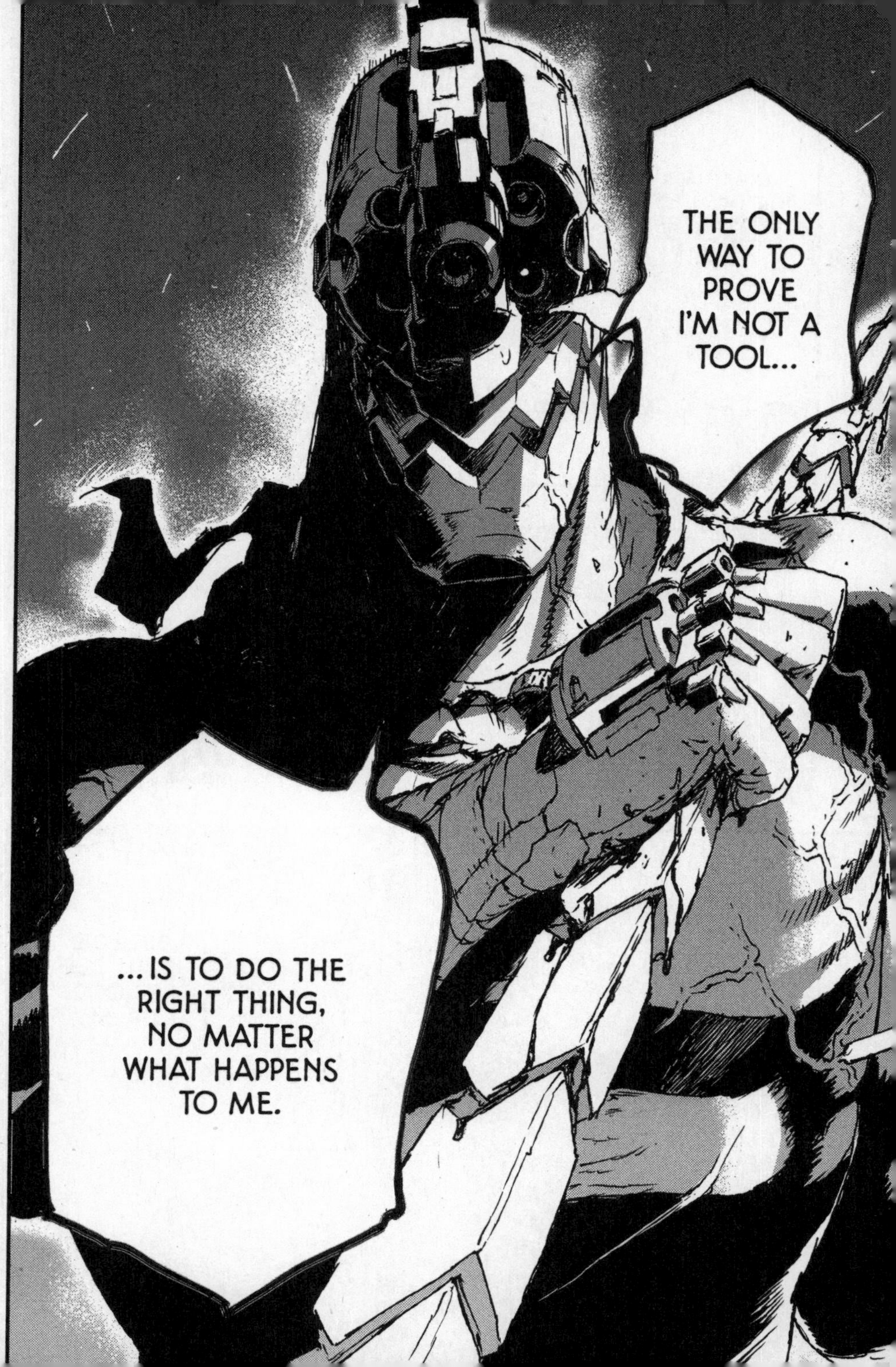
THE ONLY WAY TO PROVE I'M NOT A TOOL...
...IS TO DO THE RIGHT THING, NO MATTER WHAT HAPPENS TO ME.

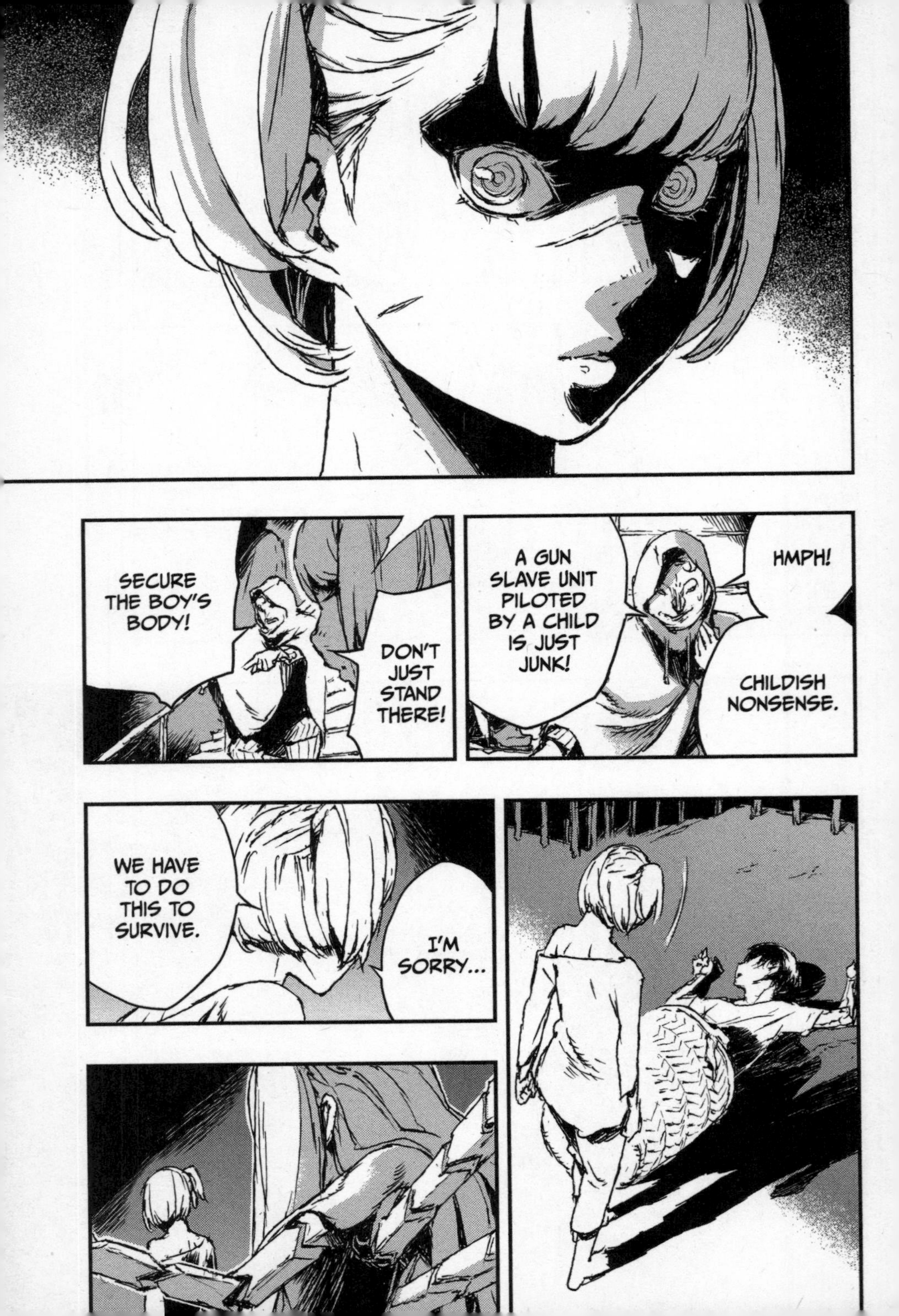
HMPH!
CHILDISH NONSENSE.
A GUN SLAVE UNIT PILOTED BY A CHILD IS JUST JUNK!
DON'T JUST STAND THERE!
SECURE THE BOY'S BODY!
I'M SORRY...
WE HAVE TO DO THIS TO SURVIVE.

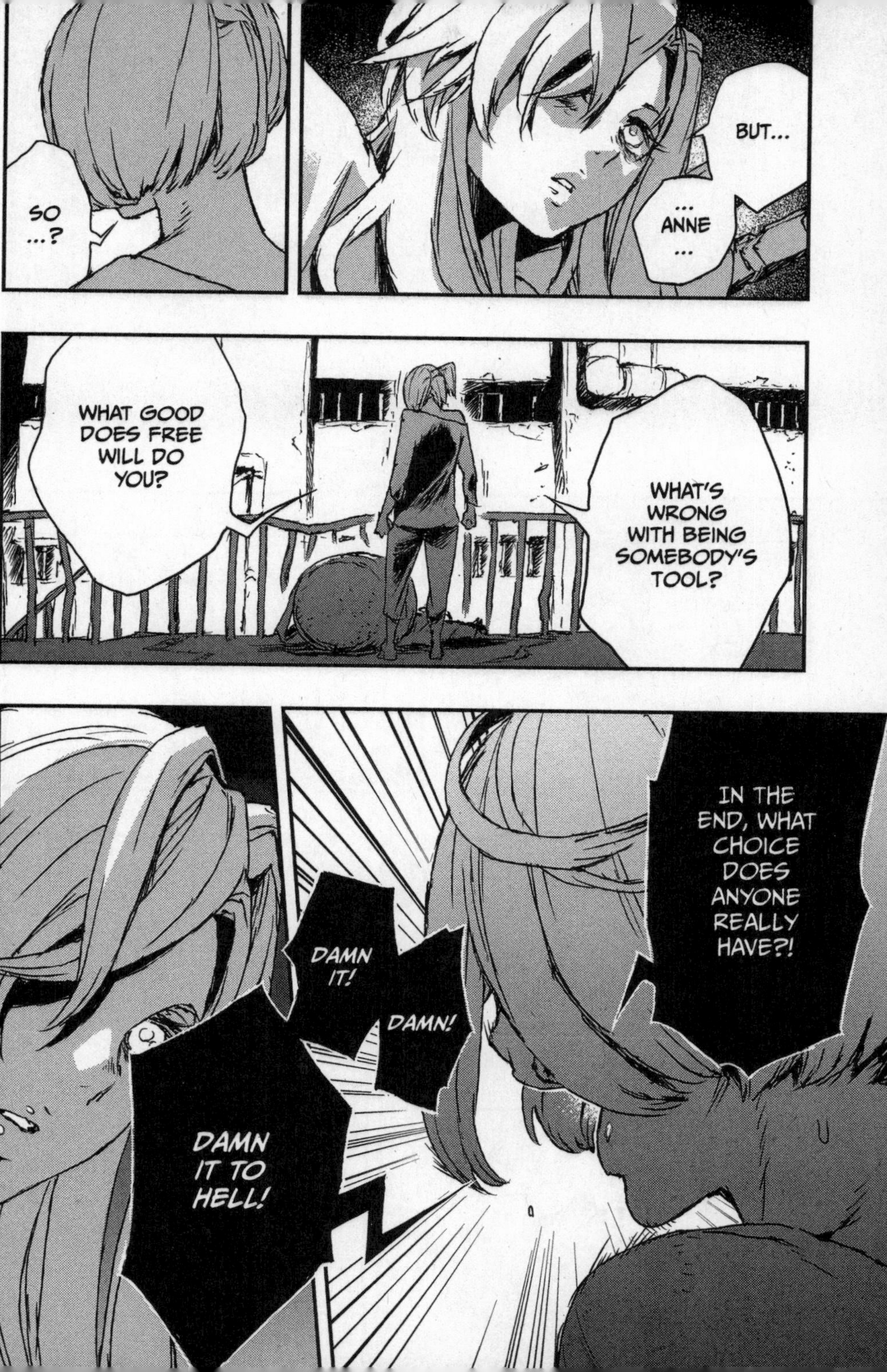
BUT...
... ANNE ...
SO ...?
WHAT'S WRONG WITH BEING SOMEBODY'S TOOL?
WHAT GOOD DOES FREE WILL DO YOU?
IN THE END, WHAT CHOICE DOES ANYONE REALLY HAVE?!
DAMN IT!
DAMN!
DAMN IT TO HELL!

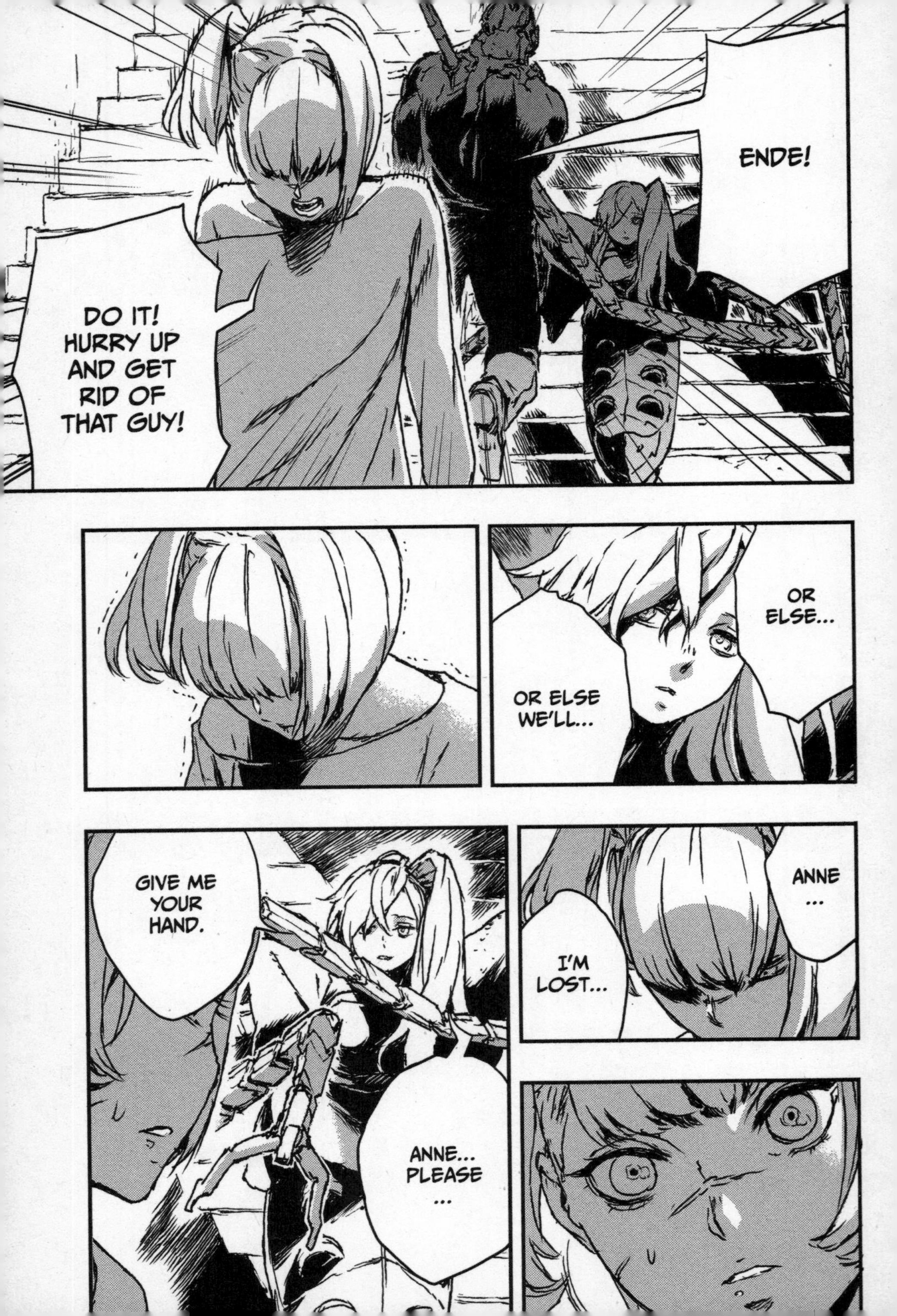
ENDE!
DO IT! HURRY UP AND GET RID OF THAT GUY!
OR ELSE...
OR ELSE WE'LL...
ANNE ...
I'M LOST...
GIVE ME YOUR HAND.
ANNE... PLEASE ...

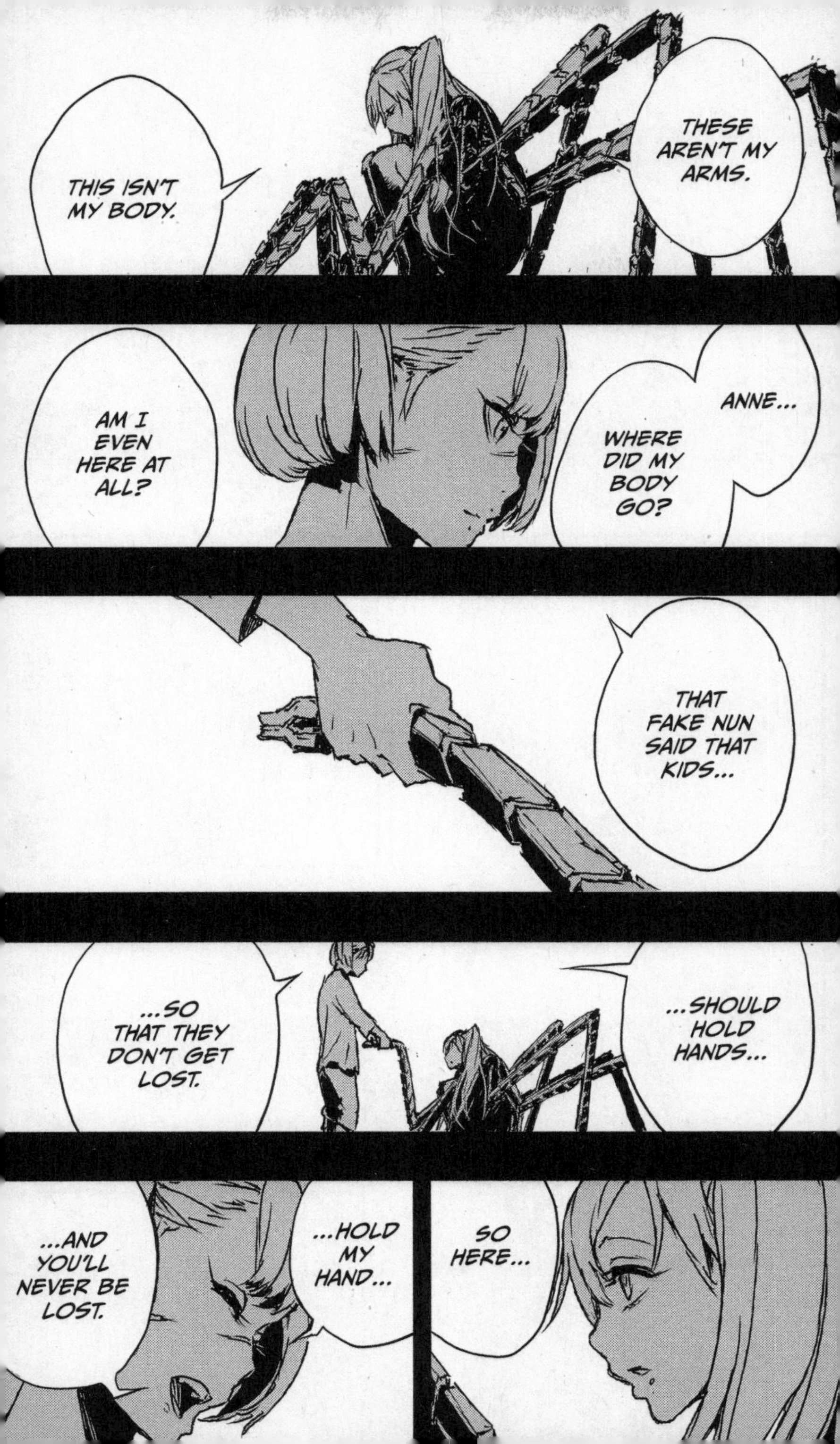
THESE AREN'T MY ARMS.
THIS ISN'T MY BODY.
ANNE...
WHERE DID MY BODY GO?
AM I EVEN HERE AT ALL?
THAT FAKE NUN SAID THAT KIDS...
...SHOULD HOLD HANDS...
...SO THAT THEY DON'T GET LOST.
SO HERE...
...HOLD MY HAND...
...AND YOU'LL NEVER BE LOST.

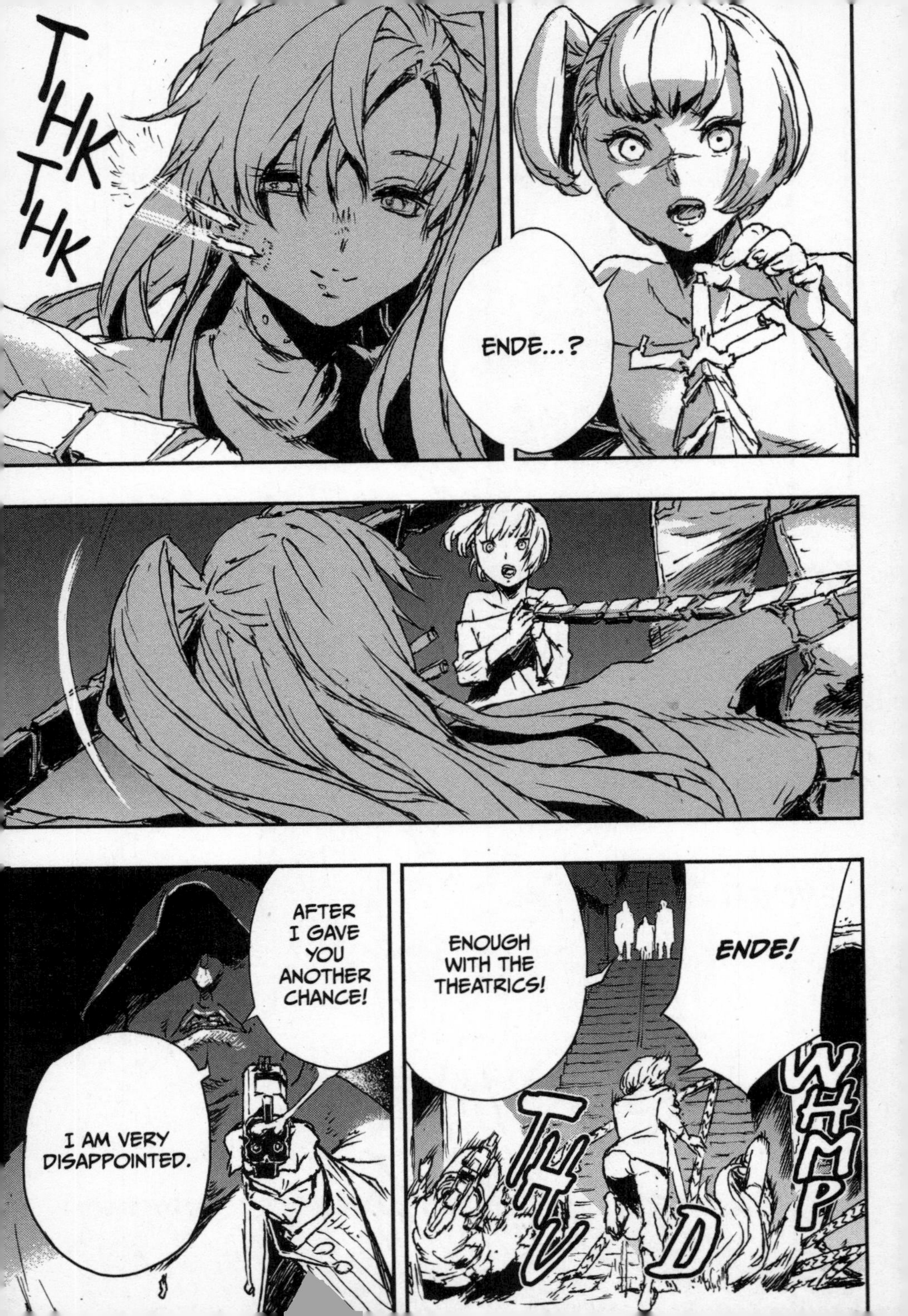
ENDE...?
THK THK
ENDE!
ENOUGH WITH THE THEATRICS!
WHMP
THUD
AFTER I GAVE YOU ANOTHER CHANCE!
I AM VERY DISAPPOINTED.

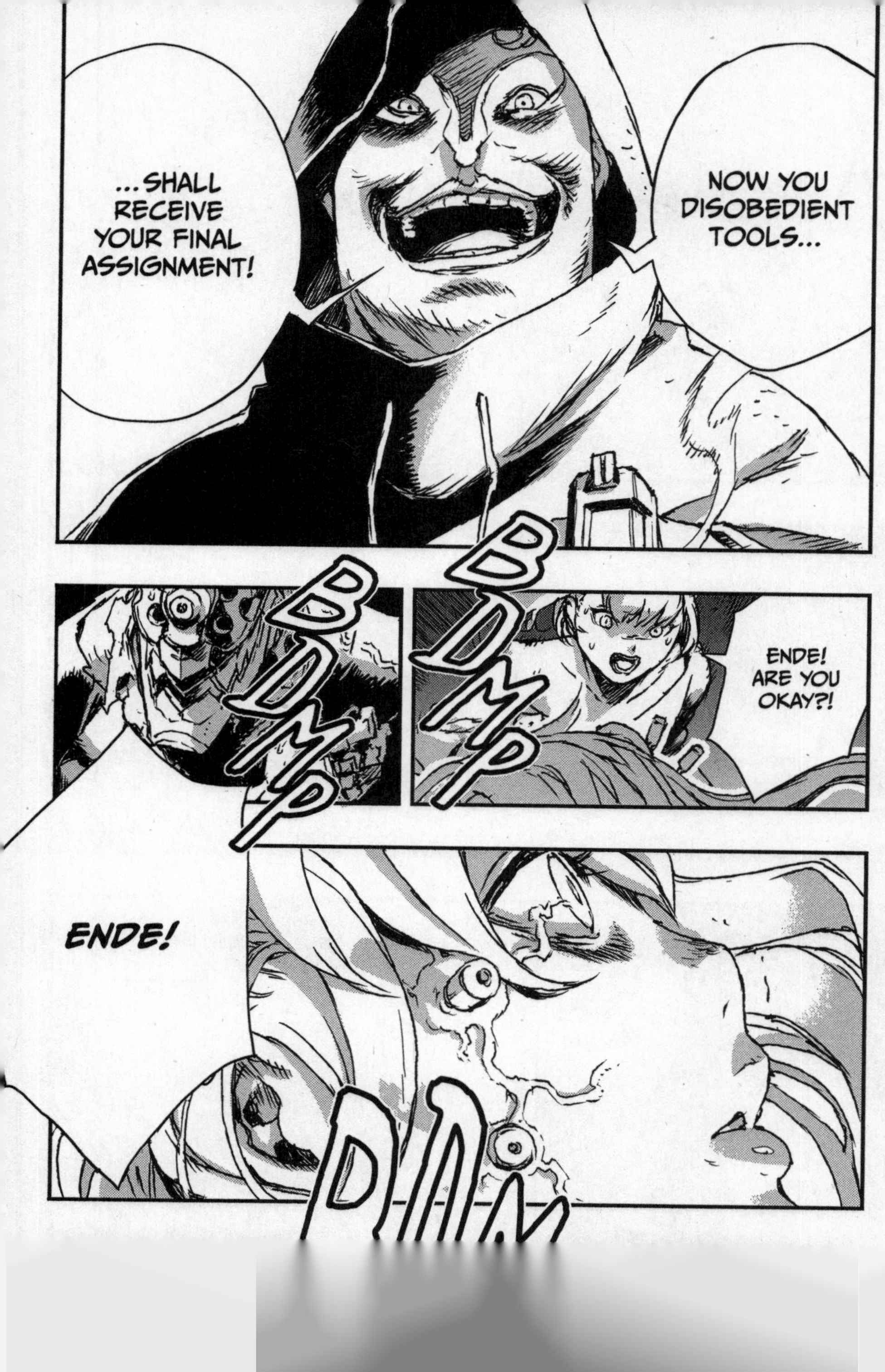
NOW YOU DISOBEDIENT TOOLS...
...SHALL RECEIVE YOUR FINAL ASSIGNMENT!
BDMP
ENDE! ARE YOU OKAY?!
BDMP
ENDE!

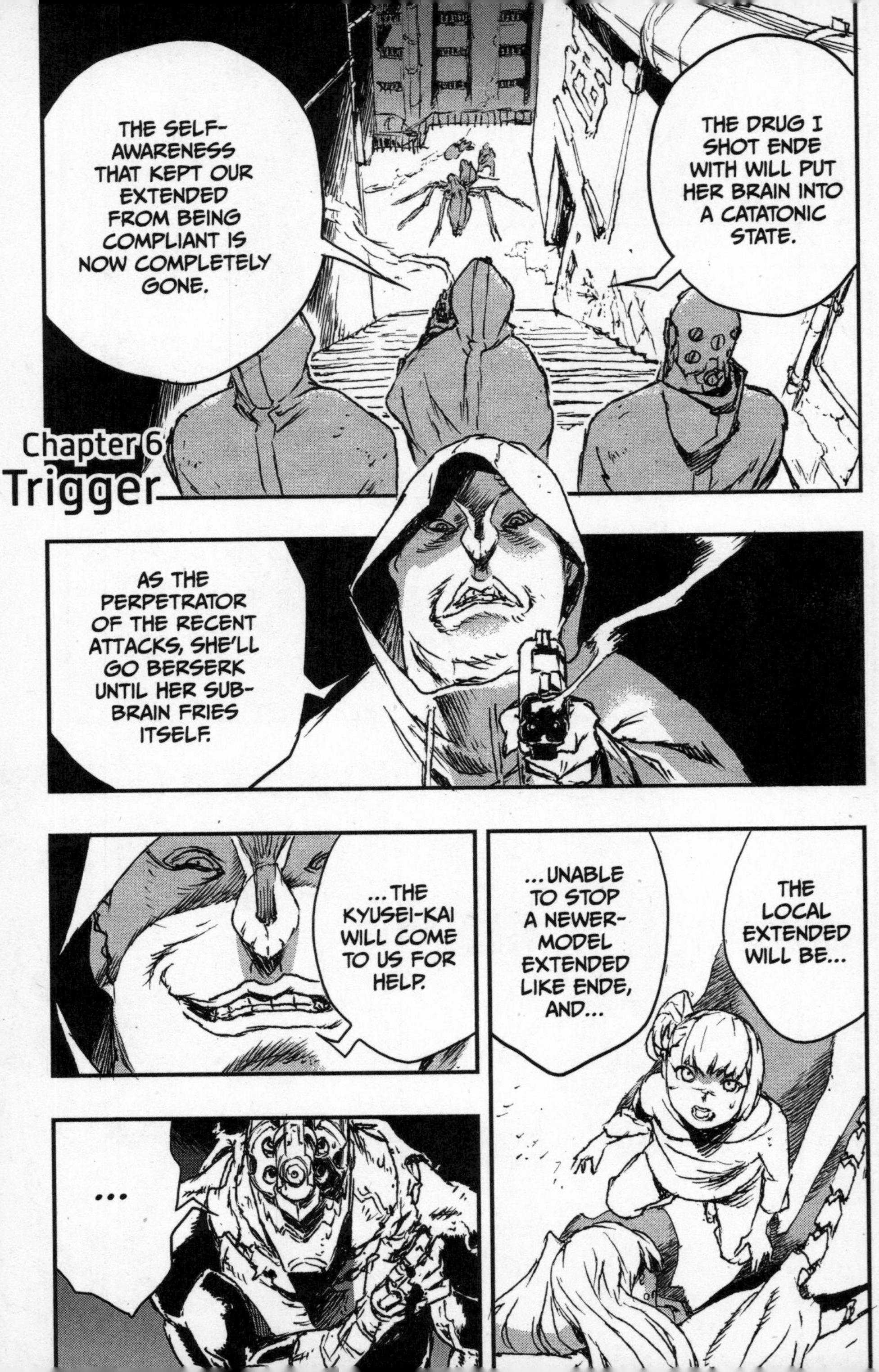
THE DRUG I SHOT ENDE WITH WILL PUT HER BRAIN INTO A CATATONIC STATE.
THE SELF-AWARENESS THAT KEPT OUR EXTENDED FROM BEING COMPLIANT IS NOW COMPLETELY GONE.
Chapter 6
Trigger
AS THE PERPETRATOR OF THE RECENT ATTACKS, SHE'LL GO BERSERK UNTIL HER SUB-BRAIN FRIES ITSELF.
THE LOCAL EXTENDED WILL BE...
...UNABLE TO STOP A NEWER-MODEL EXTENDED LIKE ENDE, AND...
...THE KYUSEI-KAI WILL COME TO US FOR HELP.
...

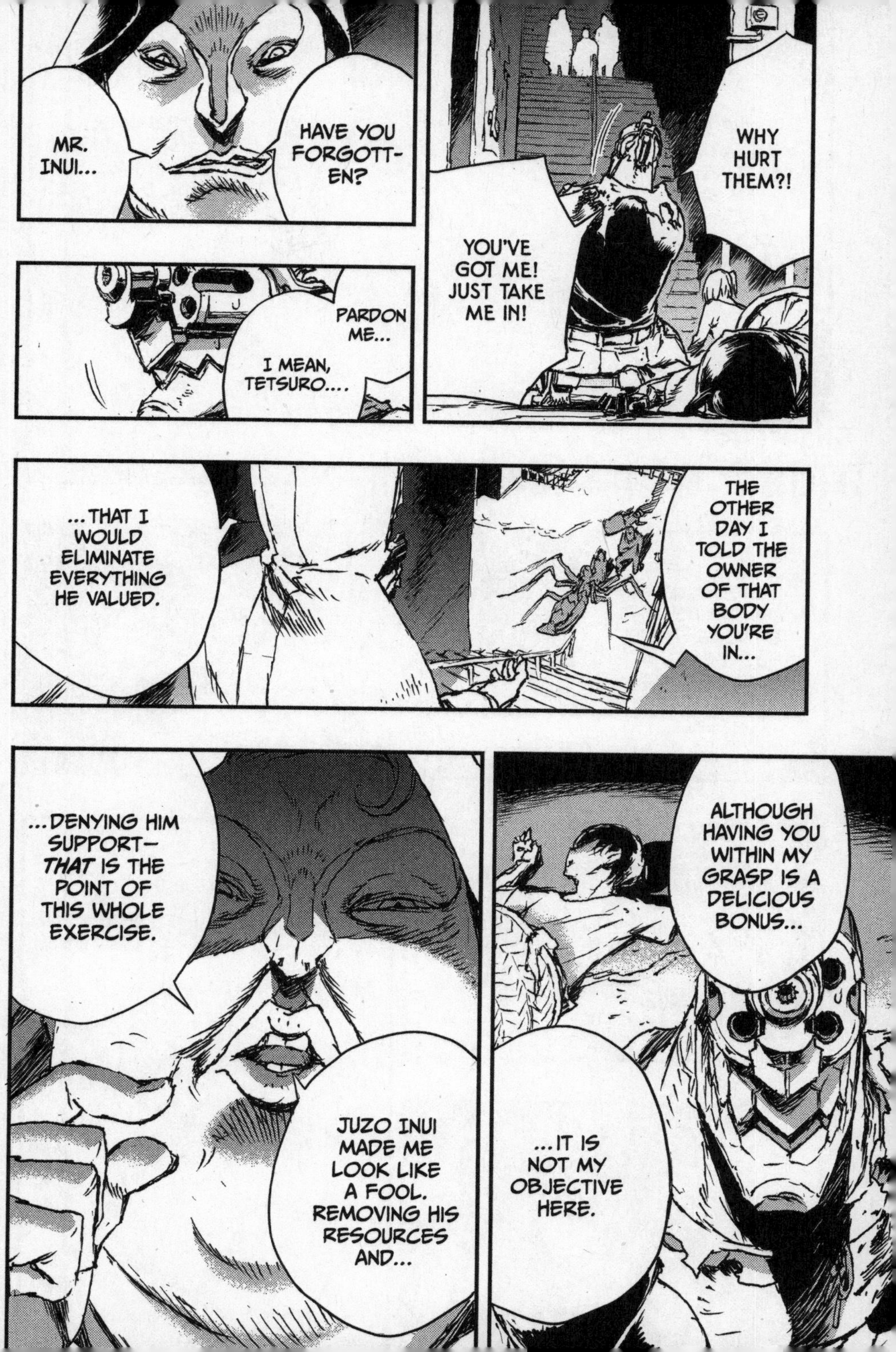
WHY HURT THEM?!
YOU'VE GOT ME! JUST TAKE ME IN!
HAVE YOU FORGOTT-EN?
MR. INUI...
PARDON ME...
I MEAN, TETSURO....
THE OTHER DAY I TOLD THE OWNER OF THAT BODY YOU'RE IN...
...THAT I WOULD ELIMINATE EVERYTHING HE VALUED.
ALTHOUGH HAVING YOU WITHIN MY GRASP IS A DELICIOUS BONUS...
...IT IS NOT MY OBJECTIVE HERE.
JUZO INUI MADE ME LOOK LIKE A FOOL. REMOVING HIS RESOURCES AND...
...DENYING HIM SUPPORT—*THAT* IS THE POINT OF THIS WHOLE EXERCISE.

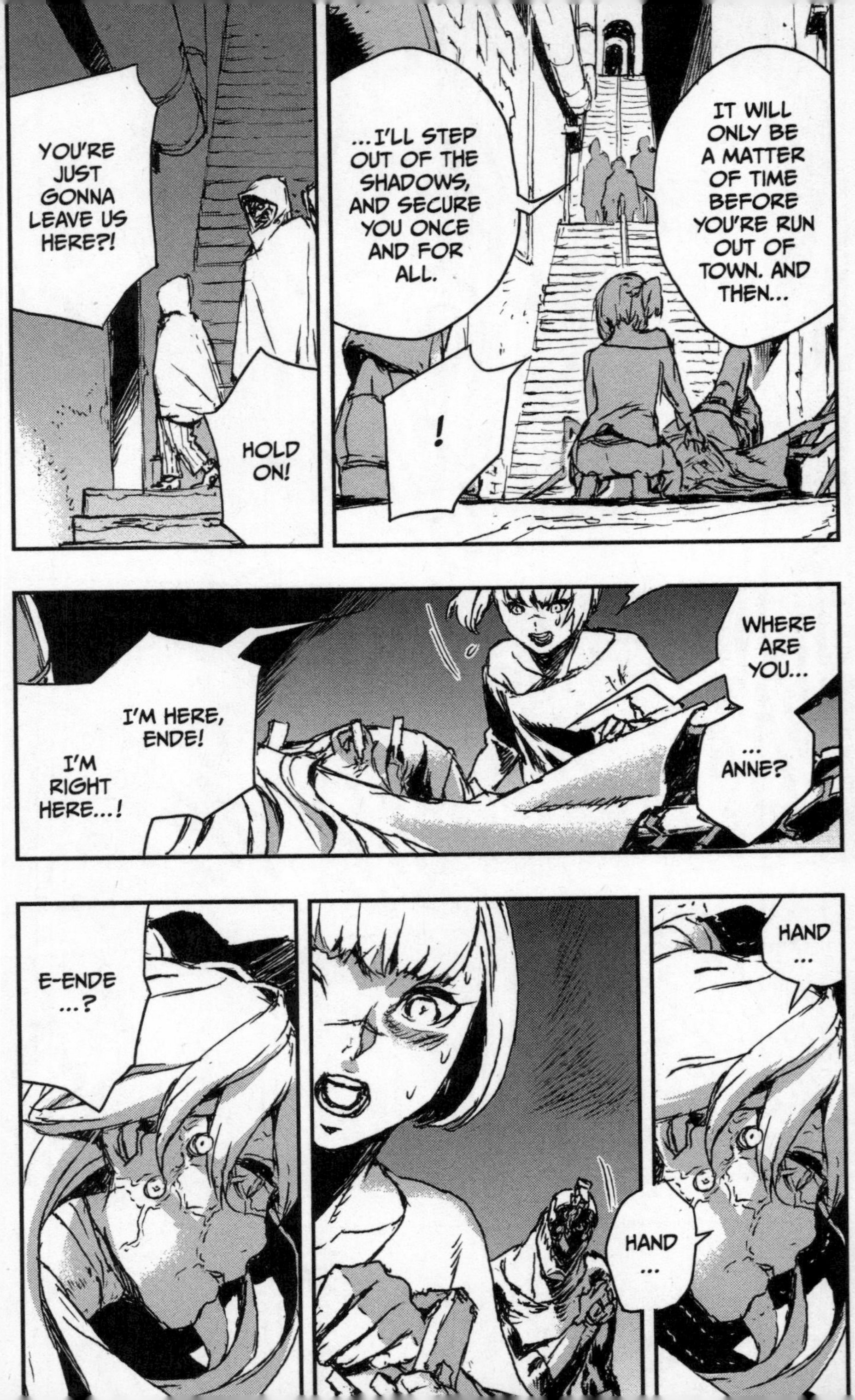
IT WILL ONLY BE A MATTER OF TIME BEFORE YOU'RE RUN OUT OF TOWN. AND THEN...
...I'LL STEP OUT OF THE SHADOWS, AND SECURE YOU ONCE AND FOR ALL.
!
YOU'RE JUST GONNA LEAVE US HERE?!
HOLD ON!
WHERE ARE YOU...
...ANNE?
I'M HERE, ENDE!
I'M RIGHT HERE...!
HAND...
HAND...
E-ENDE...?

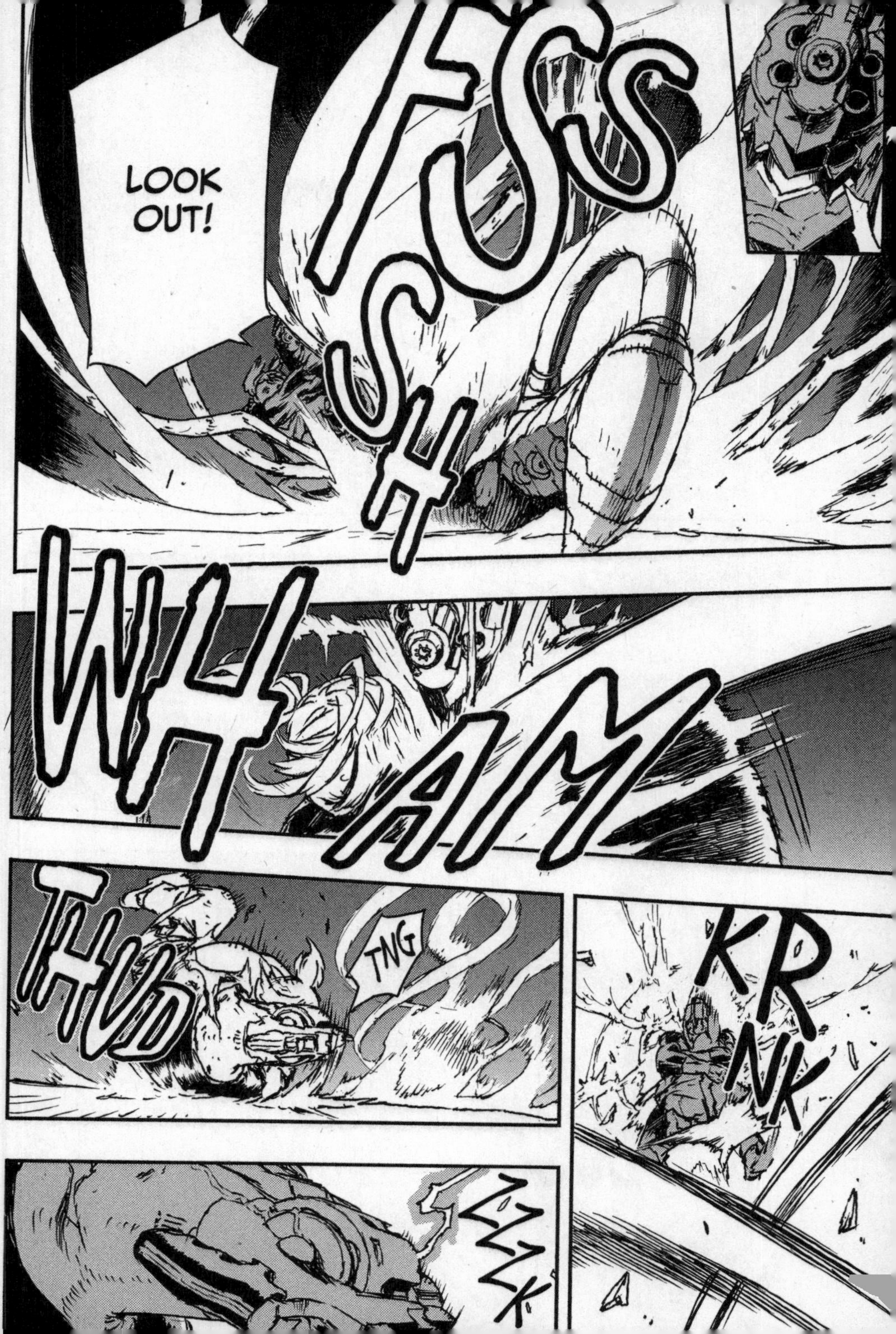
LOOK OUT!
FSSSH
WHAM
KRNK
THUD
TNG
ZZZK

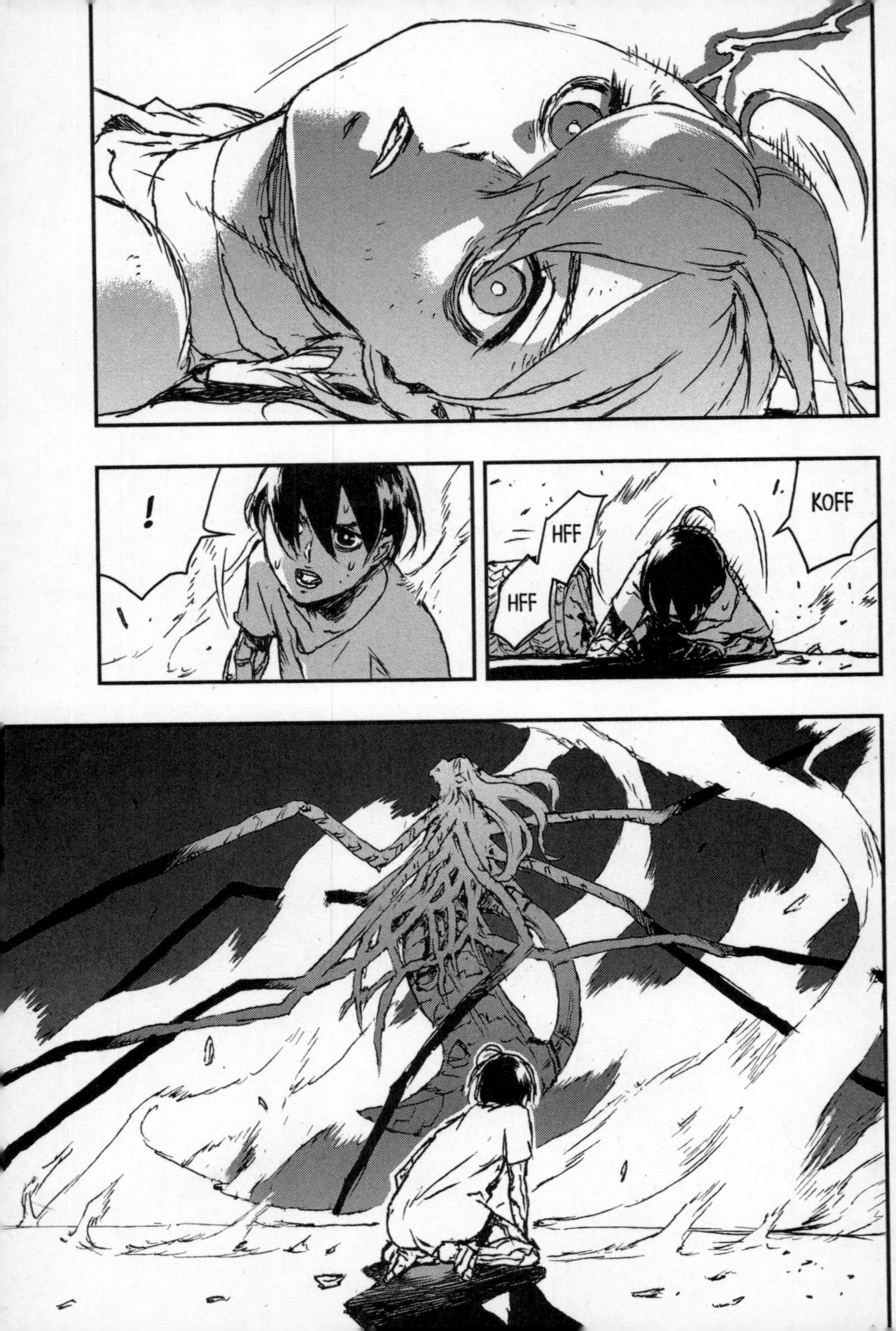
KOFF
HFF
HFF
!

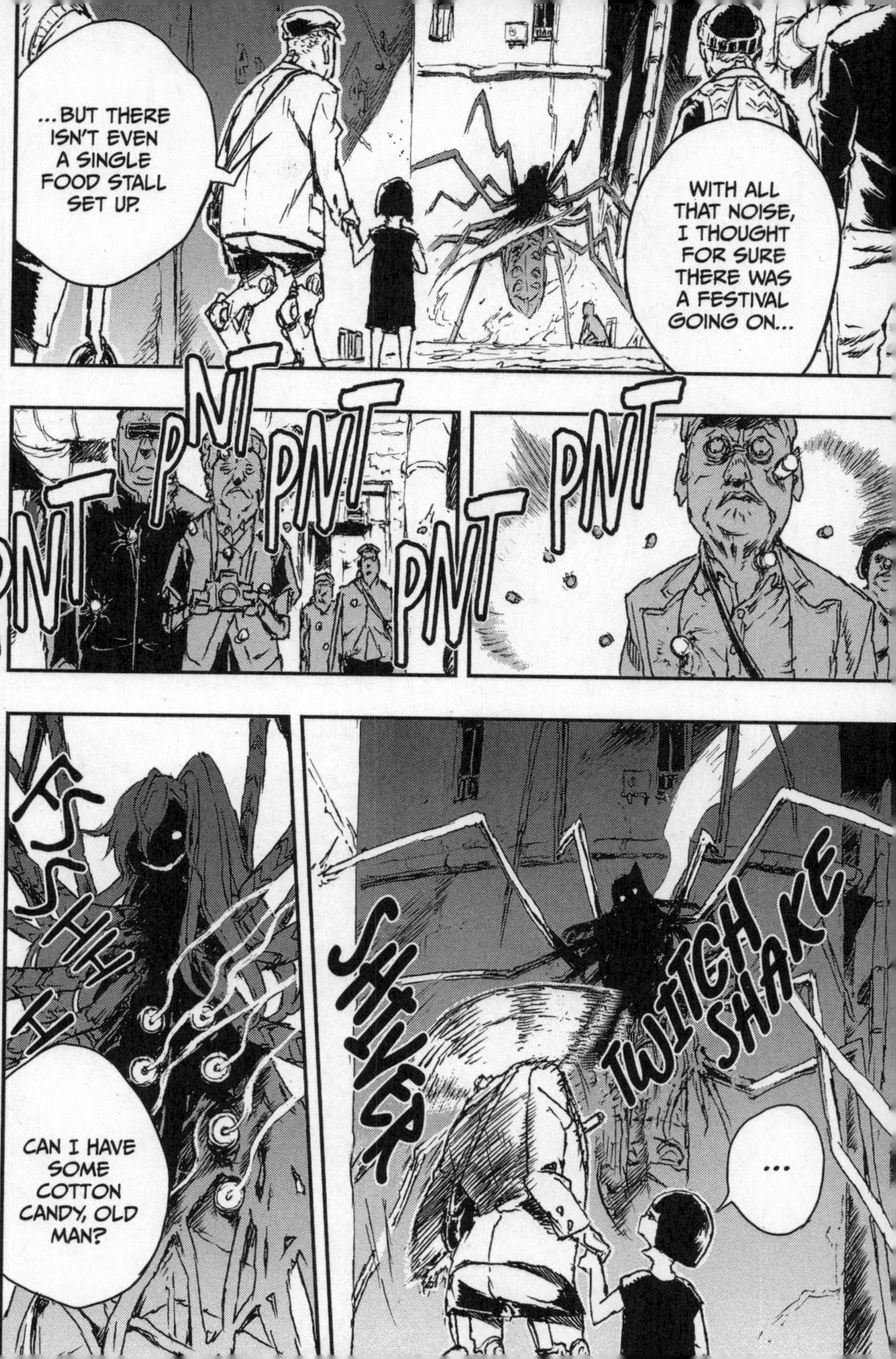
WITH ALL THAT NOISE, I THOUGHT FOR SURE THERE WAS A FESTIVAL GOING ON...
...BUT THERE ISN'T EVEN A SINGLE FOOD STALL SET UP.
PNT
PNT
PNT
PNT
PNT
TWITCH
SHAKE
SHIVER
...
FSSHHHH
CAN I HAVE SOME COTTON CANDY, OLD MAN?

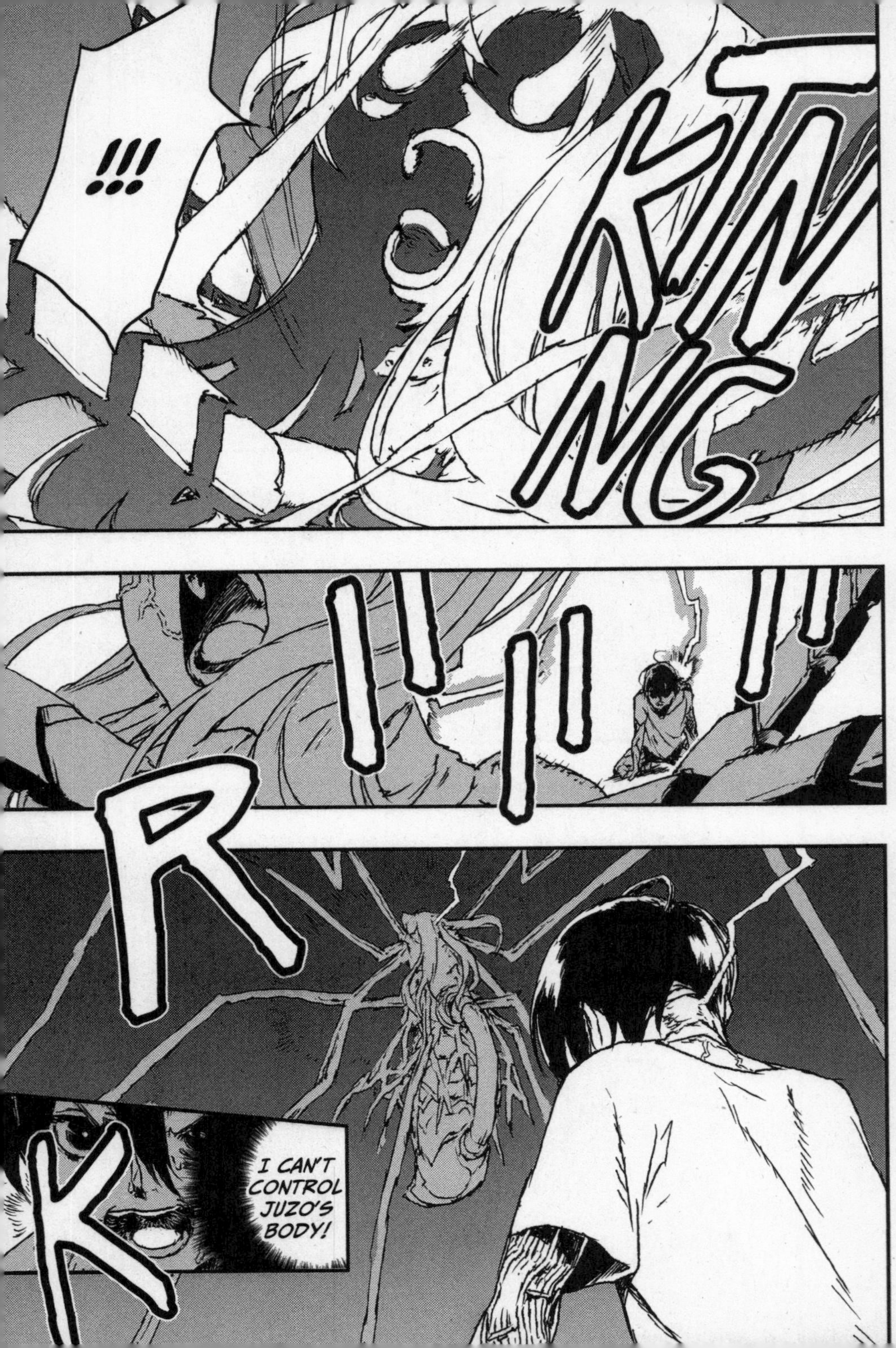
!!!
KTANG
RIIIIIIIRK
I CAN'T CONTROL JUZO'S BODY!

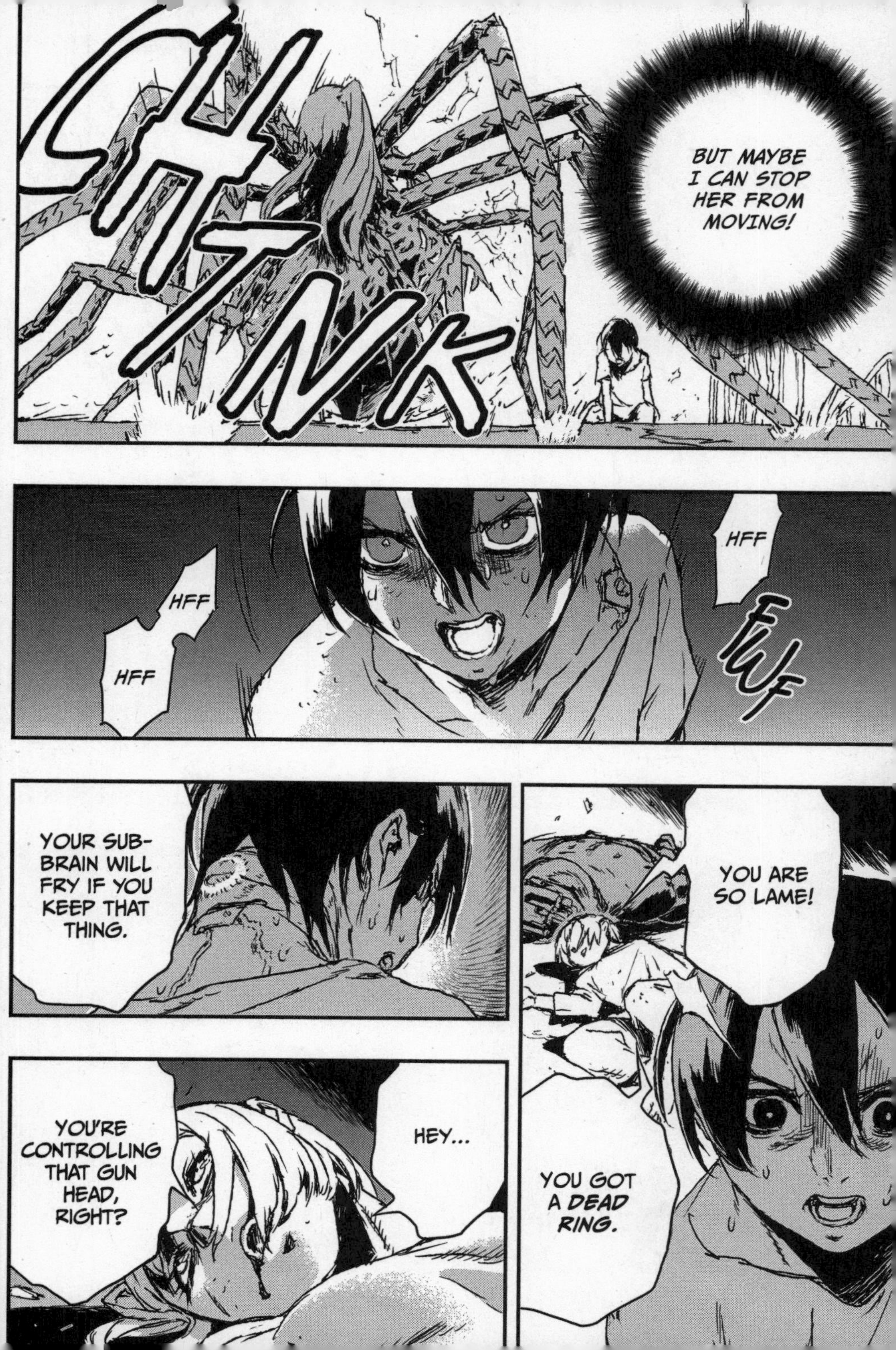
CHINK
BUT MAYBE I CAN STOP HER FROM MOVING!
HFF
FWUF
HFF
HFF
YOU ARE SO LAME!
YOU GOT A DEAD RING.
YOUR SUB-BRAIN WILL FRY IF YOU KEEP THAT THING.
HEY...
YOU'RE CONTROLLING THAT GUN HEAD, RIGHT?

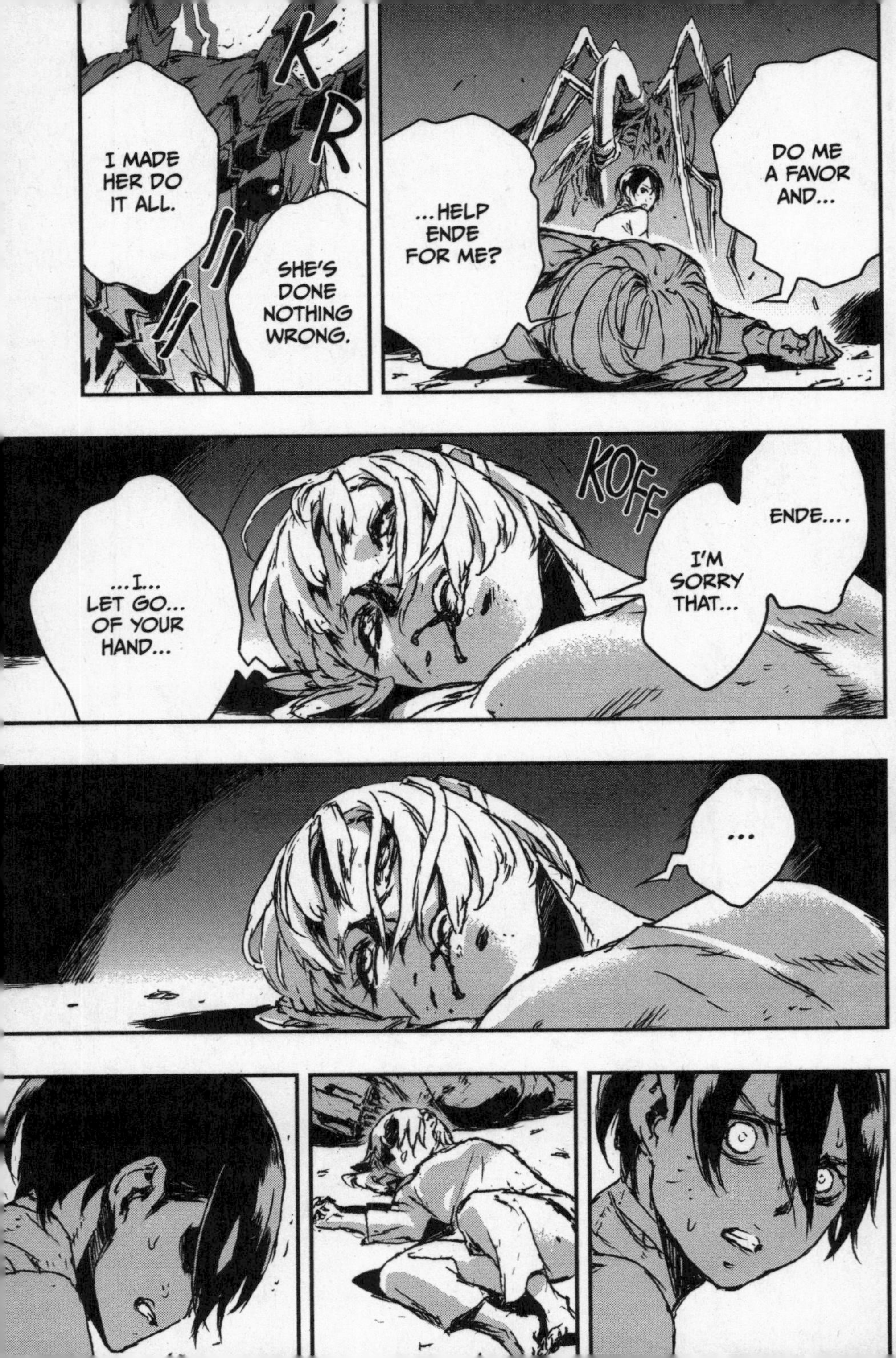
DO ME A FAVOR AND...
...HELP ENDE FOR ME?
I MADE HER DO IT ALL.
SHE'S DONE NOTHING WRONG.
KRIIII
KOFF
ENDE....
I'M SORRY THAT...
...I... LET GO... OF YOUR HAND...
...

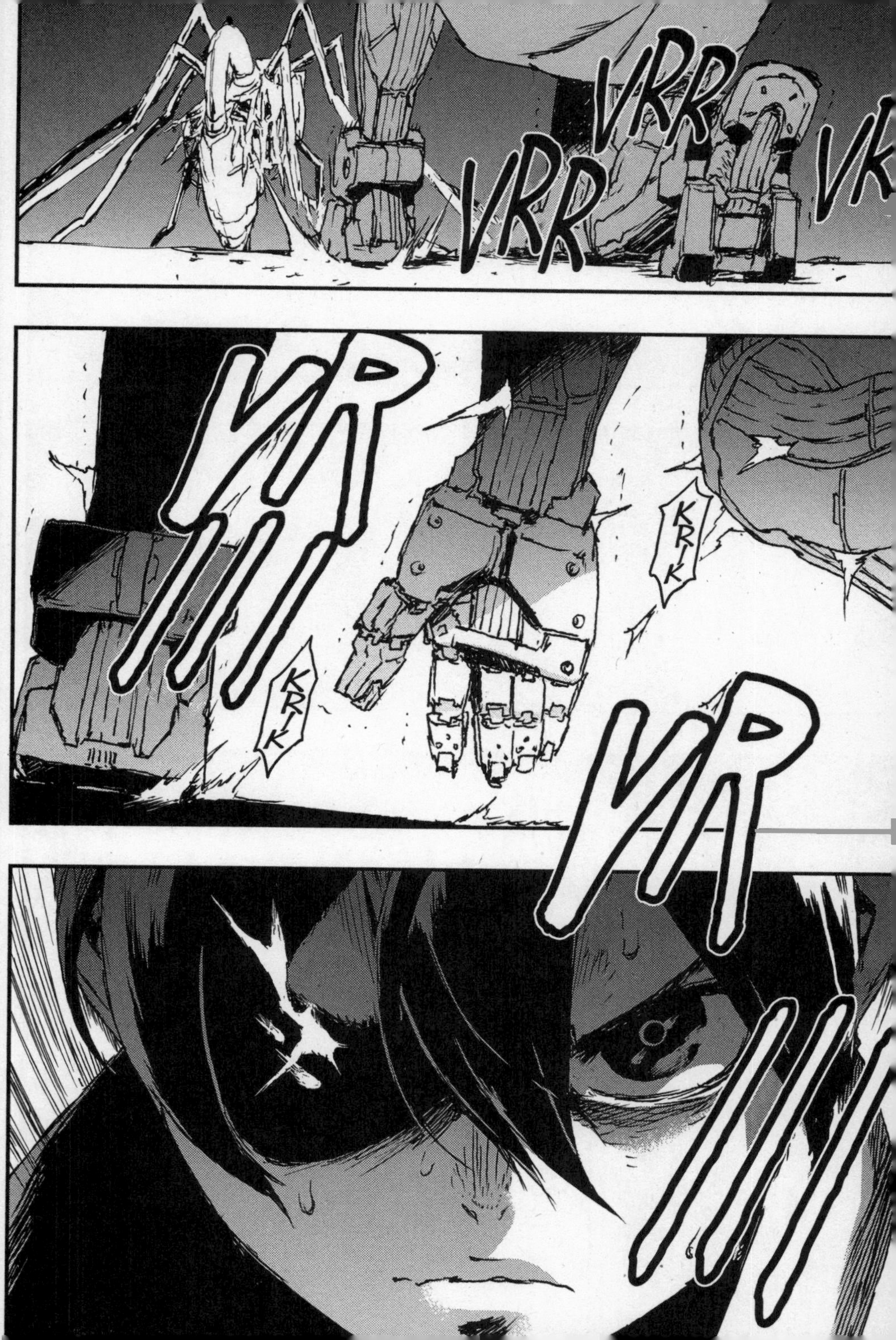
VK
VRR
VRR
KRIK
VR
KRIK
VR

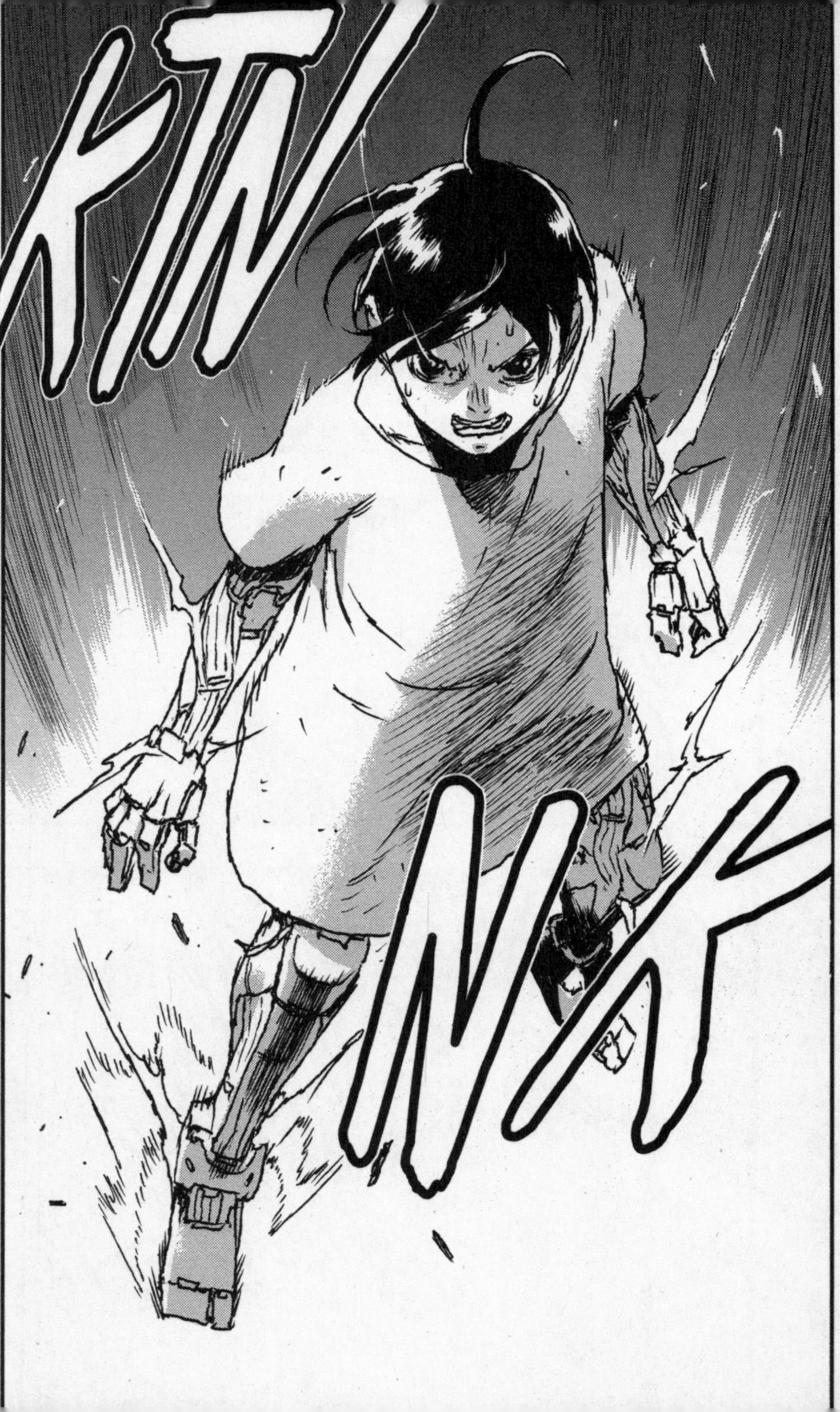

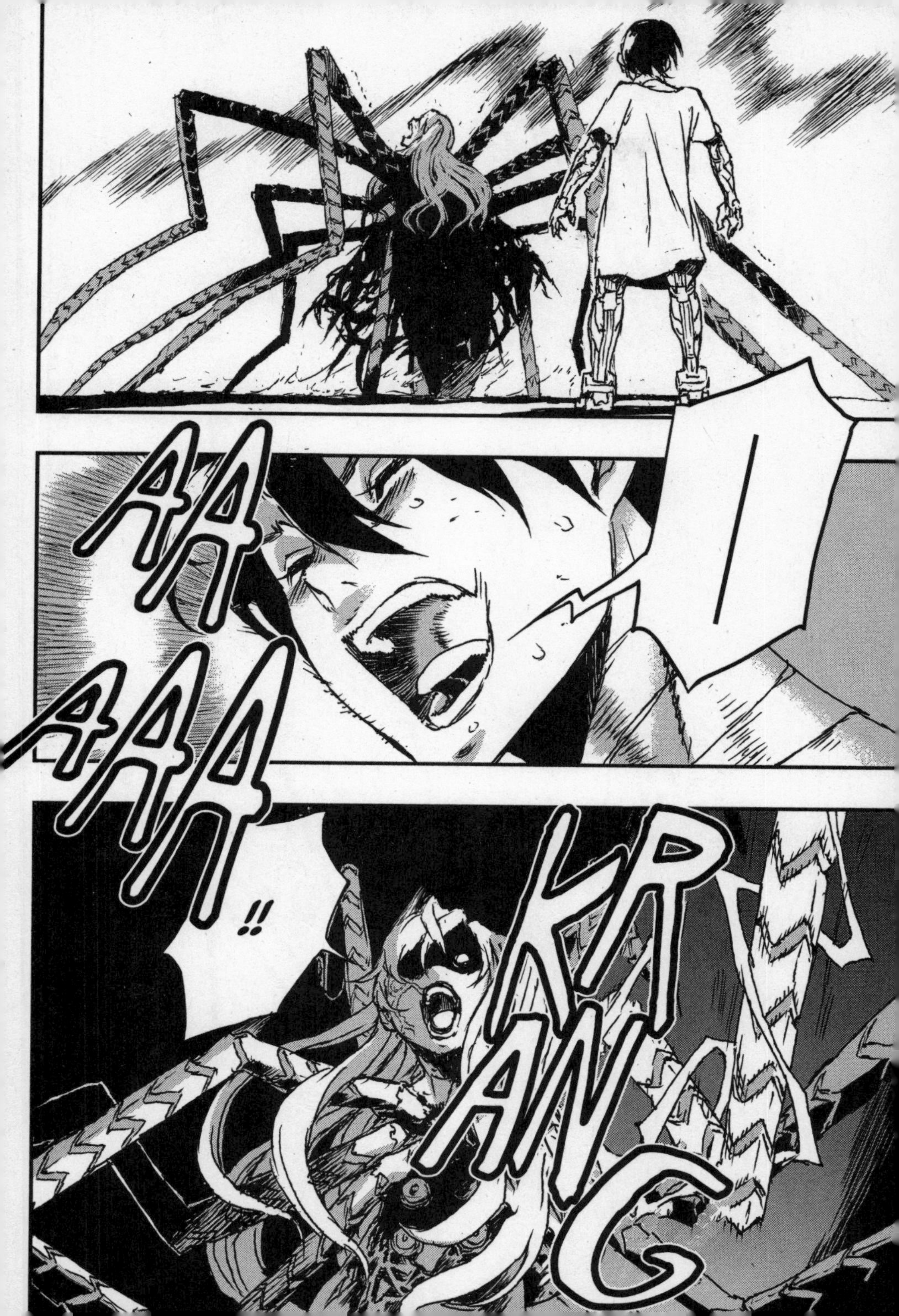
AAAAAA!!
KRANG

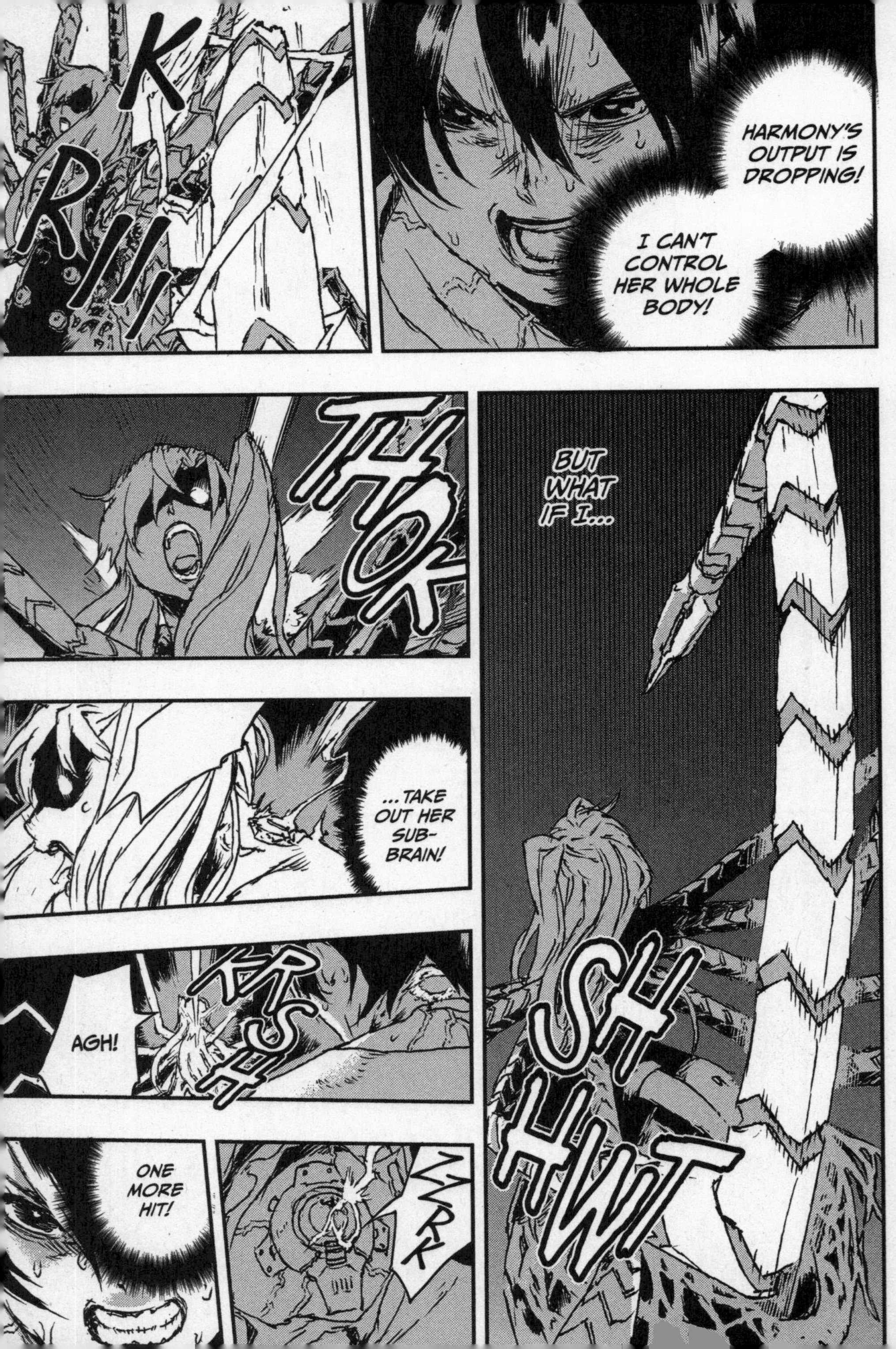
HARMONY'S OUTPUT IS DROPPING!
I CAN'T CONTROL HER WHOLE BODY!
KRIII
BUT WHAT IF I...
SHHWIT
THOK
...TAKE OUT HER SUB-BRAIN!
KRSH
AGH!
ZZRK
ONE MORE HIT!

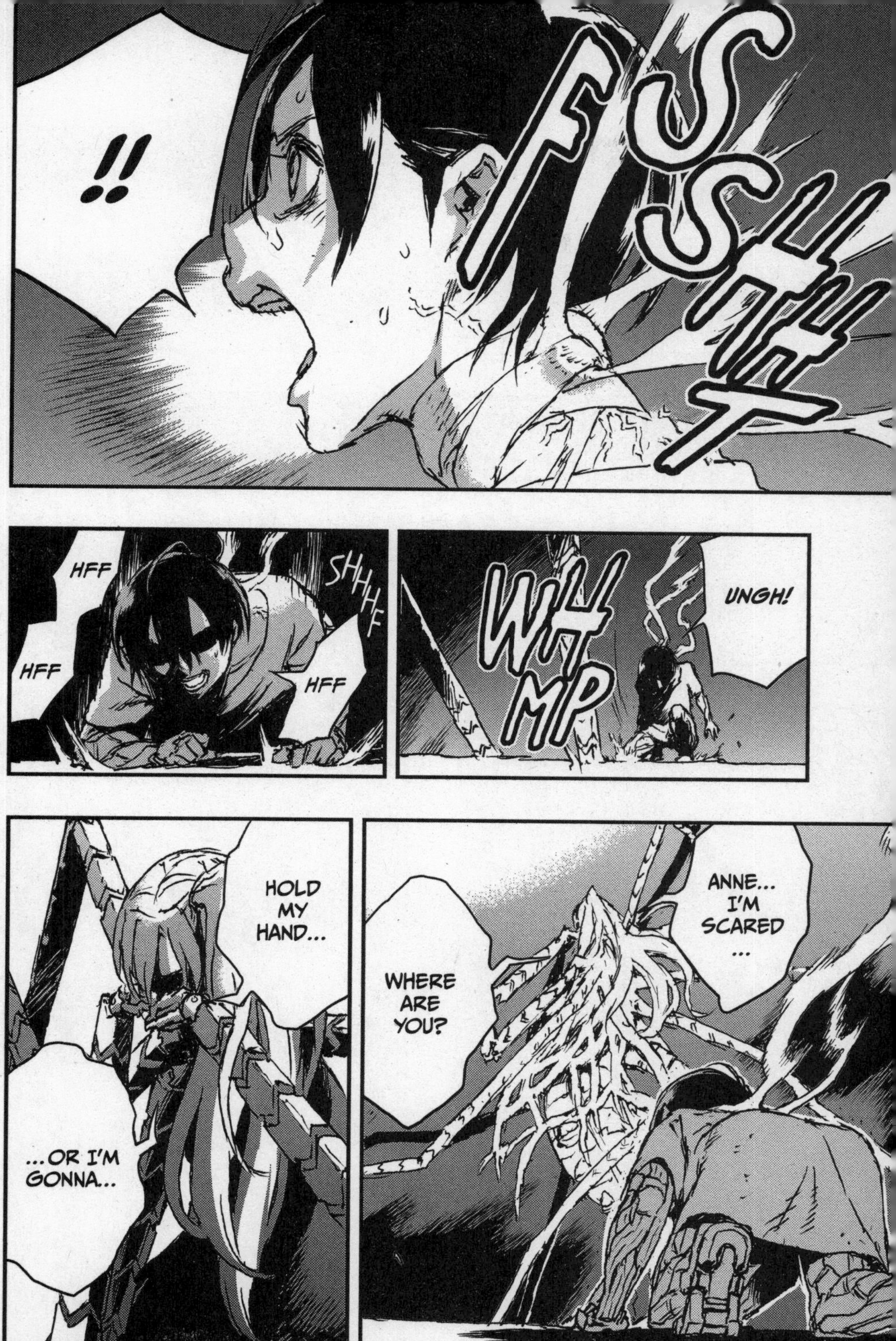
!!
FSSHHT
UNGH!
WHMP
HFF
SHHHF
HFF
HFF
ANNE... I'M SCARED ...
WHERE ARE YOU?
HOLD MY HAND...
...OR I'M GONNA...

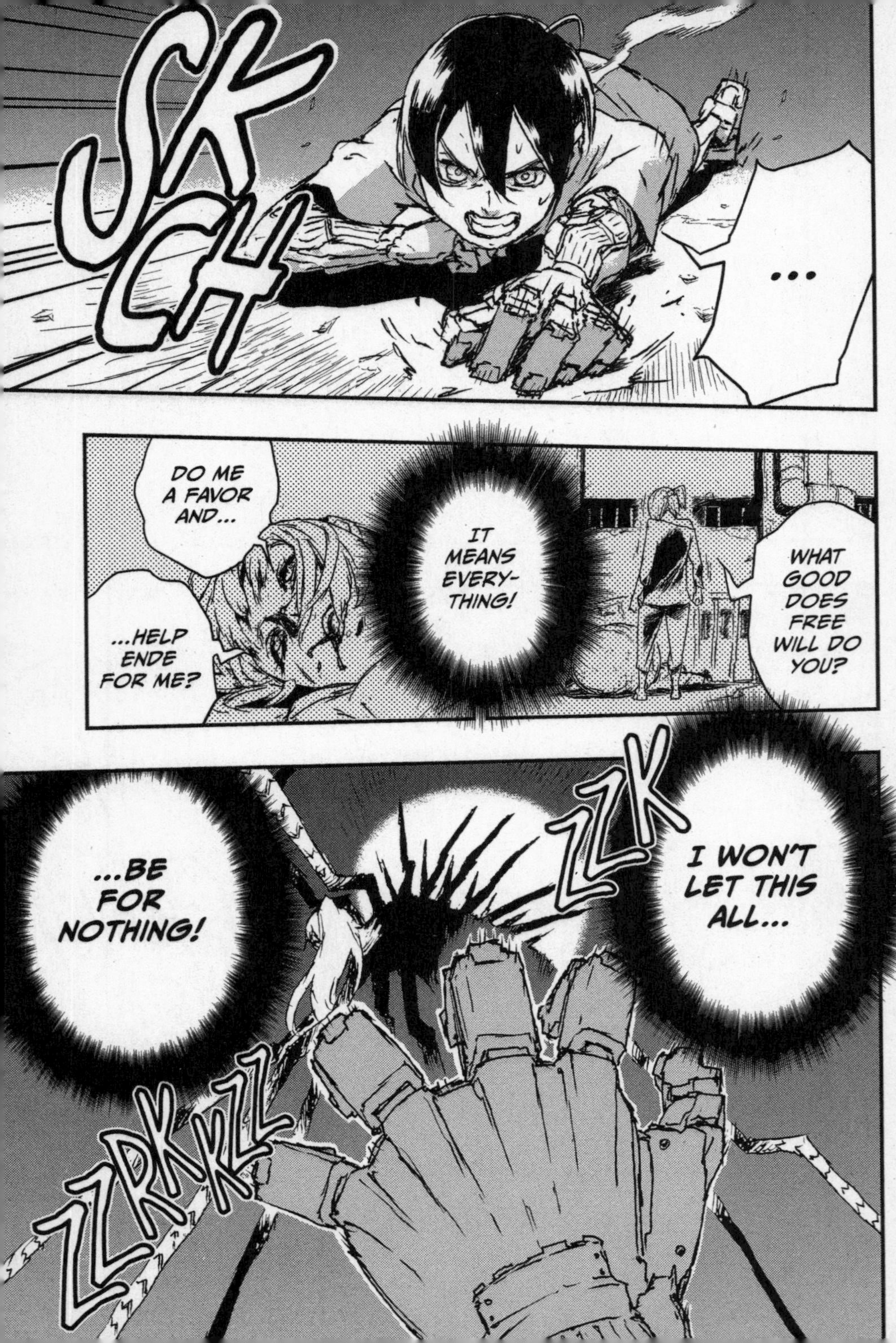
...
SKCH
WHAT GOOD DOES FREE WILL DO YOU?
IT MEANS EVERYTHING!
DO ME A FAVOR AND...
...HELP ENDE FOR ME?
I WON'T LET THIS ALL...
ZZK
...BE FOR NOTHING!
ZZRKKZZ

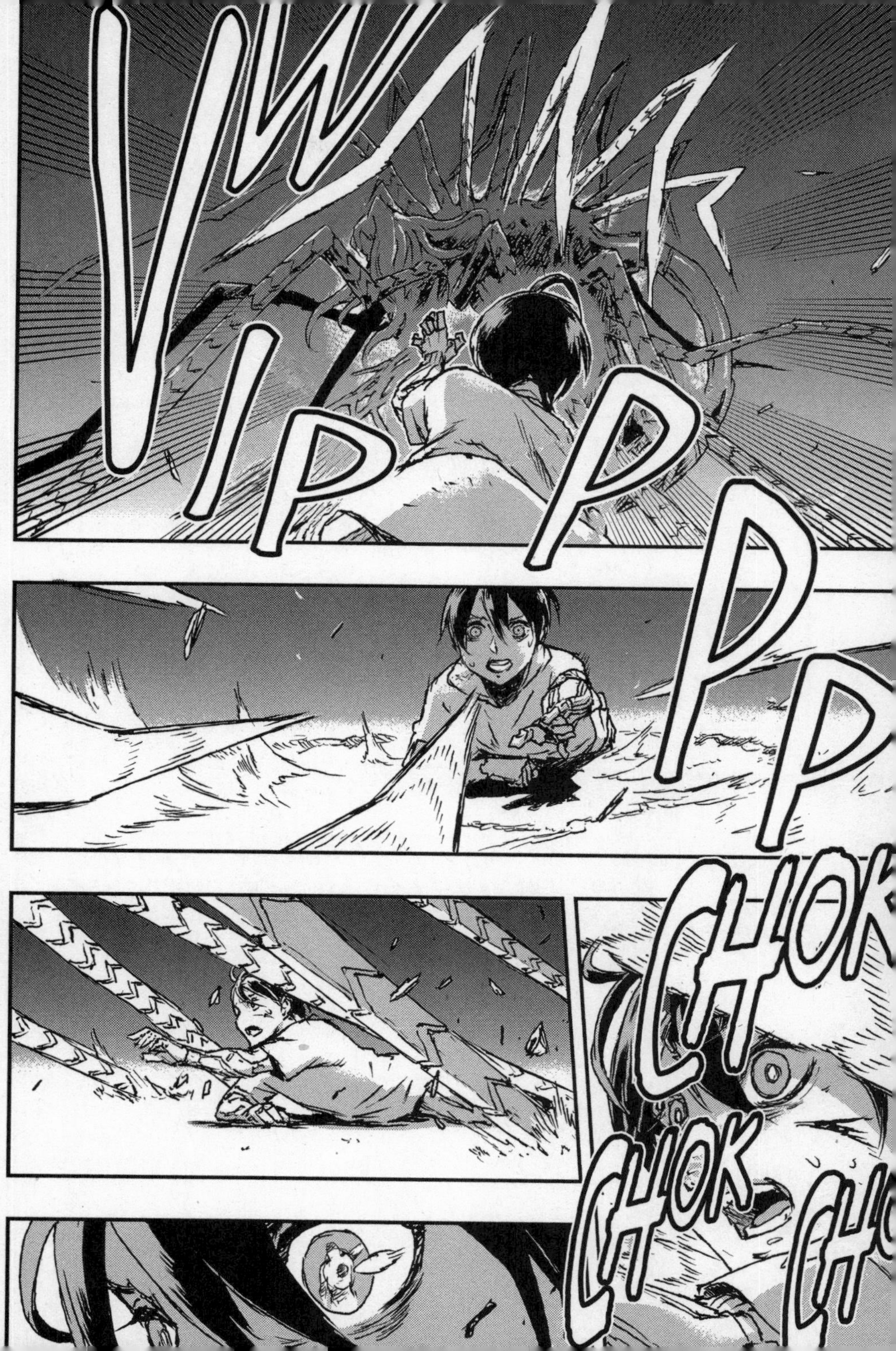
VWAM
VIPPPPP
CHOK
CHOK
CHOK
CHO

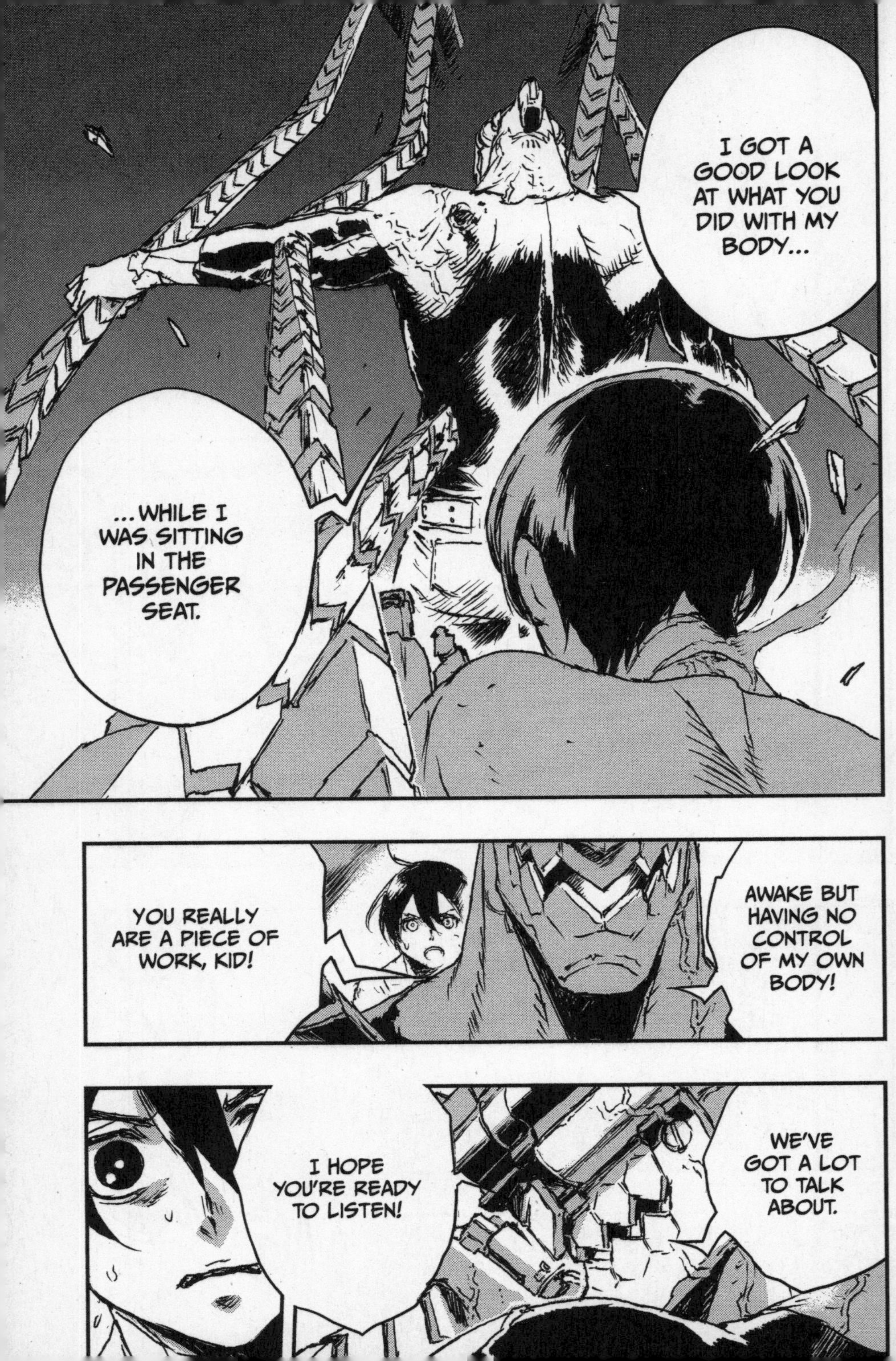
I GOT A GOOD LOOK AT WHAT YOU DID WITH MY BODY...
...WHILE I WAS SITTING IN THE PASSENGER SEAT.
AWAKE BUT HAVING NO CONTROL OF MY OWN BODY!
YOU REALLY ARE A PIECE OF WORK, KID!
WE'VE GOT A LOT TO TALK ABOUT.
I HOPE YOU'RE READY TO LISTEN!

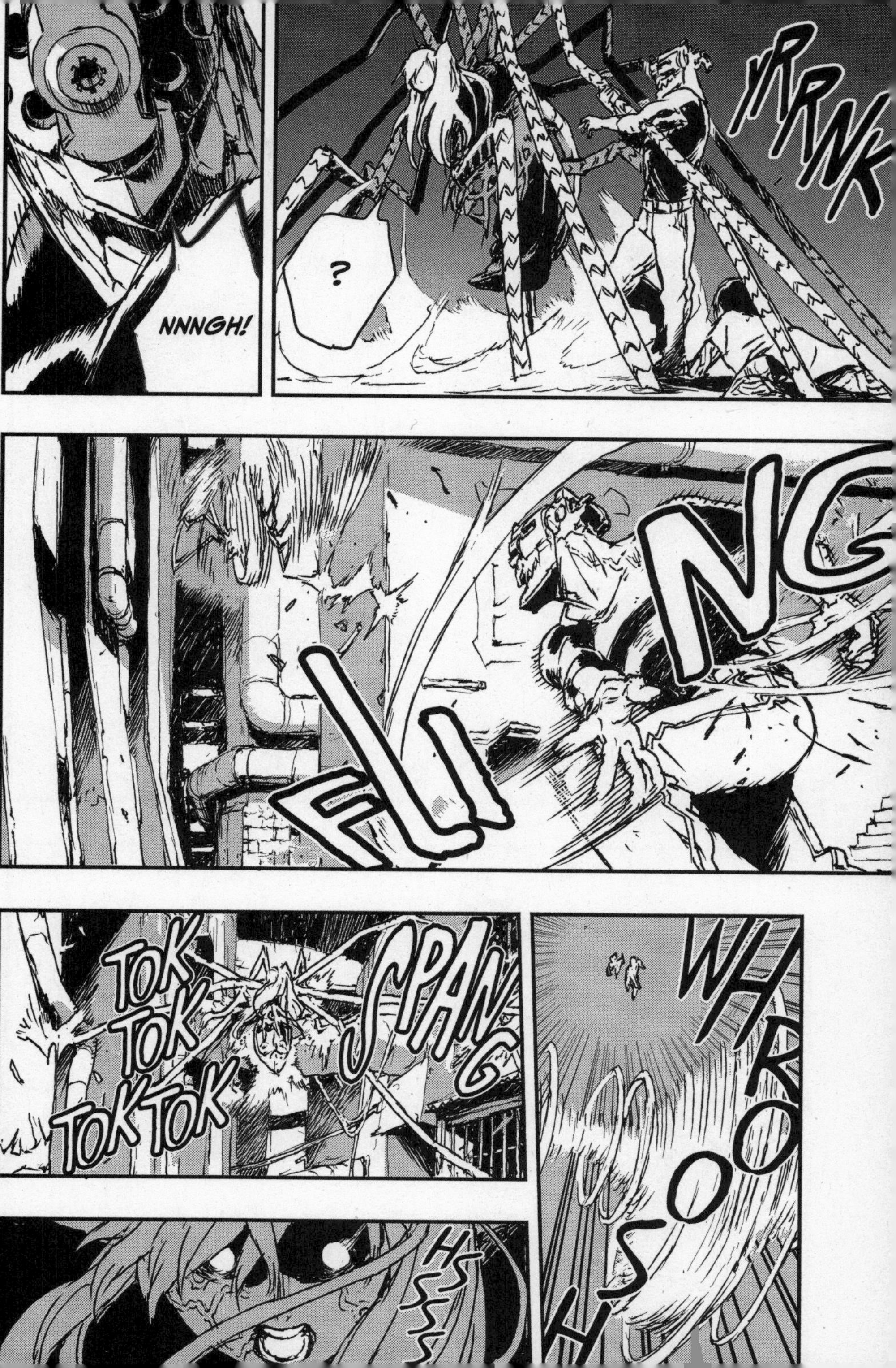
YRRRNK
?
NNNGH!
FLUNG
WHROOOSH
SPANG
TOK TOK TOKTOK
HSSSS

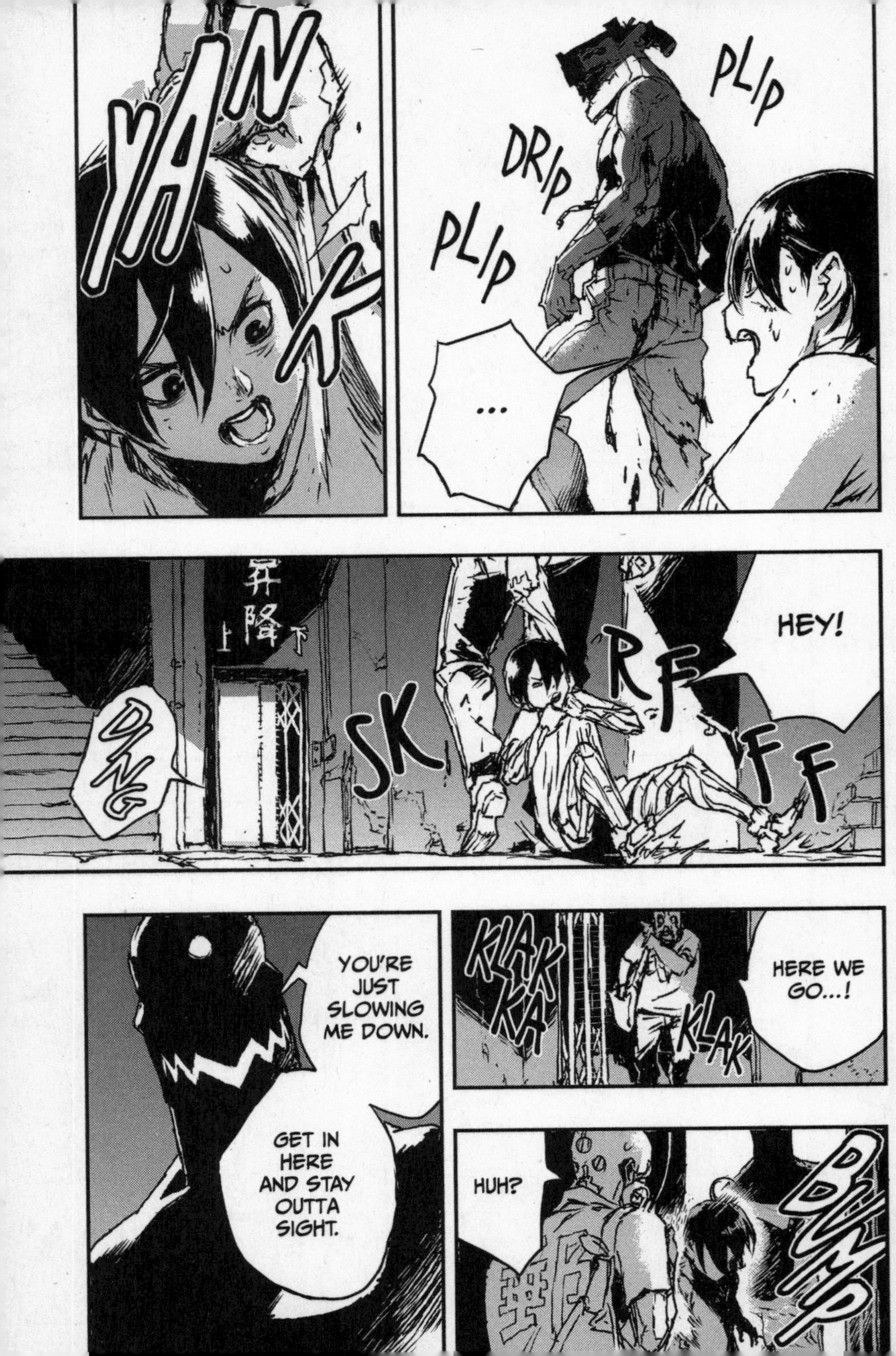
PLIP
DRIP
PLIP
...
YANK
HEY!
RFFF
SK
DING
HERE WE GO...!
KLAK
KLAKAKA
YOU'RE JUST SLOWING ME DOWN.
BUMP
HUH?
GET IN HERE AND STAY OUTTA SIGHT.

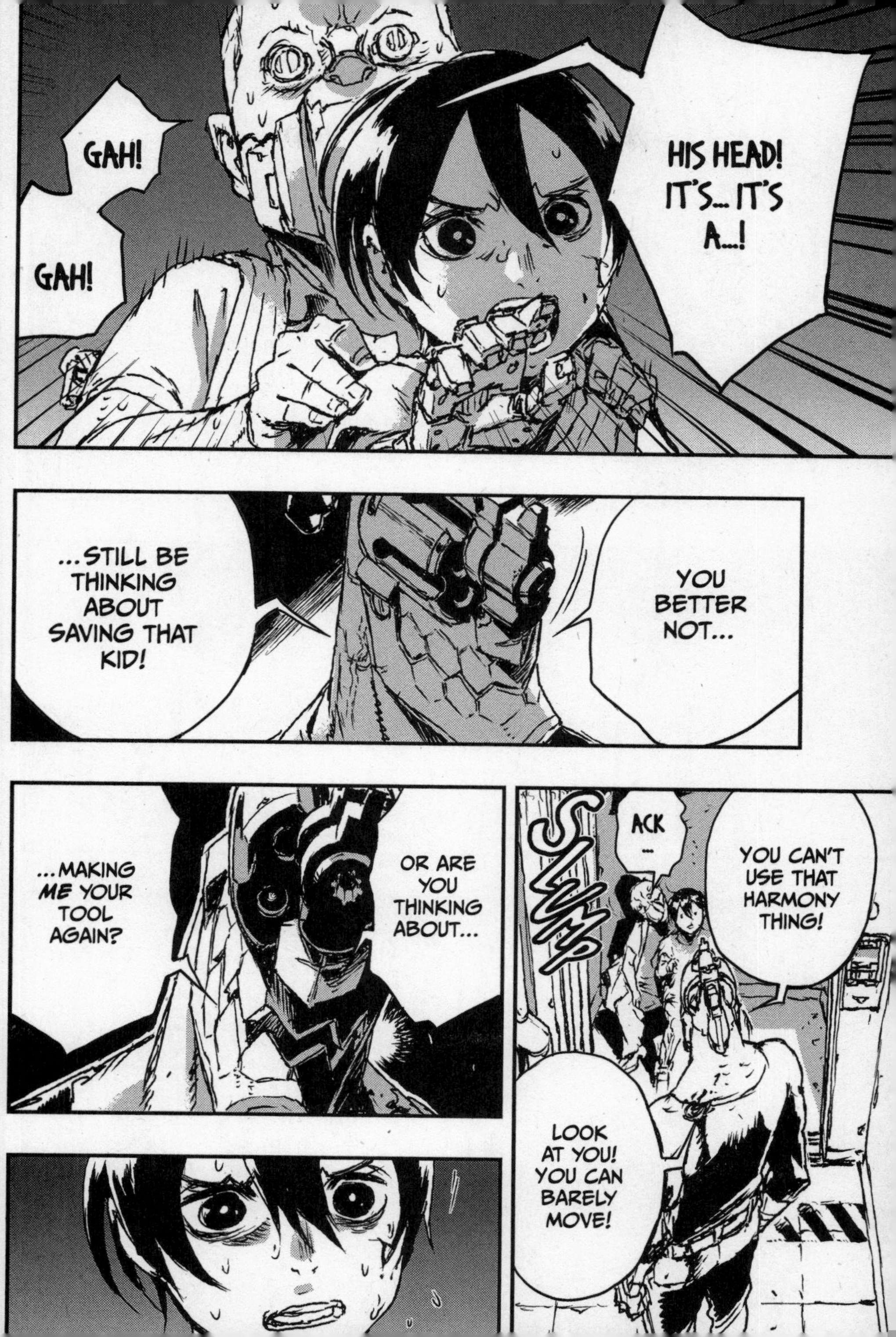
HIS HEAD! IT'S... IT'S A...!
GAH!
GAH!
YOU BETTER NOT...
...STILL BE THINKING ABOUT SAVING THAT KID!
SLUMP
ACK...
YOU CAN'T USE THAT HARMONY THING!
LOOK AT YOU! YOU CAN BARELY MOVE!
OR ARE YOU THINKING ABOUT...
...MAKING *ME* YOUR TOOL AGAIN?

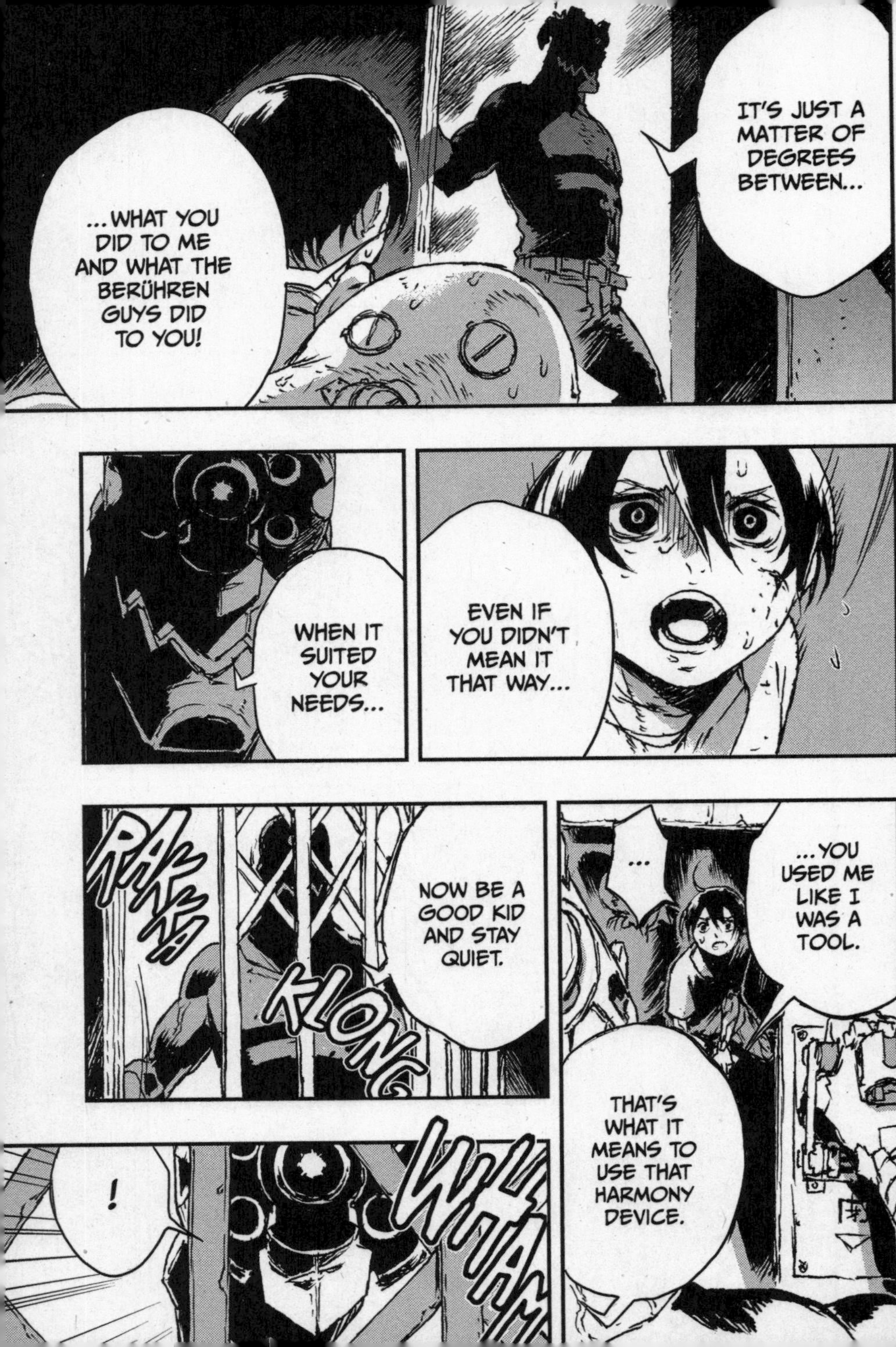
IT'S JUST A MATTER OF DEGREES BETWEEN...
...WHAT YOU DID TO ME AND WHAT THE BERÜHREN GUYS DID TO YOU!
EVEN IF YOU DIDN'T MEAN IT THAT WAY...
WHEN IT SUITED YOUR NEEDS...
...YOU USED ME LIKE I WAS A TOOL.
...
THAT'S WHAT IT MEANS TO USE THAT HARMONY DEVICE.
NOW BE A GOOD KID AND STAY QUIET.
RAKKA
KLONG
WHAM
!

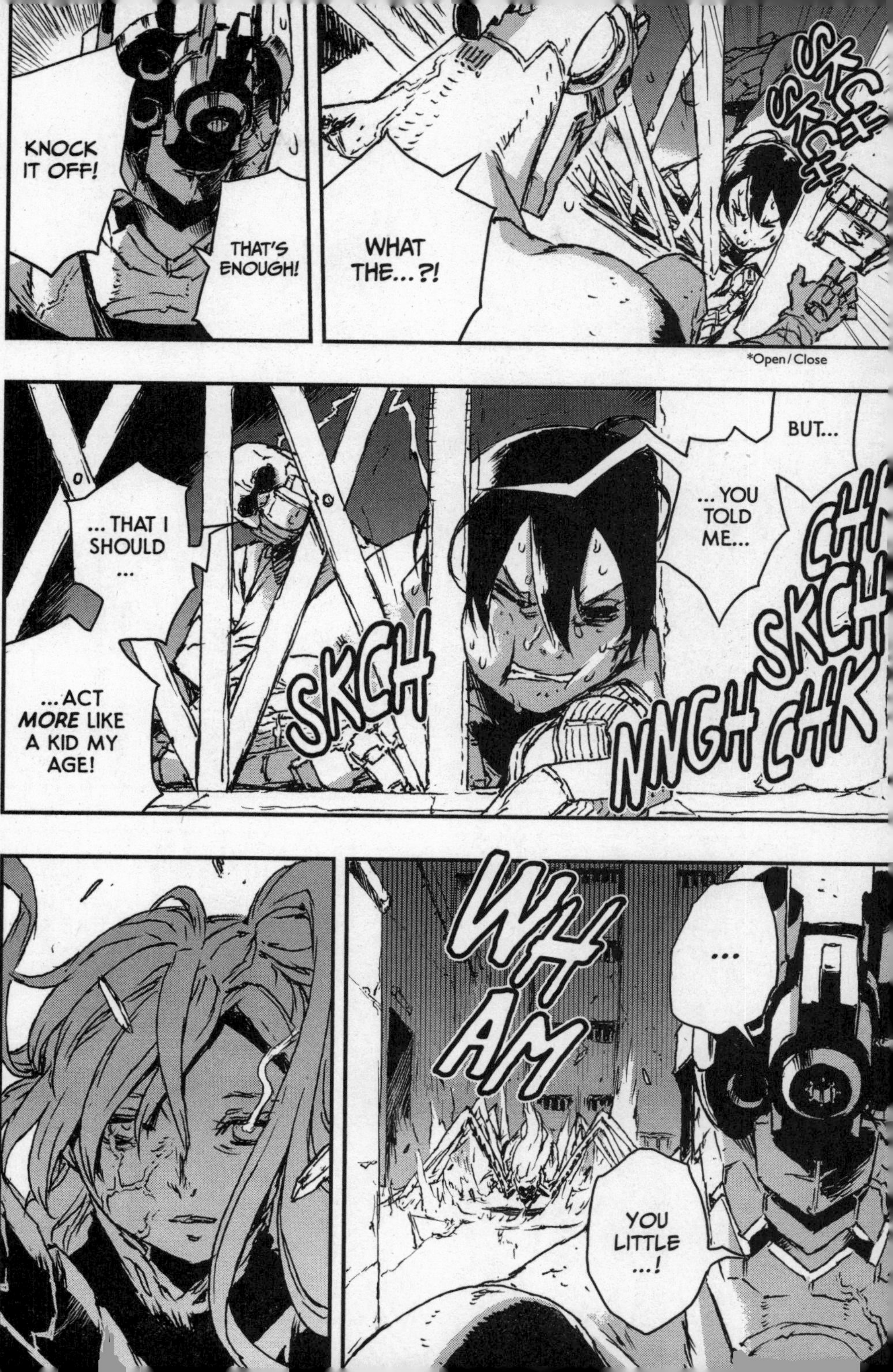
SKCH SKCH
WHAT THE...?!
KNOCK IT OFF!
THAT'S ENOUGH!
BUT...
...YOU TOLD ME...
CHK SKCH CHK
NNGH
...THAT I SHOULD...
SKCH
...ACT *MORE* LIKE A KID MY AGE!
...
YOU LITTLE ...!
WHAM
*Open / Close

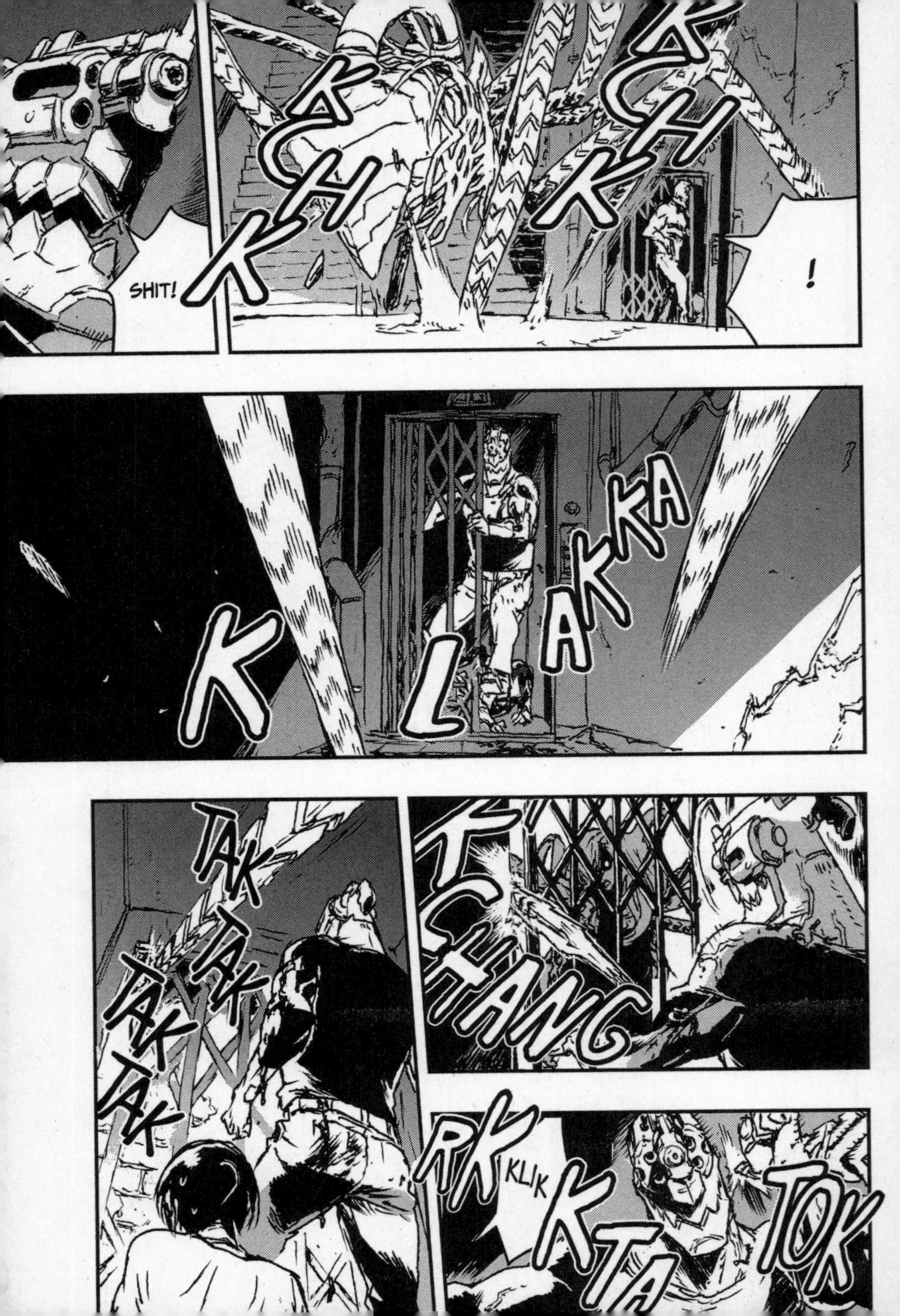
!
KACHK
KACHK
SHIT!
KLAKKA
KCHANG
TAK TAK
TAK TAK
TOK
KTA
KLIK
RYK

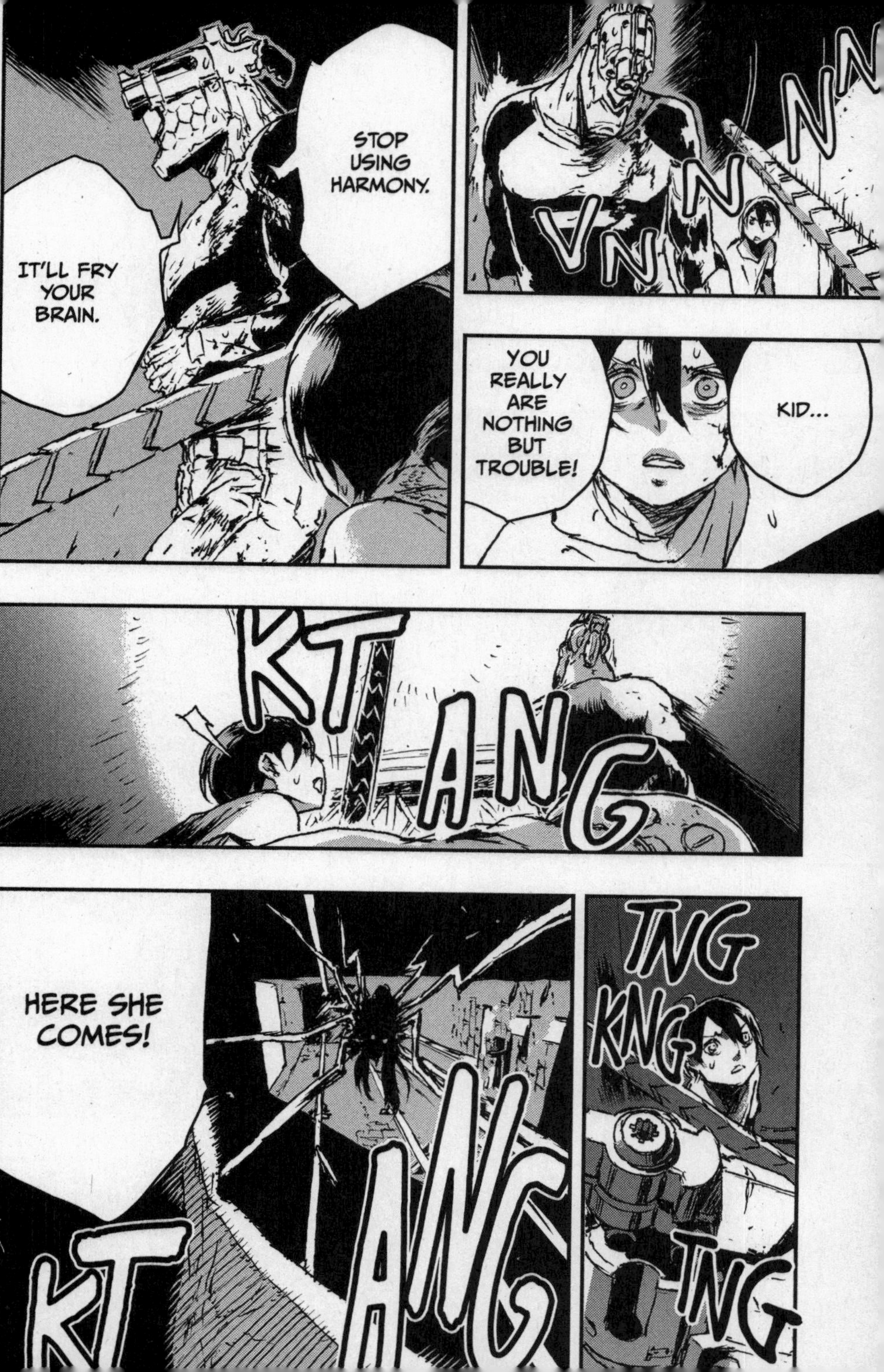
VNNNNNN
KID...
YOU REALLY ARE NOTHING BUT TROUBLE!
STOP USING HARMONY.
IT'LL FRY YOUR BRAIN.
KTANG
TNG KNG TNG
HERE SHE COMES!
KTANG

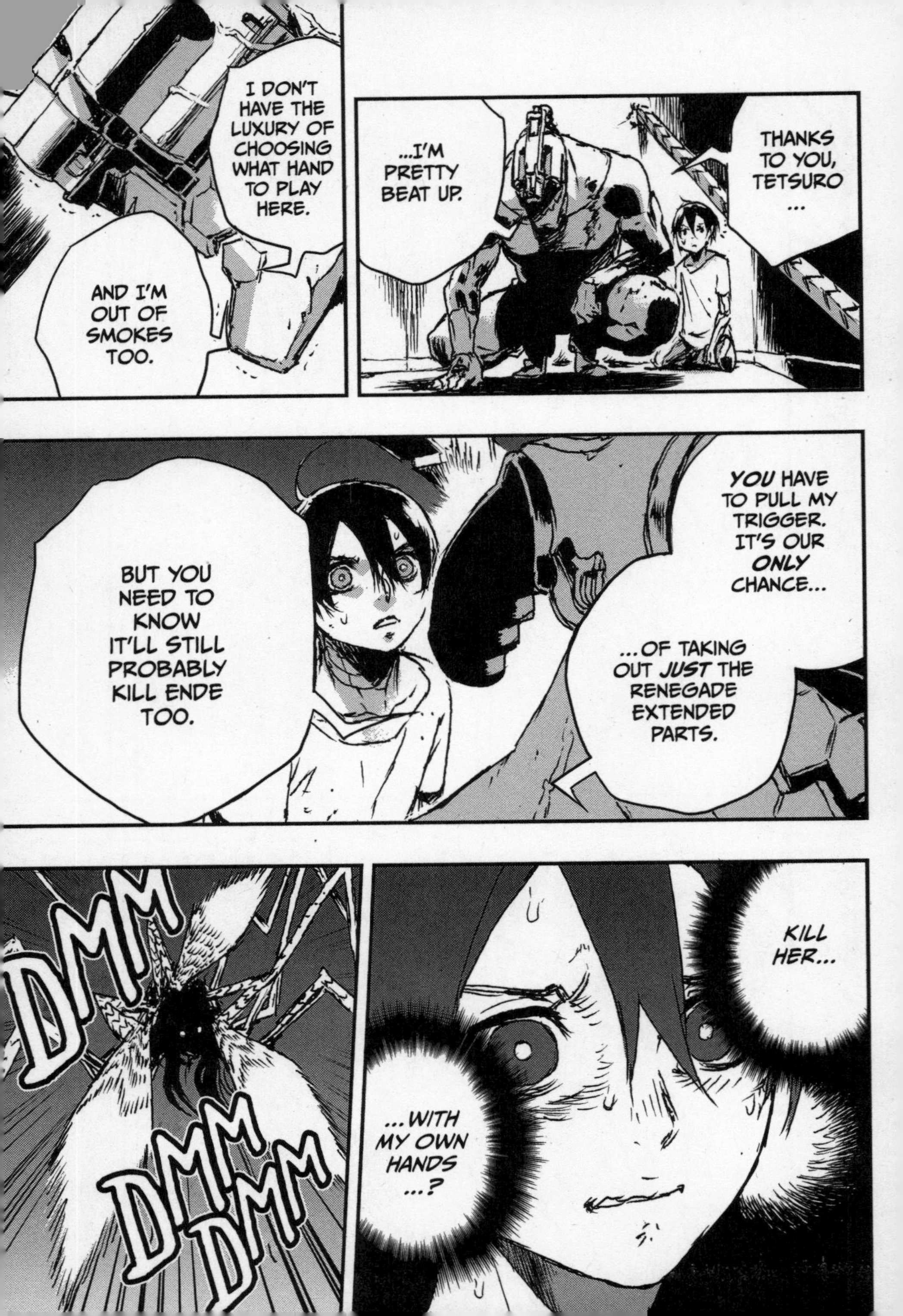
THANKS TO YOU, TETSURO ...
...I'M PRETTY BEAT UP.
I DON'T HAVE THE LUXURY OF CHOOSING WHAT HAND TO PLAY HERE.
AND I'M OUT OF SMOKES TOO.
YOU HAVE TO PULL MY TRIGGER. IT'S OUR *ONLY* CHANCE...
...OF TAKING OUT *JUST* THE RENEGADE EXTENDED PARTS.
BUT YOU NEED TO KNOW IT'LL STILL PROBABLY KILL ENDE TOO.
KILL HER...
...WITH MY OWN HANDS ...?
DMM
DMM DMM

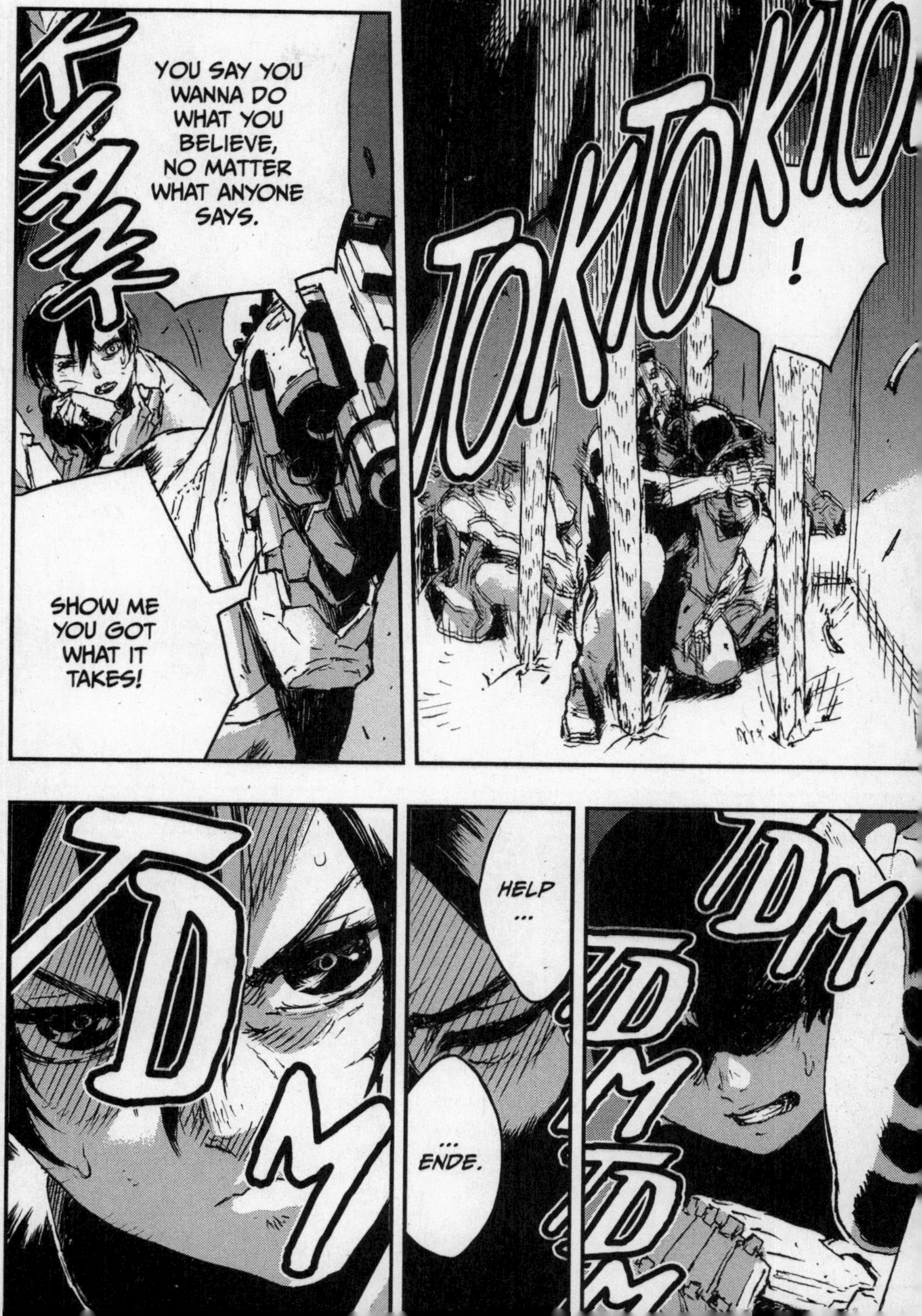
TOKTOKTO
!
KLANK
YOU SAY YOU WANNA DO WHAT YOU BELIEVE, NO MATTER WHAT ANYONE SAYS.
SHOW ME YOU GOT WHAT IT TAKES!
TDM
TDM
TDM
TDM
HELP...
...ENDE.
TDM

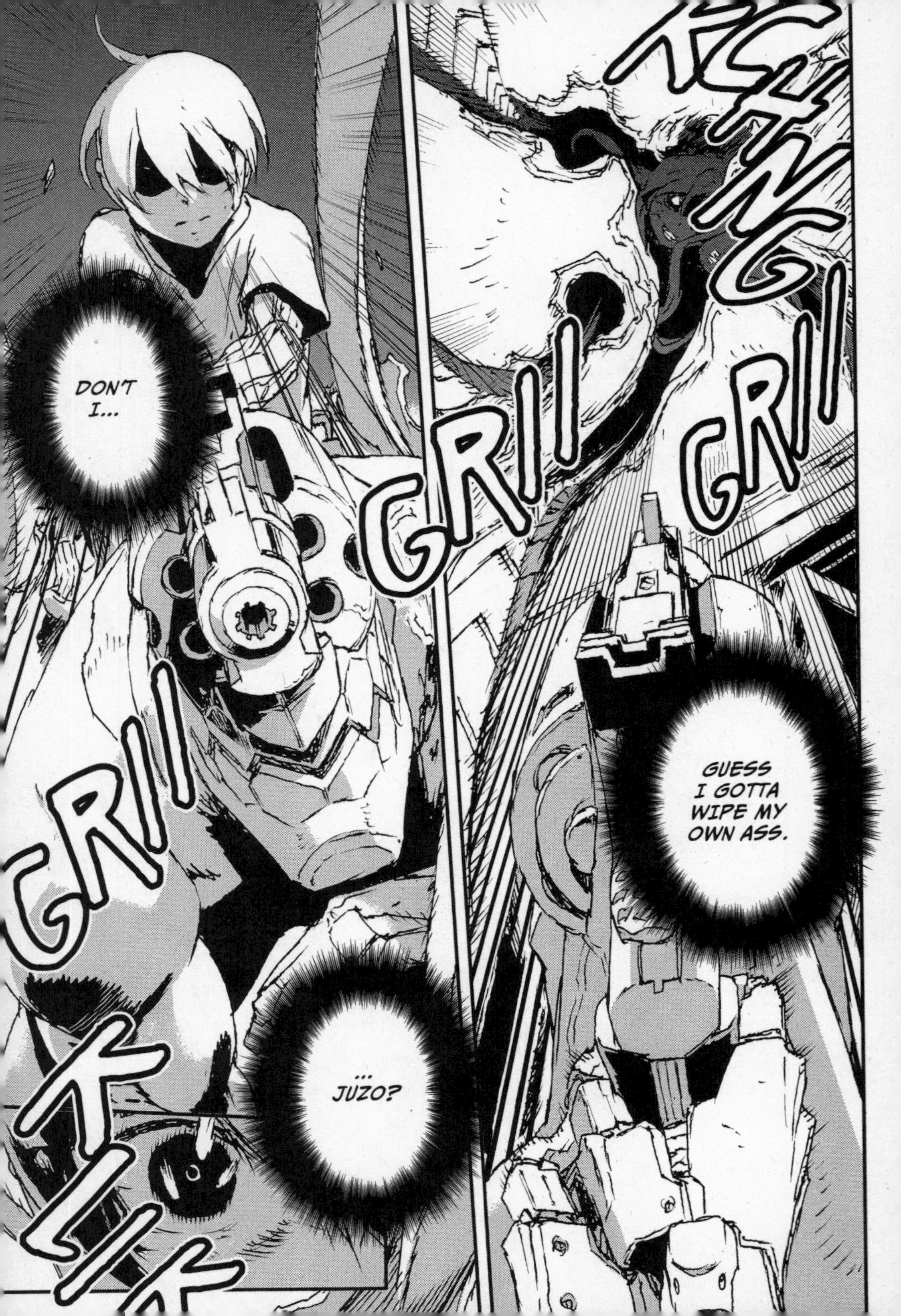
KCHNG
GRII
GRII
GUESS I GOTTA WIPE MY OWN ASS.
DON'T I...
GRII
GRII
...JŪZO?
KLIK

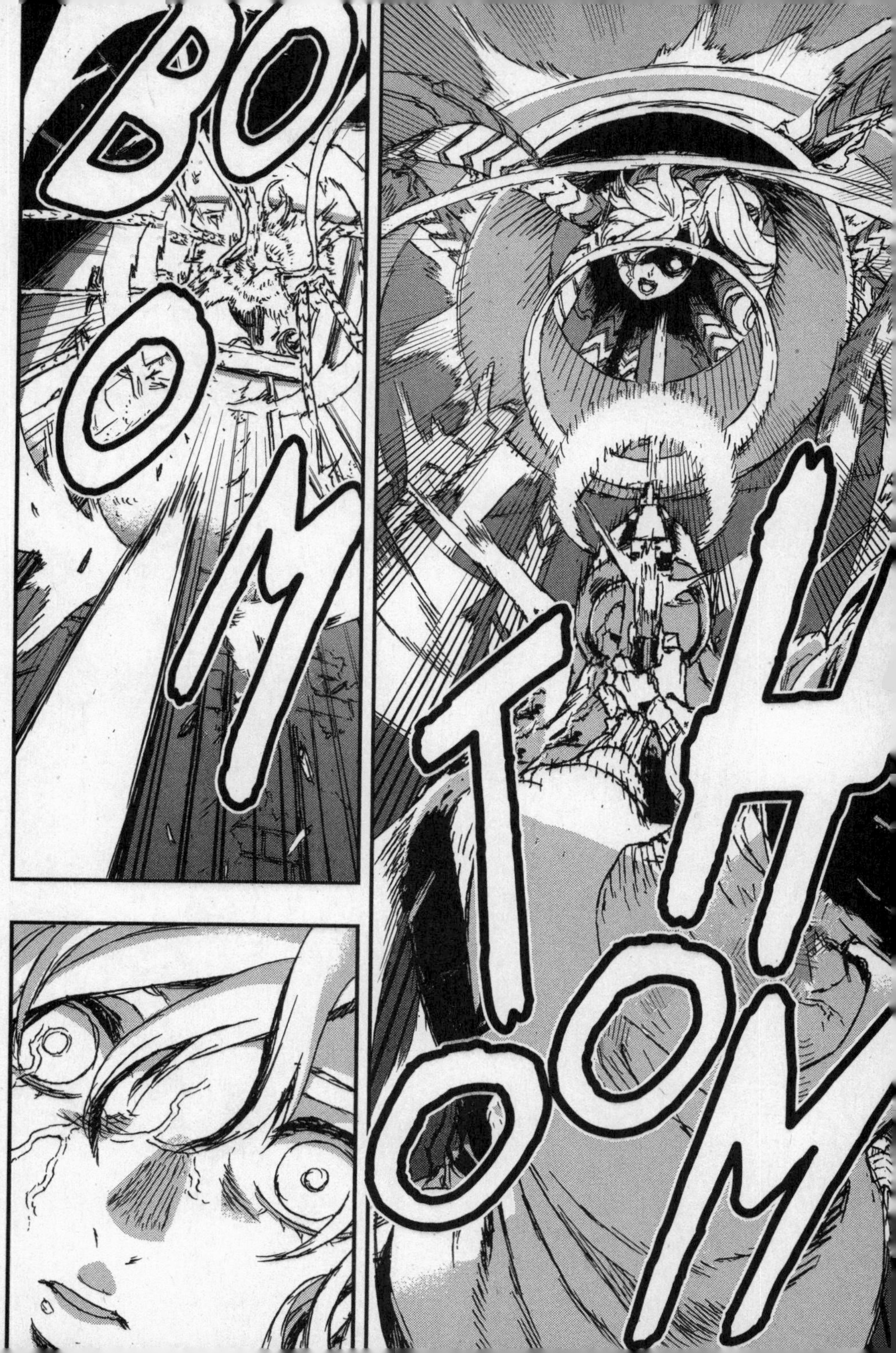
THOOM
BOOM

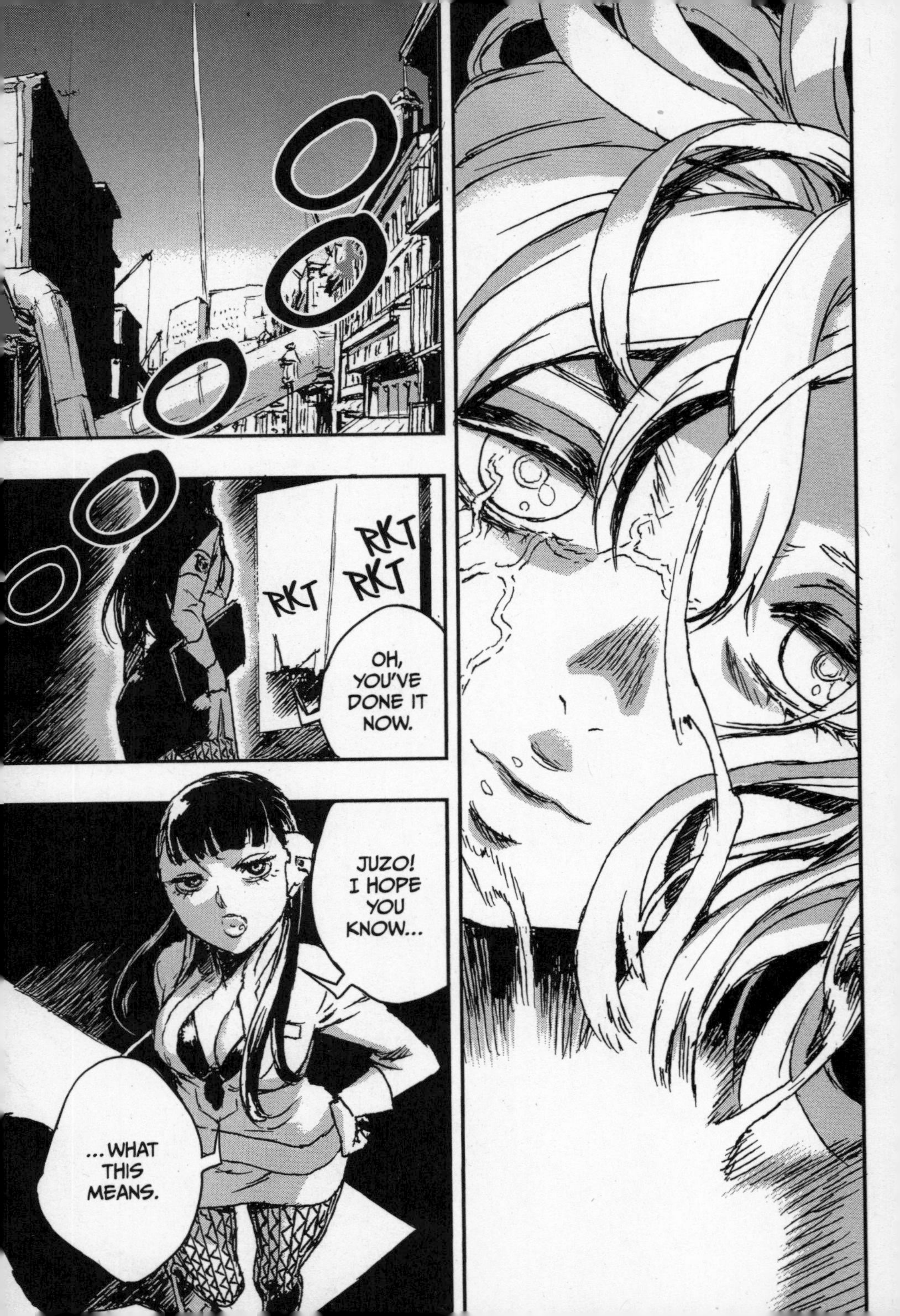

RKT
RKT
RKT
OH, YOU'VE DONE IT NOW.
JUZO! I HOPE YOU KNOW...
...WHAT THIS MEANS.

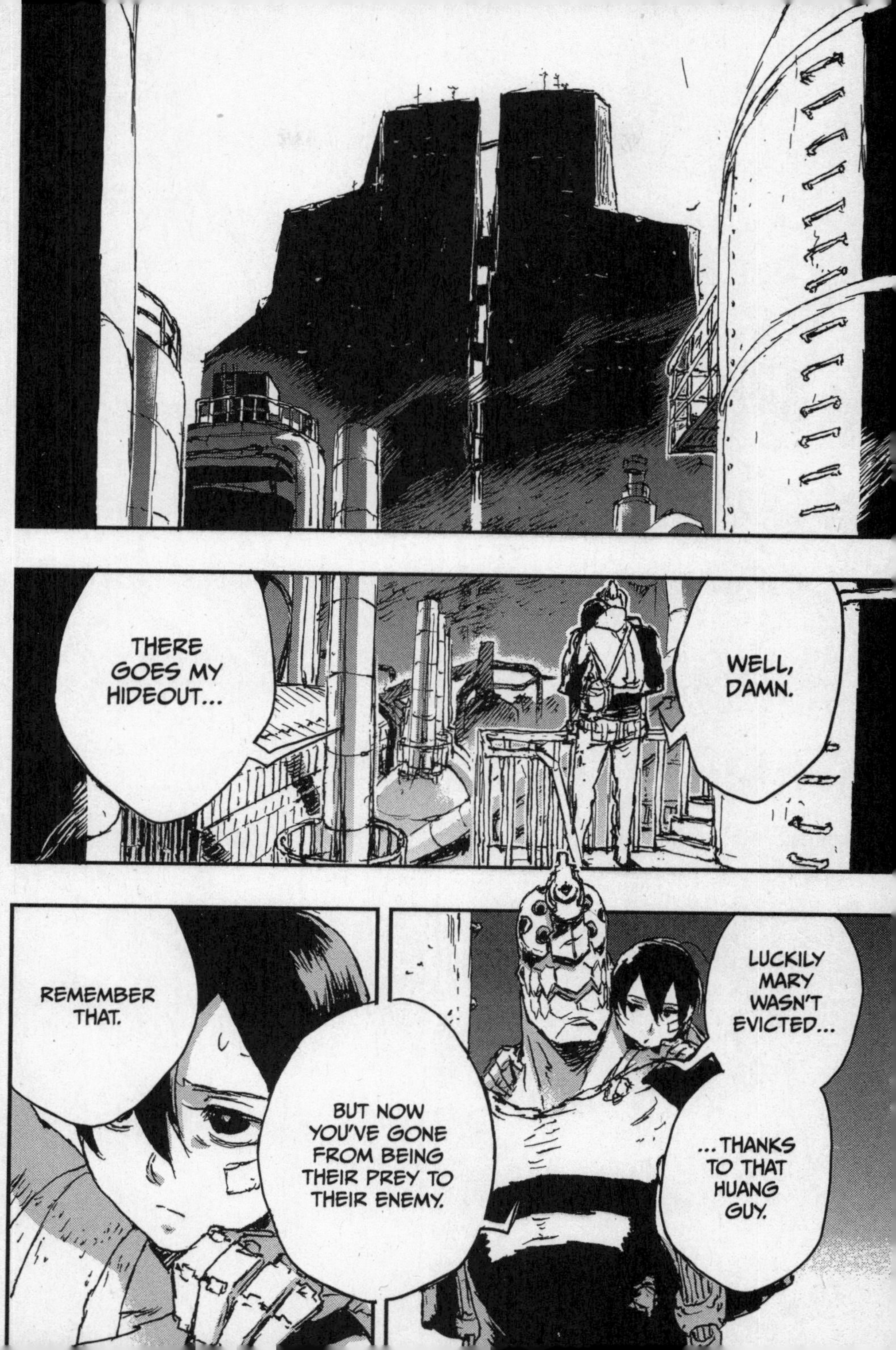
WELL, DAMN.
THERE GOES MY HIDEOUT...
LUCKILY MARY WASN'T EVICTED...
...THANKS TO THAT HUANG GUY.
BUT NOW YOU'VE GONE FROM BEING THEIR PREY TO THEIR ENEMY.
REMEMBER THAT.

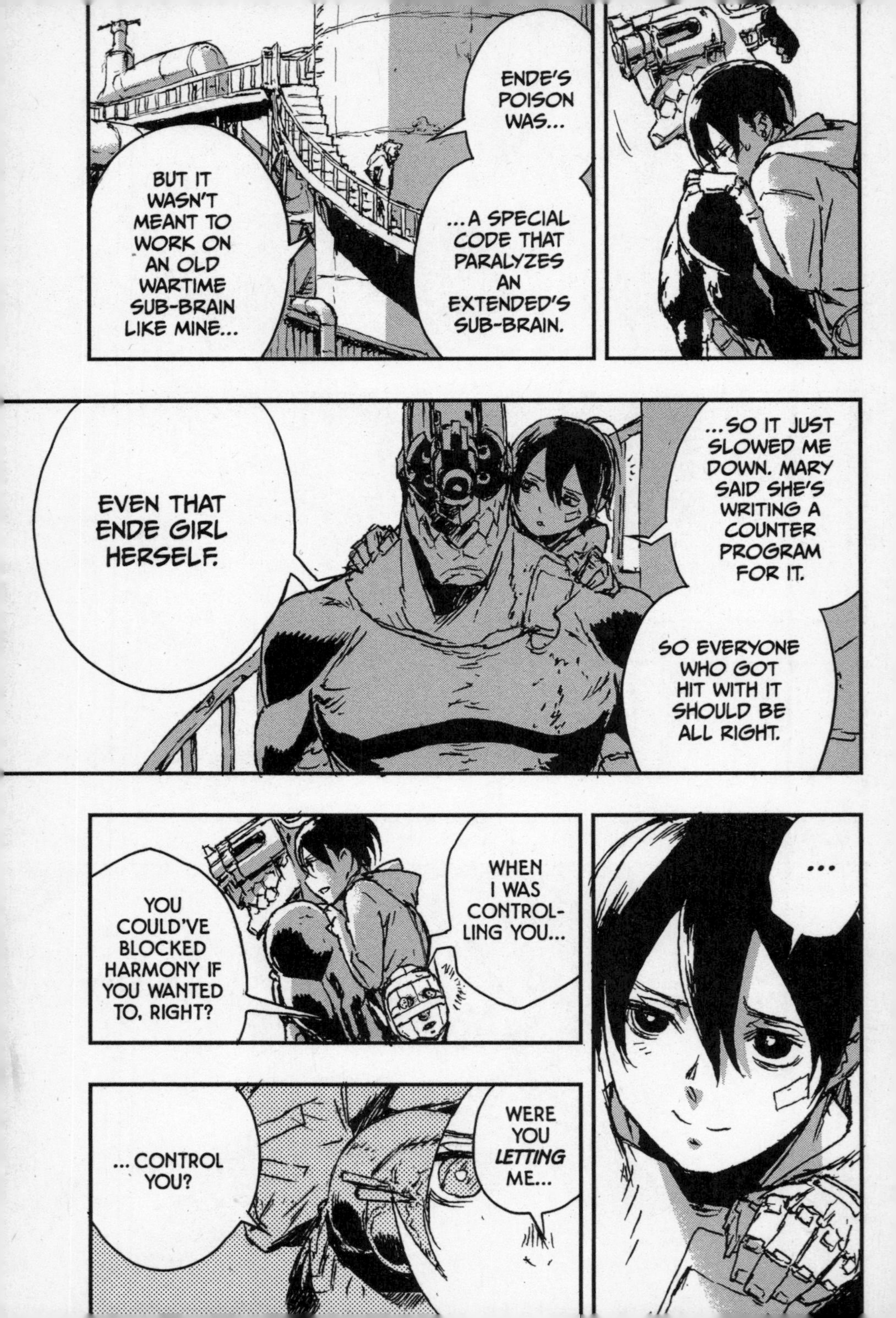
ENDE'S POISON WAS...
...A SPECIAL CODE THAT PARALYZES AN EXTENDED'S SUB-BRAIN.
BUT IT WASN'T MEANT TO WORK ON AN OLD WARTIME SUB-BRAIN LIKE MINE...
...SO IT JUST SLOWED ME DOWN. MARY SAID SHE'S WRITING A COUNTER PROGRAM FOR IT.
SO EVERYONE WHO GOT HIT WITH IT SHOULD BE ALL RIGHT.
EVEN THAT ENDE GIRL HERSELF.
...
WHEN I WAS CONTROL-LING YOU...
YOU COULD'VE BLOCKED HARMONY IF YOU WANTED TO, RIGHT?
WERE YOU *LETTING* ME...
...CONTROL YOU?

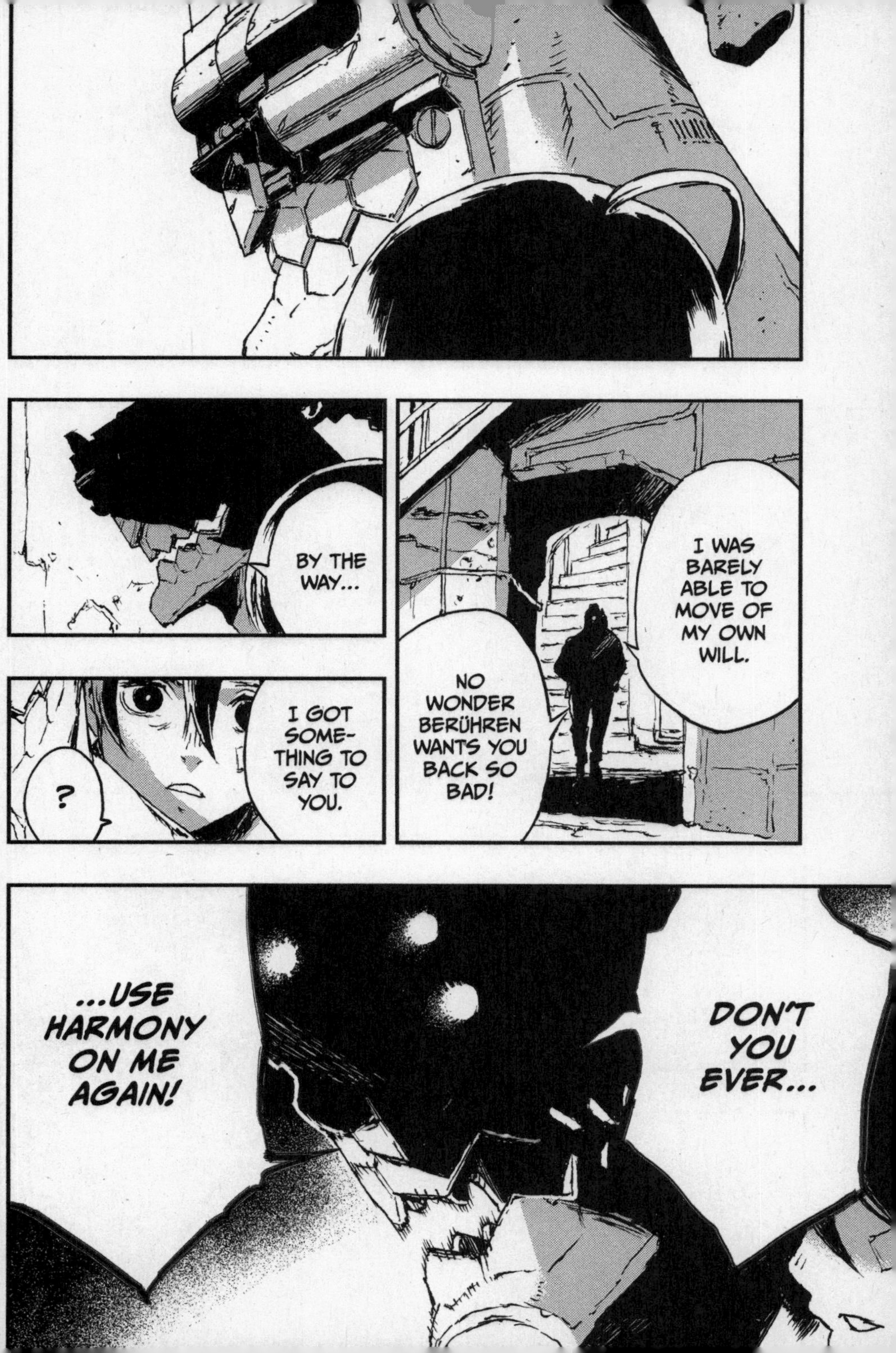
I WAS BARELY ABLE TO MOVE OF MY OWN WILL.
NO WONDER BERÜHREN WANTS YOU BACK SO BAD!
BY THE WAY...
I GOT SOMETHING TO SAY TO YOU.
?
DON'T YOU EVER...
...USE HARMONY ON ME AGAIN!

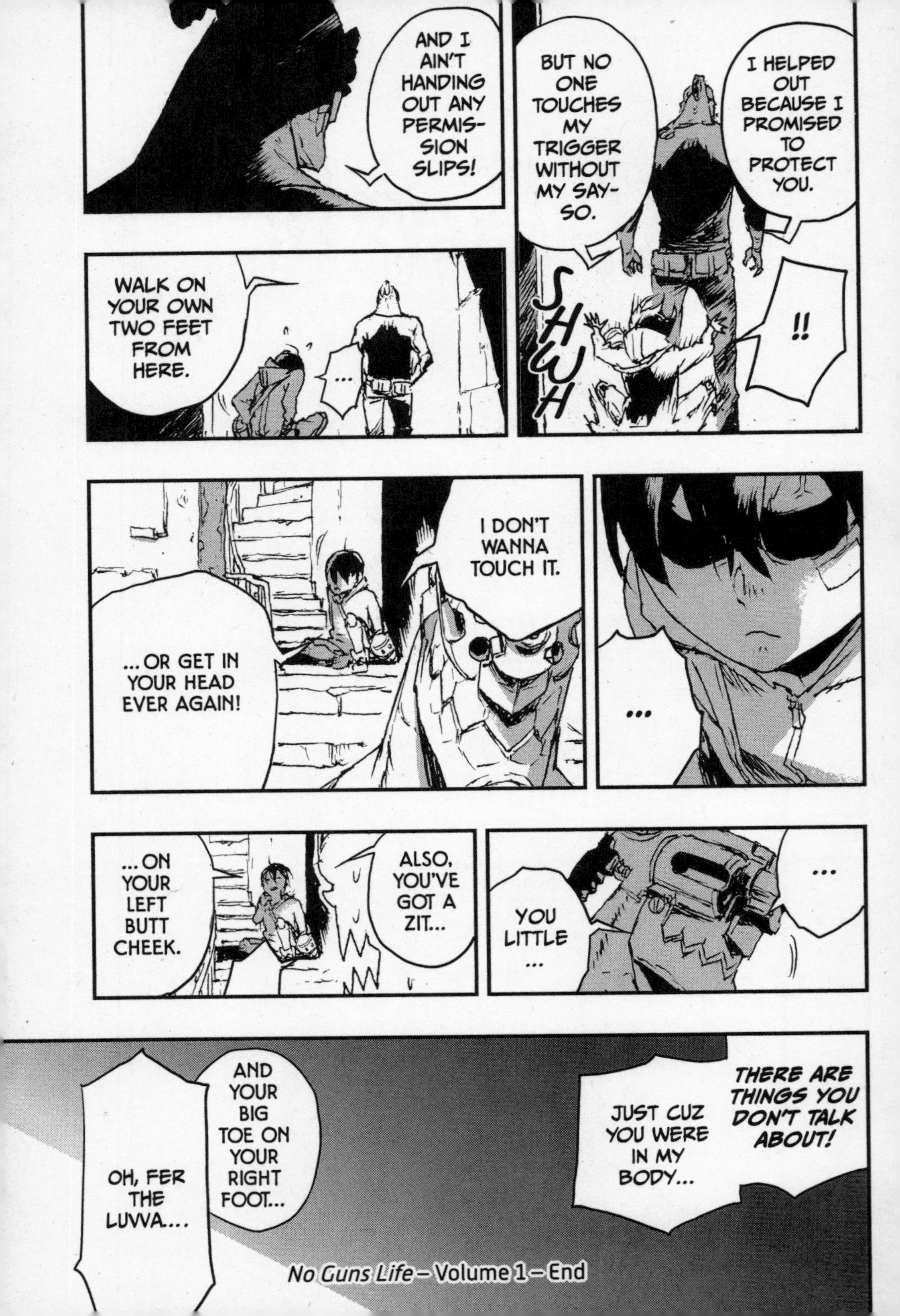
I HELPED OUT BECAUSE I PROMISED TO PROTECT YOU.
BUT NO ONE TOUCHES MY TRIGGER WITHOUT MY SAY-SO.
SHWH
!!
AND I AIN'T HANDING OUT ANY PERMISSION SLIPS!
WALK ON YOUR OWN TWO FEET FROM HERE.
...
...
I DON'T WANNA TOUCH IT.
...OR GET IN YOUR HEAD EVER AGAIN!
...
YOU LITTLE ...
ALSO, YOU'VE GOT A ZIT...
...ON YOUR LEFT BUTT CHEEK.
THERE ARE THINGS YOU DON'T TALK ABOUT!
JUST CUZ YOU WERE IN MY BODY...
AND YOUR BIG TOE ON YOUR RIGHT FOOT...
OH, FER THE LUVVA....
No Guns Life – Volume 1 – End

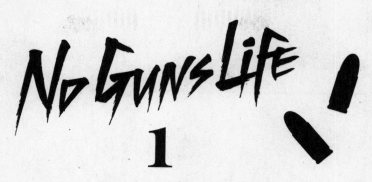

No Guns Life

1

STORY AND ART BY
TASUKU KARASUMA

VIZ SIGNATURE EDITION

TRANSLATION Joe Yamazaki
ENGLISH ADAPTATION Stan!
TOUCH-UP ART & LETTERING Evan Waldinger
DESIGN Shawn Carrico
EDITOR Mike Montesa

Printed in the U.S.A.

Published by VIZ Media, LLC
P.O. Box 77010
San Francisco, CA 94107

10 9 8 7 6 5 4 3 2 1
First printing, September 2019

VIZ MEDIA   VIZ SIGNATURE
viz.com   vizsignature.com

YOU'RE
READING THE
WRONG WAY.

NO GUNS LIFE is printed from right to left
in the original Japanese format in order to
present the art as it was meant to be seen.